Praise for *Front Lines*

"Art is not simply about what you create, it is where you situate your art and where you form community. Most artists look to the 'art world'—a location that largely serves the 1 percent. Not Susan Simensky Bietila. She has placed her art at the front lines of social justice movements since the 1960s. She is an ally in the truest sense. *Front Lines* is remarkable, and her path is a blueprint for other artists looking to do the same."
—Nicolas Lampert, author of *A People's Art History of the United States: 250 Years of Activist Art and Artists Working in Social Justice Movements*

"I have known Susan Simensky Bietila for basically my entire adult life, but until I read this book, I did not fully understand how amazing *her* life has been. *Front Lines* is an artistic autobiography of a lifetime of activist adventures, but it is so much more than this. Sue vividly narrates dozens of social struggles over the past six decades—antiwar, antiracist, feminist, working class, health care, educational, environmental, anarchist, Indigenous sovereignty, antigentrification, and beyond—centering the efforts of multiple generations of the greatest artist-activists you've probably never heard of. With vibrant prose and even more powerful images, this book provides essential history lessons and bold inspiration for our collective struggle to build a free society."
—Michael Staudenmaier, coauthor of *We Go Where They Go: The Story of Anti-Racist Action*

"Susan Simensky Bietila's art has been part of the fabric that has been elemental in expressing what they call radical ideas and communicating to the broader world about the possibilities for humanity. This is true, and will continue to be true, whether anyone knows Susan's name or not. But those who do know her name, and become familiar with more of her work and her fascinating personal story that's in the pages of this book, will be glad that they did."
—David Rovics, author of *Sing for Your Supper: A DIY Guide to Playing Music, Writing Songs, and Booking Your Own Gigs*

"Susan's artwork and community work have been such an important part of the environment, climate, and justice work shared by many in the Great Lakes region. Her designs have been spread far and wide by button, shirt, tote, and more, and her puppets have become a staple at anti–Line 5 events, uplifting (literally) all the critters who are put at risk when fossil fuel infrastructure like Line 5 continues to operate. People from communities near and far have been inspired by Susan's creativity and have learned how to make an impact with their own artwork at art builds she's led."
—Jadine Sonoda, organizer with Sierra Club Wisconsin

"Creative expression is a balm for the body and soul. Our brains are wired to secrete 'feel-good' hormones when we engage in any type of expressive activity. Susan Simensky Bietila's political cartoons reflect on the state of humanity, the state of our kinship with each other, and the natural world. As readers facing many threats to our sense of integrity, we find we are not alone. Susan's work in *Front Lines* affirms our shared values and supports our search for equity and a vital community/ecosystem. In that we stand in solidarity."
—Jan Penn, fifth-generation Wisconsin activist and
organizer against the Enbridge Line 5

"Susan Simensky Bietila is not one of those self-important 'meeting activists.' She is a hands-on artist, on the front lines with communities she's organizing with. In the old days, we'd say she was 'cadre level.' Nowadays young activists would call her 'fire.' Follow Sue in the pages of *Front Lines* through her six-decade political odyssey in the art of activism."
—Rick Whaley, coauthor of *Walleye Warriors:
The Chippewa Treaty Rights Story*

Front Lines

A Lifetime of Drawing Resistance

Susan Simensky Bietila

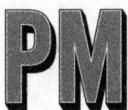

Front Lines: A Lifetime of Drawing Resistance
© 2026 Susan Simensky Bietila
This edition © PM Press 2026

All drawn stories previously appeared in *World War 3 Illustrated*.

ISBN: 979-8-88744-151-1 (paperback)
ISBN: 979-8-88744-152-8 (ebook)
Library of Congress Control Number: 2025935970

Cover design by John Yates / stealworks.com
Interior design by briandesign

10 9 8 7 6 5 4 3 2 1

PM Press
PO Box 23912
Oakland, CA 94623
www.pmpress.org

Printed in the USA.

Contents

Stories

Introduction

This book is my history of making art for the front lines of resistance and the development of this genre over the decades. I am delighted to share how I came to make movement art. The movements and events may be unfamiliar, so I have provided context in the narrative and in the captions. Most of the photographs are my own documentation. Photos by collaborators are credited in the captions. My stories are either firsthand from within movements or were told to me by friends who were on the scene. These stories are histories that were suppressed, made invisible, or defamed by the mainstream. I encourage you to rebel against the corporate media's propaganda machine by refusing social consent to crimes against humanity and the destruction of the planet.

I choose topics from the past that resonate with current crises. "Return of the Cossacks," my family's story, is also about Trump's lust to be a dictator and the current anti-immigrant vilification. "A Northwoods Tale," a history of colonialism, is also about the threats of mining in the present. "Who Are the Real Street Medics?" links street medics during past uprisings against injustice to the experience of street medics now. Knowing our history brings strength.

My artwork can be found on the streets, in books, and more recently on the shores of the Great Lakes and rivers of the Upper Midwest. I am inspired by the growing forms of collaboration between activist artists close to home and around the world. Ojibwe friends say that we work "in a good way," with many hands, to make art that says what needs to be said and that goes where it is needed. Please enjoy the many strategies and techniques throughout the book: street theater documentation, puppets, banners, posters, and installations. You'll see that I work across many different media, including stencils, paint, block printing, ink on scratchboard or silkscreen, cardboard, cloth, papier-mâché, and photography—whatever suits the project.

The Very Beginning

’m often asked how I started to make political art. My grandparents and my mother were refugees from the 1921 pogrom near Kamenetz-Podolsk, in Russia. My parents and I lived with them during the post–World War II housing shortage. I was born in 1947, and when I was four, we moved to Boulevard Houses, government housing built on landfill in East New York, Brooklyn. My favorite activity was drawing. My father brought home a ream of paper from his job at a small coffee-processing factory for me to draw on. Museums were free, and my mother enjoyed taking me to the Metropolitan Museum of Art, the Museum of Modern Art, and the Brooklyn Museum. In elementary school, I quickly finished my assignments, and the teacher would let me paint at the easel in the back of the room until the other students finished. In first grade, my teacher recommended me for a scholarship to the Brooklyn Museum Art School. At age seven, I took the New Lots Line IRT (Interborough Rapid Transit) by myself to a Saturday morning oil-painting class. In second grade, I won the award for the citywide International Brotherhood Week art competition for a drawing of a circle of people in historical costume and regalia from all over the world. I still have the heavy bronze medal.

As a preteen, I got my first job, modeling for an adult life-drawing class at the Jewish Y. I wore a leotard, with lines of masking tape placed on it to emphasize the action lines of the body. Years later, I found out that the teacher, Ralph Ortiz, was an early performance artist, famous for bloody chicken sacrifices in Santería-influenced "happenings." That year, my mother collected my best artwork, put it in a red cardboard portfolio, and took me to apply to the High School of Music & Art on 137th Street in Manhattan. I started M&A in 1961, at age fourteen. The round trip on the subway was over three hours a day, from the New Lots Avenue IRT station to Harlem. It was worth it.

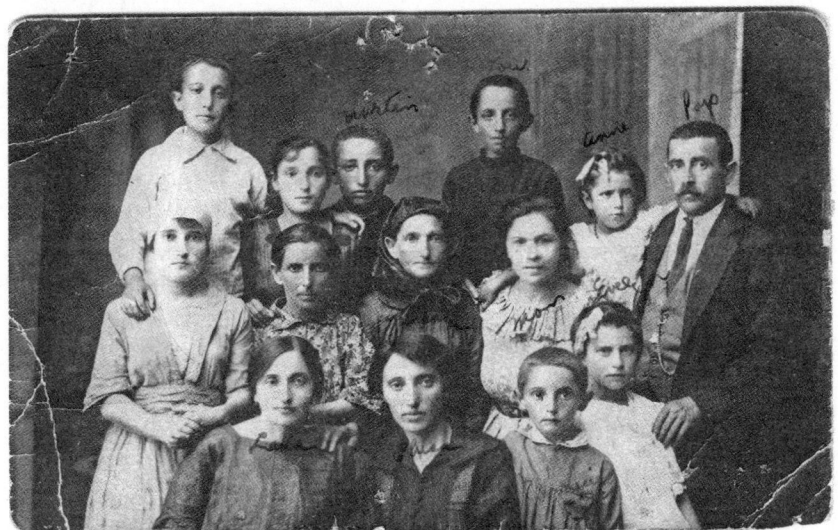

My Maternal Ancestors: These are my maternal ancestors just before they fled Bessarabia. Their town is now in Russia. My grandfather, Aaron Skolnick, is on the right, and the child he is holding is my mother, Anyuta, then age six. My grandmother, Bryna Licht, is directly to her left. Our story is too much the same today. Reactionary nationalists invade neighborhoods, street by street, killing and raping—carrying out ethnic-cleansing genocides. Those who escape carry their meager belongings wrapped in a piece of fabric, just as my grandparents did. My grandmother said that they brought a goose-down pillow and a piece of leather, thinking that these might be of value in "the land of milk and honey."

I am also often asked what historical events led me to become an activist. I grew up aware of the pogroms and the Holocaust, institutional anti-Semitism, and racism. Activism was common among Jewish refugees in East New York. My first political jolt was the 1962 Cuban missile crisis, which happened during my junior year of high school. We were all terrified. Some of the girls had sex with their boyfriends because they wanted to have that experience before the bomb fell. I just lay on the living room rug, staring out the window at the sky, waiting in dread for the blinding flash.

Despite periodic internet searches, it was only during the last decade that I found research in English about the pogroms near Kamenetz-Podolsk, during the Russian Civil War. I had only my grandmother's Yiddish pronunciation of place names to go by, but I finally figured out the transliteration. The 1917 Bolshevik Revolution is common knowledge, but not the bloody civil war that continued for six additional years.

The Pale of Settlement, a territory in the western Russian Empire where the czar allowed Jews to live, was heavily impacted.

I gave a slide presentation of the "Return of the Cossacks" story to the Summer Freedom School of Youth Empowered in the Struggle, the high school branch of the powerful Wisconsin immigrants' rights organization Voces de la Frontera. Students fluent in English translated for those newly arrived into Spanish, Arabic, Somali, Hmong, and more. They saw the similarity to their own refugee stories of forced emigration.

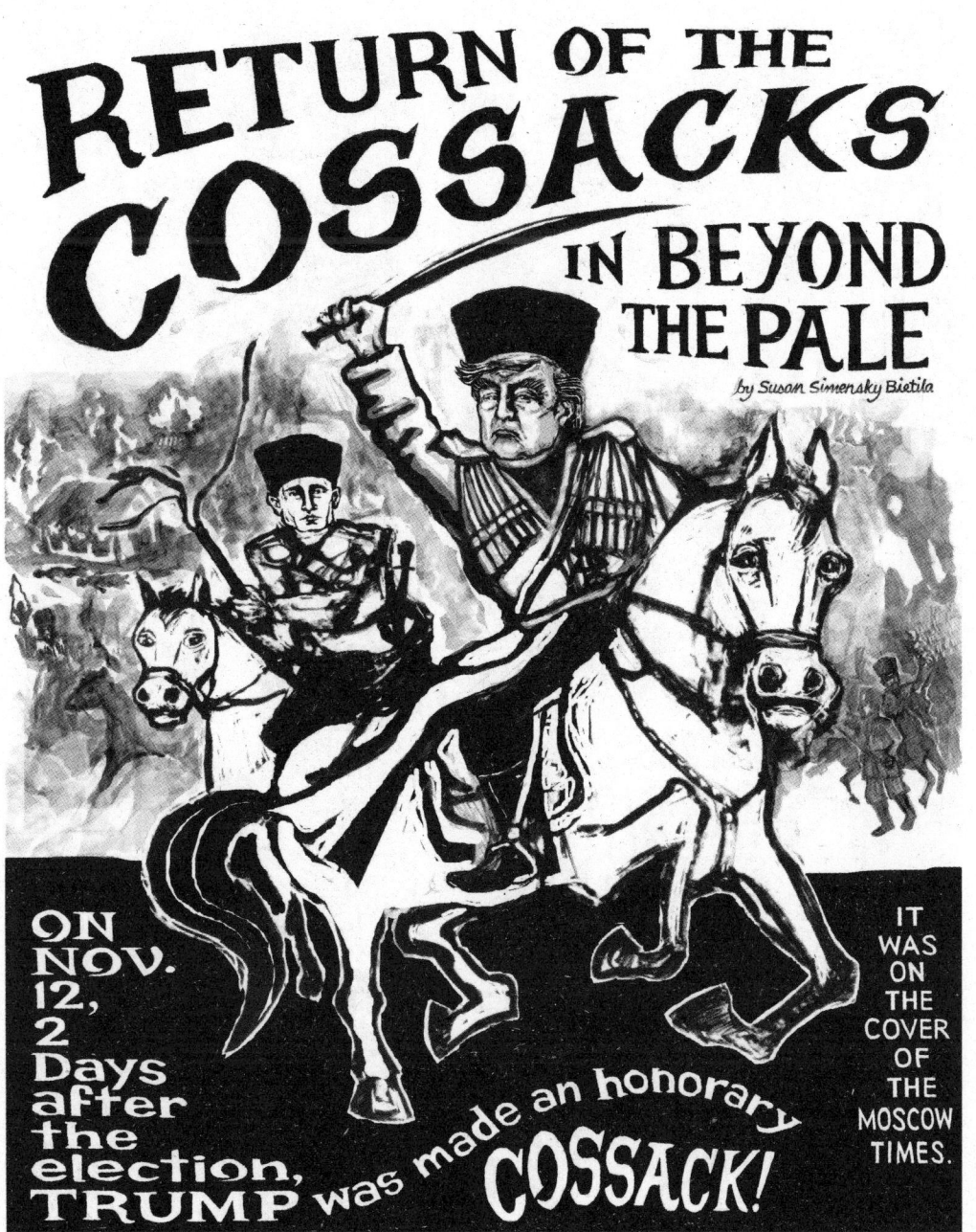

Pages 5–12: Return of the Cossacks
First appeared in *World War 3 Illustrated*, no. 48 (2017), "Fight Fascism" issue.

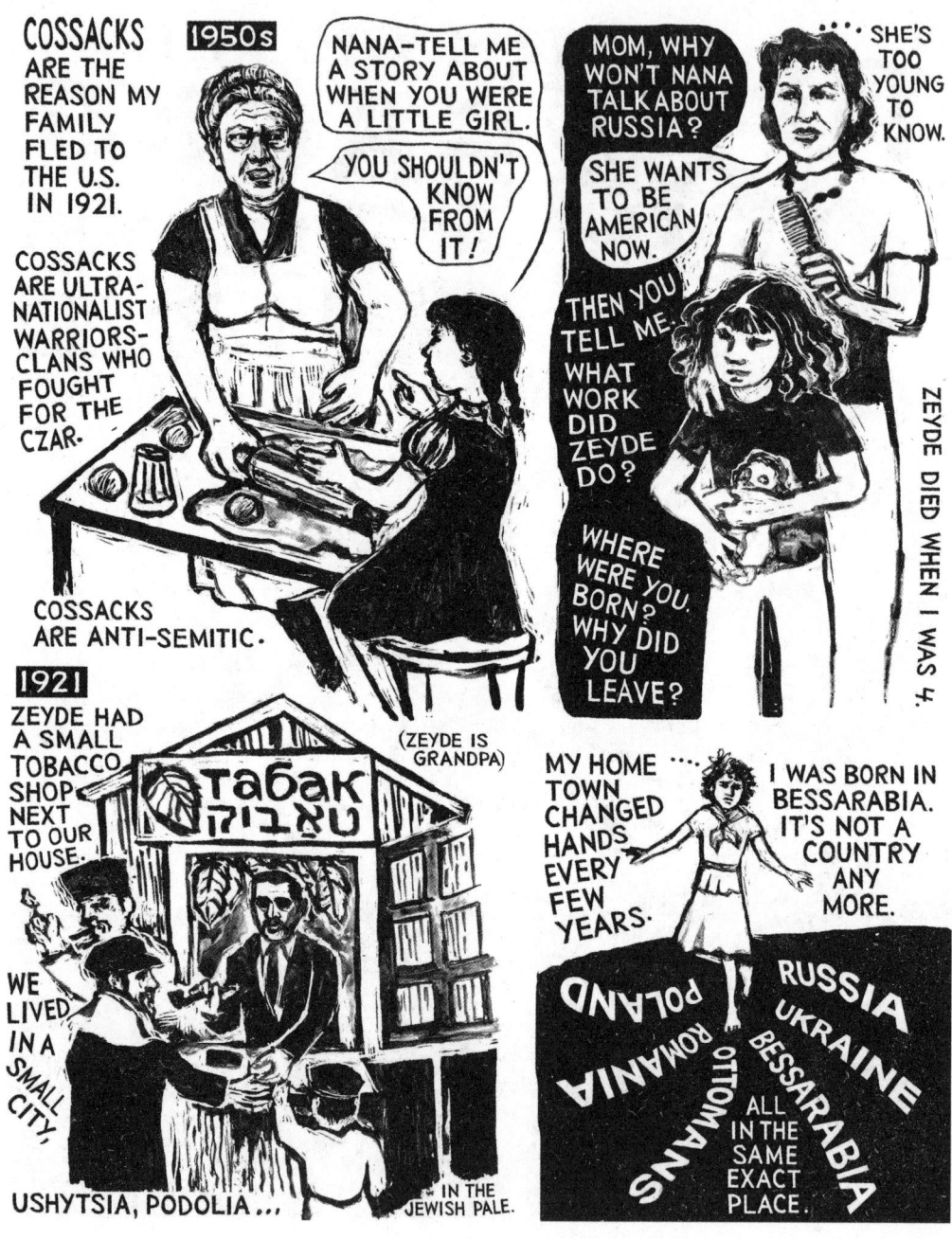

COSSACKS ARE THE REASON MY FAMILY FLED TO THE U.S. IN 1921.

1950s

NANA—TELL ME A STORY ABOUT WHEN YOU WERE A LITTLE GIRL.

YOU SHOULDN'T KNOW FROM IT!

MOM, WHY WON'T NANA TALK ABOUT RUSSIA?

SHE WANTS TO BE AMERICAN NOW.

···· SHE'S TOO YOUNG TO KNOW.

COSSACKS ARE ULTRA-NATIONALIST WARRIORS-CLANS WHO FOUGHT FOR THE CZAR.

THEN YOU TELL ME. WHAT WORK DID ZEYDE DO?

WHERE WERE YOU BORN? WHY DID YOU LEAVE?

ZEYDE DIED WHEN I WAS 4.

COSSACKS ARE ANTI-SEMITIC.

1921

ZEYDE HAD A SMALL TOBACCO SHOP NEXT TO OUR HOUSE.

(ZEYDE IS GRANDPA)

табак
טאבאק

WE LIVED IN A SMALL CITY,

USHYTSIA, PODOLIA ...

··· IN THE JEWISH PALE.

MY HOME TOWN CHANGED HANDS EVERY FEW YEARS.

···· I WAS BORN IN BESSARABIA. IT'S NOT A COUNTRY ANY MORE.

POLAND RUSSIA ROMANIA UKRAINE BESSARABIA OTTOMANS

ALL IN THE SAME EXACT PLACE.

6

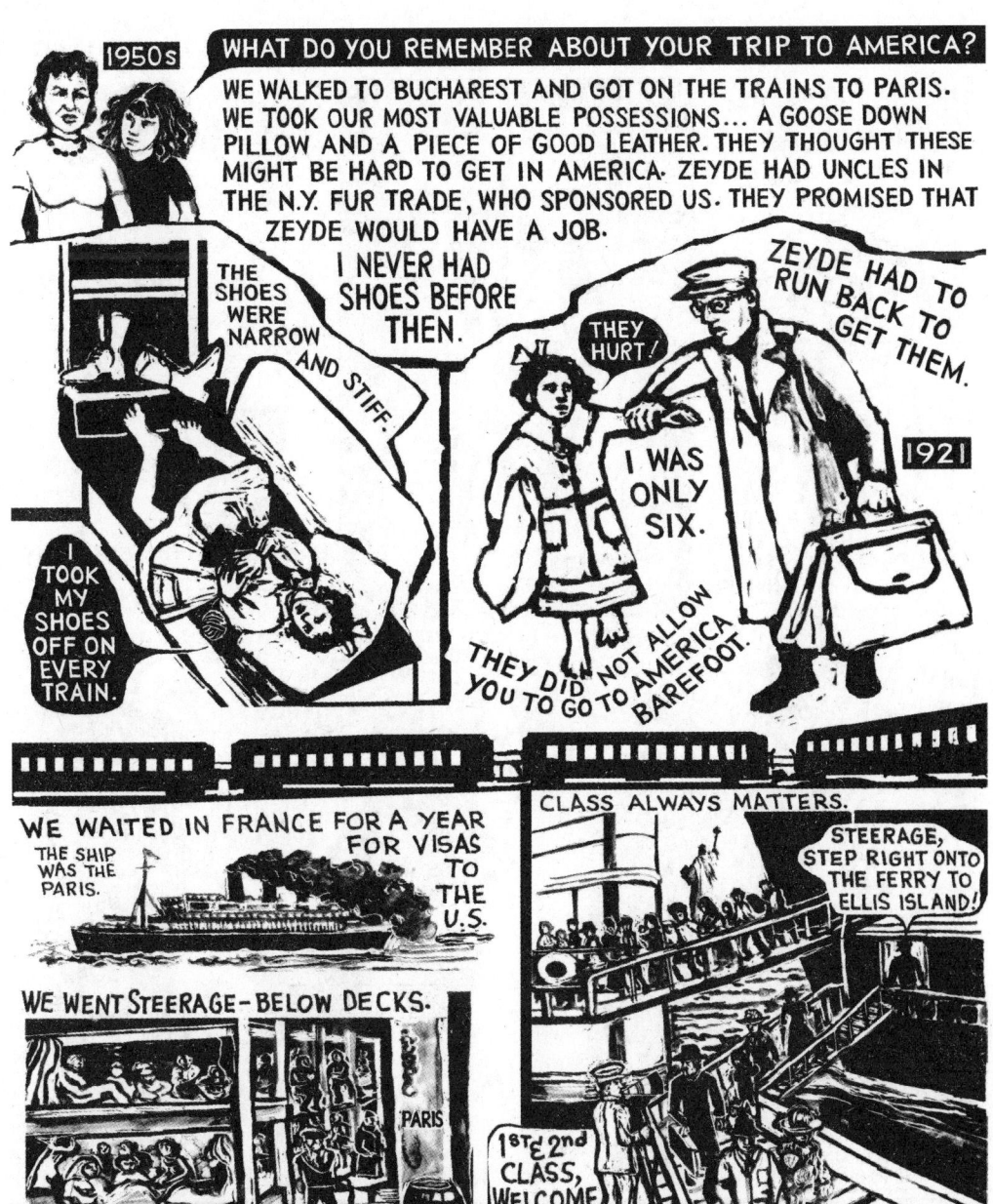

7

THE 1920s WAS NOT A GOOD TIME TO ARRIVE.

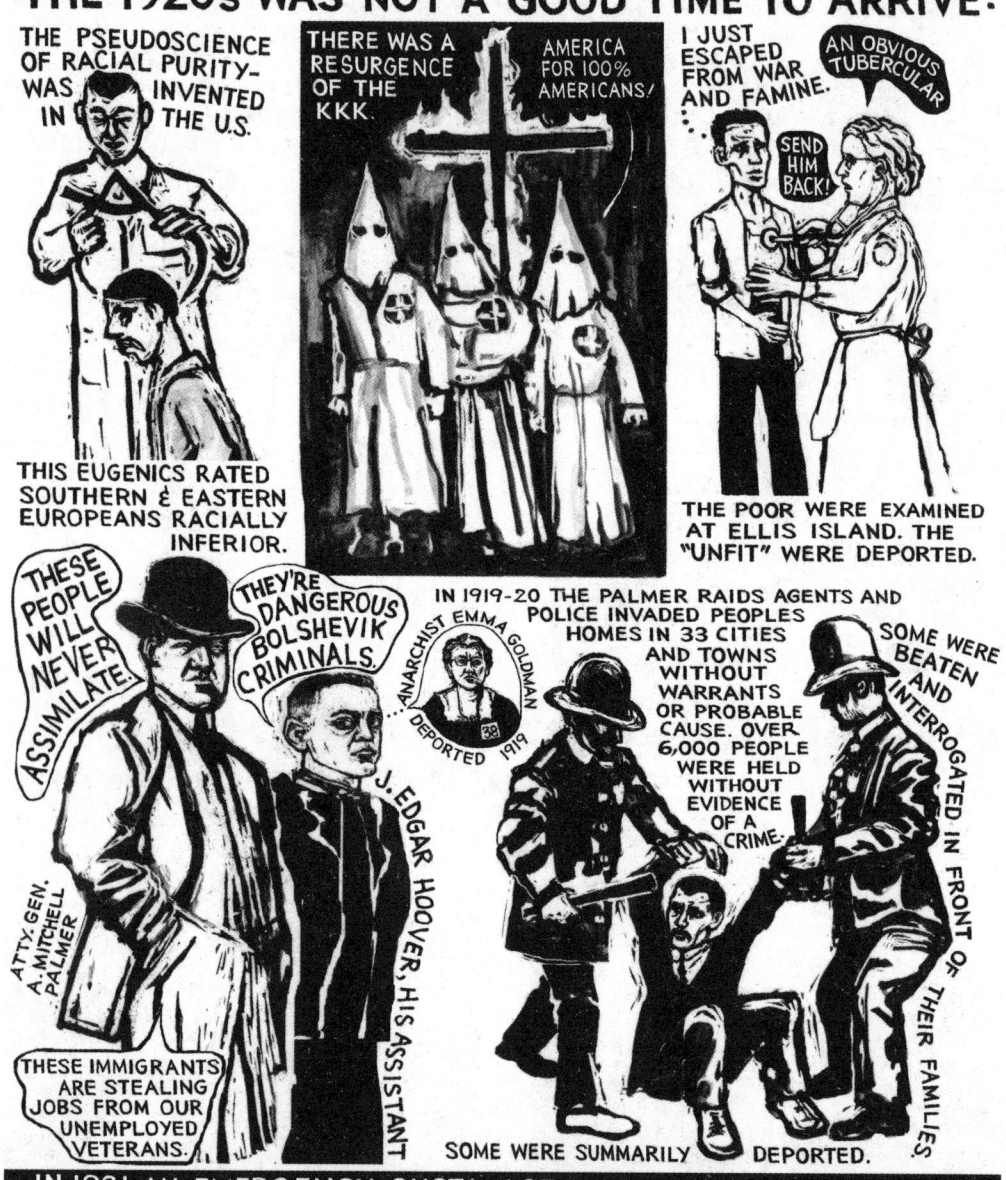

THE PSEUDOSCIENCE OF RACIAL PURITY— WAS INVENTED IN THE U.S.

THIS EUGENICS RATED SOUTHERN & EASTERN EUROPEANS RACIALLY INFERIOR.

THERE WAS A RESURGENCE OF THE KKK.

AMERICA FOR 100% AMERICANS!

I JUST ESCAPED FROM WAR AND FAMINE.

AN OBVIOUS TUBERCULAR

SEND HIM BACK!

THE POOR WERE EXAMINED AT ELLIS ISLAND. THE "UNFIT" WERE DEPORTED.

THESE PEOPLE WILL NEVER ASSIMILATE.

THEY'RE DANGEROUS BOLSHEVIK CRIMINALS.

ANARCHIST EMMA GOLDMAN DEPORTED 1919

ATTY. GEN. A. MITCHELL PALMER

J. EDGAR HOOVER, HIS ASSISTANT

THESE IMMIGRANTS ARE STEALING JOBS FROM OUR UNEMPLOYED VETERANS.

IN 1919-20 THE PALMER RAIDS AGENTS AND POLICE INVADED PEOPLES HOMES IN 33 CITIES AND TOWNS WITHOUT WARRANTS OR PROBABLE CAUSE. OVER 6,000 PEOPLE WERE HELD WITHOUT EVIDENCE OF A CRIME.

SOME WERE BEATEN AND INTERROGATED IN FRONT OF THEIR FAMILIES.

SOME WERE SUMMARILY DEPORTED.

IN 1921 AN EMERGENCY QUOTA ACT WAS PASSED TO KEEP OUT 'UNDESIRABLES'. IT WAS BASED ON COUNTRY OF ORIGIN. MADE PERMANENT IN 1924, IT REMAINED IN FORCE UNTIL 1965.

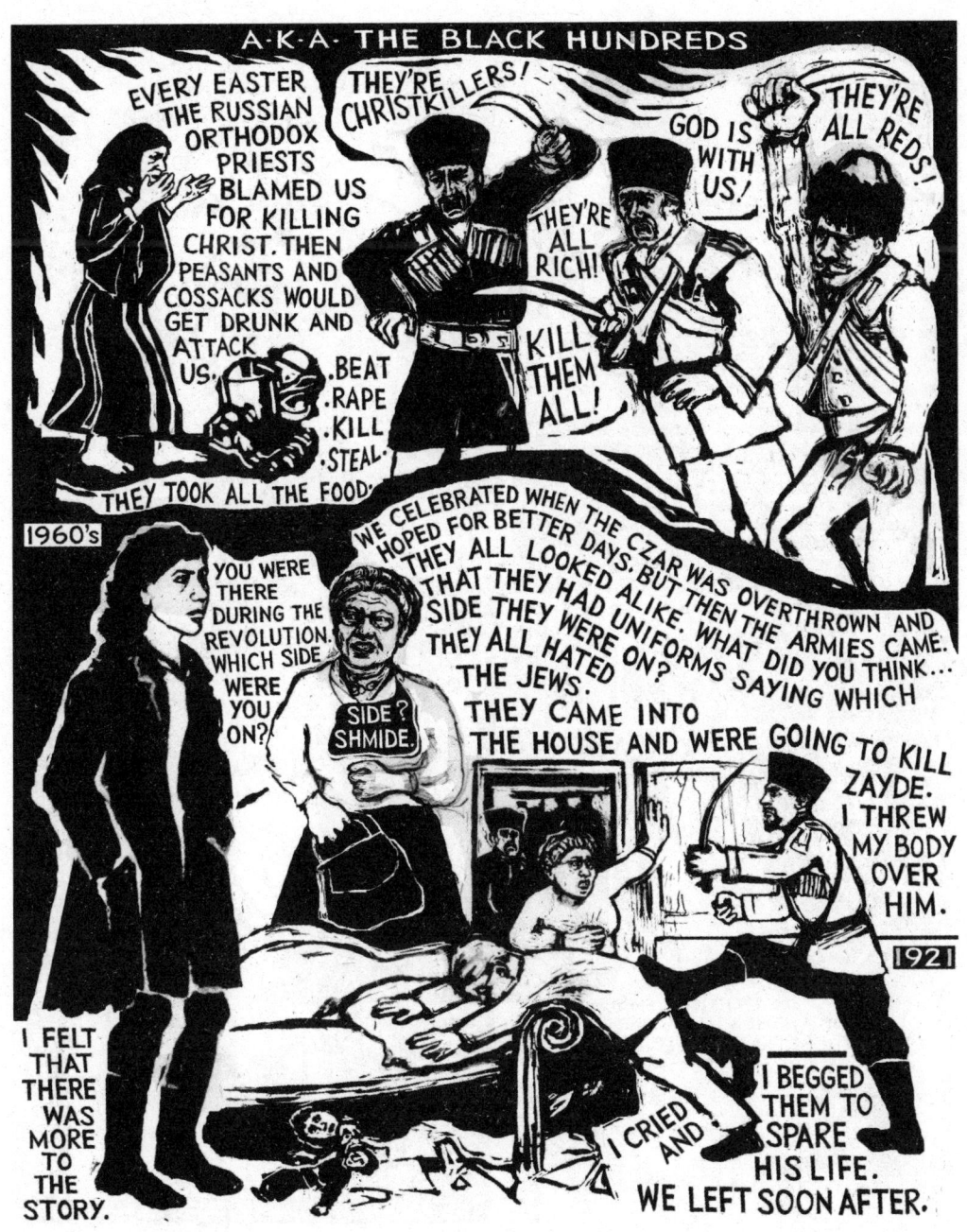

9

It's still dark far to the East.
Ancestors with secrets
Even their graves buried under water
Along with their town.

There is no place to stand where they once stood
To cry for their all but forgotten murders
No one to tell their story
Nothing solid to connect with them
Only words on paper
History chapters about the worst Pogroms
during the Russian Civil War.

Silent memories of famine
They fattened me with huge steaks
And heaps of buttery mashed potatoes
I was not allowed
To leave the table
Until I ate it all.
Then they scolded me for getting fat
But they never spoke of their starvation
When the White Armies had stolen all their food.

The lucky ones fled, carrying only their fear
Then lived their lives, screaming and vomiting up
The horrors they had seen without relief.
They burdened my generation
With grandiose expectations.
How could we not thrive here in America?

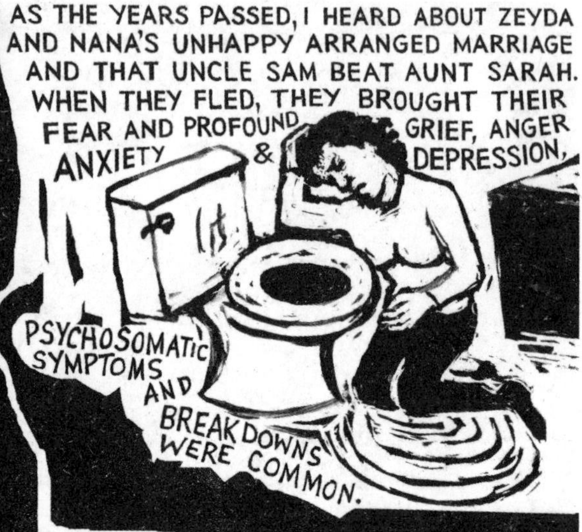

AS THE YEARS PASSED, I HEARD ABOUT ZEYDA AND NANA'S UNHAPPY ARRANGED MARRIAGE AND THAT UNCLE SAM BEAT AUNT SARAH. WHEN THEY FLED, THEY BROUGHT THEIR FEAR AND PROFOUND GRIEF, ANGER ANXIETY & DEPRESSION, PSYCHOSOMATIC SYMPTOMS AND BREAKDOWNS WERE COMMON.

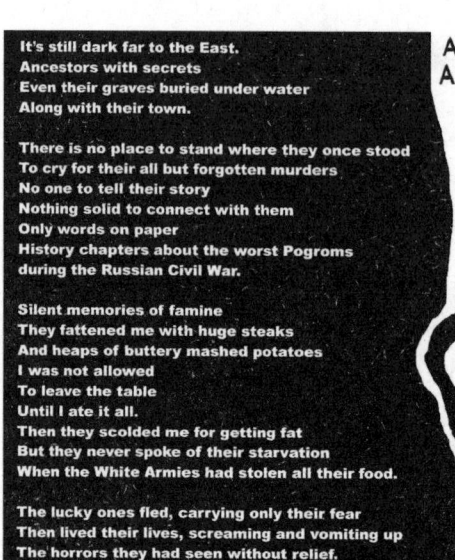

MY BROTHER OVERHEARD MORE OF THE STORY....

THEY THOUGHT THAT BECAUSE I'M BLIND, I MUST BE RETARDED! THEY SPOKE YIDDISH BUT I GOT IT ALL PERFECTLY. THERE WAS A BABY AFTER MOM. WHEN SHE WAS A FEW DAYS OLD, THE COSSACKS THREW HER TO THE GROUND AND KILLED HER. NANA'S PARENTS WERE KILLED WHEN SHE WAS NINE. SHE WAS RAISED BY HER UNCLE EDEL. THEY LEFT HOME RIGHT AFTER THAT.

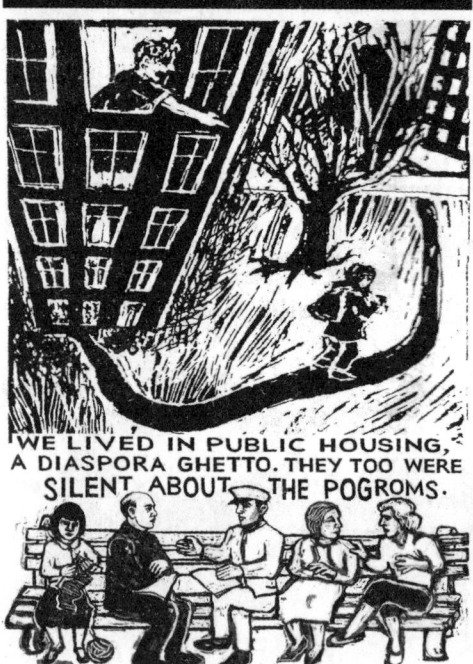

WE LIVED IN PUBLIC HOUSING, A DIASPORA GHETTO. THEY TOO WERE SILENT ABOUT THE POGROMS.

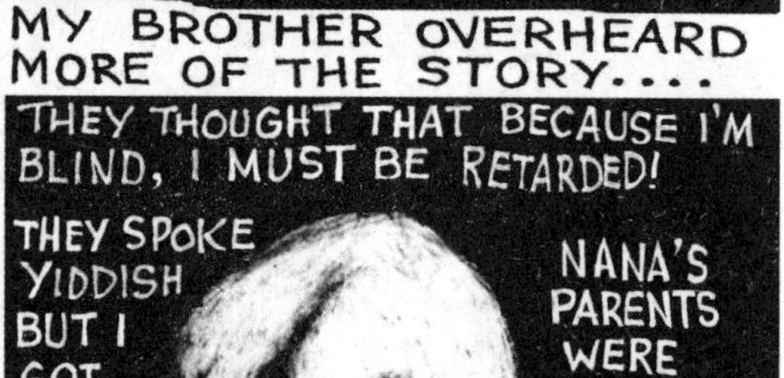

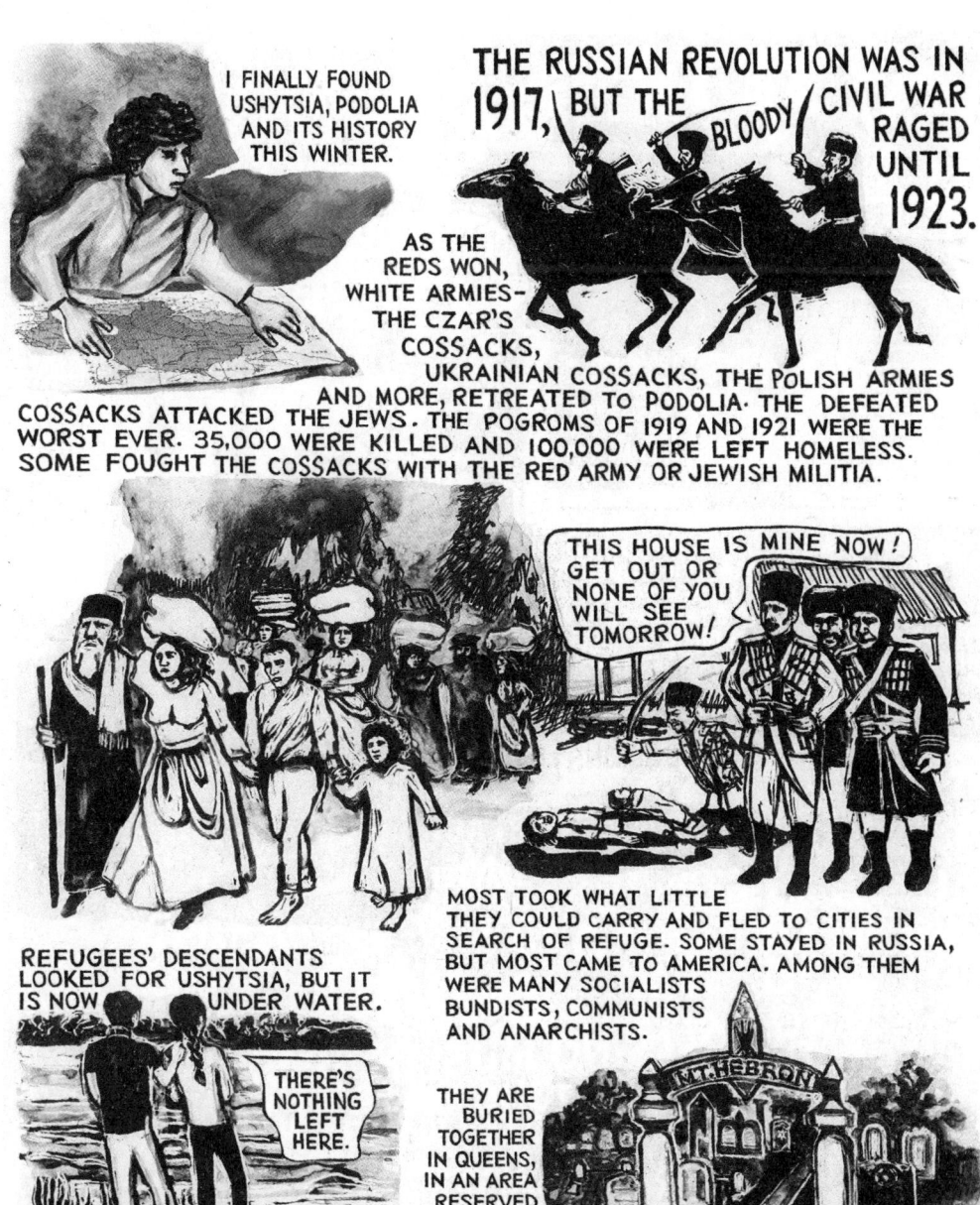

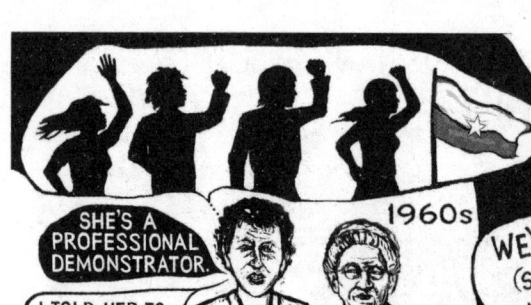

DAILY PARENT DRAMA AND CONSTANT CRISES, THE SCREAMING ARGUMENTS MADE ME HIDE IN MY BED CRYING OR RUN OUTSIDE IN THE MIDDLE OF THE NIGHT SO THAT I COULD BREATHE. I SOON LEFT HOME AND, IN TIME, CREATED MY LIFE.

1960s

SHE'S A PROFESSIONAL DEMONSTRATOR.

I TOLD HER TO MARRY A RICH MAN AND GIVE MONEY TO THE MOVEMENT AND SHE LAUGHED AT ME. OH, MAMA! WHAT CAN WE DO WITH HER?

THOSE BOYS SHE BRINGS HOME... THEY'RE TOO GOOD-LOOKING. THEY MUST BE POLICE AGENTS.

WE'RE JUST A DYSFUNCTIONAL FAMILY. (SHE SMILED AS SHE WATCHED JERRY SPRINGER.)

I SURE WISH

YOU HAD TOLD ME WHAT HAPPENED IN RUSSIA.

TRUMP FLAMBOYANTLY PROCLAIMS HIS IRRATIONAL WHIMS LIKE A TRUE CZAR. HE COMMANDS TOADIES TO SCAPEGOAT IMMIGRANTS, MEXICANS & MUSLIMS, IMPRISONING EVEN CHILDREN. WHEN HE WAS MADE AN HONORARY COSSACK IT WAS CLEAR THAT THEY RECOGNIZED ONE OF THEIR OWN.

PTSD HEREDITARY TRAUMA PANIC ATTACKS PILLS

2010

I CONTINUE TO GO TO DEMONSTRATIONS.

THIS IS HOW I HONOR MY ANCESTORS.

NOT ONE STEP BACK

BLACK LIVES MATTER

CLIMATE JUSTICE

NO TRAVEL BAN

IMMIGRANTS WELCOME HERE

NO W

NO WALLS · NO MUSLIM REGISTRY NO DEPORTATIONS OR ICE PRISONS NO PROFILING · NO POLICE KILLING PEOPLE NO FASCISTS OR OLIGARCHS · NO WARS · NO MILITARIZED POLICE · NO NAZI THUGS · NO AMERIKKKAN COSSACKS · NO WAR ON US!

Shocked, Rising Up

A chapter of the Student Peace Union, an anti-nukes group, was started at Music & Art and many other New York high schools. I was aware of this but did not join. My travel distance from school discouraged my participation in any extracurricular activities. I had not paid much attention to US politics and foreign affairs. My family read the tabloid *New York Post*, then the liberal daily. I was aware of the McCarthy hearings, the blacklists, and the Cold War.

At seventeen, I graduated with top grades and a perfect statewide test score in chemistry. I was recognized as talented in mathematics as well as art. Because of this, I was invited to a recruitment tea by the Seven Sisters colleges. I felt acutely ill at ease among the wealthy WASP alumnae and realized that being both poor and Jewish, I would be a lonely two-for-one token at those colleges. I was also recruited by the Scholars Program at Brooklyn College, part of the City University of New York, which was a prototype honors program financed by the Ford Foundation. Tuition was free, and most of the students were Jewish children of immigrants like me. I chose Brooklyn College and started there in 1964.

The summer before college, I worked at a racially integrated summer camp in the Catskills run by communist-influenced, antiracist organizers from my neighborhood. I learned about people a year or two older who had joined civil rights marches and voter registration drives in the South, as well as some guys who were moving to Canada to avoid the military draft. At night, after the campers were tucked in, the camp counselors sat around a campfire, where I learned that the US was at war with Vietnam. I felt physically shaken by the realization that the US was not a democracy but instead the number-one imperialist power after World War II's destruction of Europe. One of the other counselors was in the newly formed Students for a Democratic Society (SDS) and gave me the name of the student who was starting a chapter at Brooklyn

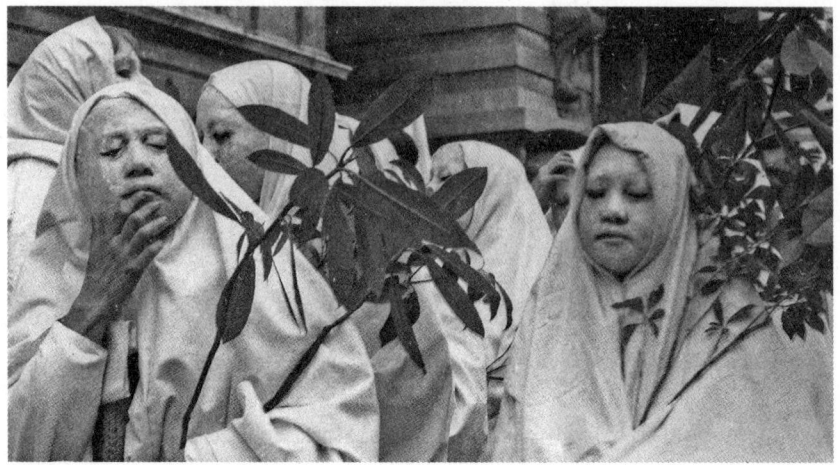

Bread and Puppet Masks: One of my first photographs ever is of Bread and Puppet Theater masks, circa 1965 at an anti-nukes march to the United Nations. This was work for photography class at Brooklyn College. The white masks represent the innocent victims of Nagasaki and Hiroshima. I attended the theater's mask-making workshop and helped to make these masks. I think they were fiberglass laid on molds. I remember the smell of the acetone used as a solvent. I now use only nontoxic materials.

College. I was encouraged to get involved. The New Left introduced me to unvarnished history and critical thinking. This changed my life.

From Berkeley to New York, the Free Speech Movement swept across campuses my first year at Brooklyn College. I joined the Faculty/ Student Ad Hoc Committee for Academic Freedom, whose purpose was to overturn the McCarthyite rules requiring students to get administration approval to host speakers, post on bulletin boards, or hold any public event on campus. During the 1940s and 1950s, faculty at the City University of New York were brought before Inquisition-like tribunals to expel professors suspected of being communist sympathizers. They required faculty to sign loyalty oaths and encouraged them to testify against one another. This intimidation continued to have an impact into the 1960s, until students stood up to the administration bullies. The college president was Harry Gideonse, a prominent figure in the Cold War–era anticommunist Freedom House who had lackey censors led by the dean of student activities. We demanded that the rights of students be the same as other citizens and that the public university should champion freedom of thought and speech. We won. Gideonse resigned in shame.

In 1966, antiwar activists were subpoenaed to appear before the House Un-American Activities Committee (HUAC) itself on August 17, in the old FBI building in Washington, DC. Many were from Berkeley. Their groups had demonstrated against the draft, blocked troop trains, and sent medical supplies to "the enemy" in Vietnam. I was invited to travel to DC in solidarity and to witness this historic event. A bus left from Union Square in the early-morning darkness, carrying New York student activists to support our comrades facing this inquisition and witness this historic event. Instead of cowering before HUAC, as so many had done in the past, these antiwar activists mocked the kangaroo court. They weren't intimidated by accusations of being communists and instead used the hearing to denounce war crimes committed by the US. Attempts by US marshals to silence them created a fracas. I was with the other college activists in the overflow crowd just outside the hearing room doors. The lawyer for one of the subpoenaed activists, Arthur Kinoy, was expelled from the proceedings and carried out over our heads by the marshals. In that instant, HUAC's power was rendered obsolete. We continued to oppose the war in Southeast Asia as the growing military draft fueled and radicalized the student movement.

After reading about my parents in the first story, you might be wondering how they reacted to this trip to DC. They raised no objection to my going to the HUAC hearing, where I would inevitably be photographed and labeled un-American. My grandmother Bryna, self-renamed Bertha, who had experienced the czarist secret police, was worried about my being targeted for being a radical leftist. Despite despising HUAC, family members encouraged keeping your head down and assimilating. My mother said, "Stop being a professional demonstrator. Why don't you just marry a rich boy and give money to the movement?" My parents were violently opposed to my going out on the subway at 2 a.m. to travel to Union Square to board the chartered bus: "Good girls don't go out in the middle of the night." Eventually my mother softened. "Okay, as long as you dress like a lady." I wore a fashionable minidress, girdle, stockings, and heels, buckling under to my mother's dress code. She was oblivious to the fact that this outfit would make my subway trip more dangerous. My father had been a trumpet player in swing bands before World War II. When he was drafted, he served in an army marching band. Musician jobs dried up with the advent of recorded music, and he ended up working as a laborer, roasting coffee for high-end restaurants in a small nonunion shop on Water Street in Lower Manhattan. He easily shouldered three-hundred-pound sacks of beans and carried them from the docks to the shop. He was a lifelong bodybuilder. When I attempted to leave for DC, he blocked the doorway, scowling, fists clenched. Somehow, I managed to dodge past him. He kicked me in the butt as I left, angry at my disobedience.

I was encouraged to start Brooklyn College as a math major in September 1964. It became obvious to several of our gifted group that we were being groomed to become the new generation of scientists and mathematicians to beat the Russians to space. We saw senior students in the program recruited by Princeton Applied Physics Lab. This validated our suspicions that we were being channeled as brain fodder for the war machine and nuclear proliferation. It was common knowledge that Einstein and Oppenheimer, whose work was pivotal to the development of the atomic bomb, grieved the unleashing of these weapons of unprecedented mass destruction. After the bombing of Hiroshima and Nagasaki, we doubted the existence of so-called pure research during the Cold War. I changed my major to studio art.

The Scholars Program excluded studio majors, but neither me nor my best friend in the program, who changed her major to modern dance, got kicked out. The Scholars Program had a spacious private lounge for students that included a full-time receptionist to make us coffee, but our perks failed to bribe us. When I was elected president of the SDS chapter and representative to regional and national meetings, my elite and somewhat mysterious Scholars Program status made it easy for me to reserve rooms for meetings. Our exclusive lounge became storage space for banners and antiwar leaflets. I was also chosen to represent the chapter in New York regional and national meetings. When seven of us packed into a VW to go to the national convention in Clear Lake, Iowa, in 1966, it was my first time away from home. My first flight was to an SDS national meeting. My ticket and that of the chapter president of Borough of Manhattan Community College were paid for by an older member.

TOPPLING TYRANTS 101

-Susan Simensky Bietila

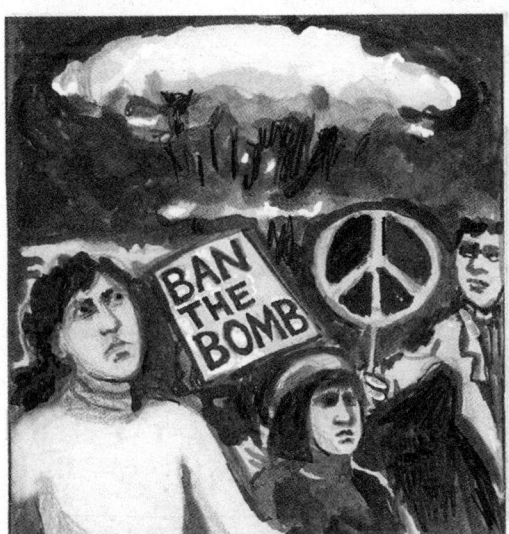

THE BOMB TERRIFIED ME.
I WAS WORKING AS A CAMP COUNSELOR DURING THE SUMMER OF 1964.

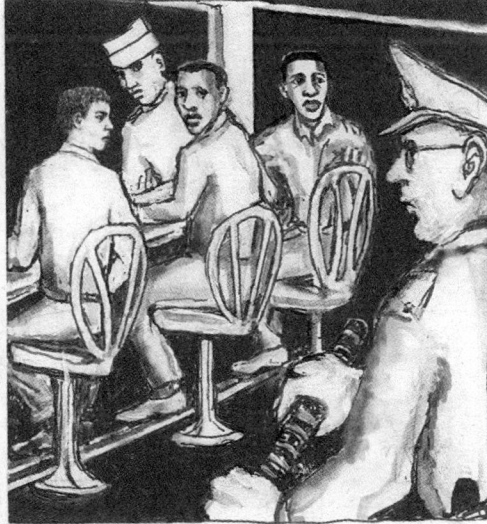

THE CIVIL RIGHTS MOVEMENT INSPIRED ME.

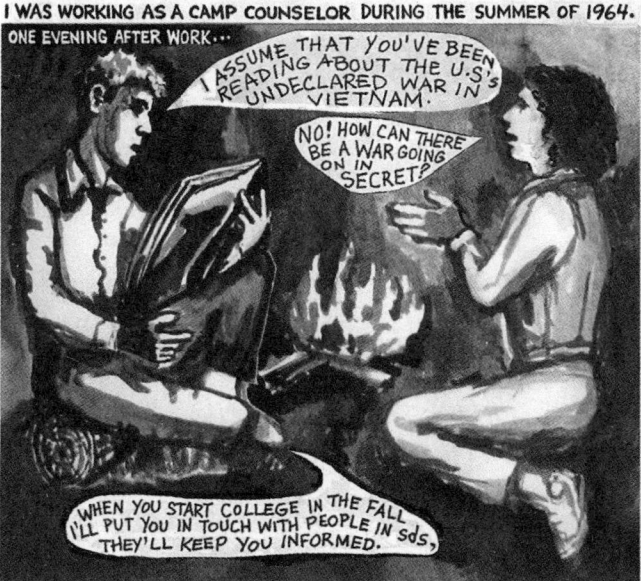

ONE EVENING AFTER WORK...

I ASSUME THAT YOU'VE BEEN READING ABOUT THE U.S's UNDECLARED WAR IN VIETNAM.

NO! HOW CAN THERE BE A WAR GOING ON IN SECRET?

WHEN YOU START COLLEGE IN THE FALL I'LL PUT YOU IN TOUCH WITH PEOPLE IN SDS, THEY'LL KEEP YOU INFORMED.

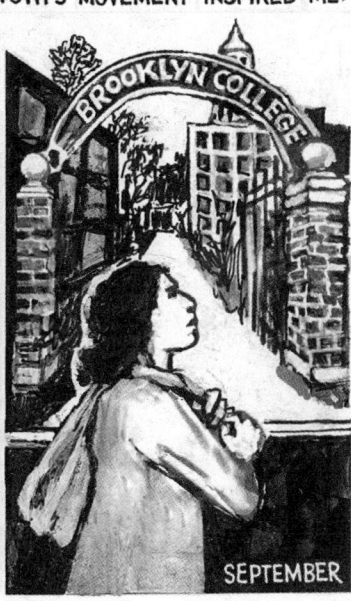

SEPTEMBER

Pages 17–24: Toppling Tyrants 101
First appeared in *World War 3 Illustrated*, no. 38 (2007), "Facts on the Ground" issue.

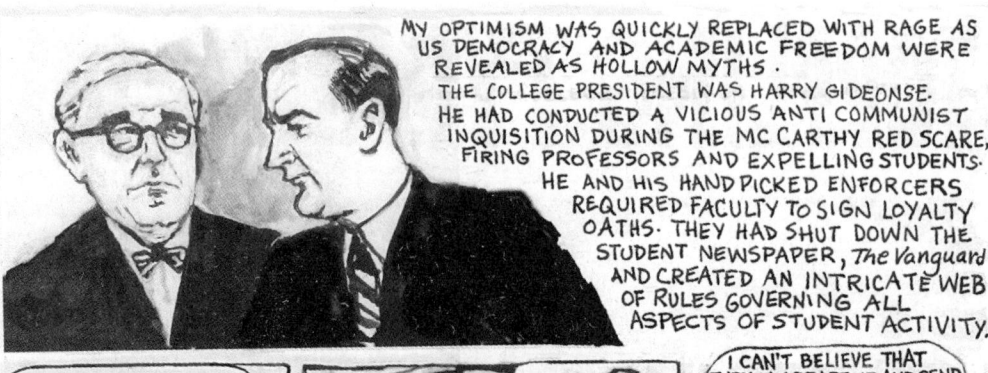

MY OPTIMISM WAS QUICKLY REPLACED WITH RAGE AS US DEMOCRACY AND ACADEMIC FREEDOM WERE REVEALED AS HOLLOW MYTHS.

THE COLLEGE PRESIDENT WAS HARRY GIDEONSE. HE HAD CONDUCTED A VICIOUS ANTI COMMUNIST INQUISITION DURING THE MC CARTHY RED SCARE, FIRING PROFESSORS AND EXPELLING STUDENTS. HE AND HIS HAND PICKED ENFORCERS REQUIRED FACULTY TO SIGN LOYALTY OATHS. THEY HAD SHUT DOWN THE STUDENT NEWSPAPER, *The Vanguard* AND CREATED AN INTRICATE WEB OF RULES GOVERNING ALL ASPECTS OF STUDENT ACTIVITY.

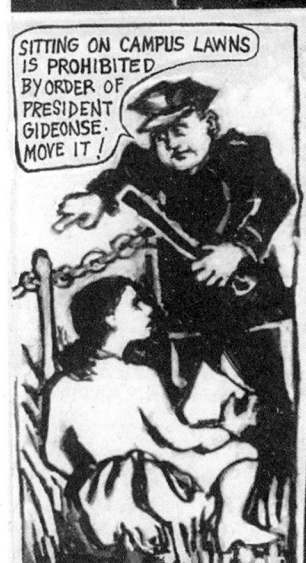

SITTING ON CAMPUS LAWNS IS PROHIBITED BY ORDER OF PRESIDENT GIDEONSE. MOVE IT!

LIBRARY RULES. FEMALE STUDENTS WEARING TROUSERS MAY NOT ENTER. BY ORDER OF PRES. GIDEONSE

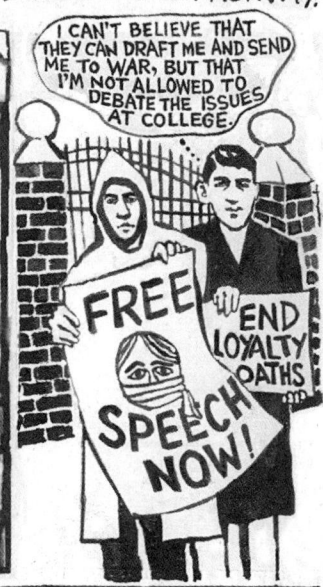

I CAN'T BELIEVE THAT THEY CAN DRAFT ME AND SEND ME TO WAR, BUT THAT I'M NOT ALLOWED TO DEBATE THE ISSUES AT COLLEGE.

FREE SPEECH NOW!

END LOYALTY OATHS

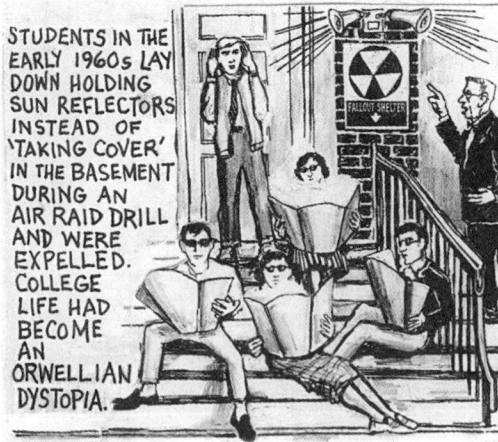

STUDENTS IN THE EARLY 1960s LAY DOWN HOLDING SUN REFLECTORS INSTEAD OF 'TAKING COVER' IN THE BASEMENT DURING AN AIR RAID DRILL AND WERE EXPELLED. COLLEGE LIFE HAD BECOME AN ORWELLIAN DYSTOPIA.

FALLOUT SHELTER

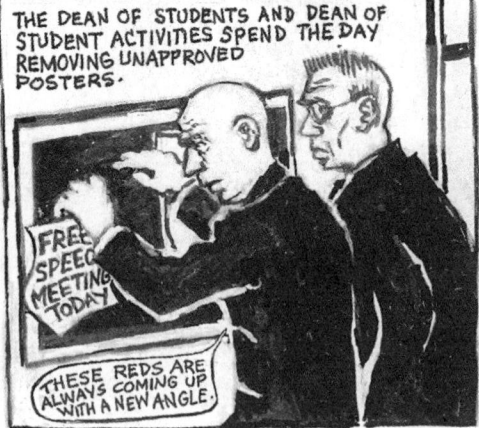

THE DEAN OF STUDENTS AND DEAN OF STUDENT ACTIVITIES SPEND THE DAY REMOVING UNAPPROVED POSTERS.

FREE SPEECH MEETING TODAY

THESE REDS ARE ALWAYS COMING UP WITH A NEW ANGLE.

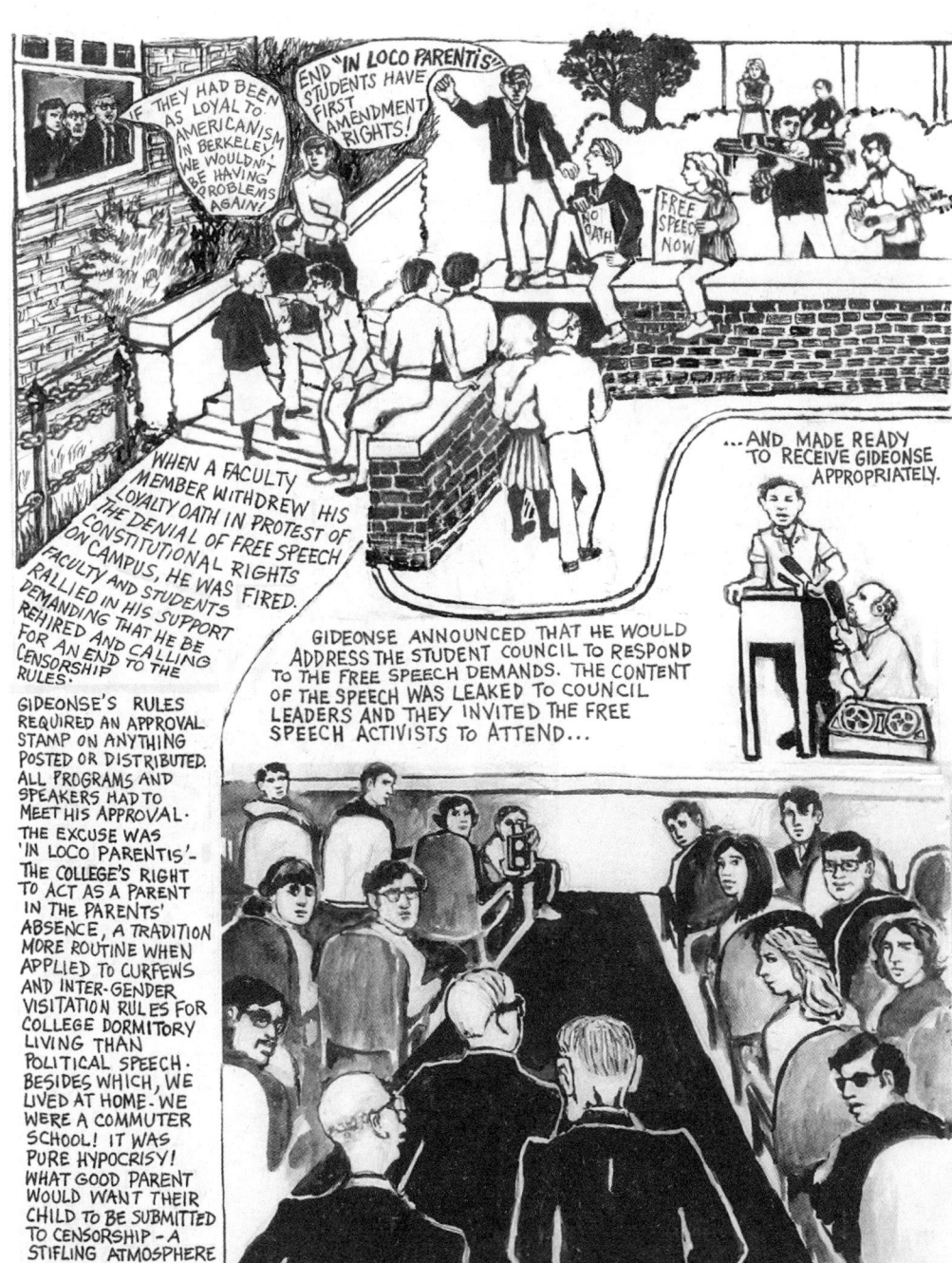

WHEN A FACULTY MEMBER WITHDREW HIS LOYALTY OATH IN PROTEST OF THE DENIAL OF FREE SPEECH CONSTITUTIONAL RIGHTS ON CAMPUS, HE WAS FIRED. FACULTY AND STUDENTS RALLIED IN HIS SUPPORT DEMANDING THAT HE BE REHIRED AND CALLING FOR AN END TO THE CENSORSHIP RULES.

GIDEONSE'S RULES REQUIRED AN APPROVAL STAMP ON ANYTHING POSTED OR DISTRIBUTED. ALL PROGRAMS AND SPEAKERS HAD TO MEET HIS APPROVAL. THE EXCUSE WAS 'IN LOCO PARENTIS'— THE COLLEGE'S RIGHT TO ACT AS A PARENT IN THE PARENTS' ABSENCE, A TRADITION MORE ROUTINE WHEN APPLIED TO CURFEWS AND INTER-GENDER VISITATION RULES FOR COLLEGE DORMITORY LIVING THAN POLITICAL SPEECH. BESIDES WHICH, WE LIVED AT HOME. WE WERE A COMMUTER SCHOOL! IT WAS PURE HYPOCRISY! WHAT GOOD PARENT WOULD WANT THEIR CHILD TO BE SUBMITTED TO CENSORSHIP — A STIFLING ATMOSPHERE HOSTILE TO THE FREE EXCHANGE OF IDEAS.

GIDEONSE ANNOUNCED THAT HE WOULD ADDRESS THE STUDENT COUNCIL TO RESPOND TO THE FREE SPEECH DEMANDS. THE CONTENT OF THE SPEECH WAS LEAKED TO COUNCIL LEADERS AND THEY INVITED THE FREE SPEECH ACTIVISTS TO ATTEND...

...AND MADE READY TO RECEIVE GIDEONSE APPROPRIATELY.

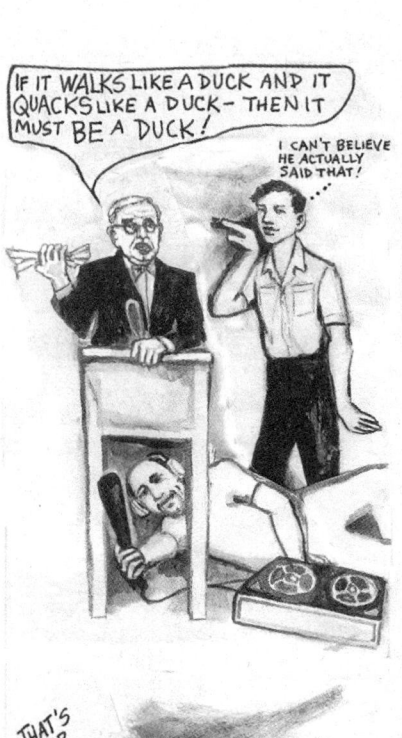

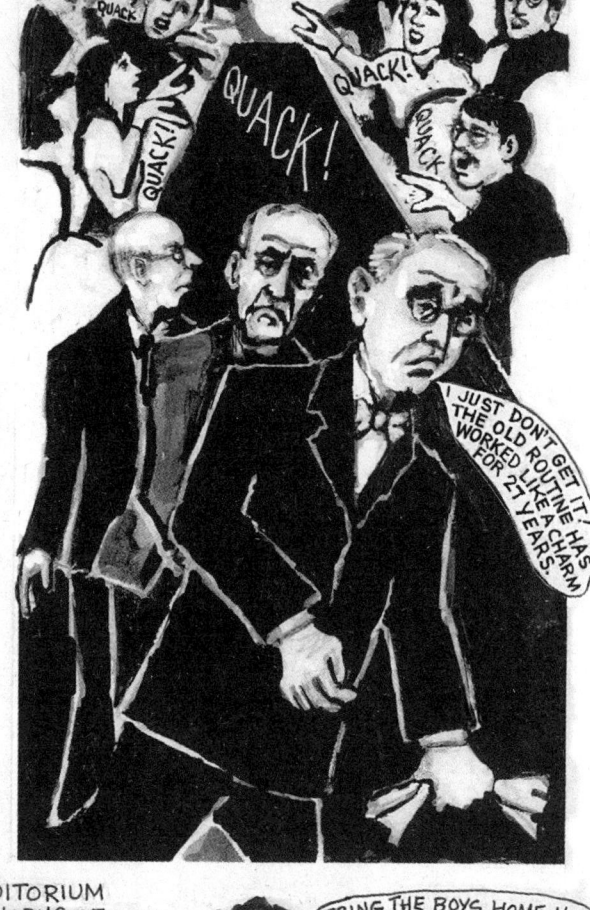

THE ENTIRE
AUDIENCE OF
THE PACKED AUDITORIUM
BROKE INTO A CHORUS OF
CACAPHONOUS QUACKING
ACCOMPANIED BY DANCE
IMPROVISATION.
   GIDEONSE AND HIS
   HENCHMEN FLED.
   HE RESIGNED SOON
   AFTER AND HIS
   ELABORATE SYSTEM
   OF REPRESSIVE RULES
   WAS QUICKLY OVERTURNED,
MAKING IT EASIER TO ORGANIZE
AGAINST THE DRAFT AND AGAINST
THE ESCALATING VIETNAM WAR

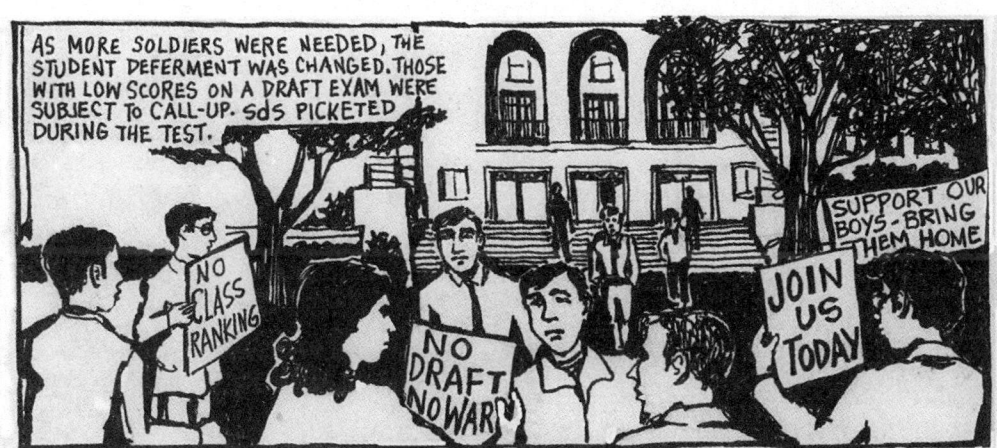

AS MORE SOLDIERS WERE NEEDED, THE STUDENT DEFERMENT WAS CHANGED. THOSE WITH LOW SCORES ON A DRAFT EXAM WERE SUBJECT TO CALL-UP. SDS PICKETED DURING THE TEST.

NO CLASS RANKING

NO DRAFT NO WAR

SUPPORT OUR BOYS - BRING THEM HOME

JOIN US TODAY

AT FIRST, STUDENTS YELLED INSULTS, THREATENED US AND TORE UP OUR LEAFLETS. BUT AS MORE BOYS WERE SENT TO WAR, PEOPLE BEGAN TO QUESTION.

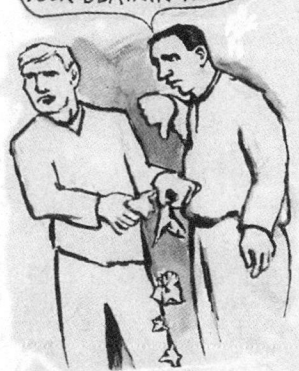

HEY COMMIE GIRL... GO BACK TO RUSSIA! NO ONE WANTS TO READ YOUR BEATNIK TRASH!

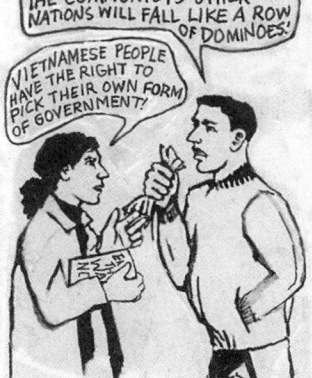

IF WE LET VIETNAM FALL TO THE COMMUNISTS OTHER NATIONS WILL FALL LIKE A ROW OF DOMINOES!

VIETNAMESE PEOPLE HAVE THE RIGHT TO PICK THEIR OWN FORM OF GOVERNMENT!

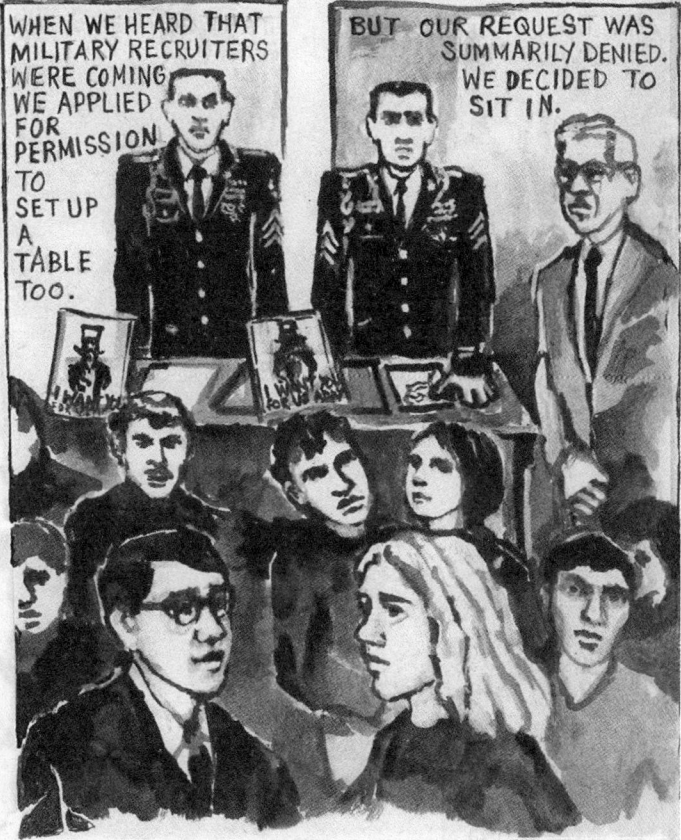

WHEN WE HEARD THAT MILITARY RECRUITERS WERE COMING WE APPLIED FOR PERMISSION TO SET UP A TABLE TOO.

BUT OUR REQUEST WAS SUMMARILY DENIED. WE DECIDED TO SIT IN.

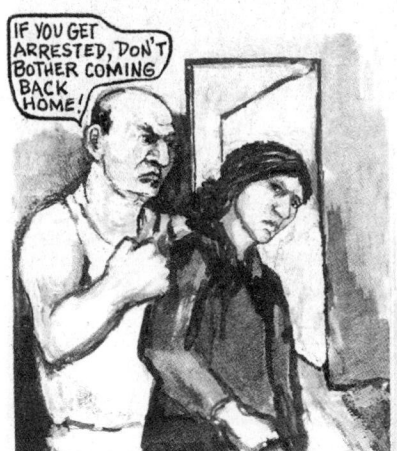

MY DAD HAD ME SHAKEN. I WENT TO CLASS ON THE FLOOR ABOVE THE SIT IN AND PLANNED TO JOIN IT NEXT HOUR.

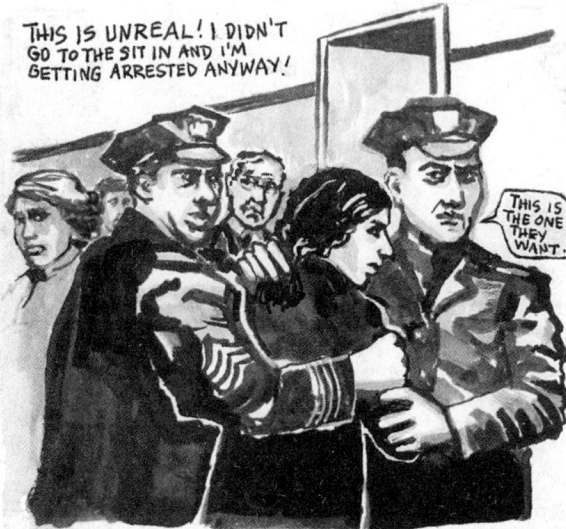

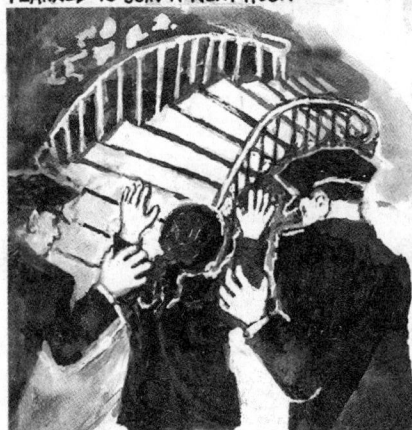

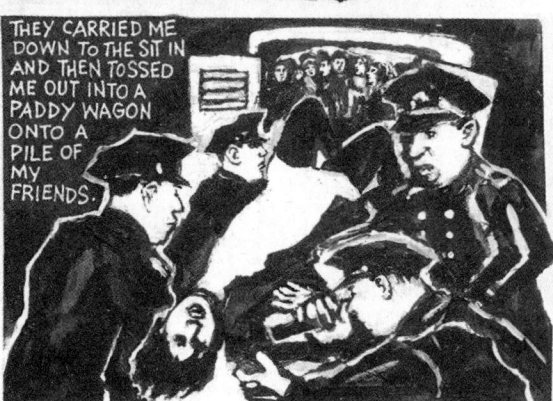

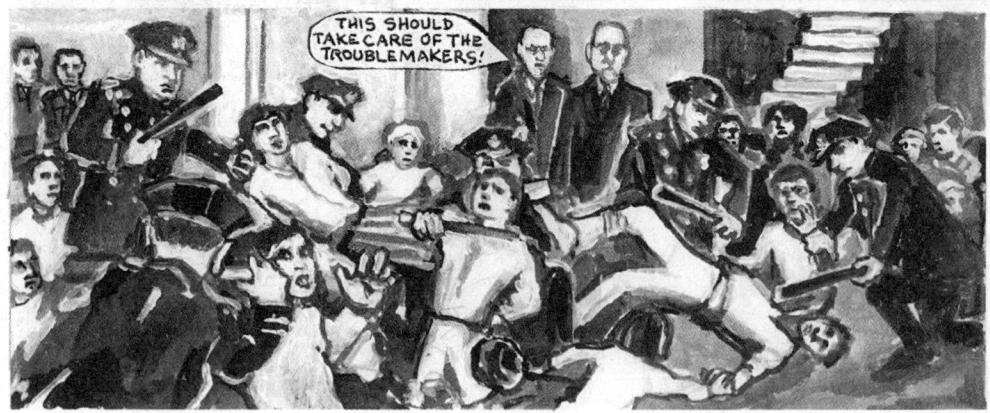

22

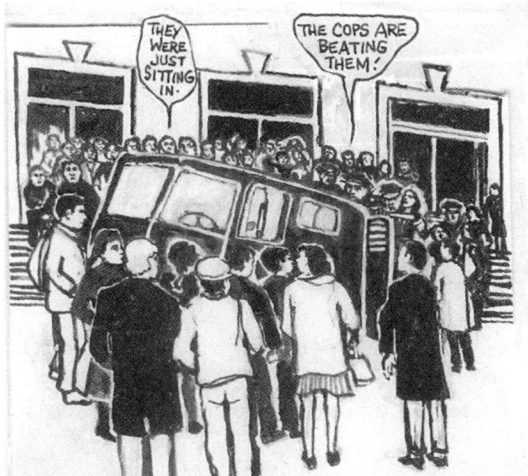

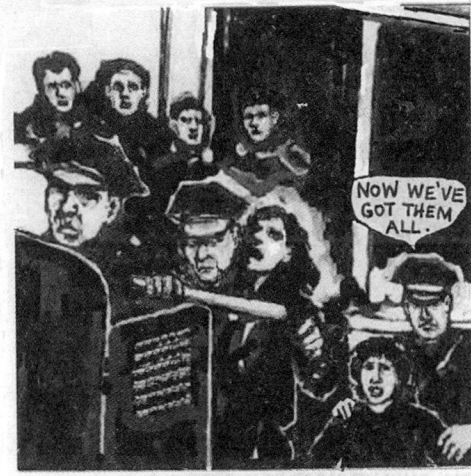

AT FIRST STUDENTS WATCHED THE ARREST AND ROUGH TREATMENT IN SILENCE. THEN THEY STOOD AROUND THE PADDY WAGONS. WORD SPREAD AND MORE STUDENTS AND EVEN FACULTY CROWDED TIGHTLY AROUND BLOCKING THE WAGONS IN.

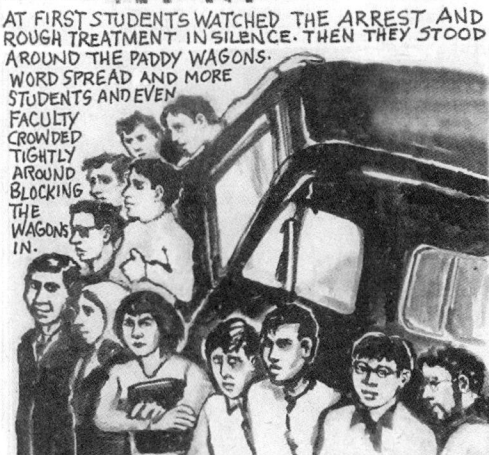

HUNDREDS OF STUDENTS AND FACULTY WHO HAD NEVER BEEN INVOLVED SAT DOWN.

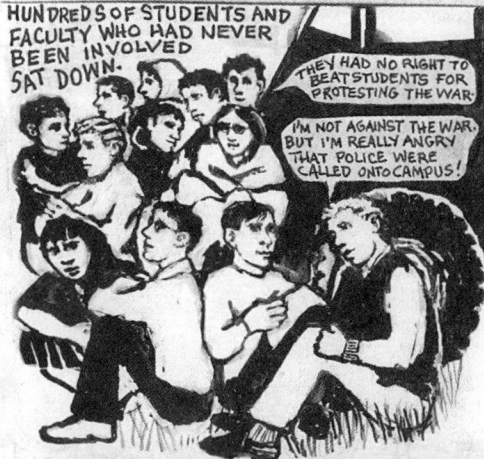

HOURS PASSED AND THE PADDY WAGONS REMAINED BLOCKED-IN WITH EVEN FRATERNITY JOCKS JOINING THE CROWD. A HAT WAS PASSED...

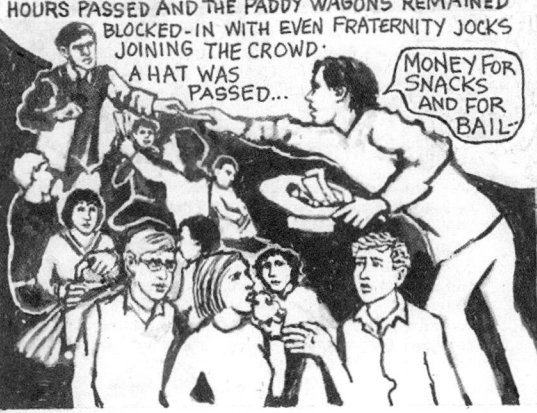

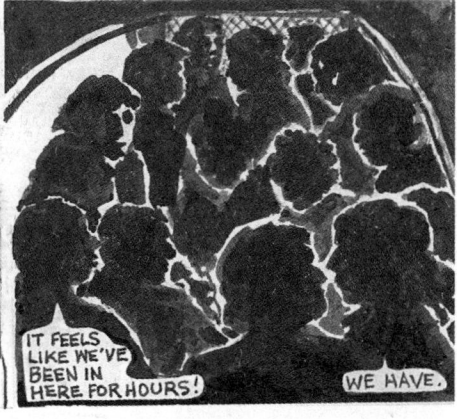

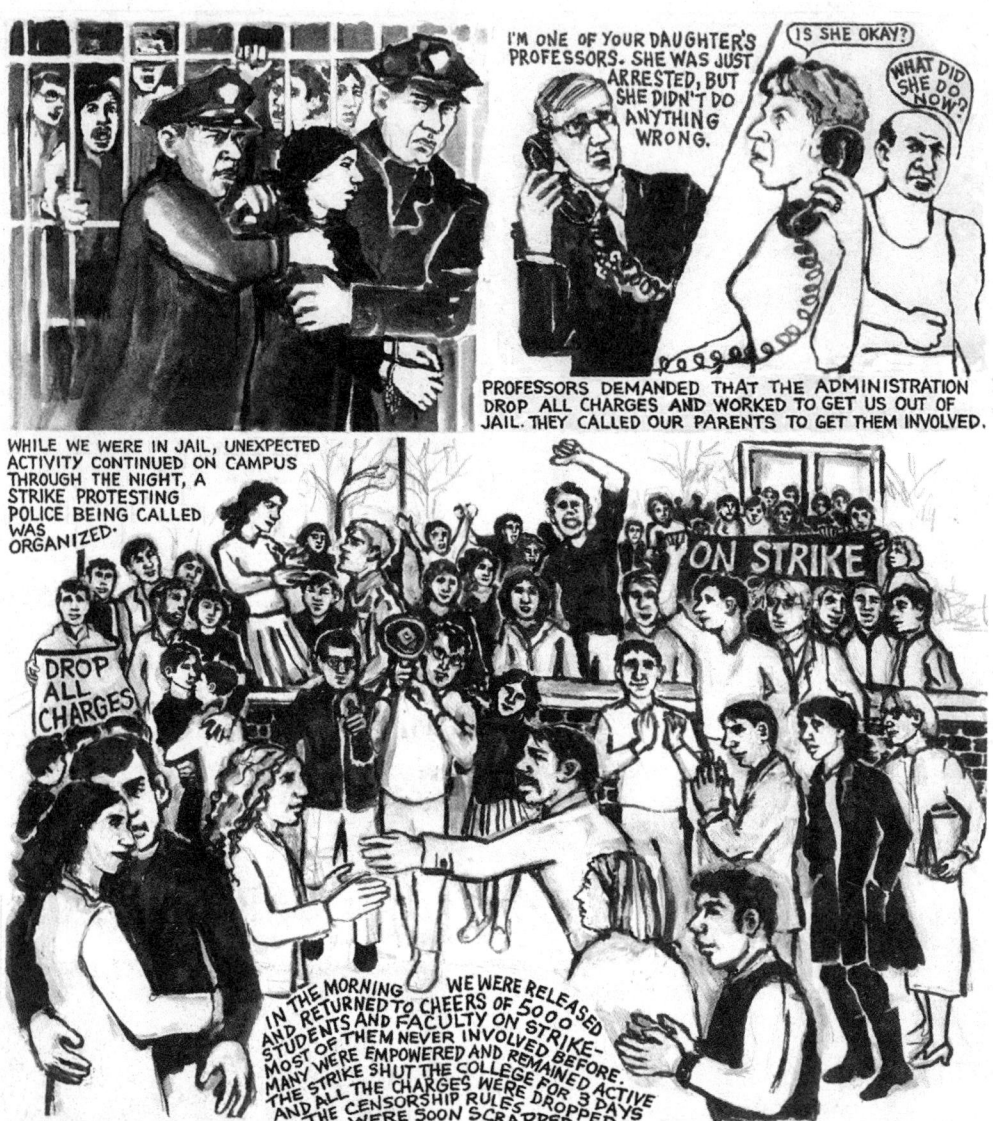

This happy ending has, for the most part, stayed with me. I am generally optimistic when it comes to the ability of people to eventually see the truth. But when I returned to Brooklyn College to research my own history for this story, I found that the library was named after, of all people, Harry Gideonse. There was a photo exhibit in the lobby of Brooklyn College History and there it was! . . . a photo of hundreds of students sitting quietly covering the quad, blocking in Paddy Wagons. The caption read "Student Riot".

How could anyone look at this picture and call it a riot? People were sitting on the grass. They weren't moving. They didn't even look angry. I brought this travesty to the attention of the archives librarians. I pointed out the obvious contradiction between what the picture showed and their caption and showed them the report in their collection documenting that it was the police who had done the rioting. I was flatly told that the caption would be changed, but I left feeling that it would not happen. This story is an effort to set the record straight.

A Bit of Art History

Many of the US schools of art merged with colleges and universities during the era of McCarthyism's blacklists, loyalty oaths, censorship, self-censorship, and Abstract Expressionism. The highest aspiration for artists was supposed to be commercial success—being represented by a major gallery that sold your work to hang in corporate offices, the homes of the wealthy, or museums. And the elite galleries and auction houses sold art as a capital investment. My gender, class background, and leftist politics made this world obviously alienating to me, with a promise of only rejection and disappointment. Narrative and figurative art was derided as communist-influenced social realism or illustration, and "commercial art." I wasn't into comic books, but for historical background, comics were not considered art at all. They were labeled lascivious, violent, indicative of low culture. In 1954, the US Senate heard testimony that comic books contributed to juvenile delinquency, a notorious boogeyman of the 1950s. A consortium of comics publishers instituted the Comic Book Code Seal of Approval, which was de facto censorship.

Art classes were organized by medium: drawing, painting, photography, and so on. There were no classes where content was discussed. We were left on our own to figure out how the "art world" functioned. There was never discussion of how we were supposed to go about making a living. I wanted my artwork and politics to be in sync. Over and over, the art professors told me that art doesn't make social change. It got ugly when I displayed my artwork from the *Guardian* at my senior show. Philip Pearlstein sneered, and Jimmy Ernst called me an illustrator and a propagandist. My answers weren't going to come from the university.

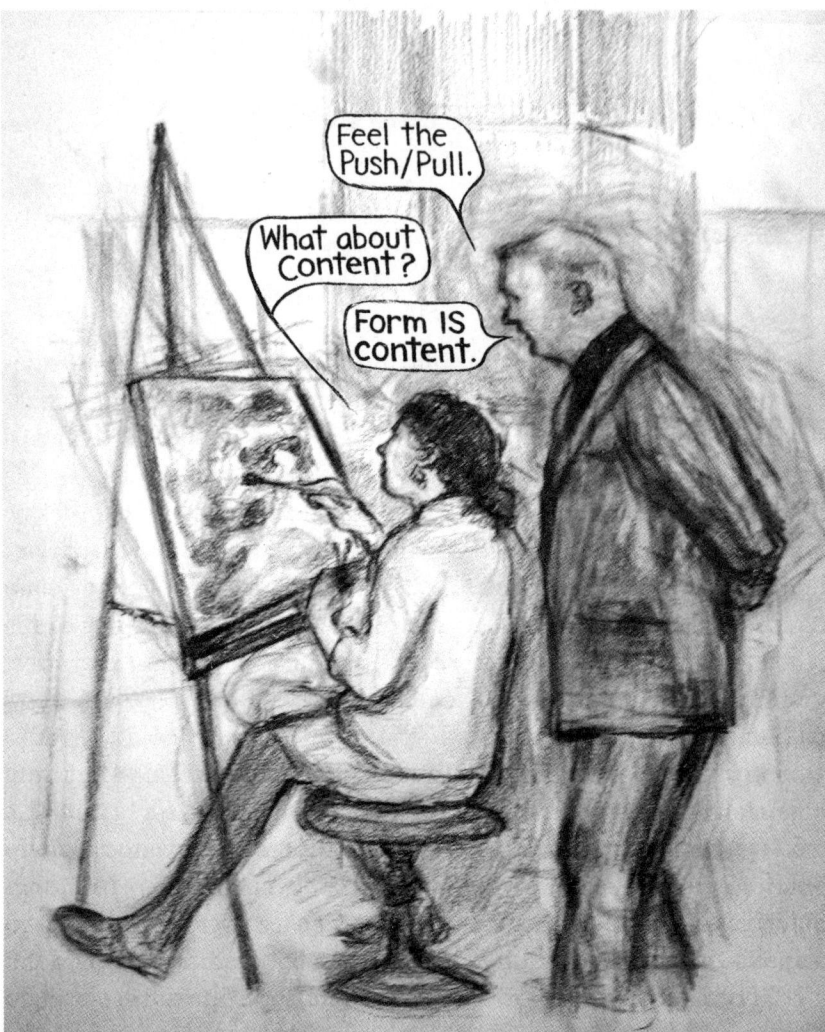

Ad and Me: It's 1966 and I am the only undergraduate with my own studio space. It was in the attic of Boylan Hall. Here is a 1:1 critique with my assigned mentor, Ad Reinhardt. A mentor relationship was part of the Scholars Program at Brooklyn College. Reinhardt is known for his black-on-black minimalist paintings. He assumed that I would be an abstract painter. His work was shown in the "best" galleries and the Museum of Modern Art. Reinhardt never told me that he was against the Vietnam War, but I found out later that he had been in the group Angry Arts Against the War. I wonder if he had been under pressure to keep his politics under wraps at the college. Inviting me to Angry Arts would have helped me find a way forward, instead of telling me to go to art show openings at the 57th Street elite galleries. He died suddenly during the summer of 1967.

My Europe Trip: Amsterdam and the Provos

In 1967, I still had scholarship money in the bank, since Brooklyn College was free. Brooklyn College had a cheap charter flight to Europe. Many people I knew were going, but I had a hard time convincing my parents to let me escape their surveillance. Finally, my nana lifted her dress and pulled out a roll of bills from under her garter, saying, "I don't know why you want to go to Europe after we had such a hard time escaping from there, but the rich people send their daughters there to learn to be ladies. My Suzele deserves only the best." Becoming a polished young lady was the last thing I had in mind.

The day after arriving at Heathrow, I found people from the English antiwar movement and the South African antiapartheid movement, including an exiled Black graduate student activist. On a hot night, my new activist friends took me to a pub, and after drinking hard cider, I was unable to walk. I had no experience with alcohol. They put me in the back of a pickup truck and took me to their apartment to sleep it off. The next day, I was introduced to Peggy Duff, a portly, tough-looking older woman who turned out to be the founder of the Campaign for Nuclear Disarmament. She took me out to her favorite pub for a pint and invited me to accompany her to the International War Crimes Tribunal in Stockholm, to hang out with Bertrand Russell. I was honored to be treated with such respect, but I decided to use my new freedom for less weighty pursuits.

I went to a rock club in a dingy black basement to hear Mick Farren and the Social Deviants. The drummer invited me to his place to crash. He was my age, a nice Jewish boy. His mother tucked me in for the night. But the next day was bad news. Another guy at the club invited me to crash at a London School of Economics building that was closed for the summer. We climbed a spiked fence into a second-story window. The next day, he took me to visit a "friend." This "friend" was a dealer, and the guy was a junkie. It was an attempt to trade me for drugs. When his hand grabbed under my skirt, I ran for the door and managed to get away. I was so traumatized that I caught the next flight to Amsterdam.

After a night in the Amsterdam Youth Hostel with calico-dressed Iowa farm girls, I set out to find *my* people. I spotted a beautiful young woman hawking a psychedelic-looking newspaper on the street corner. Adinka, an art student, was selling *Die Witte Krant* (The White Paper), Amsterdam's underground paper akin to London's *IT* (*International Times*). She told me that she was on the crew making a continuous street drawing from Amsterdam to London. I needed a place to stay, so she took me to meet Martijn Lindt. He had the key to the home of Roel van Duyn and his wife, who were on vacation in Lapland. Roel and Martijn were theoreticians of the anarchist youth movement in Amsterdam called Provo, perhaps short for "provocation." They were known for militant street demonstrations against their Princess Beatrix marrying a former Wehrmacht soldier. Provo created the White Plans, which included disarming the police, squatting, and the White Bicycle Plan, which left white painted bikes around the city that anyone could use for free. Without permits from the city authorities, they held midnight poetry performances at crowded city squares, creating the equivalent of flash mobs by word of mouth. They opened the staid culture to spontaneity. Adinka and her crowd had been part of the Provo events. They showed the way forward as an artist, making art outside of mainstream institutions to create liberatory spaces. Hakim Bey, the anarchist writer, later gave the name "temporary autonomous zones" to this way of reclaiming the commons. The Provos showed that a division into hippies and politicos, promoted in the US, was a false premise.

I crashed at Johannes's loft the rest of my time in Amsterdam. He was queer, Jewish, my age, and well known in the gay counterculture. Most of the crowd of friends were students, and they were on summer vacation too. They took me along everywhere they went. I was innocent and credulous. My new friends soon realized this, resulting in relentless teasing. Hennie, one of our group, introduced me with a smirk as "the American imperialist." They knew that I was in SDS and the antiwar movement. Because I had very short hair and dressed in clothes from the army/navy store, which was much more peculiar then than it is today, many assumed that I was a lesbian instead of a countercultural straight feminist. They took me to visit "the Qveen," a skinny albino-looking

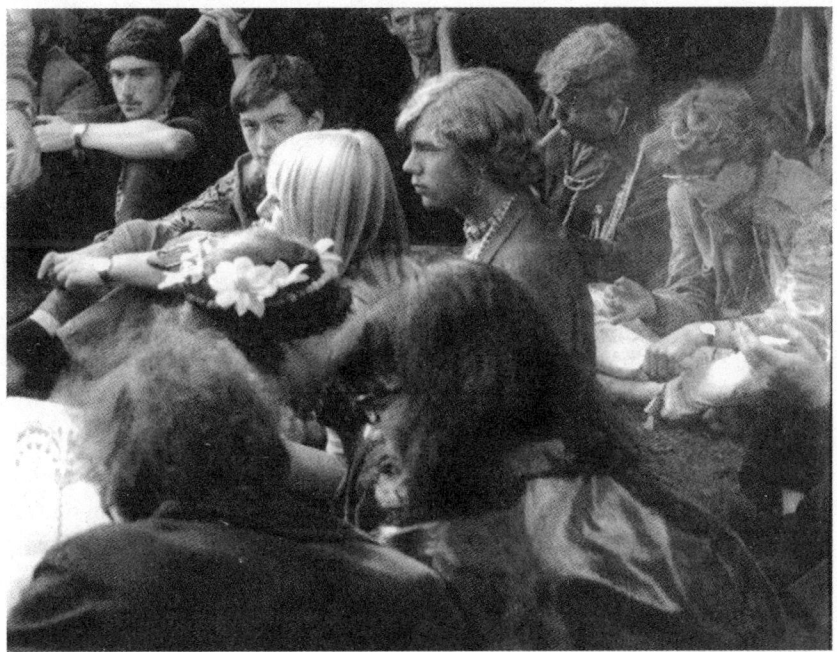

Amsterdam Be-In: In Amsterdam, in the summer of 1967, my friends took me to a Be-In in the Vondelpark. Several of them are in the picture.

boy wearing thick glasses and a shocking-pink mohair sweater. He was surrounded by his court of bodybuilder admirers. I found friendship and affinity in this crowd and a sweet boyfriend who looked like a *GQ* model. When it was time for me to leave, he proposed marriage, partly because of affection, but more to allow me to go to art school in Amsterdam for free. I was unsure of this chaste relationship with the heartthrob of many men and women.

I returned to New York and resumed organizing against the Vietnam War, which had escalated. I had new confidence and determination from my travels. My parents noticed the change and accused me of using drugs. I had already been a smoker but now hand-rolled my cigarettes in the European fashion. My father took my pipe tobacco to a lab to have it analyzed. My mother searched my room and found unopened birth control pills and hot letters from a guy I'd met at an SDS national conference. Living with parents who were angry at and suspicious of whom I had become was intolerable.

Activism had become more important than schoolwork. There were demonstrations against the draft and the Vietnam War 24/7.

At national SDS meetings, women formed a caucus to analyze our systemic oppression. From these discussions and the newly created consciousness-raising groups, I developed an understanding of gender roles as social constructions. School was on hold. I dropped out that semester and traveled to San Francisco with Paula, a friend from my home neighborhood who was enamored with Janis Joplin, free rock concerts, and the vanguard of the counterculture. We drove nonstop in a drive-away car with a speed freak. I discovered a pistol stuffed in between the cushions of the back seat. While in San Francisco, I felt isolated. I got a subsistence job sorting carnations in a refrigerated warehouse. I did visit the local underground paper, *The Movement*, and got to know some of the staff, doing a little hand-lettering and dancing in African dance sessions. I was determined to work on a similar paper. I got very sick with a kidney infection. A draft resister doing alternative service took me to the Free Clinic on the back of his motorcycle and got me to the doctor. Then the basement where I lived caught fire, and I lost my few possessions. Temporarily feeling defeated, I returned home.

From a Radical Newspaper to the Women's Underground Press

I n Amsterdam, after doing a little work on the Provos' underground paper, *Die Witte Krant*, and San Francisco's *The Movement*, I wanted to work on a political underground paper. SDS people from Austin, Texas, including a former national officer whom I didn't know well, had started *RAT Subterranean News* on New York's Lower East Side. Although the same guy who had told me about the Vietnam War and SDS back when I worked at summer camp was there, he and the others were rudely unwelcoming. They said, "We already have artists," and turned their backs to me without looking at my portfolio. Like many left groups, it was a boys' club. Most of the women were girlfriends of these movement honchos and were relegated to doing the typing and making the coffee. It was clear that I was not subservient or girlfriend material. (Spoiler alert: Two years later, women took over *RAT*. My artwork was often on the cover and throughout the paper, and the first issue after the takeover was written in my own hand lettering.)

The same day the door slammed at *RAT*, I went down East 4th Street to the *Guardian: Independent Radical Newsweekly*, the main national left-ist publication. The *Guardian* wasn't historically countercultural, but it had been recently redesigned to appeal to my New Left generation. I was hired on the spot, though only to do layout. With a condescending nod, the editors told me maybe I would eventually be allowed to try illustra-tion. Six months later, I was doing covers and illustrations that made the paper contemporary, unlike so many left publications, pages crammed with screeds in minute type and few photos or illustrations. Through my new coworkers, who were in Lower East Side affinity groups, I was introduced to the Yippies (the Youth International Party), the Committee to Defend the Panther 21, the Young Lords Party, and more.

I loved working at the *Guardian*. It was the first time that I had put my ideas into practice, and my artwork was going worldwide. It was

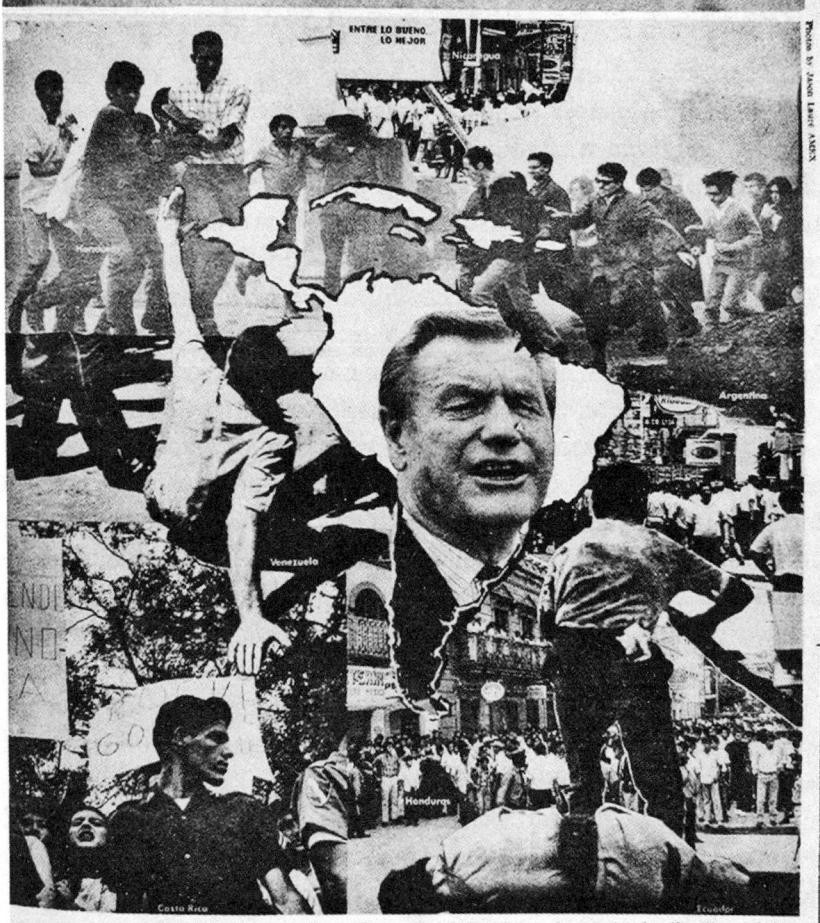

Rocky in Latin America: This July 1969 *Guardian* cover is a collage of anti-US riots that greeted New York Governor Nelson Rockefeller on his ill-fated goodwill mission to four South American nations. I continue to be a fan of collage, inspired by German revolutionary artists John Heartfield and Hannah Hoch and others from the Dada art movement.

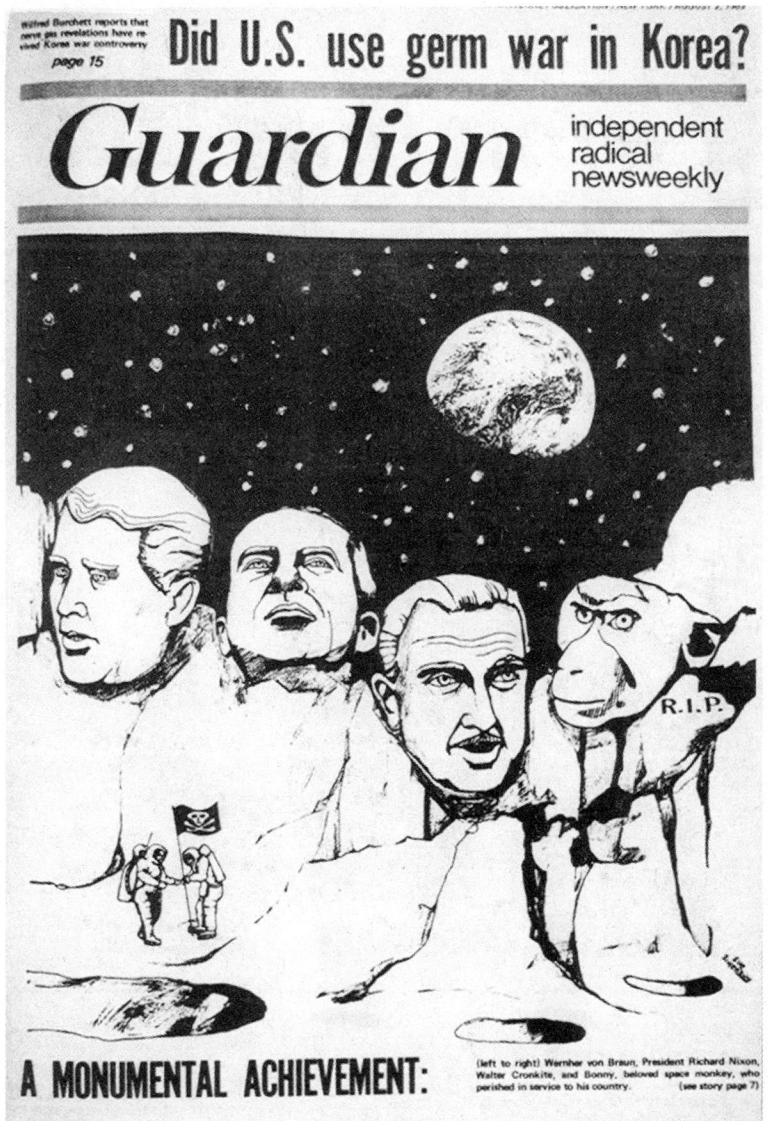

Guardian Moon Cover: The *Guardian*'s take on the 1969 moon landing was that it was part of the space race in the Cold War with Russia. Mount Rushmore references the territorial conquests. Depicted from left to right are: Wernher von Braun, the Nazi SS missile scientist brought from Germany to the US in Operation Paperclip (of *X-Files* fame); President Richard Nixon, who resigned in scandal; iconic news commentator Walter Cronkite; and space monkey Bonny, who died when sent into orbit. (Years later, she was commemorated in song by Patti Smith, the Pixies, and others.) And for a moment of truth in journalism, my astronauts are planting a pirate flag.

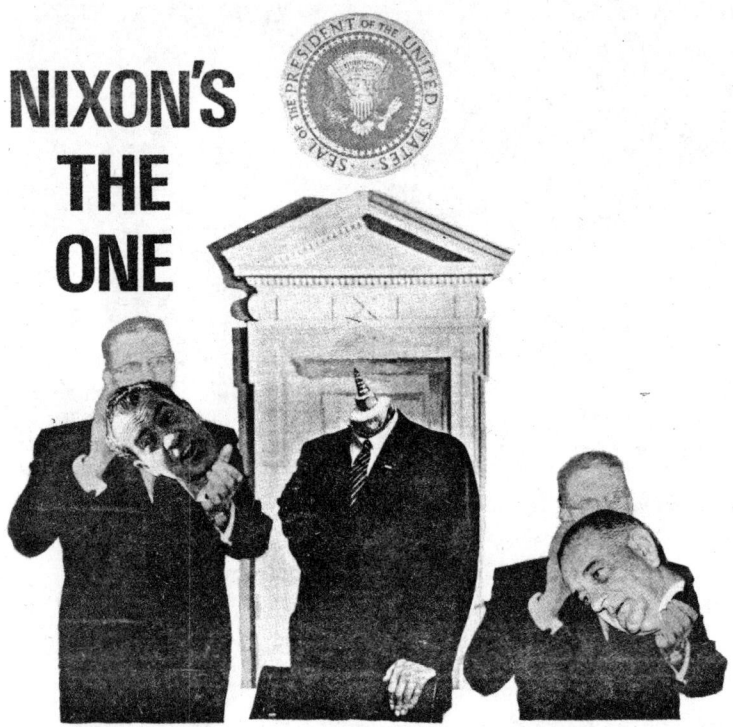

A NATIONAL PUBLICATION / NEW YORK / NOVEMBER 16, 1968 / 25¢

Guardian independent radical newsweekly

NIXON'S THE ONE

viewpoint
Nixon—a time to build:

Unable to discern a greater or lesser evil, the traditional choice of American politics, the people of the U.S. have been reduced to singing the praises of the lesser absurdity.

All power over more than half of humanity to Richard M. Nixon, President-elect of the capitalist empire by virtue of one per cent of the world's population which found him a degree less embarrassing than he who licked the tall Texan's filthy boots these four humiliating years.

In an election which gratified none but those who have abandoned hope, it was, at least, a satisfaction to witness the suffering of Hubert Horatio Humphrey.

The pity was that Lyndon Baines Johnson had the perspicacity to retire before the inevitable denouement. But he is not the first war criminal to escape the hangman.

Vietnam finished Humphrey as it finished Johnson before him. The electorate was no longer willing to tolerate a losing war in Asia, at least not in combination with a developing domestic crisis. Although Johnson attempted in the final hours of his disgrace to convey the impression that the war was nearing its end, neither he nor his minions could be forgiven.

The election changed nothing fundamental. Those who rule America continue to rule under new management.

The election was not even a clear mandate for

[Continued on page 10]

The 1968 Election of President Richard Nixon: I was thoroughly disenchanted with candidates from both parties and the electoral process itself. We get screwed either way.

thrilling. The collectivity in the *Guardian* art department was intensely satisfying. I was the only one who could draw or do collage, but everyone participated in creative discussions, analyzing the politics of the imagery. The paper's editors didn't give us much time, however, as they debated the articles' placement in the paper ad infinitum, leaving the decision about what would go on the cover until the last minute. To them, the art was an afterthought. We often had only six hours, from midnight until 6 a.m., to come up with the cover. Despite these conditions, my skills grew exponentially while I worked at the *Guardian*. I had also returned to school for my junior and senior years of college, but I was less engaged with SDS and campus activism.

The weekly layout and illustration sessions were thirty-six hours straight. We ate little but always had a cup of bad coffee or a cigarette in hand to keep alert. Whenever the Rolling Stones' song "Street Fighting Man" came onto the radio, the art crew abruptly stopped work to dance with abandon, while the somber writers and editors remained at their desks.

This was decades before the internet. We had few reference materials on hand. My visual memory of art I had seen in museums and art history classes in school served me well. Sometimes we received great photographs, but other times they were too dark or too gray to use. Drawing from these photos or tracing them and turning them into line drawings on the big light table were added to my repertoire of skills.

We got a tip that students at Boys High, a predominantly Black high school in Brooklyn, had walked out in protest against racism and the escalation of the Vietnam War. They were going to high schools all over the city and calling students to walk out. I was sent out with a camera to cover the breaking news. I hopped on the subway to Midwood High School on Flatbush Avenue in Brooklyn. It was damp and cold out. I watched as the students poured out the doors. My hands were red and had lost feeling, and the shutter of the camera froze. I realized it was a good thing I couldn't take photos. It was better that photographs of marbles tossed into the street to topple the mounted police did not exist. Photos could have been seized as evidence, used to prosecute the students, or incorporated into surveillance files by the police's anti-communist Red Squad and the FBI's COINTELPRO schemes.

Periodically, the *Guardian*'s kettle of perpetual sectarian mire boiled over. The editors and financial backers were allied with contending

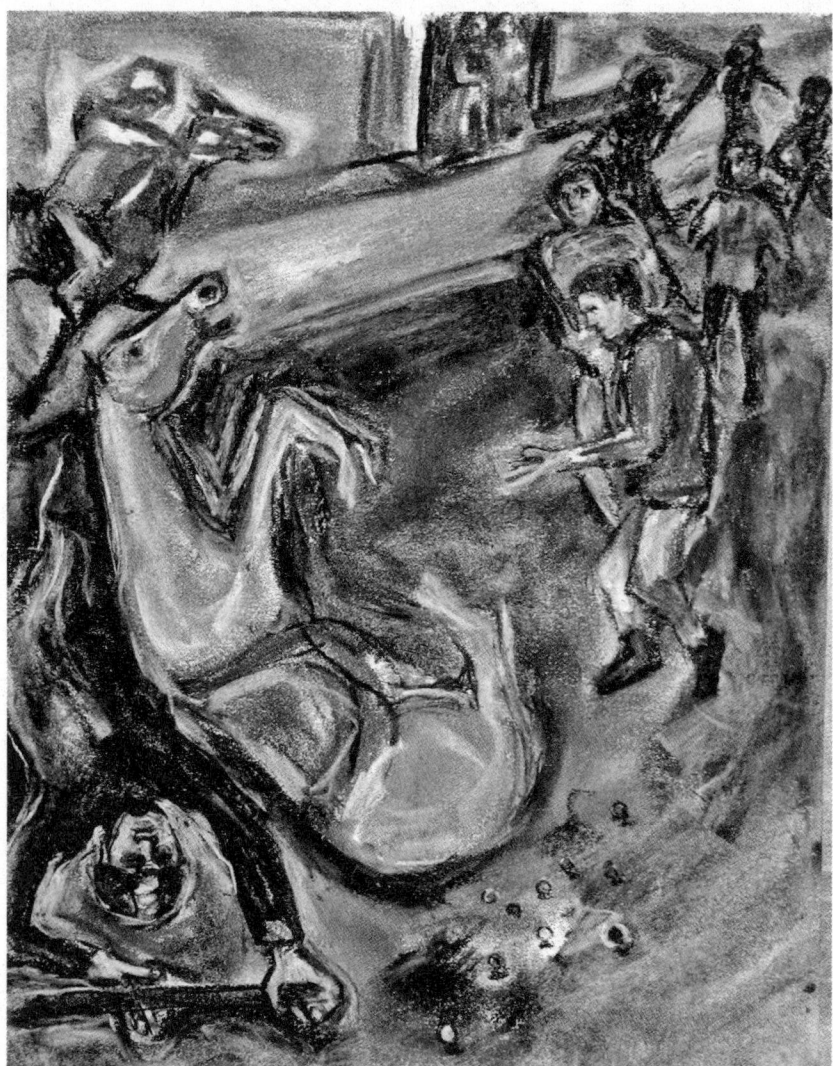

Police Horses and Marbles: When students walked out against the Vietnam War at Midwood High School in Brooklyn, they were beaten with clubs by equestrian police. In defense, they threw marbles under the horses' hooves, and horses lost footing and tumbled over. I drew the scene years later from memory.

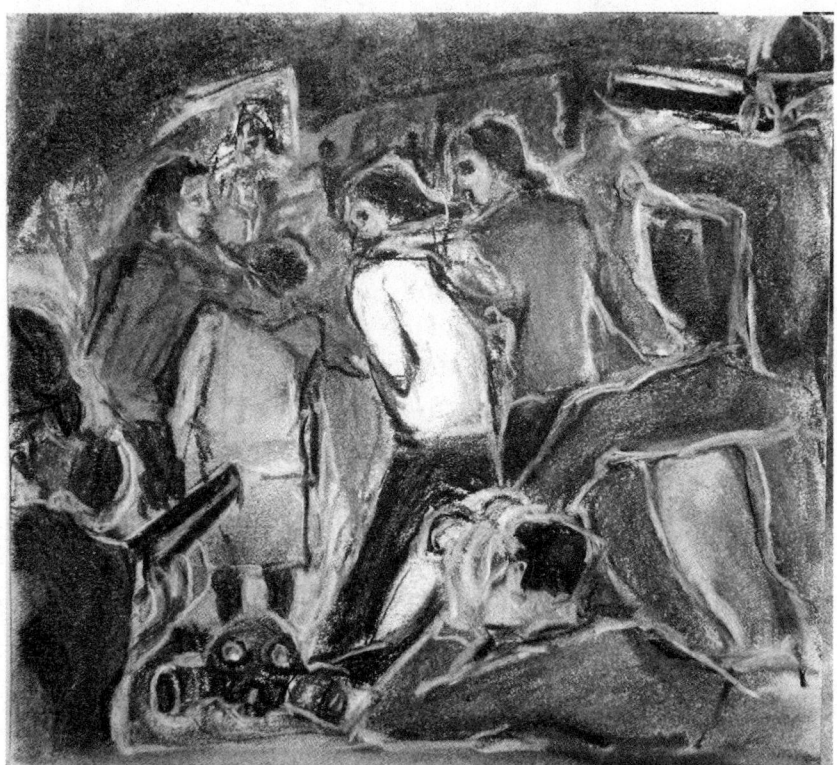

Fort Dix: On October 12, 1969, during the height of the Vietnam War, we marched onto the Fort Dix military base in New Jersey. I was with my first husband, Tom Bruni, his brother Steve, and a group of friends. We were met by a phalanx of military police, who dispensed a noxious gas over us. It was difficult to breathe and to keep our eyes open. Steve, who had been booted out of the navy, had never learned to don his gas mask properly and had been gassed numerous times during training exercises. He remained calm and led us to safety.

communist, socialist, and New Left groups. It was supposed to be a collective, but only the few top editors held power. The rest of the staff organized a walkout. Not only were we going hungry, but we were treated with little respect by a well-fed management.

The Women's Liberation Movement Begins

In September 1968, I heard about WITCH (Women's International Terrorist Conspiracy from Hell). They performed an action, No More Miss Americas, on the boardwalk outside the Miss America Pageant in Atlantic City. They hexed Wall Street on Halloween. With bold originality, they exploded second-wave feminism into the mass consciousness. I had to join.

In February 1969, I joined the "hexing" of the Bridal Fair at Madison Square Garden's Felt Forum, ironically the venue for world boxing tournaments. (You are excused if you've never heard of a bridal fair; I hadn't either.) It was a vast emporium of wedding goods and household products to promote the traditional female role in consumer culture. The event managers and security guards were paralyzed with confusion when we took over the stage and the runway, auctioning off a bride. We made them our unwitting straight men to comic political theater. The strength of this kind of action is that it is difficult for the media or the government to distort the message. Once seen, it is indelible. After participating in this action, I joined two women's liberation groups: one for consciousness raising and political analysis, and another for planning actions.

I didn't return to work at the *Guardian* after the walkout. The handful of remaining old guard had reconstituted their weekly screed and hired yet another round of hopeful young writers and artists. In 1970, the new staff, facing the same hypocrisy and oppressive working conditions, took over the building and kicked out the editor bosses and their few self-important supporters. I was there to support them at the building takeover, along with generations of former staff. They put out their own paper, the *Liberated Guardian*, and were a real collective. I had found a job typesetting the transcript of the Chicago Conspiracy Trial at the office of *The New York Review of Books*. I worked alone at night in an empty office building on 57th Street, the very same street as the elite art galleries. An appealing employee perk was free books: I could pick through the boxes of books lining the hallway. The editors treated me with kindness and respect, and they knew my politics.

One evening at home, a falling-apart fifth-floor walk-up on Avenue B and East 2nd Street, the phone rang. I didn't know the caller. She said, "Women are putting out an issue of the *RAT*. Would you like to join us?" Still stinging from the harsh rejection just a few years prior, I tasted vindication and said yes. Since that time, while *RAT* had continued excellent coverage of rock music and resistance to the war, it had come to rely on exploitative images of women to sell the paper and on sex ads to pay the bills. There was no way that politically conscious women in the movements were going to stand by. This time, I was welcomed

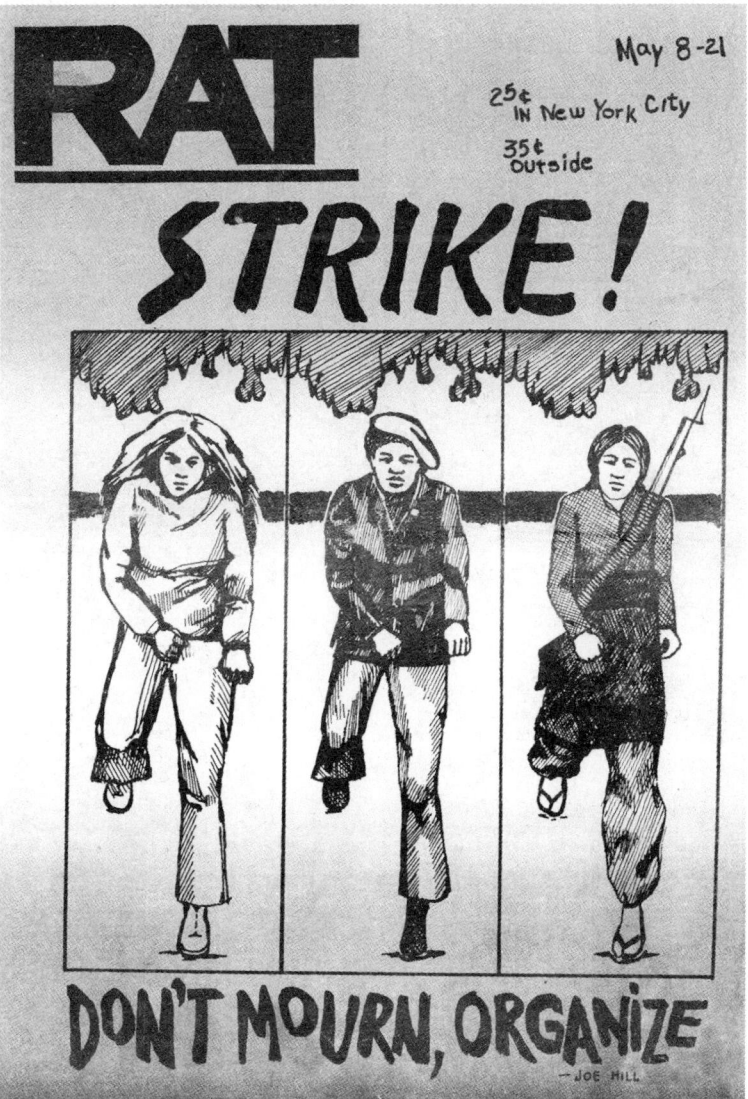

RAT "Strike!" Cover: To my surprise, this 1970 *RAT* cover was never forgotten. It came to be an iconic image chosen by women's history academia to represent the fiery beginning of second-wave feminism. The cover depicts women from the student movement, the Black Panther Party, and the Viet Cong. In the winter of 1996, I stumbled on it hanging near the entrance to the iconic show *Counterculture: Alternative Information from the Underground Press to the Internet* at Exit Art, a major New York exhibit space. The *RAT* "Strike!" cover was exhibited at the Interference Archive show *Rebel Newsprint* in 2013 as well as at Cooper Union and other New York shows celebrating the fiftieth anniversary of the women's liberation movement.

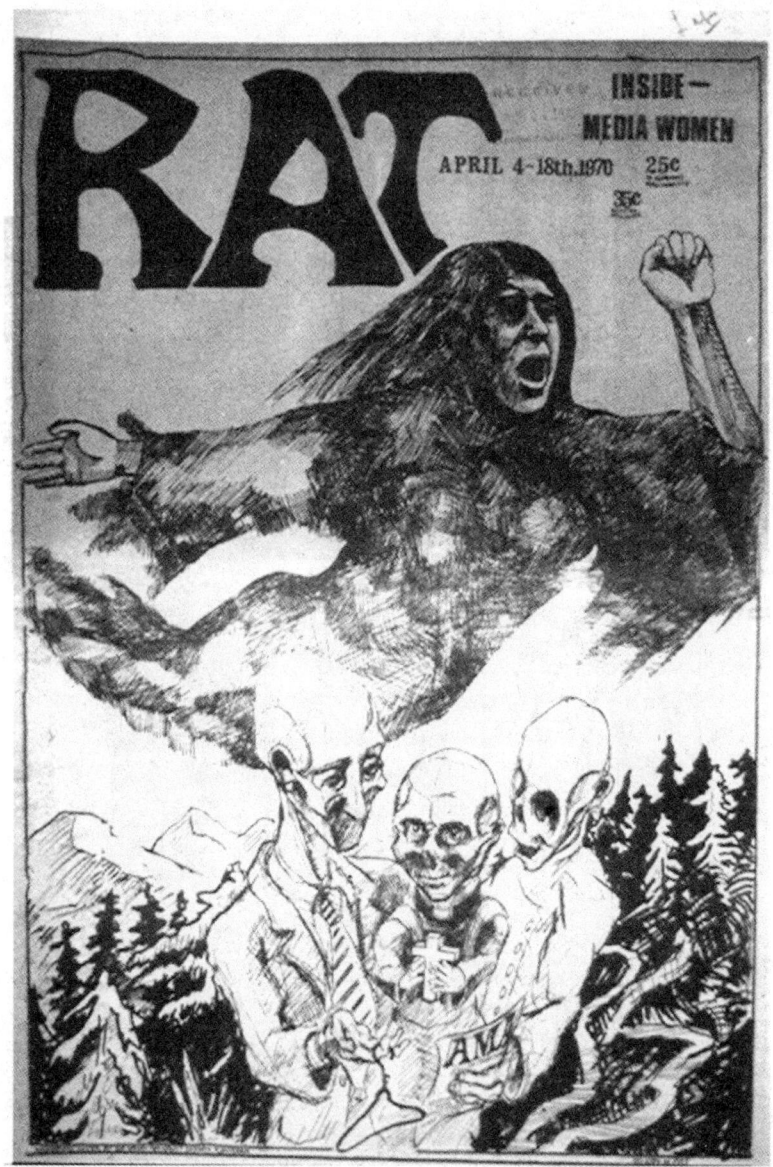

RAT Abortion Rights Cover: I was asked to add a raging witch to another woman's drawing of the misogynist triumvirate—the state, the church, and the doctors—denying women safe abortion. I never knew who dropped off that drawing at the *RAT* office. I hope she will come forward to receive thanks. Abortion was legalized in New York City in 1972. Note that the *RAT* covers didn't usually have the year on the cover and didn't come out on a consistent schedule. We were in it for the moment and didn't anticipate that the publication would have meaning in the future.

to the *RAT* office, now on 14th Street, by women from the antiwar and revolutionary movements as well as from the new women's liberation movement. We reported on the Vietnam War, the Black Panthers, and the Young Lords and wrote film reviews and cultural critiques, but we also published feminist polemics that became canon.

The original deal that had been made with the male *RAT* editorial collective was that we would put out one issue ourselves, to prove that women were more than capable of producing a radical underground publication, and then return the paper to the men. But the collective energy was so empowering, went so smoothly, and was so well received that we decided not to give the paper back. It was obvious that women being relegated to subservient traditional roles had no place in revolutionary movements. The *RAT* men's subsequent ranting, raving, and hostility lasted far beyond that moment. But the *RAT* takeover, like the street theater demonstration at the Miss America Pageant, was a clarion call. Women were rising up and resisting our deep indoctrination to behave like *ladies*. Women's *RAT* made decisions by consensus about what to include in an issue, the order of the articles, and the art content. It was so contentious as a point of women's autonomy that bitterness among many men of that generation persists to this day.

Political rifts began to emerge in the *RAT* women's collective during the second year. We were in the process of creating a way of working collectively that is now called intersectional, at a time when fracturing into identity-defined groups came to the fore. Movements were transformed and elevated by the month. Some of the *RAT* collective women became separatist feminists, and others moved primarily to the bold, "out of the closet and into the streets" gay liberation movement, all while continuing to fight the war and the draft. Others were sympathetic to SDS's Weatherman. A few *RAT* women were convicted of bombing banks, while others joined the wave of anticapitalist Maoist groups to organize with the working class and in communities of color. A few of us became health professionals. Some continued to fight the glass ceiling in publishing, while others published poetry, fiction, women's history, and political theory. Robin Morgan became a founding editor of *Ms.* magazine and edited the second-wave anthology *Sisterhood Is Powerful*.

My relationship with Tom Bruni began during the last year I worked at the *Guardian*. His best friend, Ira, was dating my roommate, Mindy. Both of the guys had been in the high school student union. They

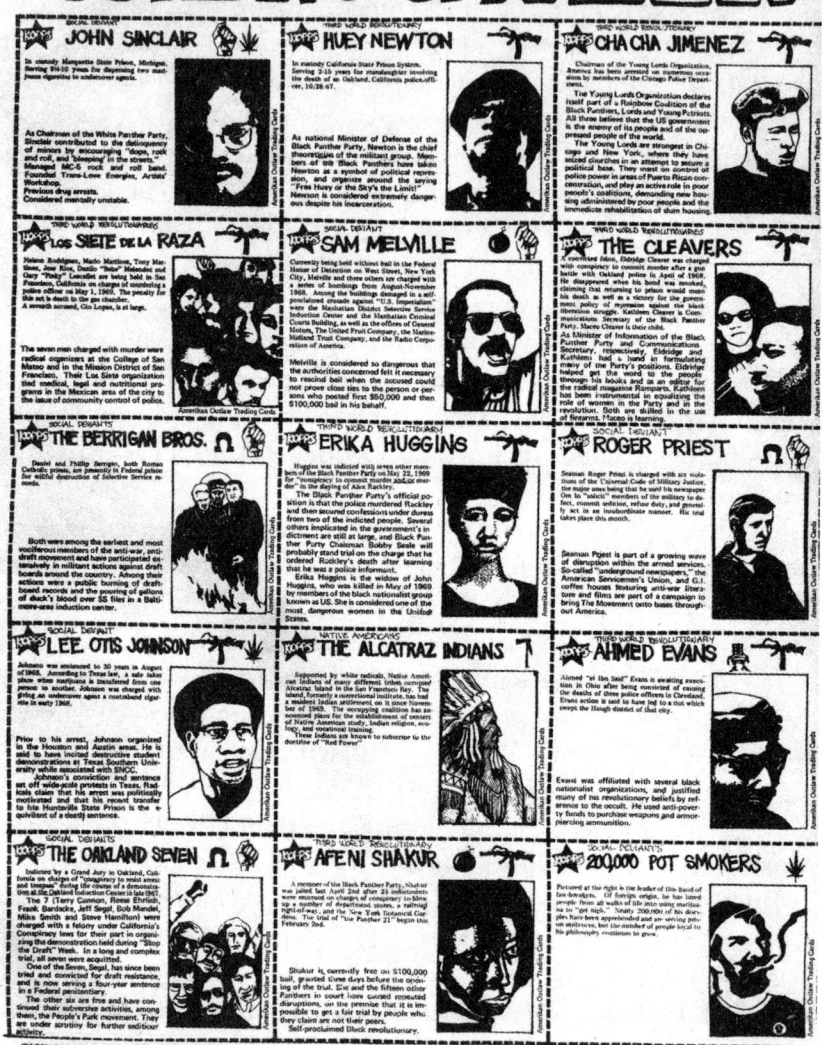

Outlaws of Amerika: The *RAT* women and a few male friends had an enthusiastic brainstorming session to decide whom to include on the *Outlaws of Amerika* trading cards. I did the drawings and layout. It was truly representative of the times. This page was reprinted in almost every book written about the underground press.

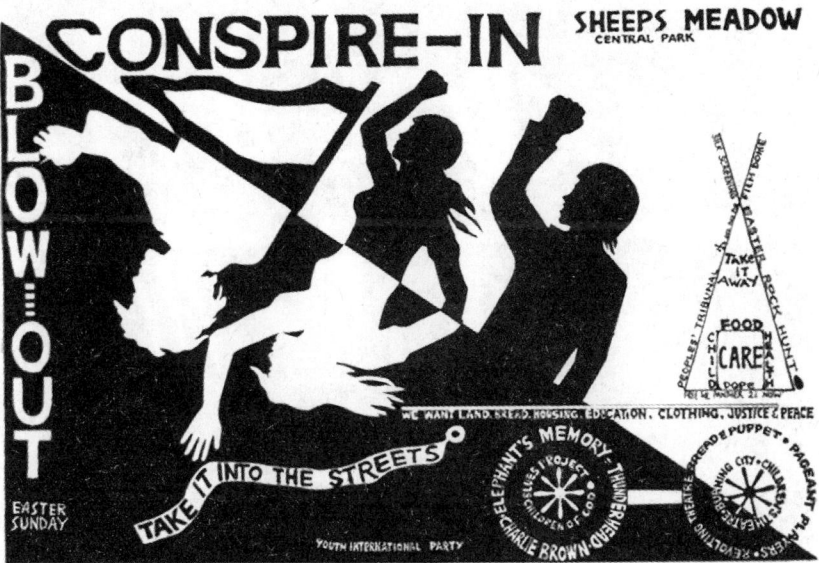

Central Park Be-In: A former *Guardian* art department friend who was a Lower East Side street anarchist stopped by the *RAT* office with an art request from Abbie Hoffman and the Yippies. They wanted me to whip up a street poster for the April 6, 1969, Be-In in Central Park on short notice. I am happy with this visual yin-yang papercut. Our crowd wore motorcycle helmets and boots to demonstrations, to protect our heads from police batons and our feet from horses' hooves. We linked arms to bolster our lines, row after row, emulating Japanese students' "snake dance" maneuver. This was a tactical predecessor of locking down in a "sleeping dragon," in which hands are chained together inside a tube or pipe.

were antiracist and antiwar and had been arrested for inciting a riot at Franklin K. Lane, their former high school, the day of the student walk-outs. Tom faced felony charges, and we thought that marriage would give him the appearance of stability. This may have worked, as he got a suspended sentence. We soon all moved into a tiny apartment on the Lower East Side. Tom built loft beds to accommodate up to four people in a room. And sometimes people crashed in the space under the lower bed. The apartment rent was sixty dollars a month. Tom and his brother Steve had grown up on welfare and had lived in the Pink Houses, to the east of Boulevard Houses, where I grew up. We subsisted on his boxes of surplus food. He was a freshman at City College and an extremely gifted craftsman and mechanic.

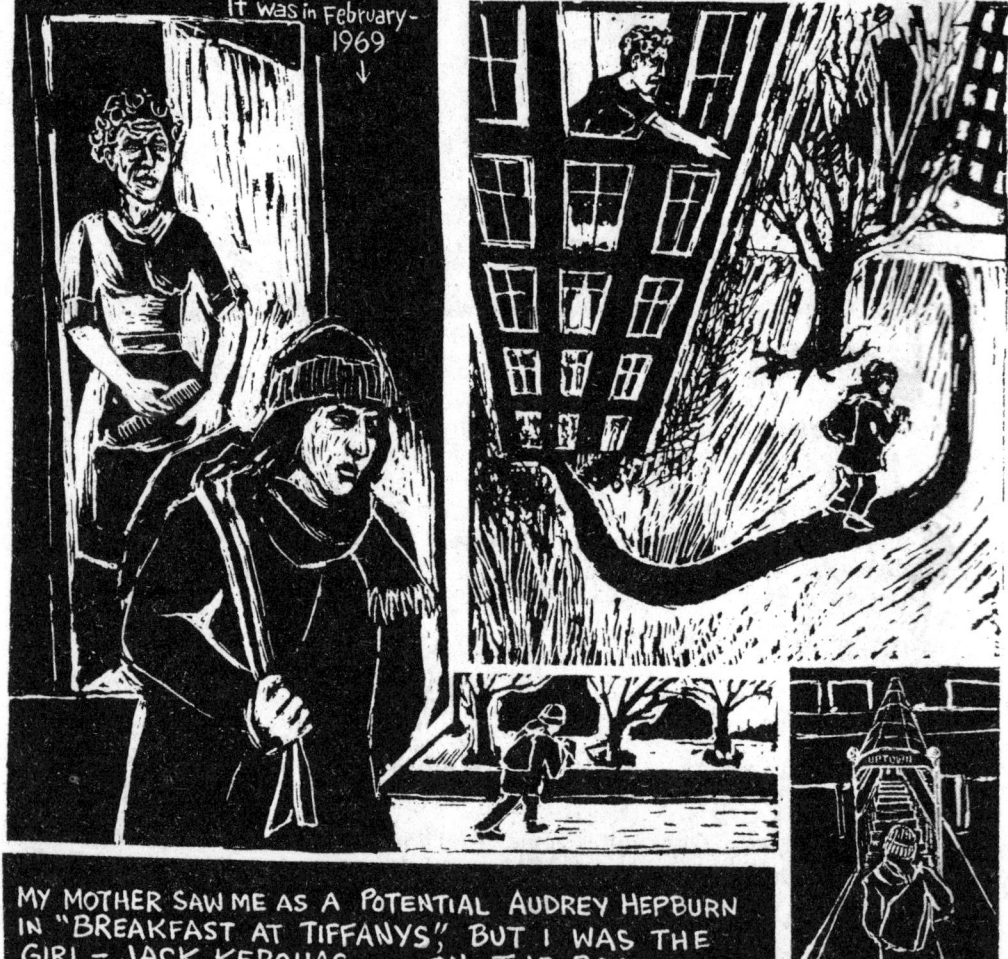

Pages 44–49: Bridal Fair

"Bridal Fair" is my second drawn story. It is not in historical sequence but depicts several events happening during a small window of time. A few feminist historians prompted me to create a documented timeline for future stories, and I took their advice. This story first appeared in *World War 3 Illustrated*, no. 30 (2000), "Bitchcraft" issue.

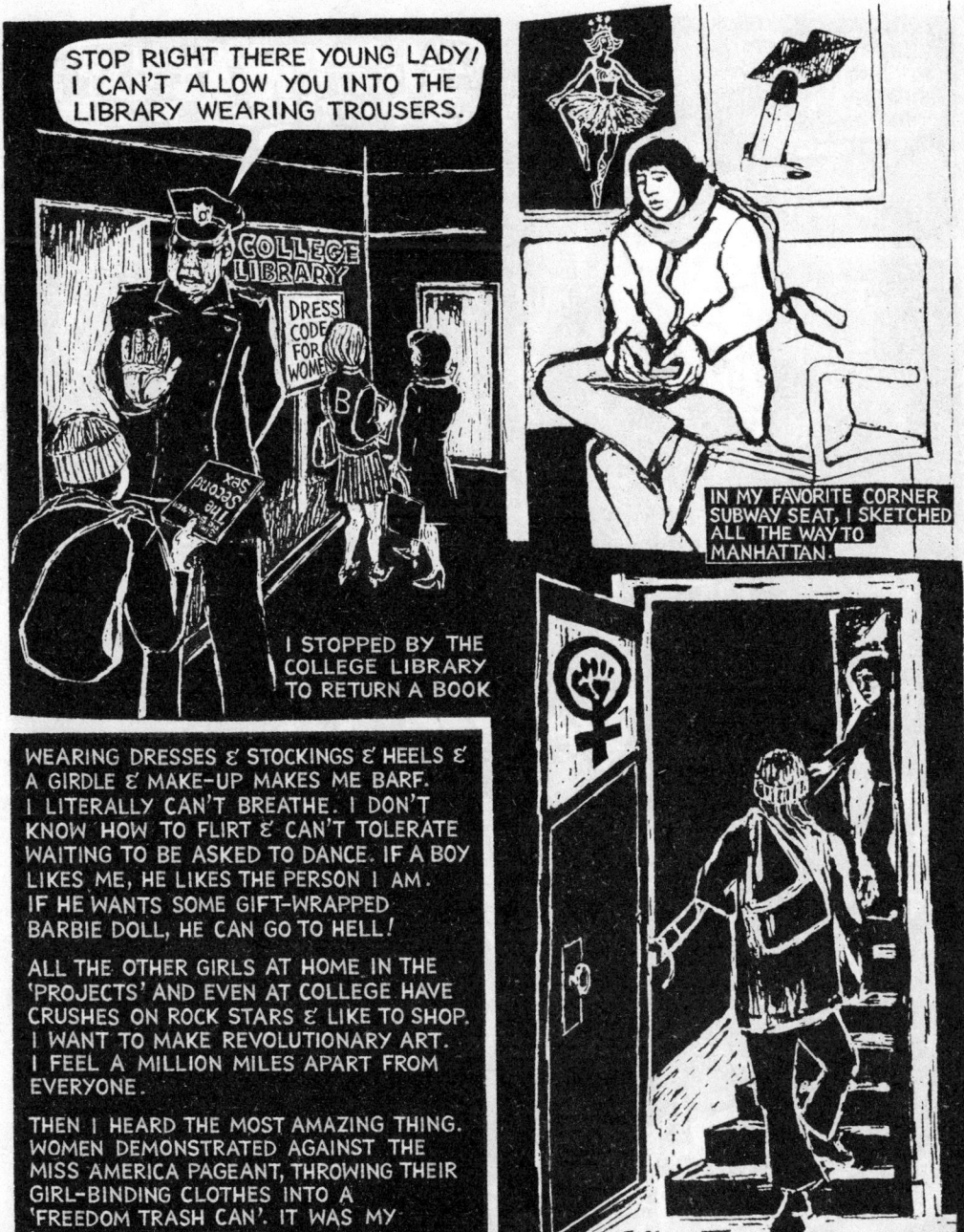

STOP RIGHT THERE YOUNG LADY! I CAN'T ALLOW YOU INTO THE LIBRARY WEARING TROUSERS.

COLLEGE LIBRARY

DRESS CODE FOR WOMEN

I STOPPED BY THE COLLEGE LIBRARY TO RETURN A BOOK

IN MY FAVORITE CORNER SUBWAY SEAT, I SKETCHED ALL THE WAY TO MANHATTAN.

WEARING DRESSES & STOCKINGS & HEELS & A GIRDLE & MAKE-UP MAKES ME BARF. I LITERALLY CAN'T BREATHE. I DON'T KNOW HOW TO FLIRT & CAN'T TOLERATE WAITING TO BE ASKED TO DANCE. IF A BOY LIKES ME, HE LIKES THE PERSON I AM. IF HE WANTS SOME GIFT-WRAPPED BARBIE DOLL, HE CAN GO TO HELL!

ALL THE OTHER GIRLS AT HOME IN THE 'PROJECTS' AND EVEN AT COLLEGE HAVE CRUSHES ON ROCK STARS & LIKE TO SHOP. I WANT TO MAKE REVOLUTIONARY ART. I FEEL A MILLION MILES APART FROM EVERYONE.

THEN I HEARD THE MOST AMAZING THING. WOMEN DEMONSTRATED AGAINST THE MISS AMERICA PAGEANT, THROWING THEIR GIRL-BINDING CLOTHES INTO A 'FREEDOM TRASH CAN'. IT WAS MY 'SHOT HEARD 'ROUND THE WORLD'.

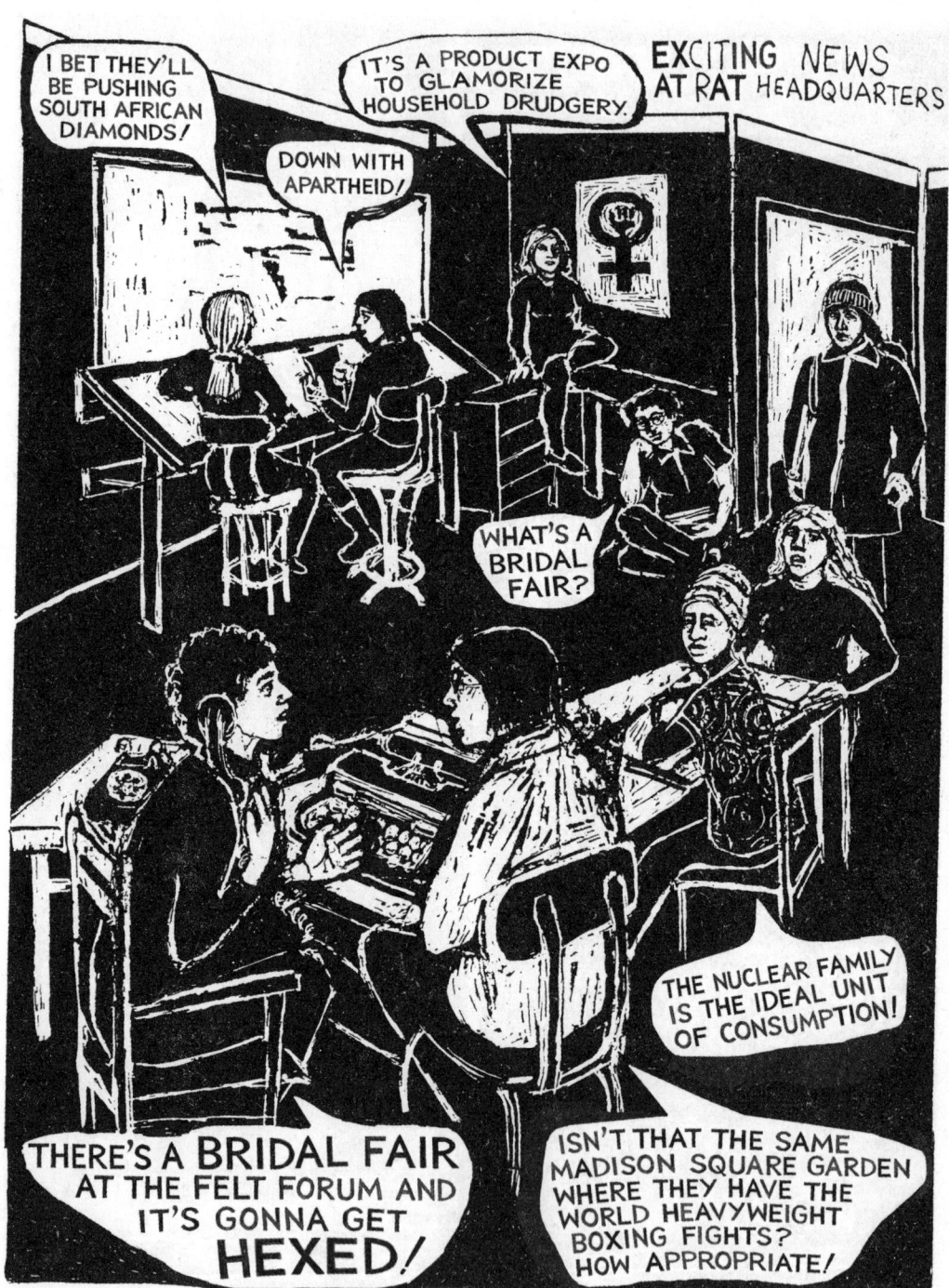

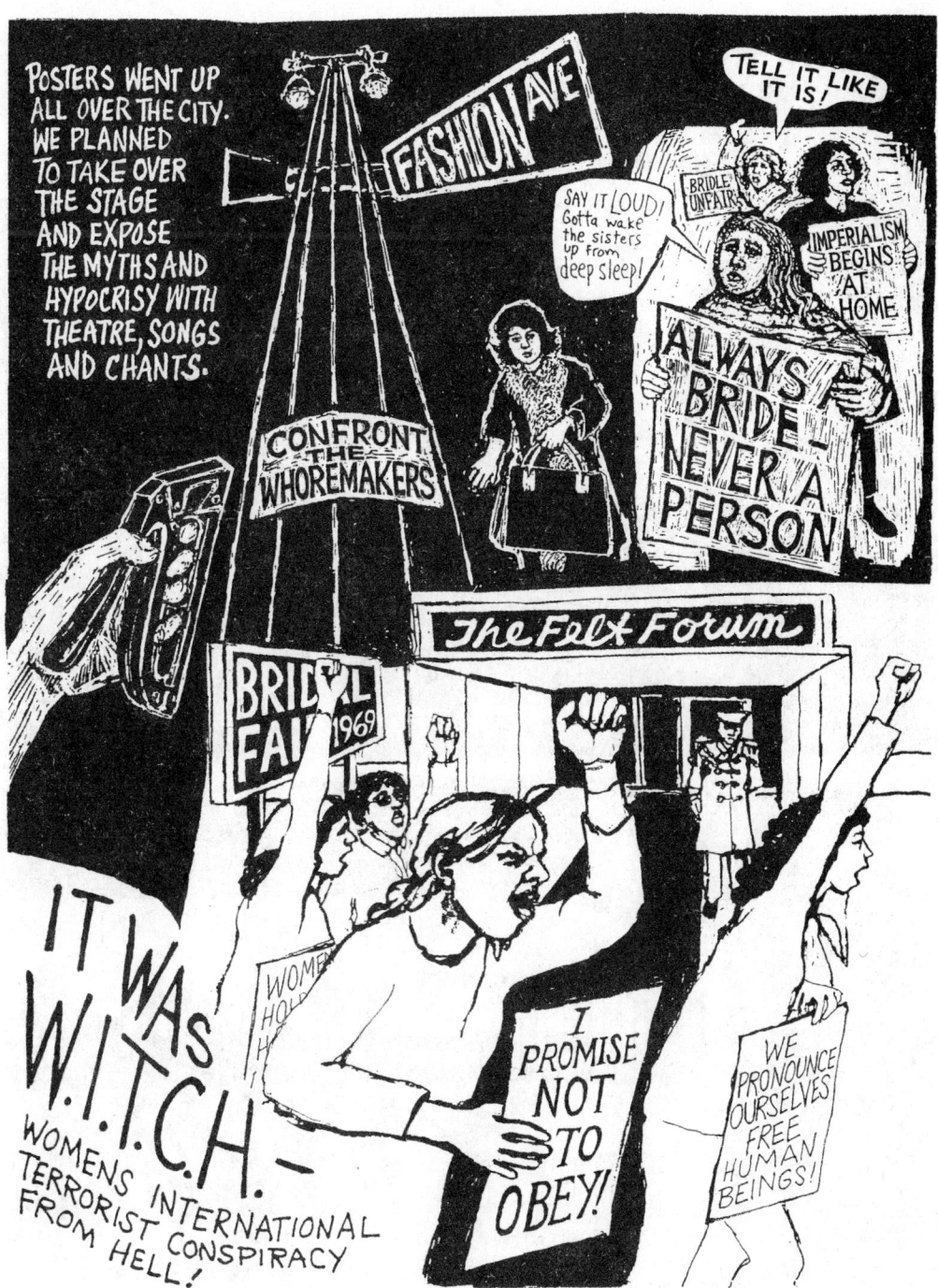

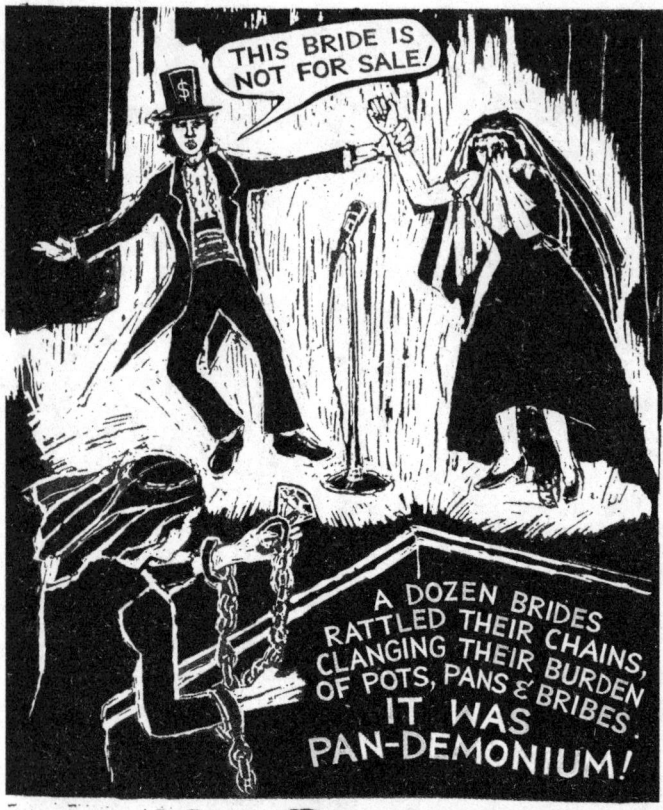

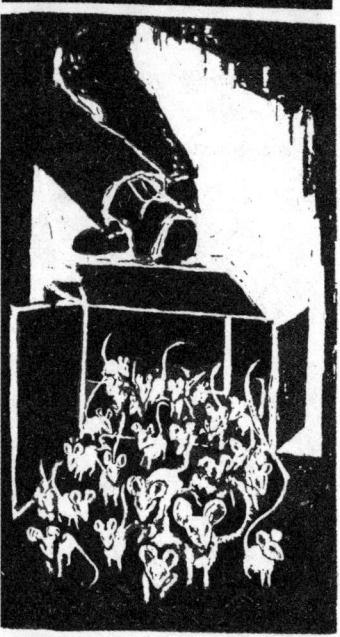

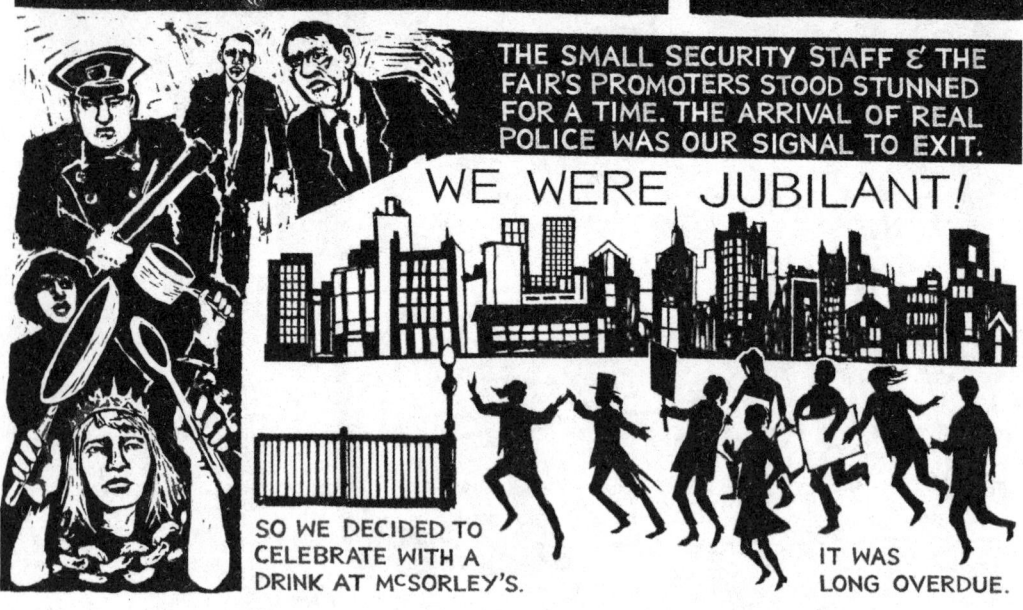

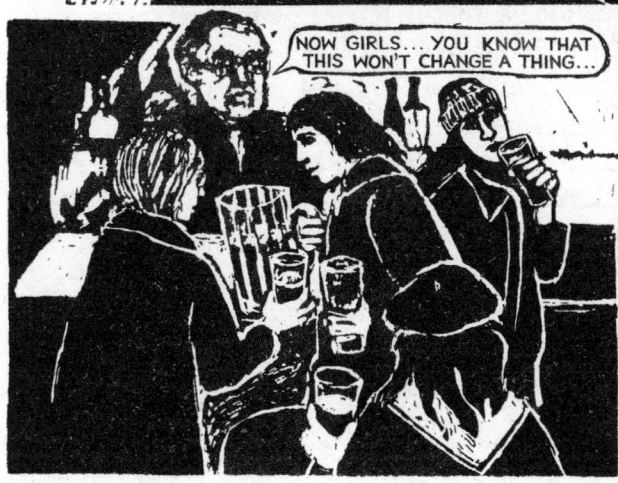

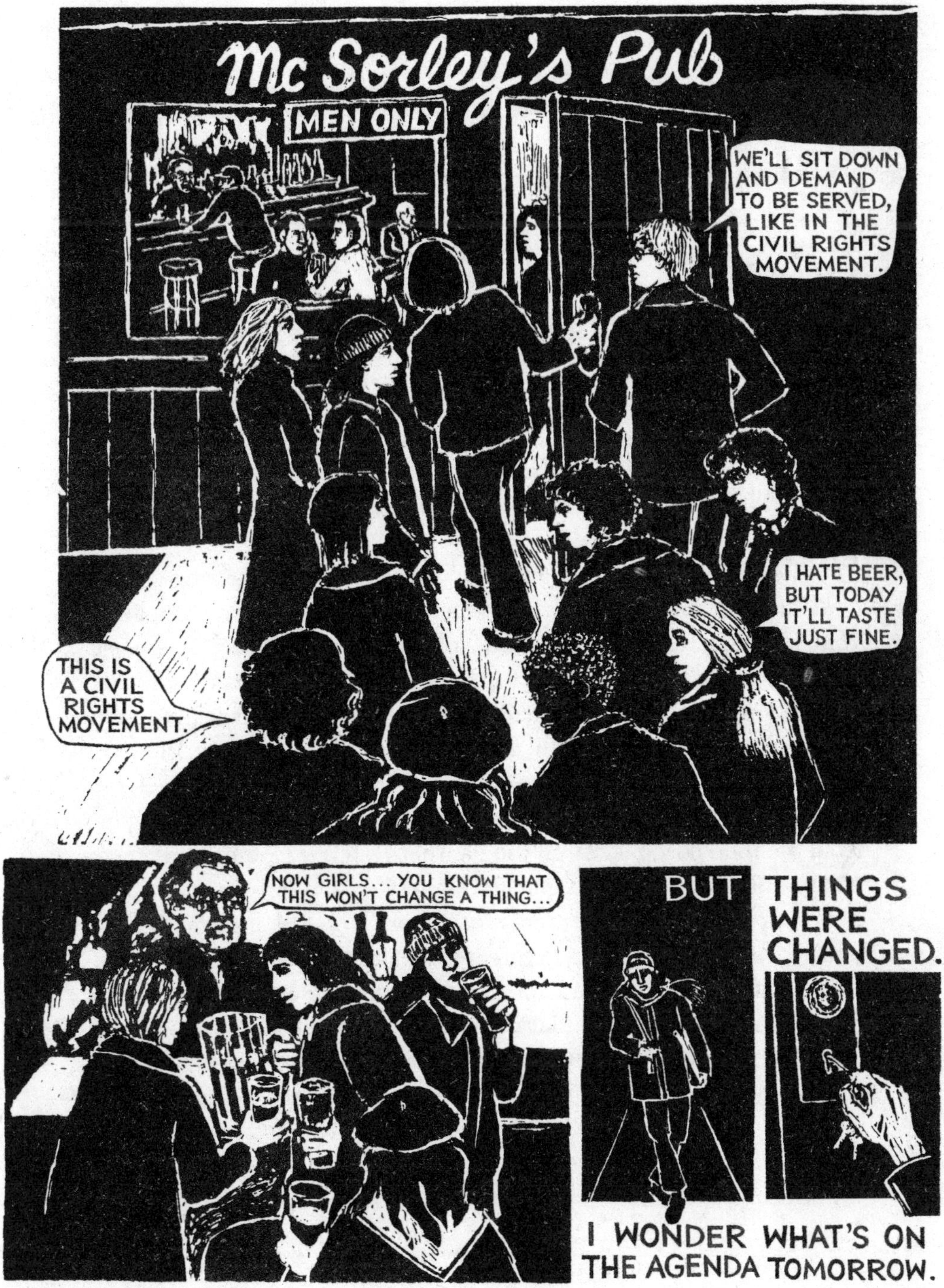

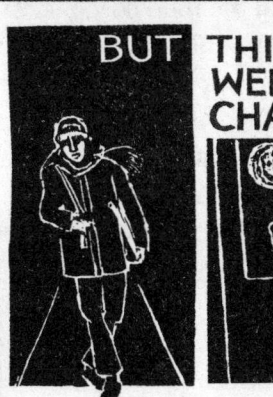

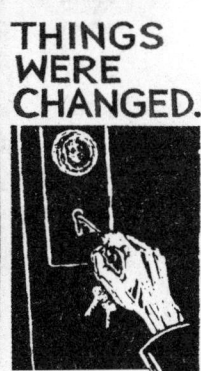

49

As the Black Panther Party Said, "Serve the People!"

Tom Bruni and I wed at the Washington Square Methodist Church, just down the street from the Women's House of Detention. His mother and grandmother were old-school Italian and wore their best clothes and covered their hair with black lace, as at Catholic Mass. The people who were picketing to free the Panther 21's Afeni Shakur, jailed at the House of Detention, joined us at the church in time for the ceremony.

The Black Panther Party and Young Lords took over the long-empty Christadora House, a high-rise social services building overlooking Tompkins Square Park, and turned it over to the community. I was part of the neighborhood collective formed to provide low-cost food to our poor and majority Puerto Rican neighborhood. Tom was then an apprentice elevator repairman and got the ancient elevators in the Christadora running. We rode the top of the Otis cab in exultation and explored the trashed upper floors. Tom and Colin, an electronics inventor we knew from the food co-op, rewired the Panther Defense Committee office and installed innovative burglar alarms in the space and on the file cabinets to protect the confidentiality of donors. The FBI and NYPD Red Squad sought these names to threaten wealthy donors, like New York Philharmonic conductor and composer Leonard Bernstein, to undermine financial support for Black Panther Party defense.

I had realized that I needed to have a way to support myself for the long haul, so during my time at the *Guardian*, I completed the required education classes to teach art in a New York City high school. When I went to take the licensing exam, the proctor was the Brooklyn College Education Department professor I had called out for being racist in a required class. He had advocated a twelve-hour school day to take African American students out of their community. (This was during the time of the NYC teachers' strike and the racially charged Ocean

Hill–Brownsville conflict about community control of schools.) He said the word "community" with a derisive sneer. The education department's chair, who was Puerto Rican, gave me credit for the class with a grade of A. This vindication was short-lived, as the record of my taking the licensing exam and my test results mysteriously vanished. I realized it was highly unlikely that I would get hired to teach in New York City.

In the consciousness-raising groups of the late 1960s, women realized that social norms denied women knowledge about the functioning of their bodies, particularly their reproductive systems. Women were empowered by research and discussion of the female orgasm and wanted to reclaim knowledge about pregnancy and birth. A women's collective in Boston was writing the classic *Our Bodies, Ourselves*, which was first published in 1970. In New York, as legalization of abortion approached, my friend Barbara and I welcomed the task of researching and writing the first abortion-counseling recommendations—accurate feminist information for women at the time of the procedure. Barbara, my closest friend in the *RAT* collective and then housemate, and also an artist, had two small children. After we researched pregnancy, birth control biology, and the social context of women's health care, I realized that becoming an RN would be a way to immerse myself in organizing women while earning a decent living. At the time, only 5 percent of doctors were women, due to quotas in medical schools, as compared with over 50 percent today. Barbara, whose mother was Haitian, became a childbirth educator and worked at Roosevelt Hospital in Manhattan, which served predominantly women of color.

Becoming a Nurse

At the end of August 1970, I went to check out the only nursing school I knew of, Downstate Medical Center in Crown Heights, Brooklyn. I was admitted the very same day, with a full scholarship, into their accelerated program for people with college degrees in unrelated fields. It was a brand-new program and they were short of students. While in nursing school, I met Ann Hirschman, RN, an original street medic who introduced me to the Medical Committee for Human Rights (MCHR). When I finished nursing school, my marriage with Tom Bruni ended. I had been his only girlfriend ever, and he wanted to date other women. It broke my heart for a time. We both ended up living in the same neighborhood in Baltimore, Maryland, and were in the same activist circles. He remained part of my life for several years.

I first worked as a labor and delivery RN at Downstate's high-risk OB unit in January 1972. New York's governor was Nelson Rockefeller, the same one who had been met with riots all over Latin America a few years before. He declared a hiring freeze, and it impacted the state hospitals. As a new graduate, I worked night shifts all alone, the only person on the unit with the women in labor. No unit clerk, no one else. Most of the patients spoke little English, so I urgently gained key word proficiency in Puerto Rican Spanish and Haitian Creole (Kreyol). When delivery was imminent, I had to go and find the OB resident, sleeping in his on-call room, and shake him awake. The short staffing was dangerous for patients in this high-risk birth unit and frightening for me. Realize that there were no fetal monitors or IV pumps to accurately titrate medications. The baby was immediately whisked off to the nursery. The idea of bonding with your baby was little known, and breastfeeding was not facilitated.

At the time, women were given a cleansing enema and had their pubic hair shaved off. They were often drugged with "twilight sleep" into amnesia and remembered nothing of giving birth. Their wrists and ankles were buckled to metal handles and stirrups with thick leather restraints. Women in labor were not allowed to have any support people, partners, or family members in the labor or delivery rooms. Women soon defied this antiquated birth regimen. Natural childbirth and breastfeeding continue to gain popularity.

In January 1973, I left New York and moved to Baltimore and went to work in one of the best public health departments in the US. In the Western District, I worked alongside nurse midwives in the OB clinic, taught childbirth classes, and worked in satellite well-baby clinics, giving immunizations. In my classic blue uniform, I made home visits to Black women and girls who were recent migrants from the South and white women who had recently arrived from rural West Virginia. The Western District was the same area featured on the TV series *The Wire*. I lived in the Mother Jones house. The Mother Jones Collective was one of Baltimore's post-SDS collectives doing working-class organizing. The 1960s wave of radical energy still energized activism through the 1970s and into the 1980s.

Always ready for a new adventure, I volunteered to be the union negotiator for nurses working at the Baltimore Health Department and Baltimore City Hospital, including the supervisors, and to chair the education program for the Maryland Nurses Association convention. Our keynote speaker was from the Health Policy Advisory Committee (Health PAC), a left-issues think tank, and spoke about the universal right to health care. When sanitation workers went on strike, the mayor, William Donald Shaeffer, ordered the public health nurses to pick up the trash. Obviously, this did not go over well. Several nurses joined the sanitation workers as we dumped trash on the steps of city hall. We spoke in solidarity at their press conference. Then Ronald Reagan was elected. He cut funding for the maternal health and child health programs to privatize these services, which health departments nationwide had provided for free. He promised that the private sector, HMOs, would provide comprehensive health care. I was hired by the huge Johns Hopkins Hospital, a famed research center. During the first few weeks at that job, nursing administrators followed me around, worried I was there to organize a union.

A group of radical health professionals, two former nuns who were medical social workers, a family practice doctor who had marched against the Vietnam War in uniform, and a nursing student who had served time in federal prison for pouring blood on draft records joined

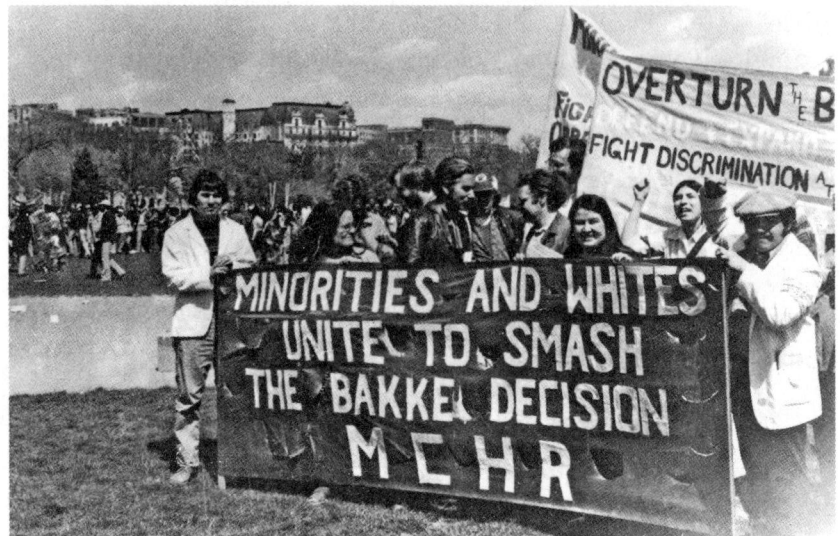

Medical Committee for Human Rights Marching for Affirmative Action:
MCHR marched in Washington against the anti–affirmative action wave
of that time. Claiming that "reverse racism" had twice denied him his
rightful place in the medical school of the University of California, Davis,
Allan Bakke, a white California man, sued. His case went to the Supreme
Court. The court was split and ruled that race could be one factor in
college admissions but that the University of California could not have
quotas for admissions based on race. Bakke was ultimately admitted to
the medical school. I am second from right, fist raised, wearing my public
health summer uniform.

me in organizing the Baltimore chapter of the Medical Committee for
Human Rights. MCHR had chapters throughout the country, and growing
membership was fueled by the continuing resistance to the Vietnam War
and inspired by the Black Panther Party's free clinics and the Young Lords
takeover of Lincoln Hospital in the Bronx. MCHR was also nationally
against the anti–affirmative action Supreme Court decision in the *Bakke*
case of 1978.

The only artwork I did during this time was a series of linoleum
block print posters to publicize events—among them, programs about
the United Farm Workers' lettuce boycott and the boycott of Rhodesian
chrome. The posters were quickly taken down, not censored but collected
by people who wanted them. I realized this when I saw them framed in
the offices of the National Lawyers Guild and other radical groups.

Around this time, friends introduced me to Paul Bietila, a draft
resister and antiwar activist. They thought we would make a good pair.

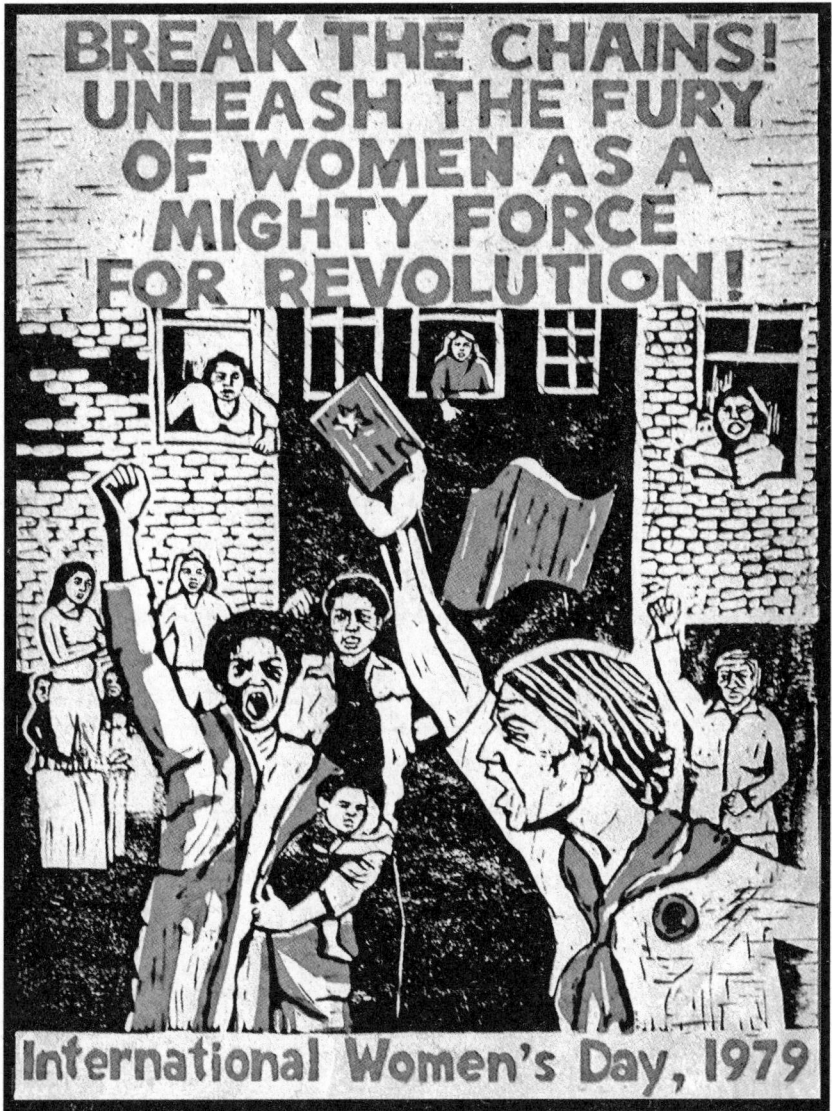

Break the Chains!: A Maoist International Women's Day block print poster featuring the Little Red Book.

As reluctant as I was to accept their matchmaking, they were right. Paul moved into the Mother Jones house two weeks after we met. We married a year later, when we planned to have children. We wanted to prevent custody issues in case either of us ended up in jail. Our first son was born in 1976 and the second in 1979.

Paul was from an iron-mining town in the Upper Peninsula of Michigan, a place where everything is covered in red dust. Like many Finns, his family worked in the mines. His sister and brother-in-law were miners, and Paul had worked in the mines during summer vacation while he was in high school. Most of the mines have closed, leaving lakes contaminated with mercury and other toxic metals. For me, it was an introduction to the effects of mining's archetypal boom and bust and to the culture of this remote Snow Belt region. There are few jobs remaining, so most of the young people left for cities near and far.

Paul's parents approved of our marriage, because they thought I would keep Paul out of trouble. Paul and his father, who had been an Olympic ski jumper, were eager hiking guides to remote Northwoods places where we could pick wild blueberries. Only familiar with cities, I was delighted by the vast forests and wildlife. My parents approved of Paul and thought that marriage and children would keep me away from the front lines.

Based near Washington, DC, our Baltimore MCHR chapter was often called on to be street medics for demonstrations at the Capitol. Ambulance units are not permitted to enter an area where there is active conflict going on, so activists who are medical professionals or have been trained to provide first aid are an important part of demonstrations. It is a special skill to handle injuries from confrontations between demonstrators and police, a skill not taught in medical or nursing schools.

In 1978, the five-month Indigenous cross-country march from Alcatraz Island to Washington, DC, demanding that Indigenous treaty rights be recognized, arrived in Maryland. The Longest Walk was organized in response to proposed legislation to eliminate treaties between the US and Native nations, which would have effectively ended the right to hunt and fish in ceded territories. I was pleasantly surprised when an organizer from one of the Sioux nations knocked on my door. He asked if I would help by joining their camp in Greenbelt, Maryland, as an RN. It was only forty miles away, and I had the days off work. With several thousand Indigenous people at the park campground, two RNs with Maryland licenses were required to be on site. The organizer said

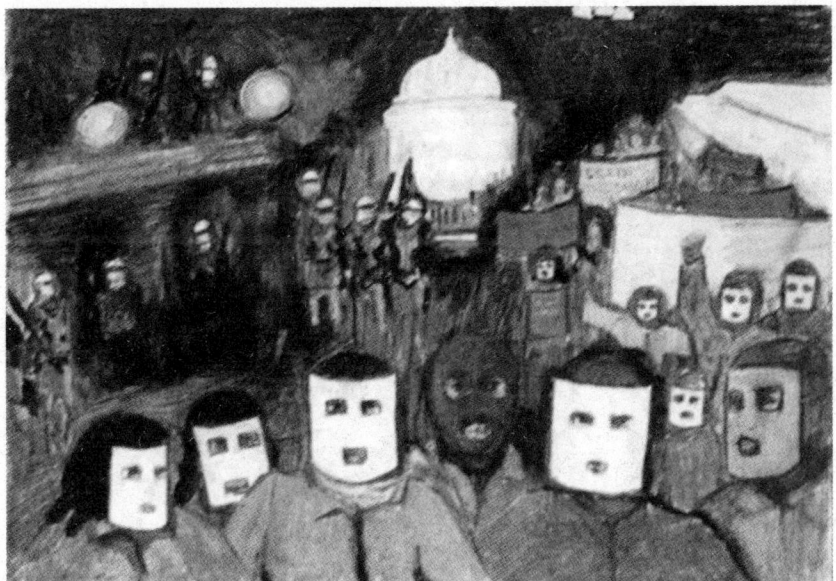

Down with the Shah: This drawing shows the 1977 demonstration of Iranian students against the Shah of Iran, Mohammad Reza Pahlavi, on an official visit to Washington, DC. They wore masks to protect their families in Iran from retribution. Savak, Iran's dreaded secret police, stood on roofs of surrounding US government buildings, with telephoto lenses, snapping pictures. The Shah, famous for his bloody reign and lavish lifestyle, was installed in 1953 by the CIA and the British Secret Intelligence Service (better known as MI6) in a coup, unseating the democratically elected prime minister, Mohammad Mosaddegh. Savak tortured and killed many opponents, filling dungeons with political prisoners. The CIA did the same in Chile in 1974, where popularly elected President Salvador Allende was overthrown and replaced with bloody dictator General Augusto Pinochet. At this national march, I was in the front line without a mask, as a medic, arms linked with several unmasked resistance leaders. Other MCHR medics were on the periphery.

we wouldn't need to do medical care, that their own medicine people were on hand for that. I quickly found another MCHR nurse willing to go. We borrowed tents and sleeping bags and packed up my toddler. We set up camp next to the Farm, the famed Tennessee birthing collective. I remember the camp as beautiful people in vivid regalia, huge bonfires, drumming and singing, saffron-robed Buddhist monks clanging cymbals at sunrise, and a child who was too excited to sleep. Before that week, I knew about the treachery of the smallpox blankets and the United States' genocide of the Indigenous population, common knowledge among sympathetic Jewish refugees. But I had a lot more to learn.

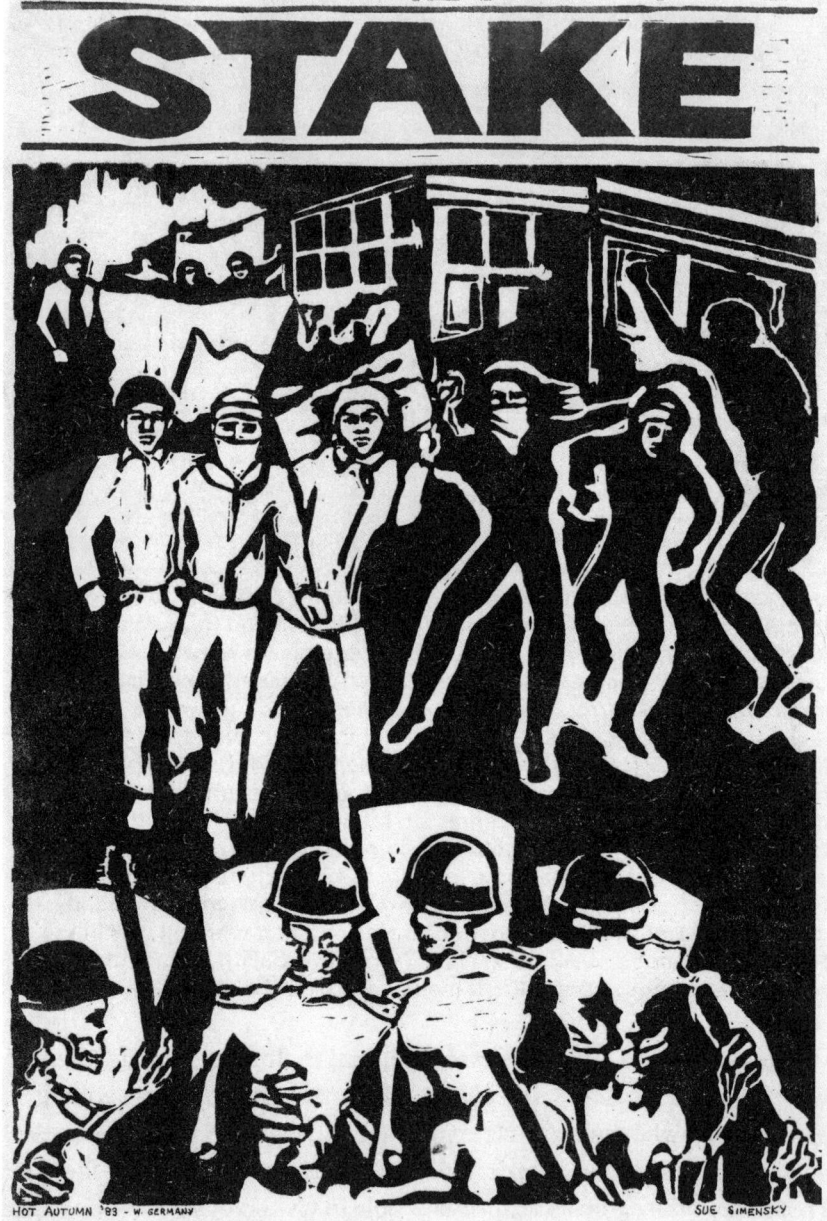

The *Stake* Cover: In 1981, there was an uprising in Kreuzberg, a poor neighborhood in Berlin, Germany. Demonstrations of thousands demanded that old buildings not be razed. Squatters occupied vacant apartments and fought the police at barricades to defend their gains.

Paul and I and a group of Baltimore writers and artists started a zine called the *Stake*, as in "the stake to drive into the heart of the vampire, capitalism," borrowing from an apt metaphor used by Karl Marx. Capital *is* an undead parasite extracting the value of our labor and leaving us drained. The zine was pirate-xeroxed at night by a poet with Lou Reed–style black nail polish who worked at the copy center at Johns Hopkins University. The *Stake* was a do-it-yourself project that lasted three issues. We collated and stapled the issues ourselves and hawked them on the street. With money from these sales, we paid a movement printer to make more copies.

In the mid-1980s, MCHR worked with the African Liberation Support Committee antiapartheid movement, meeting with students from Morgan State and joining with Johns Hopkins students building a shantytown on the quad, prefiguring the Occupy movement of 2011 to 2016 and the present-day Palestine support encampments.

Our family lived in a row house next door to organizers of Rock Against Racism and went to punk shows at the Marble Bar, a black-painted club in the basement of a down-and-out hotel. Around this time, I came across a copy of *World War 3 Illustrated*. When Paul and I went to visit my parents, we visited the *WW3* office, which was just a room in one of the editors' Brooklyn apartment.

Moving to Milwaukee

In those days, Paul worked at a small spice company, until he started to cough up blood, then at a foam rubber factory where the male workers, an international crew, found out they were all having difficulty urinating. With the help of occupational health doctor friend Jim Keogh, we called in the federal worker protection team, and the catalyst causing the problem was taken off the market. Paul then got a "good" union job, shoveling mud on top of the steaming coke ovens at Bethlehem Steel's Sparrows Point mill. The steel mill was a hotbed of radical activism, with several left groups organizing politically conscious rank-and-file caucuses in the steelworkers' union. It was a dangerous job with horrific accidents. During a coal miners' wildcat strike, there was a scarcity of high-quality coal. Bethlehem Steel management substituted inferior quality, and it exploded, leaving a severely burned comrade trapped in the pit. His life was saved by another worker, who dived into the conflagration and pulled him out.

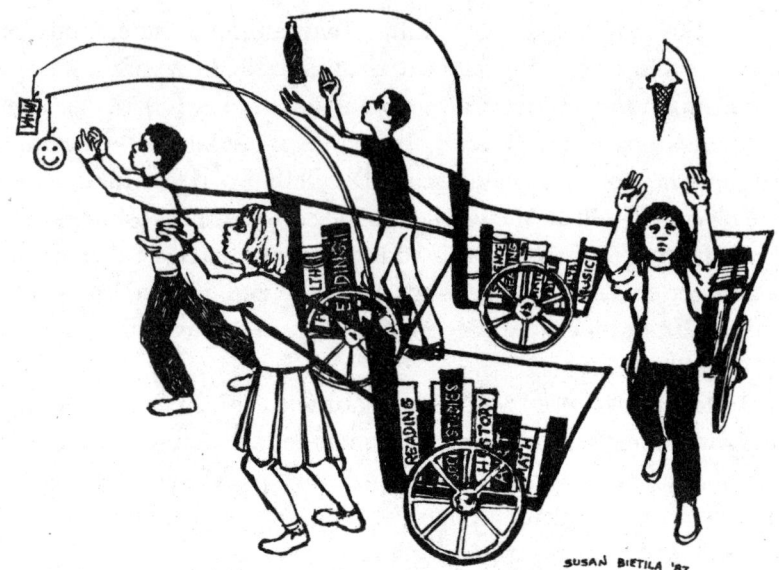

SUSAN BIETILA '87

A Parent's View of Assertive Discipline

Assertive Discipline Illustration for *Rethinking Schools*: Paul and I, with our older son, analyzed assertive discipline and published it in the teacher/activist magazine *Rethinking Schools*. Assertive discipline was a repressive behaviorist method of classroom control. Our son loved learning but, for good reason, hated school. Paul organized a Paulo Freire study group and invited Ira Shor, Freire's translator and spokesperson in the US, to speak at UW–Milwaukee. In 1988, we joined other parents, teachers, and Spanish-speaking community groups in the movement to found Fratney Elementary/La Escuela Fratney, a public school with a two-way bilingual, whole-book-approach, multicultural-antiracist curriculum.

In the early 1980s, automation eliminated thousands of jobs, and Paul was laid off permanently. He returned to college and graduated from the University of Maryland with honors in poetry and creative writing. In 1986, we moved to Milwaukee for Paul to go to graduate school at the University of Wisconsin–Milwaukee (UWM), where he worked as a teaching assistant in the English department. We drove a U-Haul cross-country with our two children, a cat, and our car in tow. We saw Paul's family more often, since Milwaukee was closer to the Upper Peninsula of Michigan and they had come to terms with his long hair and politics and his refusal to fight in Vietnam. I had a job waiting for me at a birth center. It was a good deal, with two twelve-hour weekend shifts, five days off, and pay for thirty-six hours and full benefits. I had five days a week to be with my young children and continue to be immersed in activism.

I was pleasantly surprised to find that, after a decade away from drawing, I could capture likenesses, something I couldn't do before but had always wanted to. I used this new talent to become a "stringer" artist for NBC in federal court, a gig I'd learned about from a nurse anesthetist at Johns Hopkins labor and delivery whose boyfriend did court drawings. In Milwaukee, I was on cases that went on for weeks. I drew a Nazi deportation trial, where the accused was proved to have been an SS guard. The Nazi was a tiny old man, but his presence made the hairs on the back of my neck prickle. Next was a school desegregation case between the suburban school districts and Milwaukee Public Schools, which opened my eyes to the etiology of Milwaukee's hypersegregation. When many African American veterans moved north after World War II to work in industrial factories, redlining in federal mortgage lending became common practice to prevent integration.

Once we caught our breath from the move, Paul and I explored activist groups in town. We decided, as parents, to join the editorial staff of *Rethinking Schools*, the progressive teachers' periodical.

In the early 1990s, I took monoprint and etching classes at UWM to get my hands on printmaking equipment and explore new ways of making political art. Soon after, I started graduate school, which was fully funded in exchange for working as a project assistant in printmaking. Printmaking faculty approved of my technique but couldn't understand the content. The postmodern theory professor argued that I was wrong to cite Michel Foucault's *Discipline and Punish* as an influence. The hourglass from the *On Time* series (see page 64) has been on the cover of *Anarchist Studies* magazine and in many shows.

The Central America Solidarity Movement

At UWM, Paul and I joined the Latin America Solidarity Committee (LASC), organizing programs to educate the community about the US-backed wars. The CIA and US military were behind the overthrow of democratically elected governments, installing "friendly" brutal and corrupt dictatorships and bringing death squads targeting labor unions, farmers' organizations, student activists, and even nuns in Nicaragua, El Salvador, and Guatemala. (The Clash song "Washington Bullets" on the 1980 album *Sandinista!* is about the US Contra wars against the elected socialist government of Nicaragua. Definitely listen to it, if you haven't.)

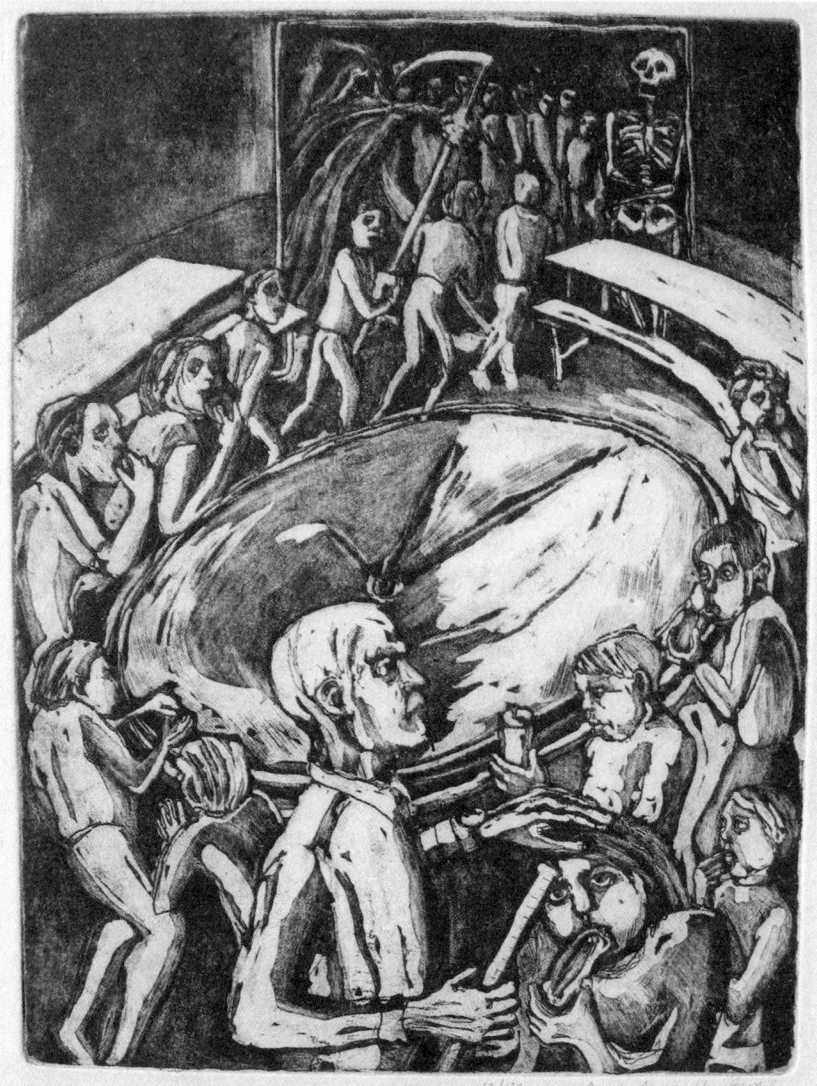

On Time: **This series in etching and aquatint with stenciled color is titled *On Time*. The anxious theme was triggered by my younger son getting sick at lunch due to being timed and rushed to eat as quickly as possible. After all, living by the clock is innate to social control.**

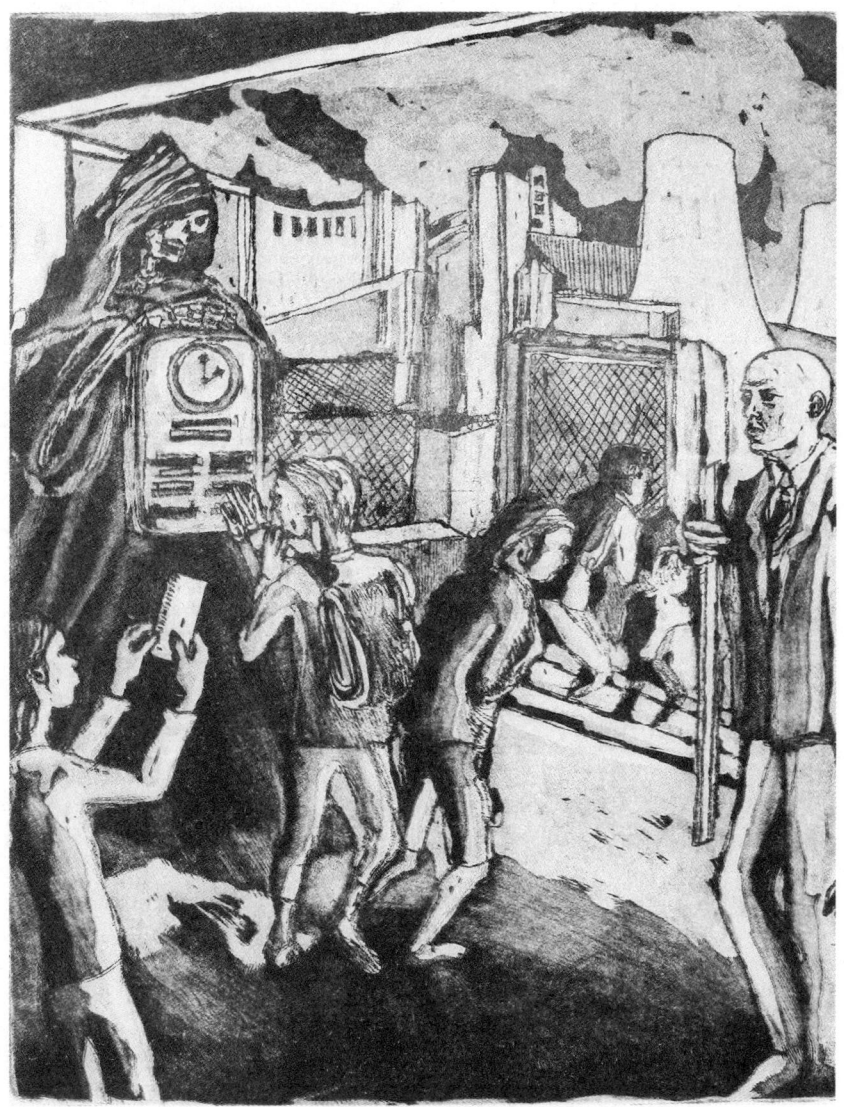

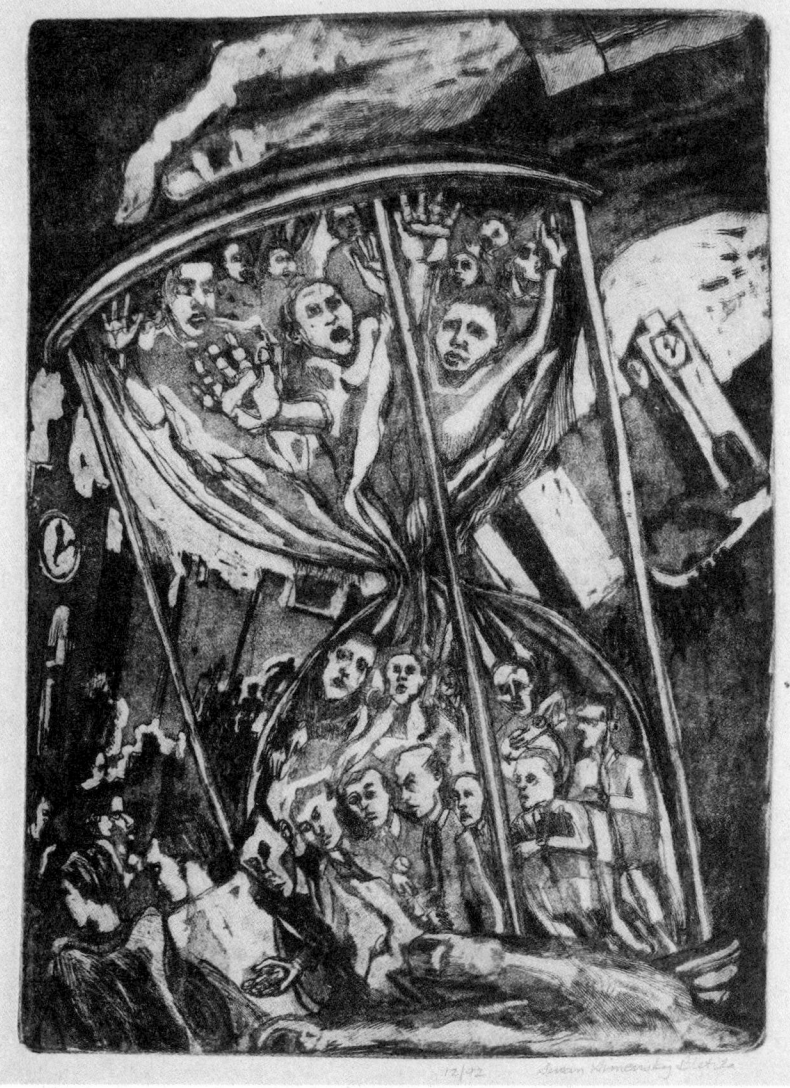

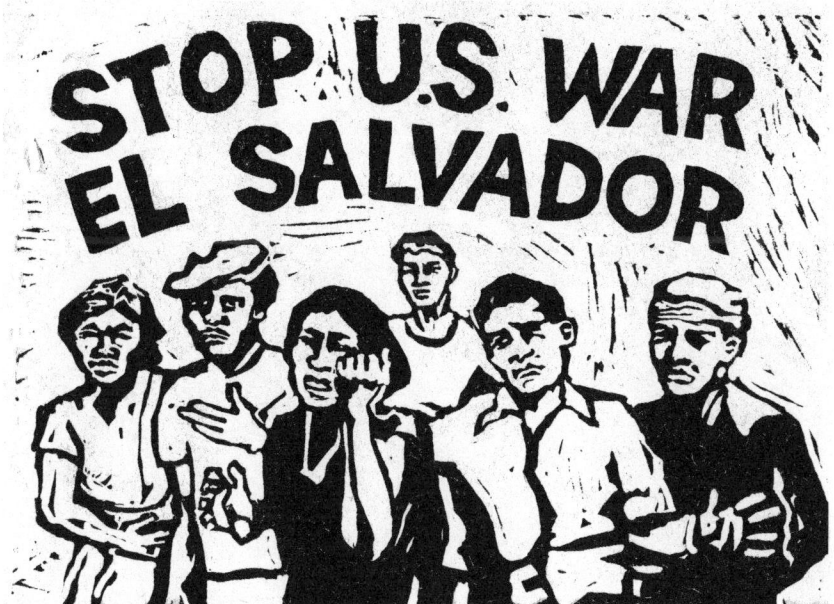

Stop US War in El Salvador: A block print advocating for the end of the US-backed war in El Salvador.

LASC joined a usual Saturday picket line in front of the Federal Office Building in an empty downtown Milwaukee. Walking in a circle, grimly droning familiar slogans, it looked like religious penance. We suggested that we march through actual neighborhoods and engage with people, but we were voted down by the citywide peace groups. It had worked well during the open housing marches in 1967 and 1968 in Milwaukee and would go on to prove extremely effective when Black Lives Matter marches, following the murder of George Floyd, went through neighborhoods all over the city and into the suburbs.

Activists for a US Out of Central America march had heard that I might be able to build horses for a Four Horsemen of the Apocalypse street performance on stilts. Although I had never done anything like it, I said, "Sure." I constructed armatures of chicken wire and applied plaster cloth. The horses were too heavy, but not unwieldy. Paul suggested we start a Central America antiwar street theater group, the logical next step. The response was enthusiastic. The group quickly grew, attracting UWM students, artists, and activists. We built puppets out of cardboard and papier-mâché with wood frames and sewn clothing. We wrote scripts as a group and constructed props collectively at rollicking meetings. The

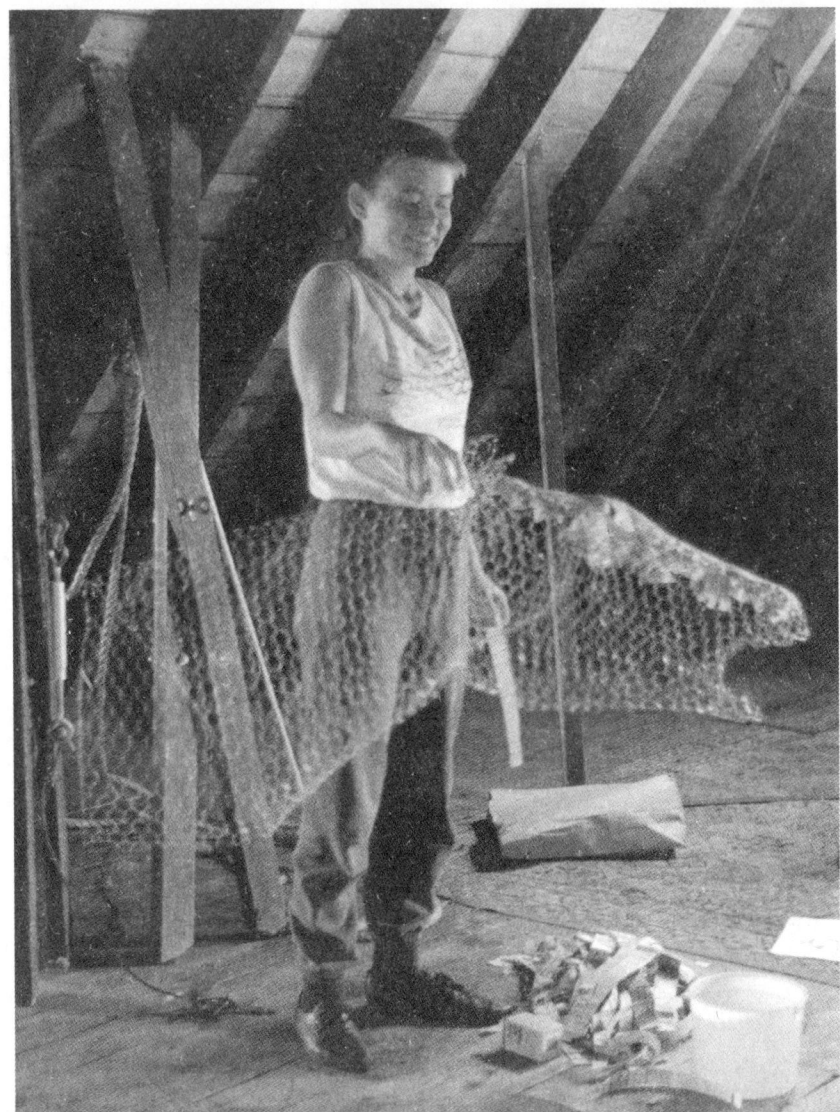

Debbie and the Armature for a Horse: Debbie Davis holds the chicken-wire armature for our first puppet, a horse for an equestrian stilt walker.

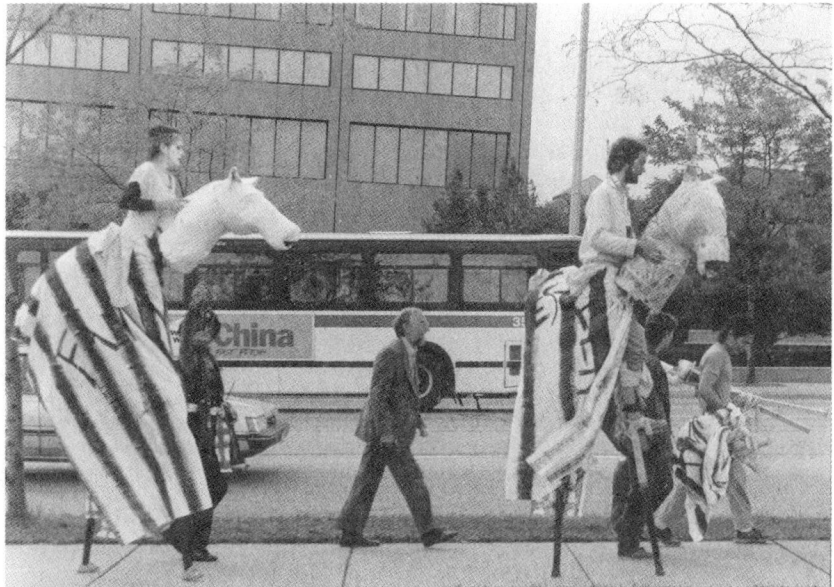

Horses and Riders: The horses and "riders" walk down Wisconsin Avenue in Milwaukee to join the rally at the Veterans Memorial Building on Lake Michigan.

cast of puppets we made included an Ollie North of the Iran-Contra drugs-for-weapons scandal, a corrupt, drug-trafficking Panamanian president and dictator Manuel Noriega, and a stilt-walking Uncle Sam.

My favorite performance happened when the CIA came to campus to recruit. Instead of demonstrating *against* the CIA, as would be expected, we paraded *for* them, dressed as "Friends of the CIA." This strategy was called *détournement* by the French Situationists of the 1960s. It included death squads, murdered *campesinos*, dictator General Augusto Pinochet of Chile (who took over in a US-supported coup d'état that deposed the democratically elected socialist President Salvador Allende), kleptocrat Imelda Marcos of the Philippines trailing a string of a hundred high-heeled shoes, a government spook creeping through the bushes with an enormous cardboard camera, and a businessman chained to his briefcase. Ron as General Pinochet accompanied Debbie Davis as a bloodsucking *Military Mosquito*, a dystopian insect she created out of decaying khaki military surplus that walked on stilt arms and stilt legs—the military-industrial complex personified (see page 68).

UWM campus police could not fathom what we were doing or figure out how to respond. Much like the WITCH action at the Bridal Fair, we

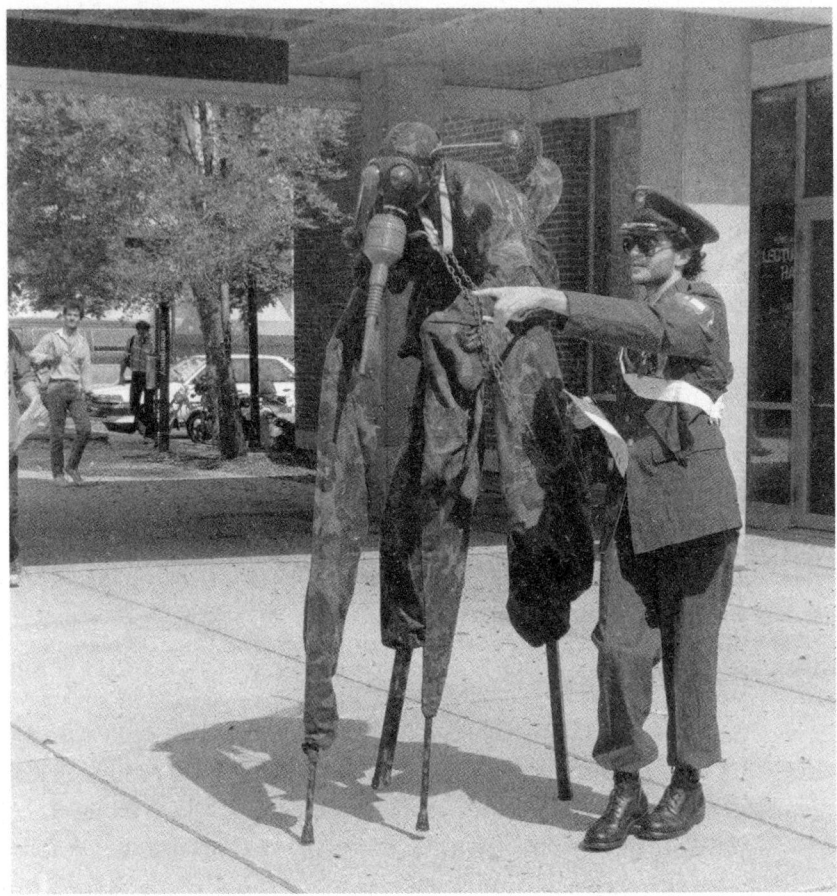

The CIA Comes to UWM to Recruit: The military-industrial complex itself welcomed the CIA to the UW–Milwaukee campus. The bloodsucking *Military Mosquito* was accompanied by General Augusto Pinochet.

made our point and walked away, leaving the representatives of the oppressors gaping in our wake. Years later, in a 2008 interview with David Solnit of Art and Revolution by writer and zinester Jen Angel, they identified the type of activism we were doing as "a laboratory of resistance," the concept of constant innovation and evaluation. Solnit and Angel discussed combining art and organizing as "audacious experiments [by the people] that have put the authorities on unfamiliar terrain.... If you do the same thing over and over again, they know how to respond to it."*

---

* Jen Angel, "David Solnit and the Arts of Change," *Journal of Aesthetics & Protest*, 2008, http://www.joaap.org/webonly/solnit_angel.htm.

World War 3 Illustrated Magazine and Graphic Nonfiction Art

While I was visiting my parents, who remained in Brooklyn, I went to an opening at the gallery Exit Art, which had an exhibit of art by Seth Tobocman, cofounder of *World War 3 Illustrated*, the confrontational comics anthology. It was early and only a few people had gathered. Seth came over to me and said, "So, who are you?" I told him my name and he said, "I know who you are." It turned out that Seth and several other *World War 3* artists worked at the *Guardian* a decade after I had left New York. "Why aren't you working with us?" he asked. I replied that I didn't do comics. He said, "Well, you could!" And so, with a place for my art to go out into the world, and new supportive friends, I started drawing stories for *World War 3 Illustrated*. The story about my neighborhood, Riverwest, fighting against a big-box grocery with an immense parking lot next to the Milwaukee River was my first comic.

The Humboldt Yards Story

Milwaukee remains one of the most segregated cities in the US. The North Side, where redlining concentrated the African American population, is subjected to fresh-food apartheid. Corner stores carry chips, soda, and products with long shelf life while access to fruits and vegetables and other fresh foods are a car or bus ride away. In 1998, our diverse Riverwest neighborhood had four supermarkets and a food co-op within walking distance. We wanted trails and woods along the Milwaukee River to continue through our neighborhood. We love the beavers, the otters, and the blue heron stalking fish in the river, and we love the raccoons and opossums on the banks. Jewel-Osco, a predatory Chicago-based supermarket and drugstore chain, wanted to build a big-box store there.

Neighbors organized to stop not just the store but the vast concrete parking lot, which would funnel pollutants into the river. Jewel-Osco

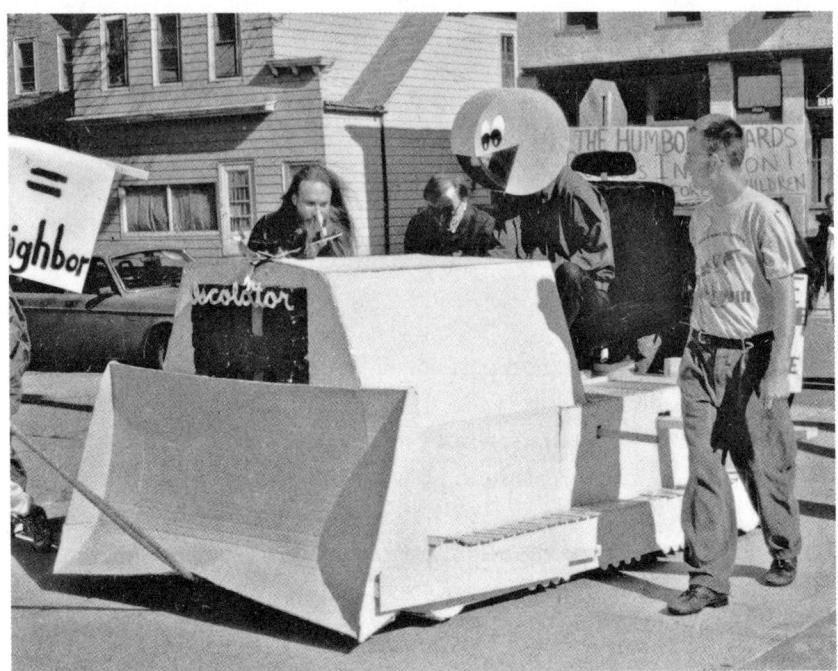

The *Oscolator*: A puppet bulldozer built by John Augustine and friends, rolled by people power, in a No Jewel-Osco parade.

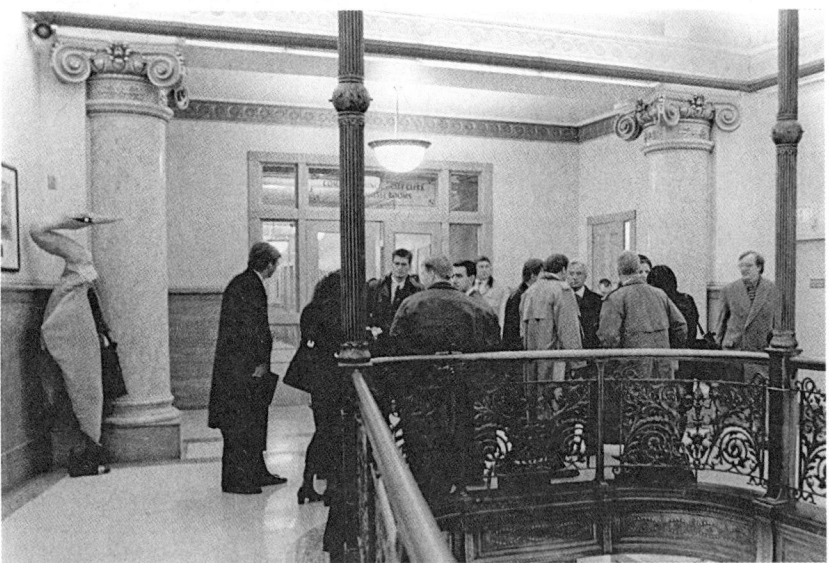

A Heron Puppet Witnesses a City Hall Hearing: The first of several Milwaukee River heron puppets peers suspiciously at the trenchcoated Jewel-Osco company men outside one of the numerous hearings in Milwaukee City Hall.

flew in a flock of beige-trenchcoated corporate henchmen and bused in employees from Chicago to pack city council hearings. They went to a nearby senior center and put out a cold-cut buffet to lure in elderly African Americans, and then transported them to city hall to make it appear that opposition to their store was racist. Despite our perseverance, the store was built. Jewel-Osco built their stores not in the African American communities where they were needed but right next to the other large grocery stores and drugstores, hoping to compete them out of business. See a Walgreens, across the street a new Osco. Their corporate warfare strategy provided no advantage to shoppers. In 2007, the Jewel-Osco chain suddenly shut down all their grocery stores, but the green space was gone.

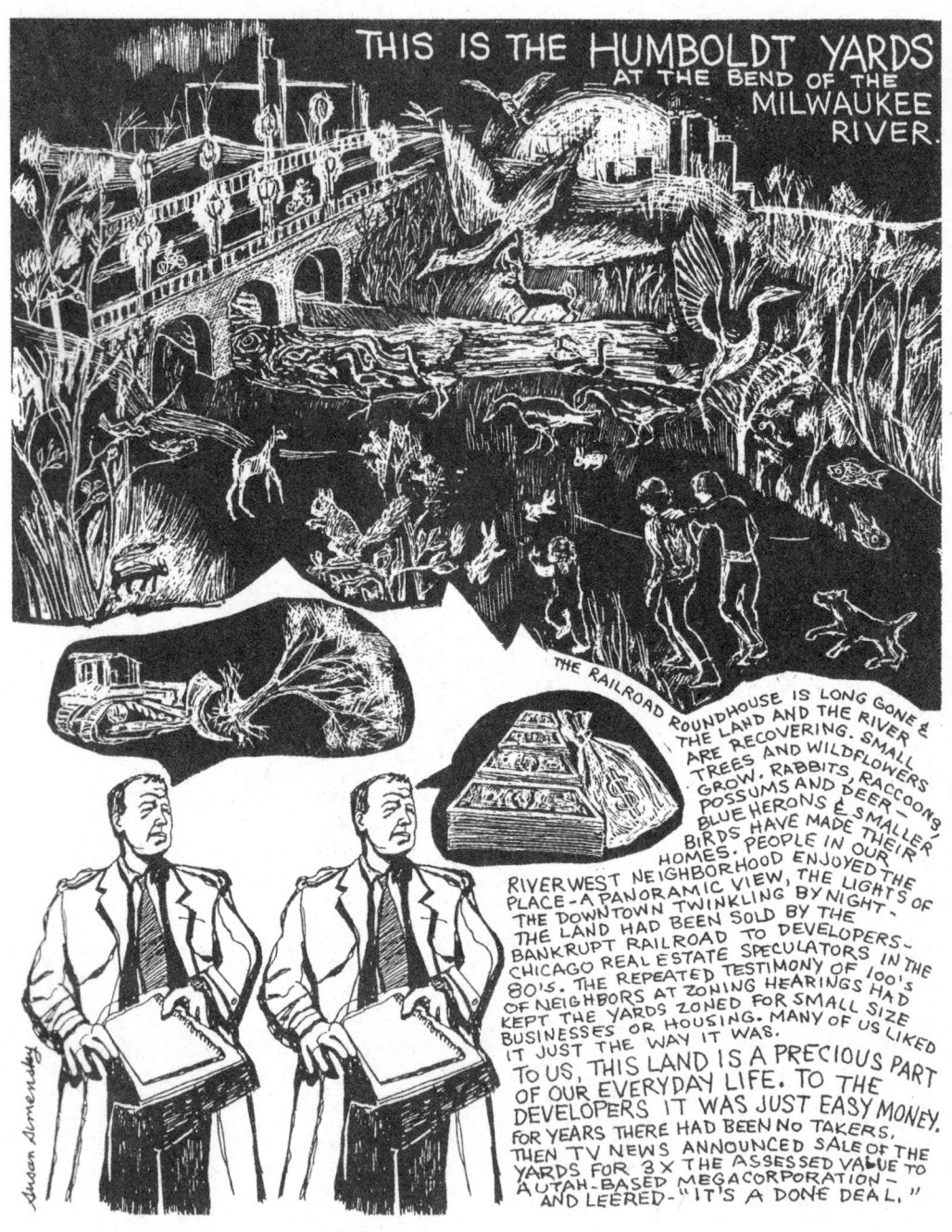

Pages 72–77: This Is the Humboldt Yards
First appeared in *World War 3 Illustrated*, no. 29 (2000), "Land" issue.

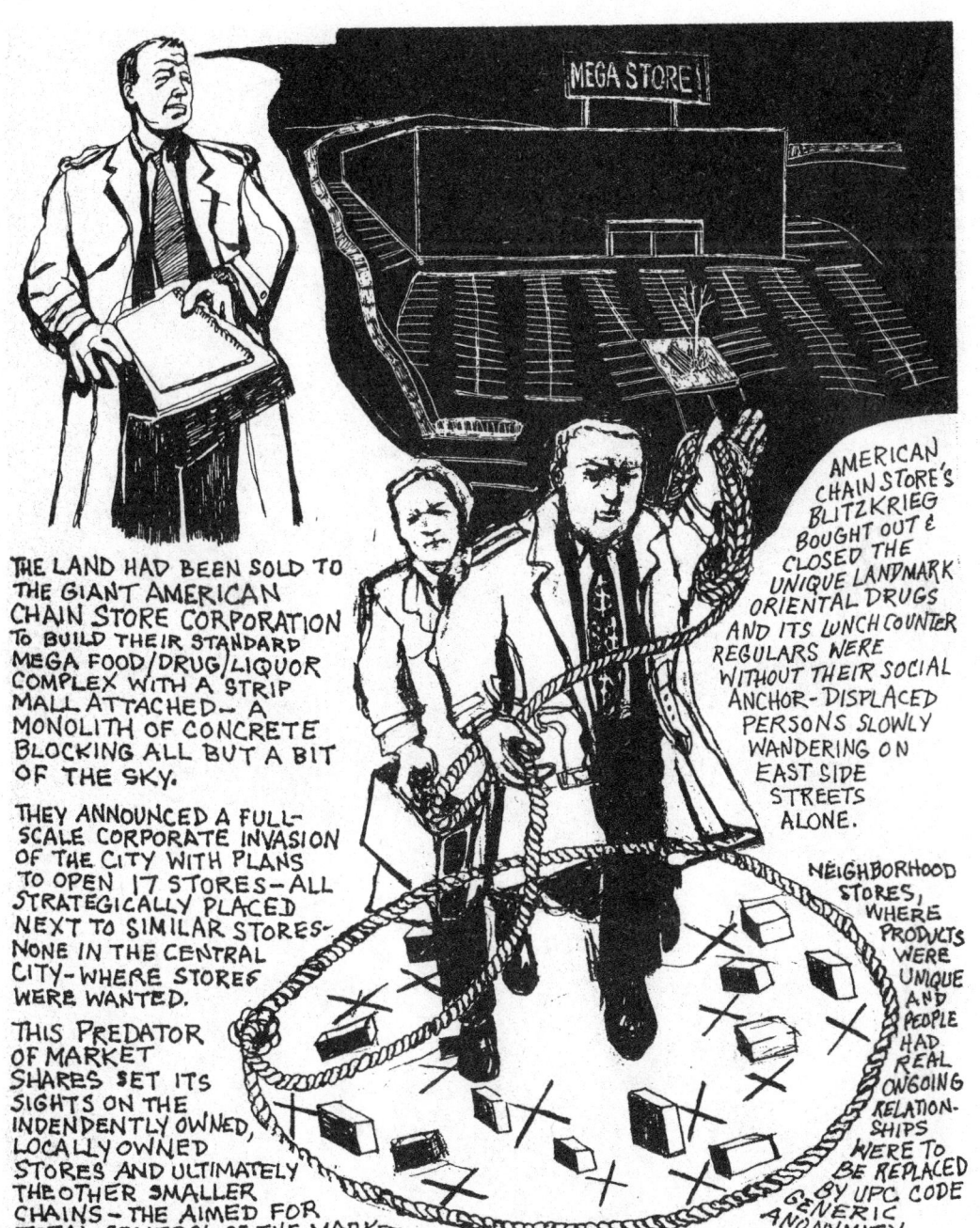

THE LAND HAD BEEN SOLD TO THE GIANT AMERICAN CHAIN STORE CORPORATION TO BUILD THEIR STANDARD MEGA FOOD/DRUG/LIQUOR COMPLEX WITH A STRIP MALL ATTACHED— A MONOLITH OF CONCRETE BLOCKING ALL BUT A BIT OF THE SKY.

THEY ANNOUNCED A FULL-SCALE CORPORATE INVASION OF THE CITY WITH PLANS TO OPEN 17 STORES—ALL STRATEGICALLY PLACED NEXT TO SIMILAR STORES— NONE IN THE CENTRAL CITY—WHERE STORES WERE WANTED.

THIS PREDATOR OF MARKET SHARES SET ITS SIGHTS ON THE INDENDENTLY OWNED, LOCALLY OWNED STORES AND ULTIMATELY THE OTHER SMALLER CHAINS — THE AIMED FOR TOTAL CONTROL OF THE MARKET.

AMERICAN CHAIN STORE'S BLITZKRIEG BOUGHT OUT & CLOSED THE UNIQUE LANDMARK ORIENTAL DRUGS AND ITS LUNCH COUNTER REGULARS WERE WITHOUT THEIR SOCIAL ANCHOR— DISPLACED PERSONS SLOWLY WANDERING ON EAST SIDE STREETS ALONE.

NEIGHBORHOOD STORES, WHERE PRODUCTS WERE UNIQUE AND PEOPLE HAD REAL ONGOING RELATION-SHIPS WERE TO BE REPLACED BY UPC CODE GENERIC ANONYMITY.

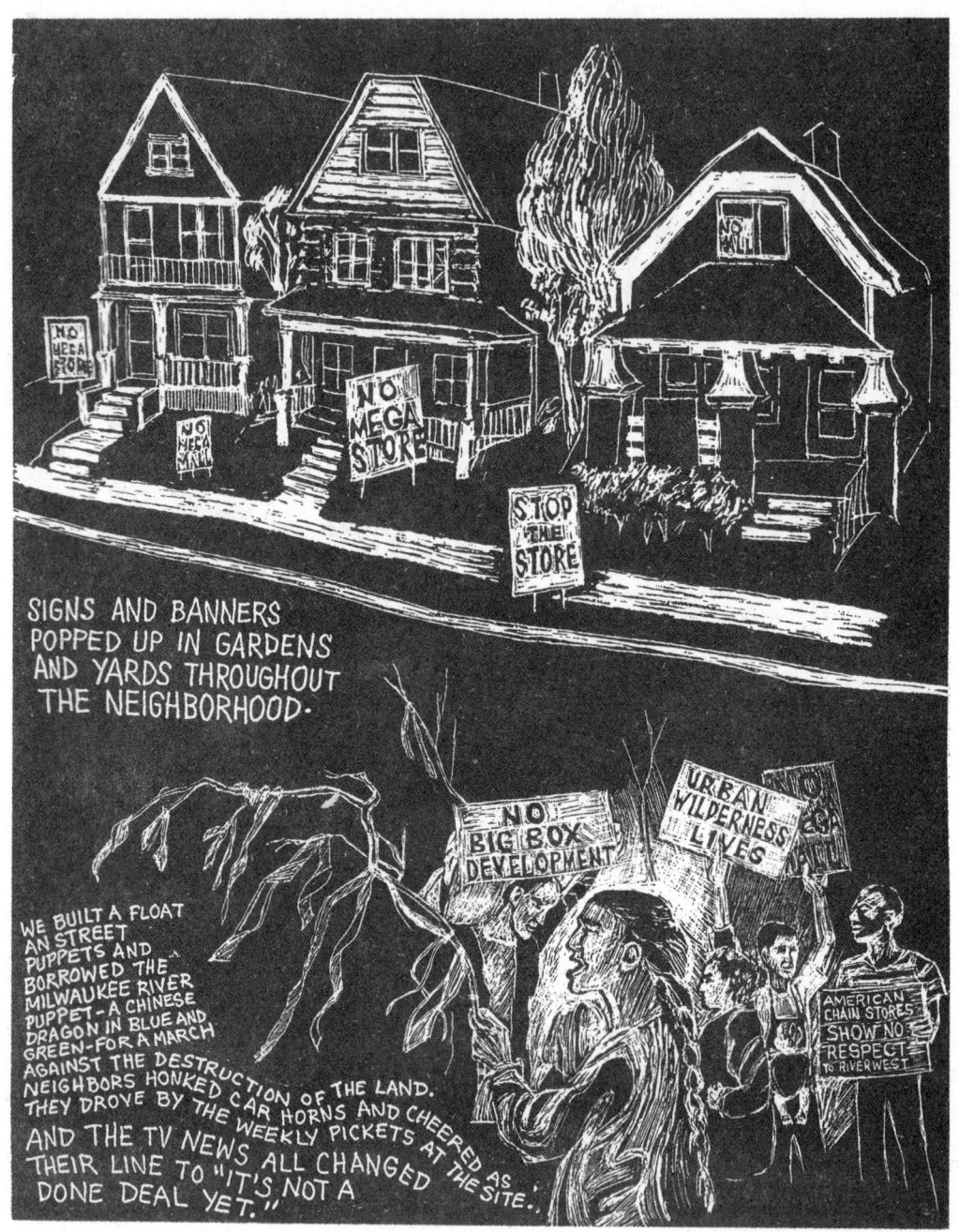

SIGNS AND BANNERS
POPPED UP IN GARDENS
AND YARDS THROUGHOUT
THE NEIGHBORHOOD.

WE BUILT A FLOAT
AN STREET
PUPPETS AND
BORROWED THE
MILWAUKEE RIVER
PUPPET - A CHINESE
DRAGON IN BLUE AND
GREEN - FOR A MARCH
AGAINST THE DESTRUCTION OF THE LAND.
NEIGHBORS HONKED CAR HORNS AND CHEERED AS
THEY DROVE BY THE WEEKLY PICKETS AT THE SITE.
AND THE TV NEWS ALL CHANGED
THEIR LINE TO "IT'S NOT A
DONE DEAL YET."

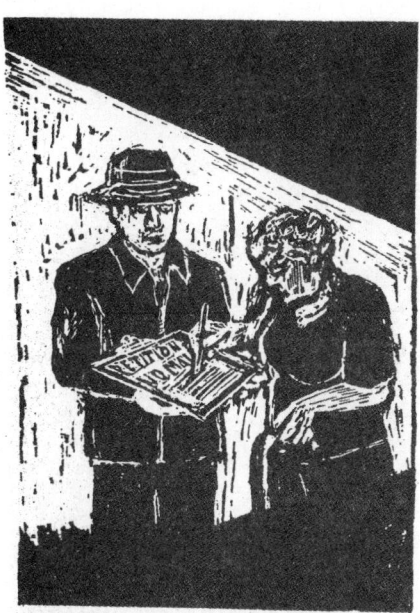

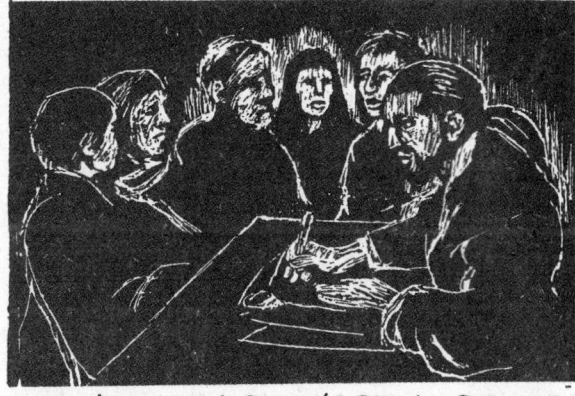

WHEN WE FINALLY SEE THE PLANS FOR THE COMPLEX WHICH THEY PROMISED WAS FULL OF GREEN SPACE, FEATURING A "TOWN SQUARE" AND HAD BEEN SPECIALLY DESIGNED AFTER INTENSIVE MEETINGS WITH THE COMMUNITY— "PEDESTRIAN FRIENDLY"— IT WAS ALL WE FEARED — THEIR GENERIC BIG BOX & VAST PARKING LOT, 1/4 MILE UPHILL TO THE BUS STOP. THEIR PLAN WAS RUBBER-STAMPED BY THE CITY PLAN COMMISSION BUT AFTER DAYS OF TESTIMONY VOTED DOWN 4:1 BY THE CITY ZONING COMMISSION — AS INAPPROPRIATE FOR THE SITE. WE

THOUSANDS OF NEIGHBORS SIGNED ANTI MEGASTORE PETITIONS. HUNDREDS CAME TO EACH HEARING TO TESTIFY— CITY DEVELOPMENT COUNCIL, ZONING COMMISSION, COMMON COUNCIL... MEANWHILE THE ARMY OF P.R. FLUNKIES, LEGAL & ARCHITECTURAL LOBBYISTS RIPS OFF OUR LAWN SIGNS ON THEIR WAY UP FROM ILLINOIS & SPEND HUNDREDS OF THOUSANDS GREASING PALMS & SPREADING LIES.

CELEBRATED, BUT NOT FOR LONG... THE CITY COUNCIL PRESIDENT MADE UP NEW RULES. TO JAM ZONING PAST THE OPPOSITION.

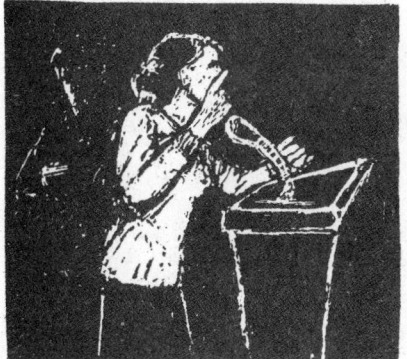

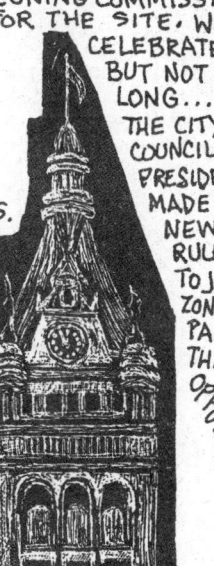

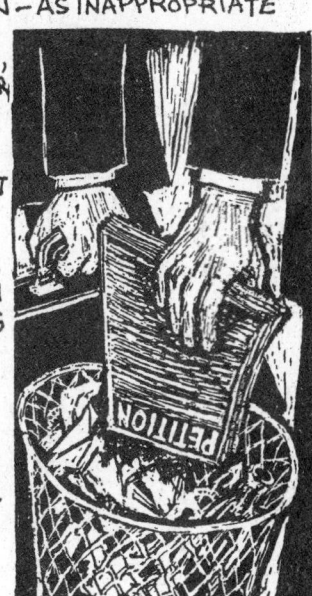

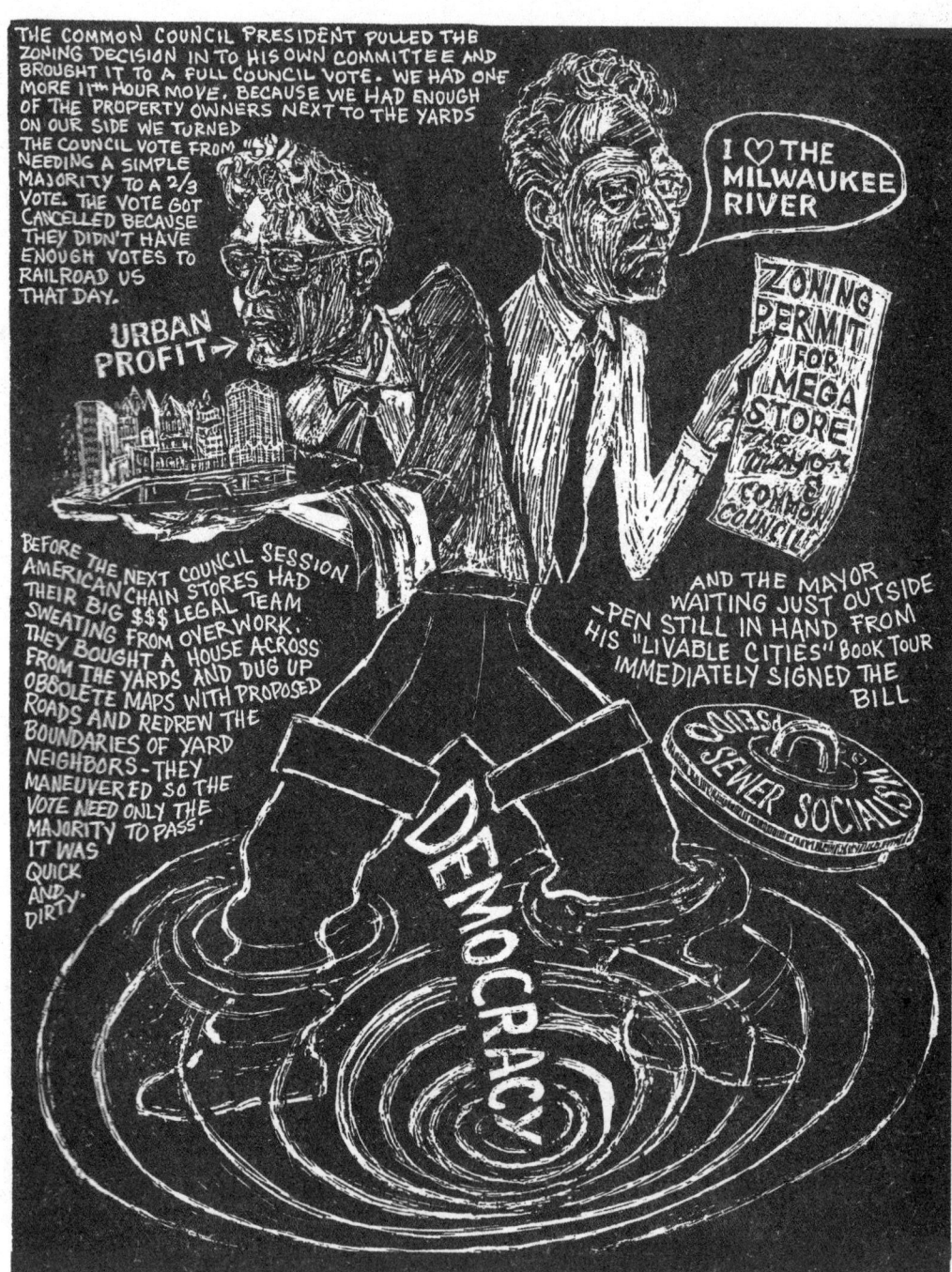

THE COMMON COUNCIL PRESIDENT PULLED THE
ZONING DECISION IN TO HIS OWN COMMITTEE AND
BROUGHT IT TO A FULL COUNCIL VOTE. WE HAD ONE
MORE 11th HOUR MOVE, BECAUSE WE HAD ENOUGH
OF THE PROPERTY OWNERS NEXT TO THE YARDS
ON OUR SIDE WE TURNED
THE COUNCIL VOTE FROM
NEEDING A SIMPLE
MAJORITY TO A 2/3
VOTE. THE VOTE GOT
CANCELLED BECAUSE
THEY DIDN'T HAVE
ENOUGH VOTES TO
RAILROAD US
THAT DAY.

URBAN
PROFIT→

I ♡ THE
MILWAUKEE
RIVER

ZONING
PERMIT
FOR
MEGA
STORE
The Mayor
& Common
Council

BEFORE THE NEXT COUNCIL SESSION
AMERICAN CHAIN STORES HAD
THEIR BIG $$$ LEGAL TEAM
SWEATING FROM OVERWORK.
THEY BOUGHT A HOUSE ACROSS
FROM THE YARDS AND DUG UP
OBSOLETE MAPS WITH PROPOSED
ROADS AND REDREW THE
BOUNDARIES OF YARD
NEIGHBORS - THEY
MANEUVERED SO THE
VOTE NEED ONLY THE
MAJORITY TO PASS.
IT WAS
QUICK
AND
DIRTY.

AND THE MAYOR
WAITING JUST OUTSIDE
- PEN STILL IN HAND FROM
HIS "LIVABLE CITIES" BOOK TOUR
IMMEDIATELY SIGNED THE
BILL

PSEUDO
SEWER SOCIALISM

DEMOCRACY

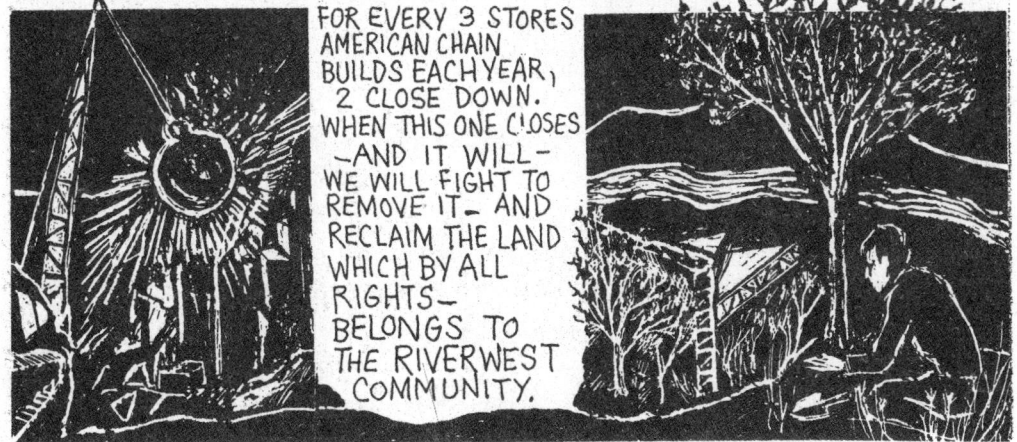

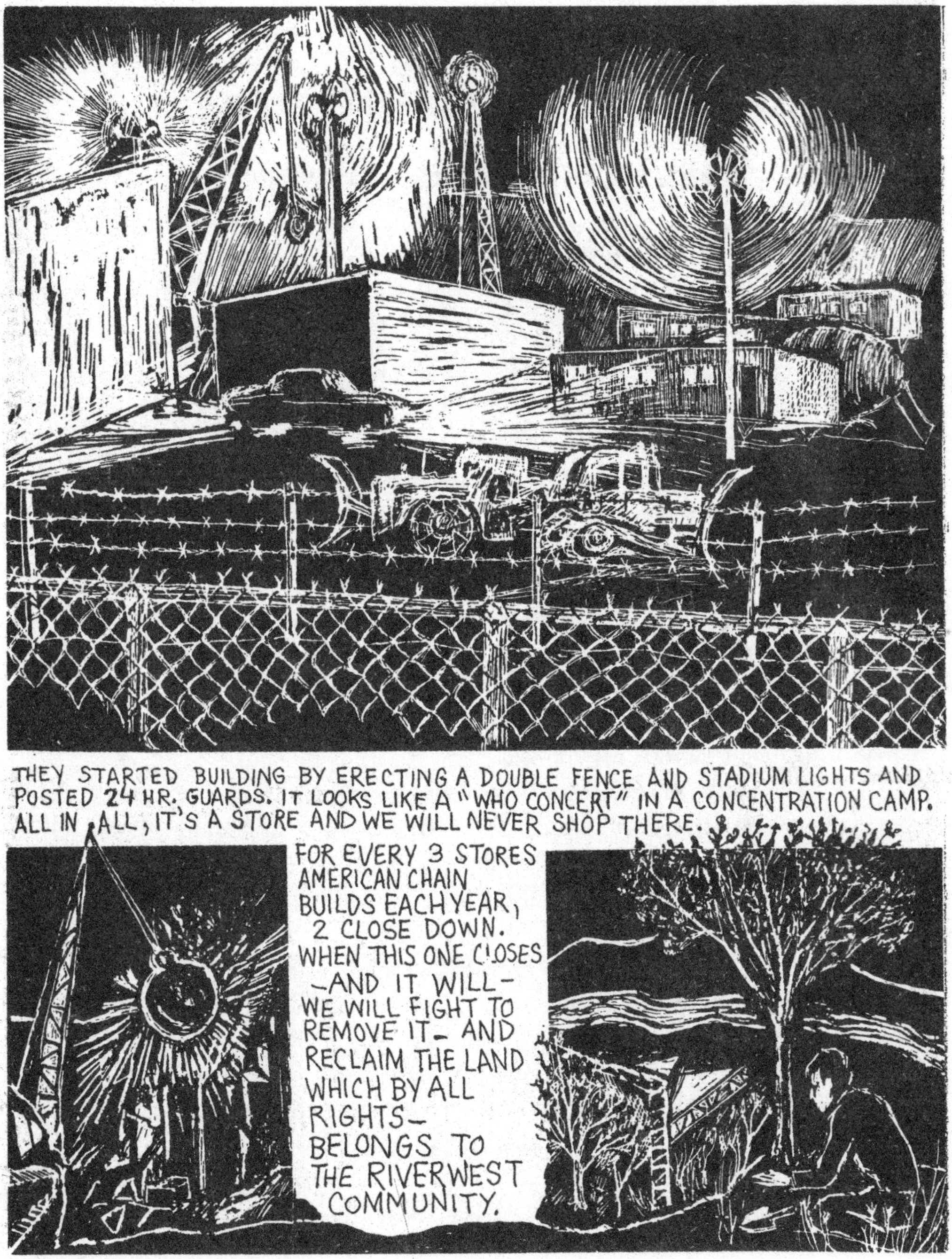

THEY STARTED BUILDING BY ERECTING A DOUBLE FENCE AND STADIUM LIGHTS AND POSTED 24 HR. GUARDS. IT LOOKS LIKE A "WHO CONCERT" IN A CONCENTRATION CAMP. ALL IN ALL, IT'S A STORE AND WE WILL NEVER SHOP THERE.

FOR EVERY 3 STORES AMERICAN CHAIN BUILDS EACH YEAR, 2 CLOSE DOWN. WHEN THIS ONE CLOSES —AND IT WILL— WE WILL FIGHT TO REMOVE IT— AND RECLAIM THE LAND WHICH BY ALL RIGHTS— BELONGS TO THE RIVERWEST COMMUNITY.

Art and Revolution and the Antiglobalization Movement

I n 1996, my sixteen-year-old younger son, Smitty, told me that he was going to Active Resistance (AR), an international anarchist gathering being held in Chicago that he had read about in the *Fifth Estate*, Detroit's underground anarchist paper. Smitty assured me that he would be safe. "You would really like the people there, Mom." Smitty wanted to help make giant puppets with David Solnit, a California activist who was leading what is now called an art build. With all the risks I'd taken and close calls I'd had when I was young, the overprotective mother mode kicked in with a vengeance. So I went to AR too and brought several friends from the UWM street theater group. The gathering was much more than an art build. It was a weeklong event with workshops and strategizing sessions, delicious vegan meals, and mass camping inside a closed spice factory. My son was right. It was wonderful.

I watched as the *Corporate Power Tower* was built during the art build at the AR gathering. This is where I first met David and so many others. Giant puppets became a worldwide phenomenon during the time of the antiglobalization movement. This was also the beginning of our access to the internet at home. Paul and I collected the images of these wonderful floats and puppets.

In 1998, Active Resistance was in Toronto. Because we had heard that cars heading for AR were getting turned back at the Canadian border, I wore an uncharacteristic pink flowered dress and shared the front seat with Patti, whose van bore a handicapped license plate and who traveled with her wheelchair and an aide. With the young punks hidden in the darkened back seats, we were waved right through at the border. We met hundreds of activists from all over so-called North America. There were people from the Ontario Coalition Against Poverty, a powerful housing movement that converted unused buildings into affordable housing. There were youth from anabaptist communitarian

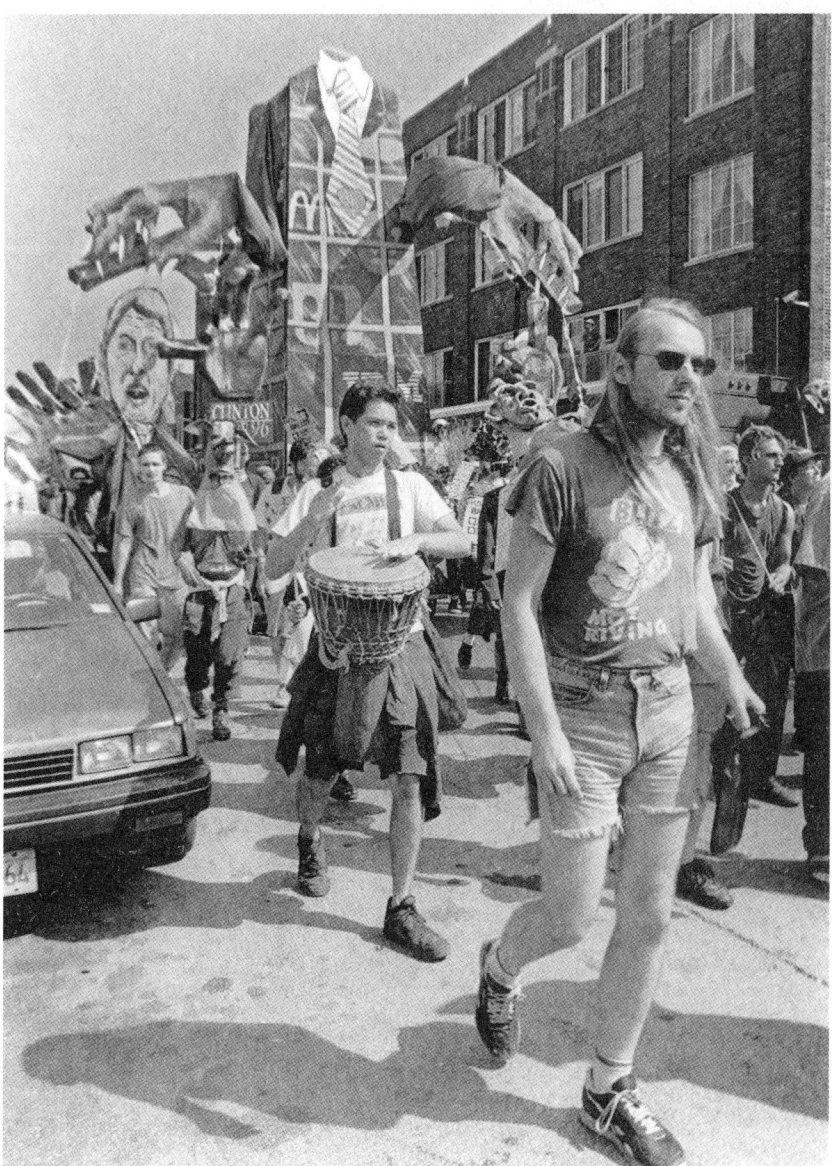

The *Corporate Power Tower*: This headless businessman emblazoned with corporate logos dangles marionette-like puppets with spinning heads of the 1996 Democratic presidential candidate Bill Clinton on one side and Republican candidate Bob Dole on the other. This enormous structure, built at Active Resistance in Chicago, was pulled on a dolly base for the 1996 Democratic National Convention in Chicago. And there is more: When the structure stopped at a crossroads, the walls of the tower folded down upon themselves as a giant red fist rose toward the sky. I didn't do any building but made sure to take photos to share.

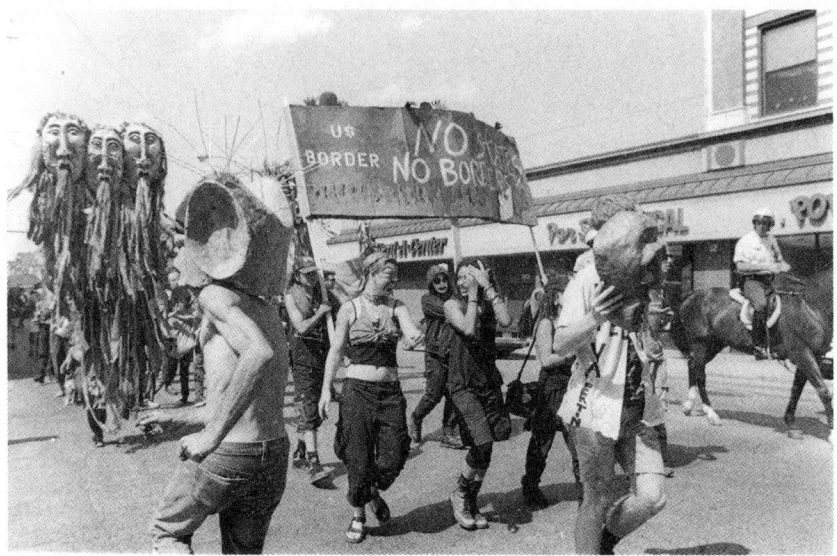

No Borders: Here is the No Borders section of the march during the 1996 DNC in Chicago. The winds blow and the giant ears conduct surveillance.

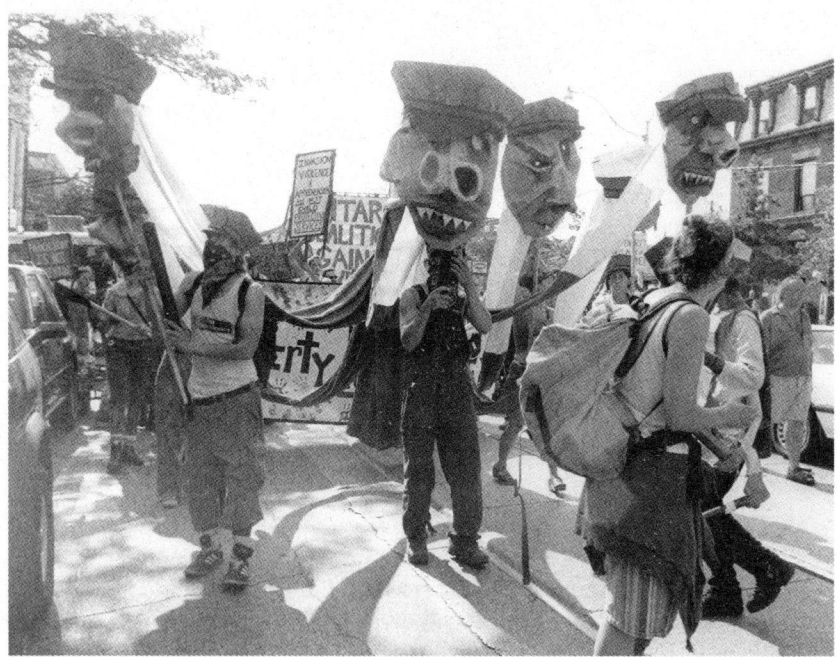

Chicago Pigs March: The renowned puppet police with giant pig heads at the 1996 DNC.

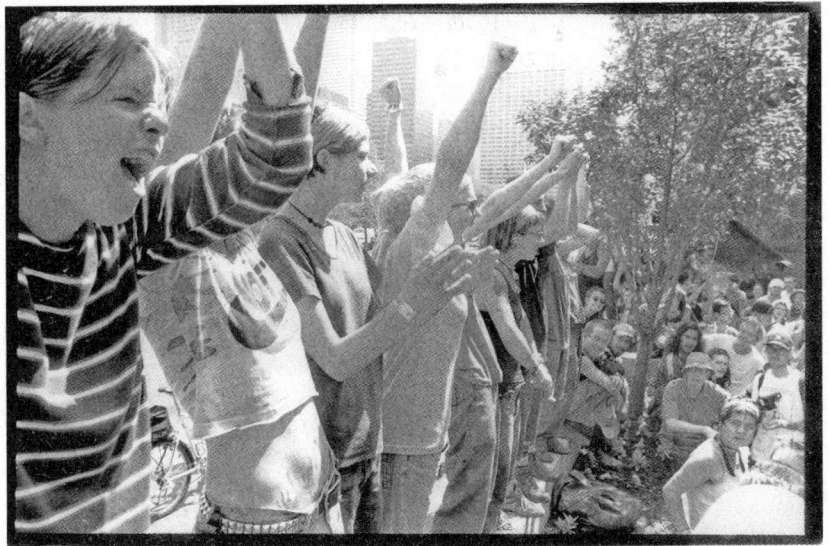

Radical Cheerleaders: Let me introduce the Radical Cheerleaders, who performed synchronized chants, cheers, and dance moves at demonstrations. Here they perch on the wall outside the United States Embassy in Toronto at a picket against new US troop deployments to Africa and South Asia. The Radical Cheerleaders were a worldwide wave of ironic political punk feminist performance, combining anarcha-feminism with Riot Grrrl culture.

groups, francophone crust punks with their shaggy dogs from northern Quebec, and many other activists and artists.

During the Active Resistance years, David Solnit and Allie Starr came to Milwaukee on their Art and Revolution tour. David taught techniques for making giant puppets at the Riverwest Artists Association's old sheet-metal-factory gallery, while Allie led a contact improvisation workshop outside in the shadowy yard. A group of young people from the neighborhood anarchist DIY punk scene traveled to dance with her in the San Francisco May Day parade. The Art and Revolution Convergence Collective was a group started in San Francisco to organize gatherings to explore new ways to combine art with direct action. It referenced Reclaim the Streets in the UK, which was akin to the impromptu night events in Amsterdam.

There Will Be No Crandon Mine

When a friend became editor in chief of the University of Wisconsin–Milwaukee's independent newspaper, *The UWM Post*, he invited me to write opinion pieces and then editorials. He said that he liked what I had to say but that I needed to learn how to put it into written form. I wrote about the first Gulf War raging in the Middle East and advocated for a free Palestine, refusing to publish vile Zionist opinion pieces or letters to the editor. This provoked Tagar, the Zionist student group (who were pro-war and allied with the College Republicans) to threaten to beat me up. They wore buttons calling me an anti-Semite. I had the support of the others at the *Post* and progressive campus groups and was not harmed.

I also wrote about the spearfishing war in Wisconsin. Indigenous people in the state had started openly exercising their treaty rights to fish, hunt, and gather in the ceded territories off the reservations. This area, with many lakes and forests, encompasses most of the northern half of Wisconsin. I did an interview with Rick Whaley, who joined other nonviolent activists to stand on the docks on the northern lakes to block attacks by vile, racist thugs against Indigenous people who were spearing walleye with tridents. Together with Red Cliff Ojibwe Walt Bresette, he coauthored *Walleye Warriors*, which tells this story.

At that time, a series of multinational mining corporations sought permits to mine metallic sulfide ore along the Wolf River near the town of Crandon in central Wisconsin, in the same region where the conflict over off-reservation fishing was taking place. This proposed mine endangered the water and land of the nearby Mole Lake Sokaogon Chippewa (Ojibwe) and their wild rice beds as well as the area ecosystem. The Midwest Treaty Network's Wolf Watershed Educational Project (WWEP) worked with a diverse alliance of rural Indigenous and white communities against construction of the Crandon Mine. The Milwaukee branch asked me to join, particularly because they had heard that I had experience as a street medic. They were worried about potential gunfire in the Northwoods between Indigenous warriors standing against Exxon and the litany of foreign mining corporations that followed in Exxon's wake. There had been armed standoffs in the recent past: in 1975, when the Menominee Warrior Society occupied the Alexian Brothers Novitiate near the tribe's reservation, and in 1996, when Ojibwe activists blocked railroad tracks on the Bad River Reservation to stop train cars carrying sulfuric acid to a copper mine in White Pine, Michigan, to the east. This second standoff ended when police stood down, not wanting a confrontation with what they thought would be armed warriors in the woods. The mining company stopped the shipments to White Pine.

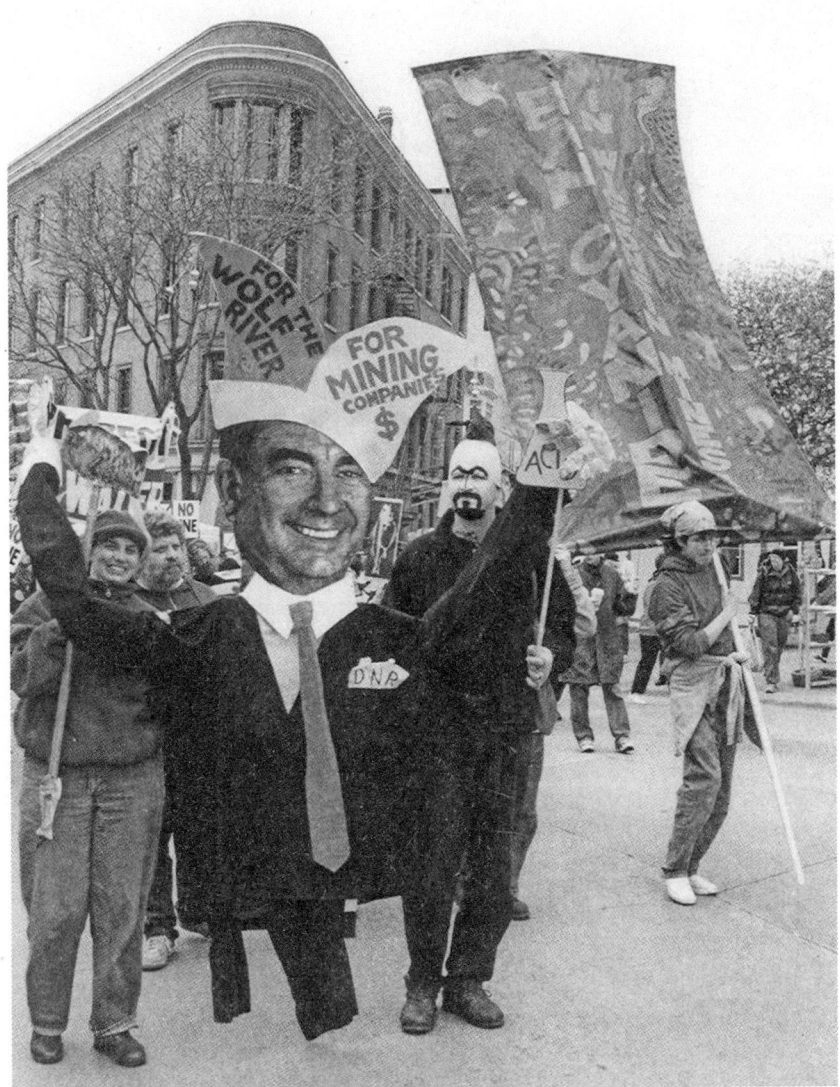

Flat Toxic Tommy: For this puppet of pro-mining Republican Wisconsin Governor Tommy Thompson, *Flat Toxic Tommy*, his fool's cap and beaker labeled "acid" make an apt ensemble. When David Solnit visited Milwaukee during the Art and Revolution tour, he taught us how to construct this type of effigy. The experimental "BAN CYANIDE" vertical banner (right), inspired by Kurosawa's samurai-movie battle flags and referring to the poison used to leach gold, copper, and zinc out of sulfide ore, proved unwieldy.

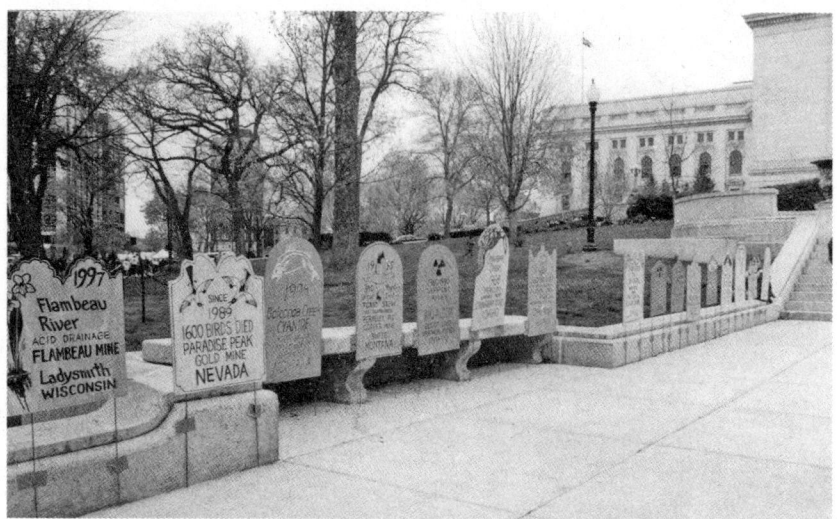

Tombstones at the Wisconsin Capitol: The Milwaukee Mining Impact Coalition (part of the WWEP) taught me about the dangers of mining metallic sulfide ore and compiled a list of rivers poisoned by mining worldwide. To make this visible, we made a mobile graveyard, with tombstones dedicated to these rivers. The group scavenged wires from election signs and recycled bicycle-box cardboard. With the group's research, I came up with motifs reflecting the location of these rivers in the world. We used latex housepaint as an undercoat, and I painted most of the lettering on the faux stone. We installed the tombstones along roadsides and where Wolf River communities were organizing against the Crandon Mine. Here, a few of the tombstones are posted along a walkway to the Wisconsin Capitol, after a graveyard-shaped installation on the lawn was stopped by Capitol Police. Despite being made of cardboard, the latex paint sealed them well, and they lasted for years.

Two of the women in the Milwaukee Mining Impact Coalition (part of the WWEP) were registered nurses but worked processing insurance claims. I had never seen a gunshot wound and also wasn't prepared to be a medic in the woods. I traveled with these new friends to testify at Department of Natural Resources hearings and interviewed them for our local pirate radio station, the Wireless Virus, during a long drive. They explained the chemistry of sulfide mining and the history of this unique Native/non-Native alliance, quickly bringing me up to speed. The history of Paul's hometown had given me an intimate understanding of the boom-and-bust economy of mining in the Upper Midwest, as well as the effect of toxic tailings that poisoned the beautiful local lakes. I joined the movement to do artwork for education and agitation, convinced that the power of this unlikely alliance would win.

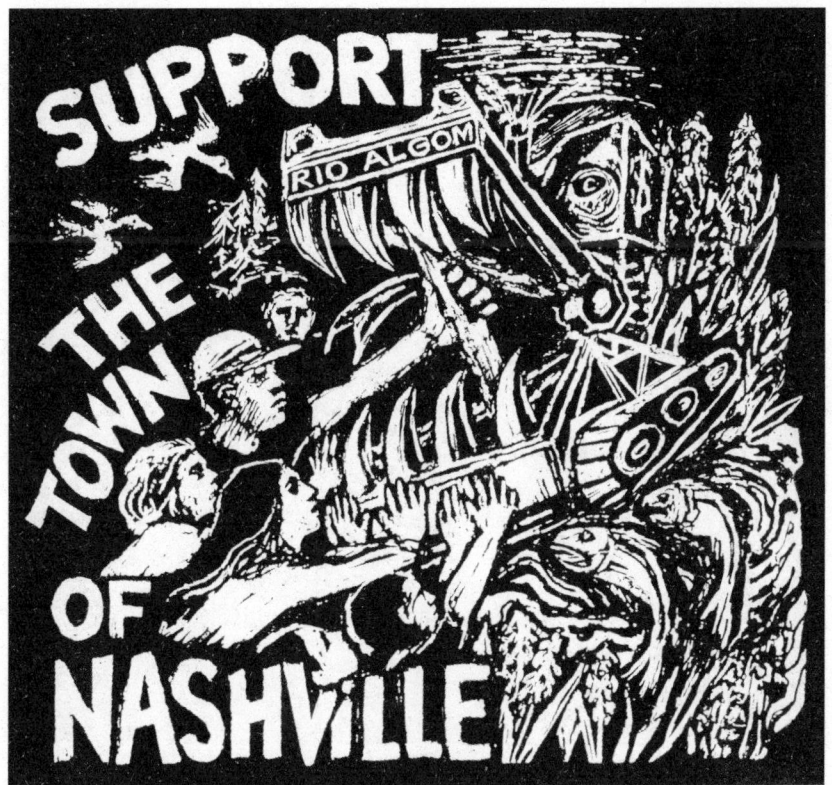

Nashville Township: The town of Nashville, Wisconsin, was one of so many small towns and townships along the Wolf River that passed resolutions against the mine. The coalition was exceptional for its diversity. The mayor of Nashville (a retired Chicago cop), Trout Unlimited, hunters' organizations, and tourism businesses joined the Mole Lake Sokaogon Chippewa, Menominee, Potawatomi, and other Indigenous and non-Native environmental activists against the mine.

In 2008, Nicolas Lampert curated an art show, *Seeing Green*, at the Woodland Pattern Book Center gallery and invited me to paint a mural. Paul and I traveled to the Wolf River to get to know the lay of the land and to research Mole Lake and the Sokaogon Chippewa wild rice beds. We were given a tour by a young boy, the only one around that day.

I painted the Crandon Mine victory mural in acrylics on plywood six feet by twenty-four feet, the size of the outside wall of the building where it would be displayed. I worked on it in the art room of Milwaukee's Bay View High School, where I was the school nurse. Students eagerly painted along with me. The mural was mounted on the front of Woodland Pattern Book Center building on Locust Street, the heavily trafficked

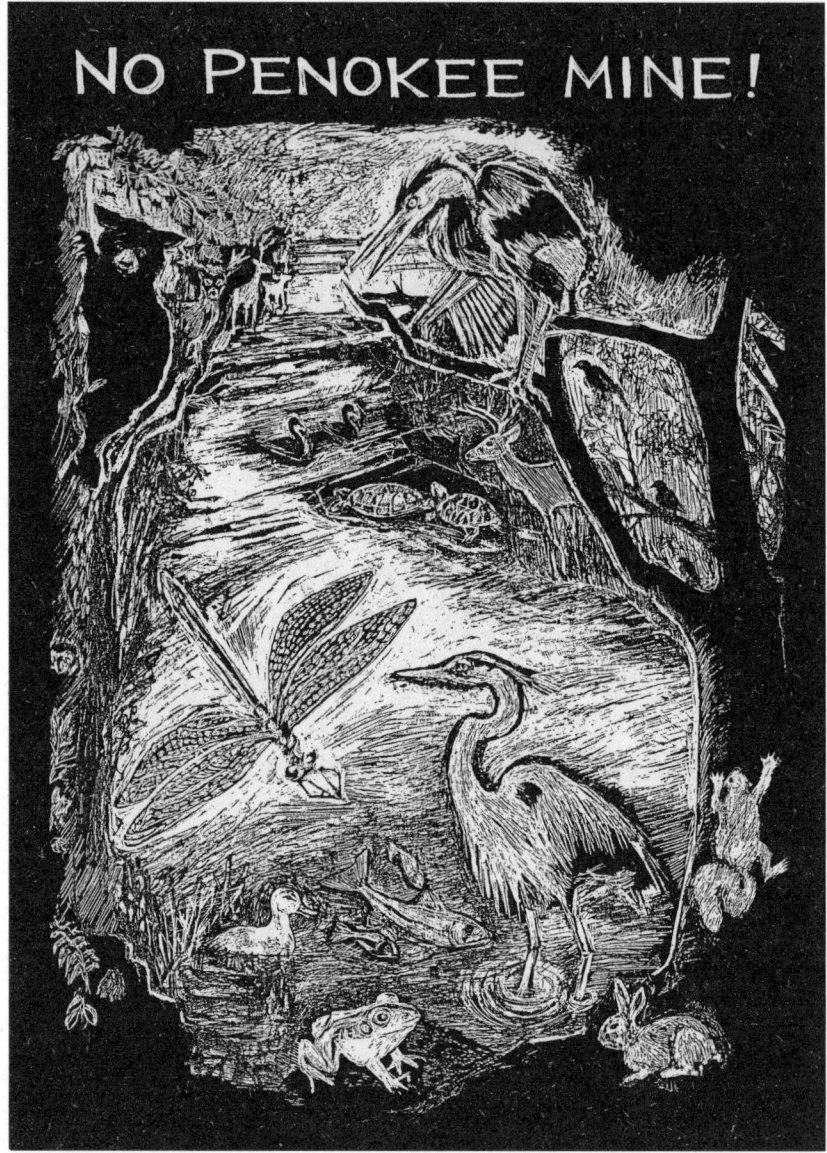

No Penokee Mine Poster: My scratchboard and ink page for "A Northwoods Tale" traveled far. I saw it worn on T-shirts at marches in Chicago and Oklahoma. Nicolas Lampert and Paul Kjelland silk-screened the poster at an art build. The proposed Penokee Mine, an immense open-pit iron mine in the ancient Penokee Mountains south of Lake Superior, was defeated by public opposition in just five years. The silk-screen posters traveled widely when I donated them for fundraising events to support the No Dakota Access Pipeline occupation at Standing Rock in 2016.

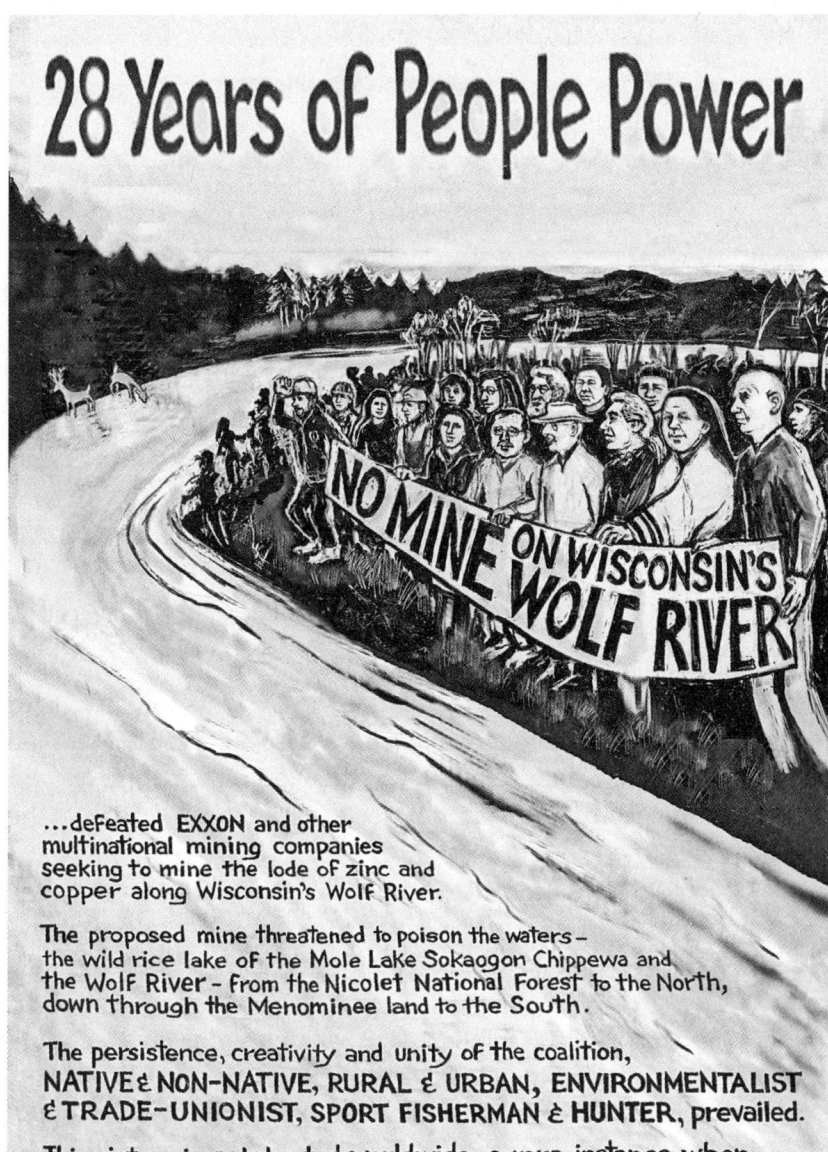

28 Years of People Power

NO MINE ON WISCONSIN'S WOLF RIVER

...defeated EXXON and other
multinational mining companies
seeking to mine the lode of zinc and
copper along Wisconsin's Wolf River.

The proposed mine threatened to poison the waters –
the wild rice lake of the Mole Lake Sokaogon Chippewa and
the Wolf River – from the Nicolet National Forest to the North,
down through the Menominee land to the South.

The persistence, creativity and unity of the coalition,
NATIVE & NON-NATIVE, RURAL & URBAN, ENVIRONMENTALIST
& TRADE-UNIONIST, SPORT FISHERMAN & HUNTER, prevailed.

This victory is celebrated worldwide, a rare instance when
grassroots citizens defeated corporate mining interests.

Crandon Mine Victory Art: This is a vertical reworking of the Crandon
Mine victory mural in black and white.

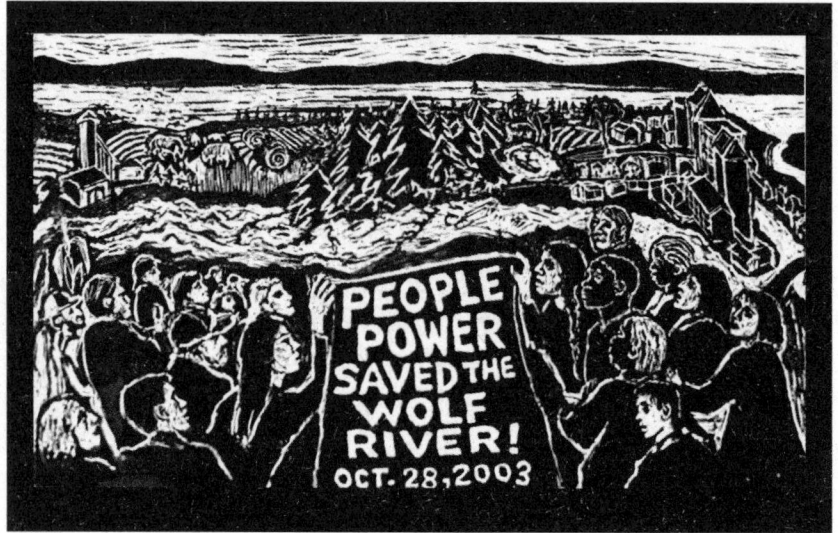

People Power: The *People Power* scratchboard graphic was my first experiment with scratchboard. I found that white scratchboard works better for me. I draw most of my stories using brush and india ink and then scratch into the drawing to refine it.

route between UWM and the interstate. The students who helped to paint it told me that they had their parents drive over to see the finished work. It was up for over a year and was popular in the neighborhood. Please read the words on the mural (see the vertical reworking of the mural on page 87).

There are advantages to doing public artwork in a smaller city or town. Whatever you do is remembered and likely to lead to invitations for other worthwhile collaborations. If the art speaks to heartfelt concerns, it is greatly appreciated.

In October 2023, I was invited to the twentieth anniversary celebration of stopping the Crandon Mine, hosted by the Mole Lake Sokaogon Chippewa and the Forest County Potawatomi. It was a joyous reunion. My artwork was included in the display of artifacts and in photographs. Speakers told the history of "a thousand cuts" that drove away multinational mining corporations one by one. Leaders with diverse skills, retired mine engineers, lawyers, and Indigenous treaty experts and grassroots organizers described their collaboration and the fluid improvisation of successful tactics. For instance, when Exxon Mining Company produced a full-color glossy brochure, it was mysteriously replaced with a shiny antimine doppelgänger.

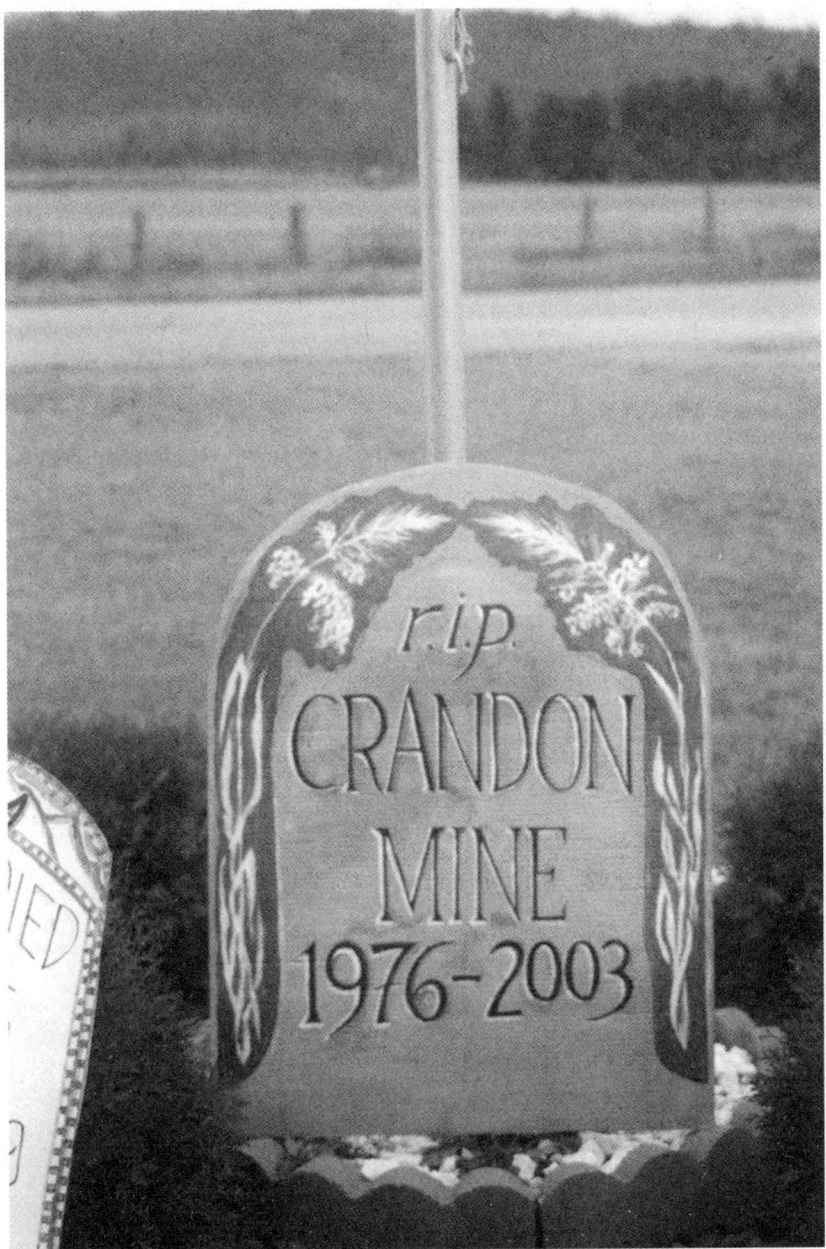

A Victory Monument: This is the last tombstone. It marks the death of the Crandon Mine. It was propped against the flagpole at Mole Lake Sokaogon Chippewa Reservation at the victory celebration in 2003, with the rest of the tombstones assembled on the lawn.

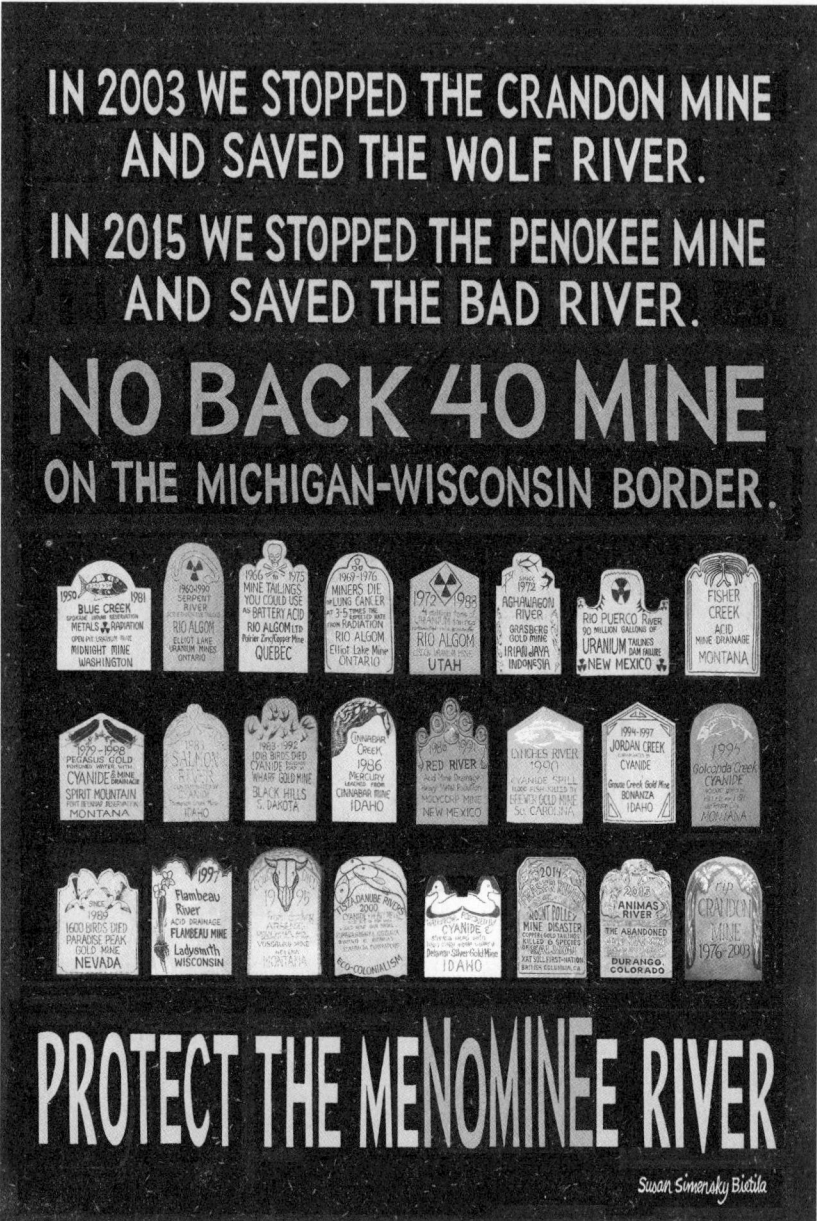

Tombstones Poster: This poster shows all the tombstones dedicated to rivers poisoned by mining worldwide.

The corporations present permission to mine as a "done deal," when that could not be further from the truth. Al Gedicks, emeritus professor of environmental sociology at the University of Wisconsin–La Crosse, is known for the analysis that our victory was achieved by denying the mine "social license to operate." This strategy has helped stop new mines from opening. The ore is still there, and proposals continue to pop up, Whac-a-Mole style, in northern Wisconsin and the Upper Peninsula of Michigan.

The movement against the Crandon Mine did not end anti-Indigenous racism in the Northwoods, but it created awareness that if rivers and lakes were polluted by mining, no one would want to eat the contaminated fish. Clean water is central to the economy of the Northwoods. Racist agitators had some of the wind knocked out of their sails. Hurley, Wisconsin, is just across the Montreal River from the Upper Peninsula, in Iron County. It was the town that lured the iron miners to spend their meager pay on booze and whores. To this day, it has well-deserved notoriety for having more strip clubs per population than anywhere in the US. Back in the day, Al Capone and the Chicago mob vacationed nearby. Today, the area is a haven for fishing and snowmobiling tourists and for persistent racist hate groups. In the late 1990s, the KKK held a rally there. Afterward, Red Cliff Ojibwe civil rights activist Walt Bresette and friends opened the fire hydrants and scrubbed Main Street with mops and pails.

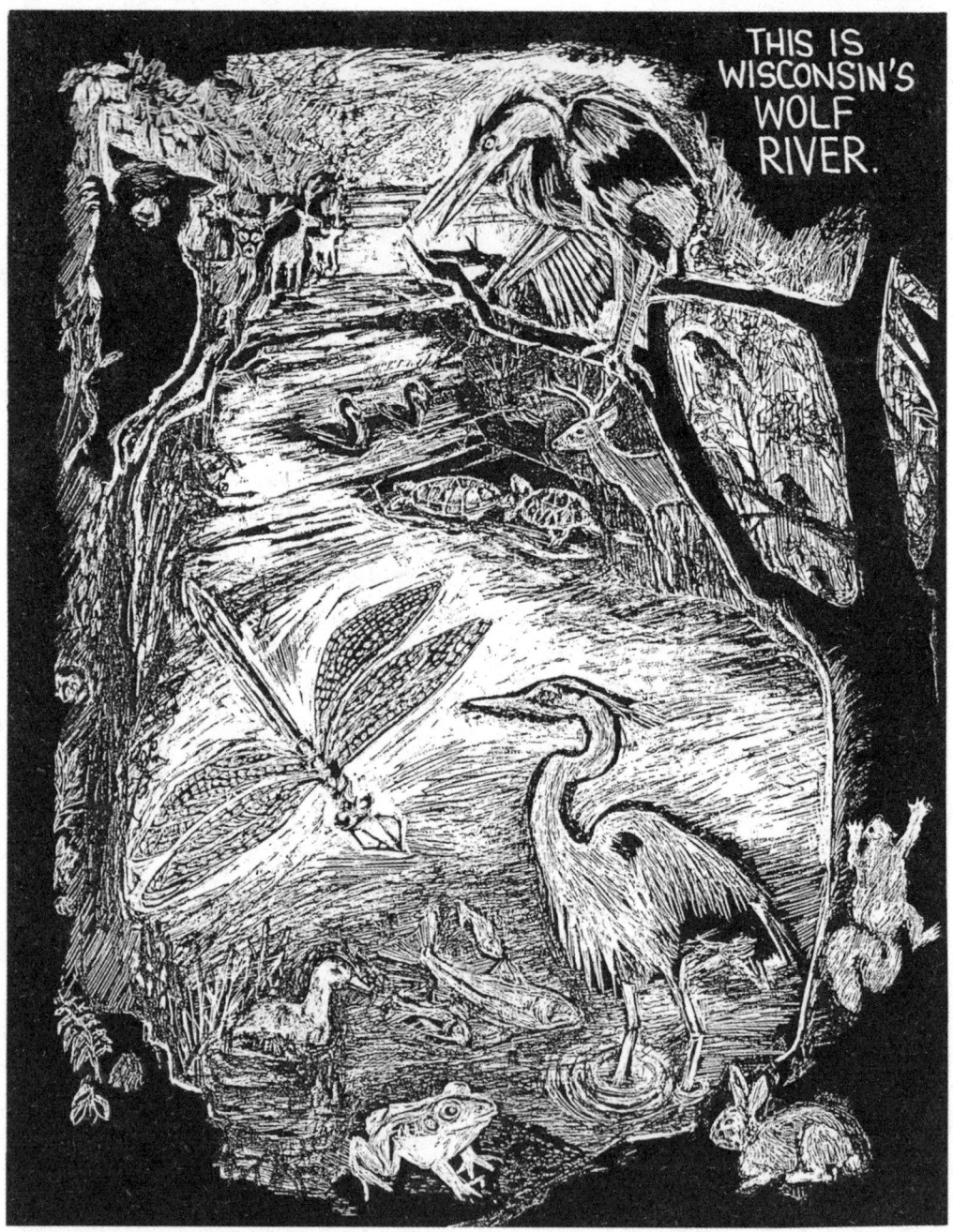

Pages 92–101: A Northwoods Tale
First appeared in *World War 3 Illustrated*, no. 33 (2002), "The Situation" issue.

IN 1975 EXXON MINERALS DISCOVERED A RICH DEPOSIT OF ZINC, COPPER AND OTHER PRECIOUS METALS AT THE WOLF RIVER'S HEADWATERS NEXT TO MOLE LAKE SOKAOGON CHIPPEWA RESERVATION.

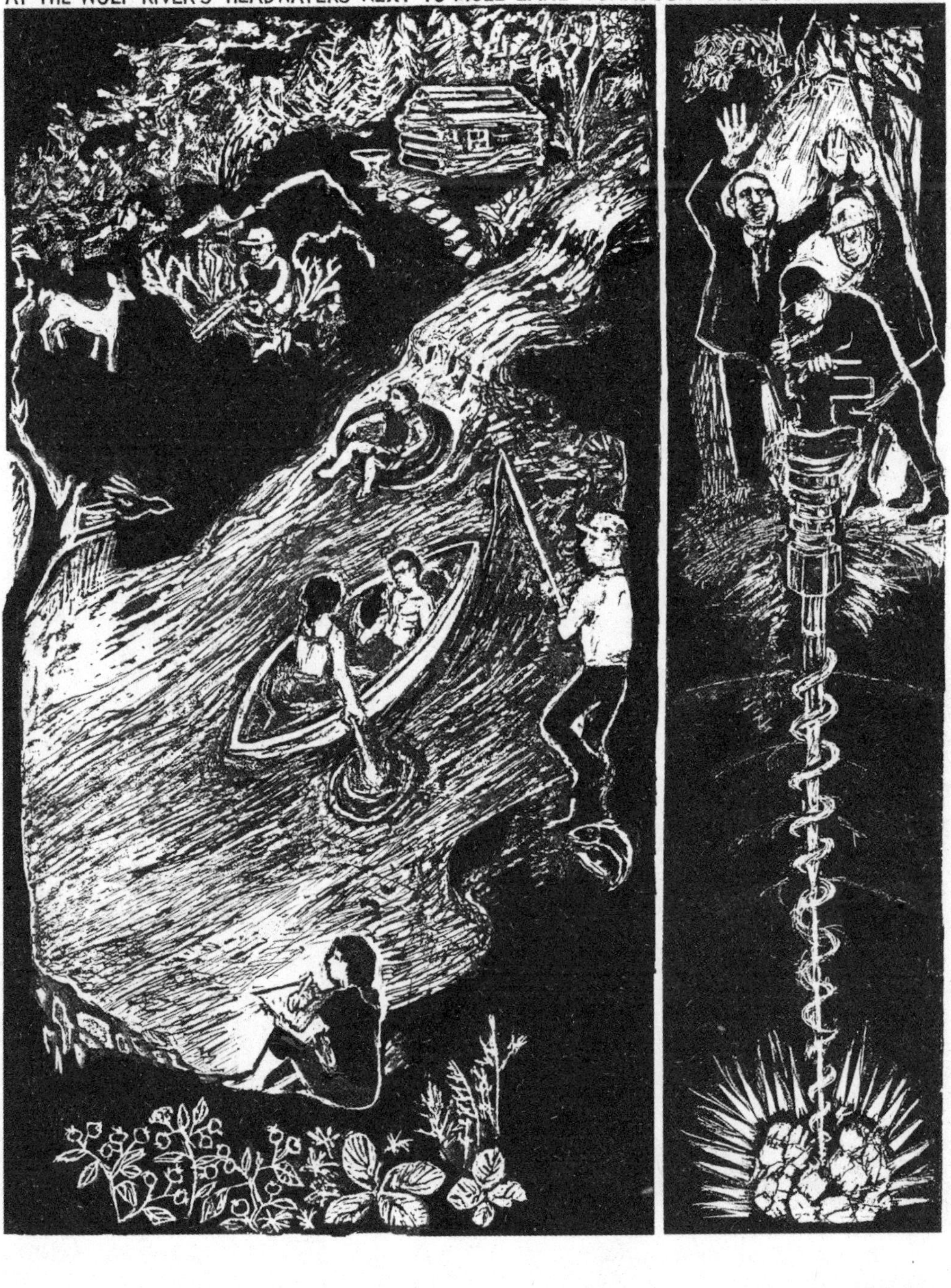

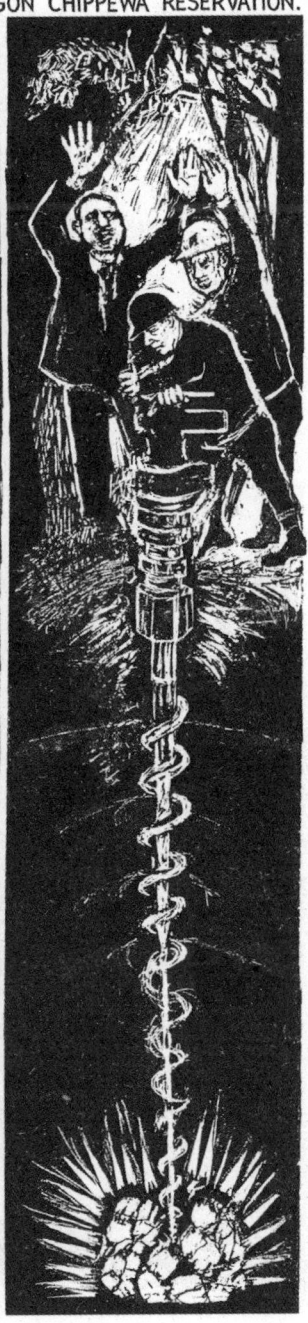

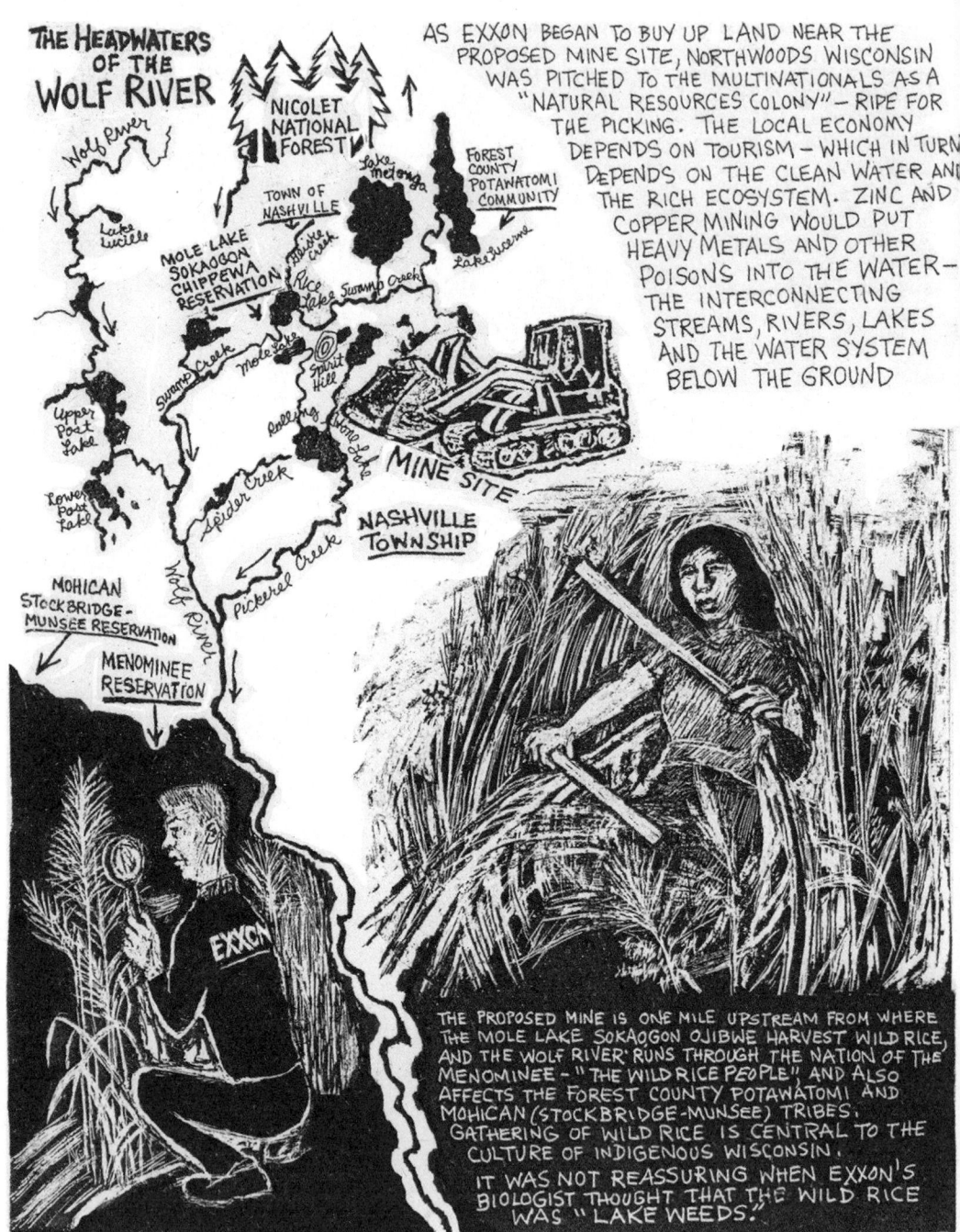

THE HEADWATERS OF THE WOLF RIVER

Wolf River

NICOLET NATIONAL FOREST

Lake Lucille

TOWN OF NASHVILLE

Lake Metonga

FOREST COUNTY POTAWATOMI COMMUNITY

MOLE LAKE SOKAOGON CHIPPEWA RESERVATION

Little Creek

Rice Lake Swamp Creek

Lake Lucerne

Swamp Creek

Mole Lake

Spirit Hill

Oakspring

Mole Lake

Upper Post Lake

Spider Creek

MINE SITE

NASHVILLE TOWNSHIP

Lower Post Lake

Pickerel Creek

Wolf River

MOHICAN STOCKBRIDGE-MUNSEE RESERVATION

MENOMINEE RESERVATION

AS EXXON BEGAN TO BUY UP LAND NEAR THE PROPOSED MINE SITE, NORTHWOODS WISCONSIN WAS PITCHED TO THE MULTINATIONALS AS A "NATURAL RESOURCES COLONY" — RIPE FOR THE PICKING. THE LOCAL ECONOMY DEPENDS ON TOURISM — WHICH IN TURN DEPENDS ON THE CLEAN WATER AND THE RICH ECOSYSTEM. ZINC AND COPPER MINING WOULD PUT HEAVY METALS AND OTHER POISONS INTO THE WATER — THE INTERCONNECTING STREAMS, RIVERS, LAKES AND THE WATER SYSTEM BELOW THE GROUND

EXXON

THE PROPOSED MINE IS ONE MILE UPSTREAM FROM WHERE THE MOLE LAKE SOKAOGON OJIBWE HARVEST WILD RICE, AND THE WOLF RIVER RUNS THROUGH THE NATION OF THE MENOMINEE — "THE WILD RICE PEOPLE" AND ALSO AFFECTS THE FOREST COUNTY POTAWATOMI AND MOHICAN (STOCKBRIDGE-MUNSEE) TRIBES. GATHERING OF WILD RICE IS CENTRAL TO THE CULTURE OF INDIGENOUS WISCONSIN.

IT WAS NOT REASSURING WHEN EXXON'S BIOLOGIST THOUGHT THAT THE WILD RICE WAS "LAKE WEEDS."

EXXON GLOATED OVER POTENTIAL FOR HUGE PROFITS.

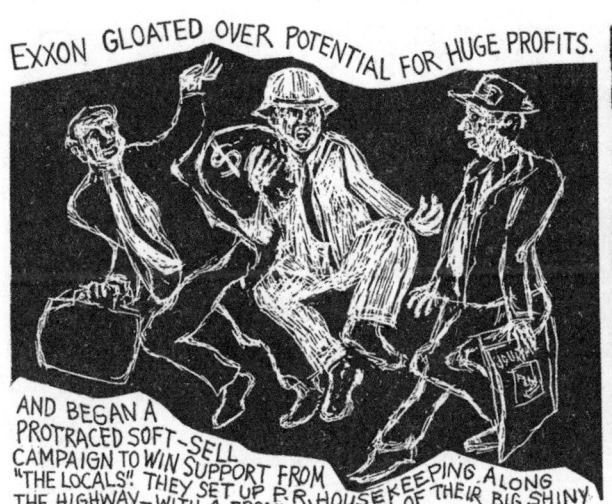

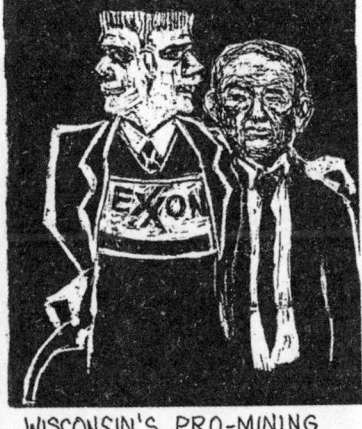

AND BEGAN A PROTRACTED SOFT-SELL CAMPAIGN TO WIN SUPPORT FROM "THE LOCALS". THEY SET UP P.R. HOUSEKEEPING ALONG THE HIGHWAY—WITH A FRONT YARD FULL OF THEIR BIG SHINY YELLOW MINING MACHINES AND FLOODED SCHOOLS AND COMMUNITY GROUPS WITH PRO-MINING PROPAGANDA. THEY GAVE MONEY TO LITTLE LEAGUE TEAMS AND HELD OUT A PROMISE OF JOBS IN THIS REGION WITH HIGH UNEMPLOYMENT.

WISCONSIN'S PRO-MINING GOVERNOR, TOMMY THOMPSON APPOINTED FORMER EXXON LOBBYIST, JAMES KLAUSER AS HIS #1 ASSISTANT.

IN 1983 FEDERAL COURTS RECOGNIZED THE OJIBWE'S LEGAL RIGHT TO HARVEST, FISH AND HUNT IN THE "CEDED TERRITORIES" VAST AREAS OF THE FOREST'S SOLD TO THE FEDERAL GOVERNMENT BEFORE THEY WERE FORCED ONTO RESERVATIONS.

BEGINNING IN 1986, WHEN TRIBE MEMBERS WENT TO THE LAKES TO HARVEST WALLEYE. THEY WERE HARASSED AND ATTACKED BY MOBS OF RACISTS WHO PACKED BOAT LANDINGS USED SPEED BOATS TO CREATE WAKES TO TRY TO SWAMP SPEARFISHERS' BOATS.

MOST POLICE STOOD BY, HANDS IN THEIR POCKETS, BLIND EYES TO DEATH THREATS, PIPE BOMBINGS, GUNSHOTS AND STONINGS INTENDED TO INTIMIDATE THE NATIVE AMERICANS.

RACIST AGITATORS SEIZED UPON THE SPEARFISHING AS THEIR WEDGE TO TRY TO OVERTURN TREATY RIGHTS (WHICH REMAIN A THREAT TO MINING). GOV. THOMPSON'S SPECIAL ASSISTANT KLAUSER CALLED ON THE CHIPPEWA 'TO END THE VIOLENCE' BY SELLING THEIR TREATY RIGHTS FOR A LUMP SUM OF CASH.

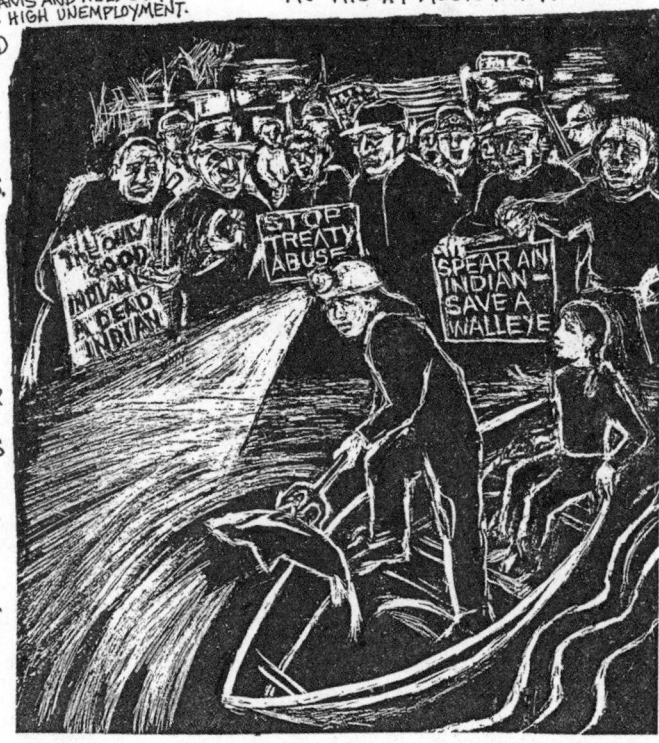

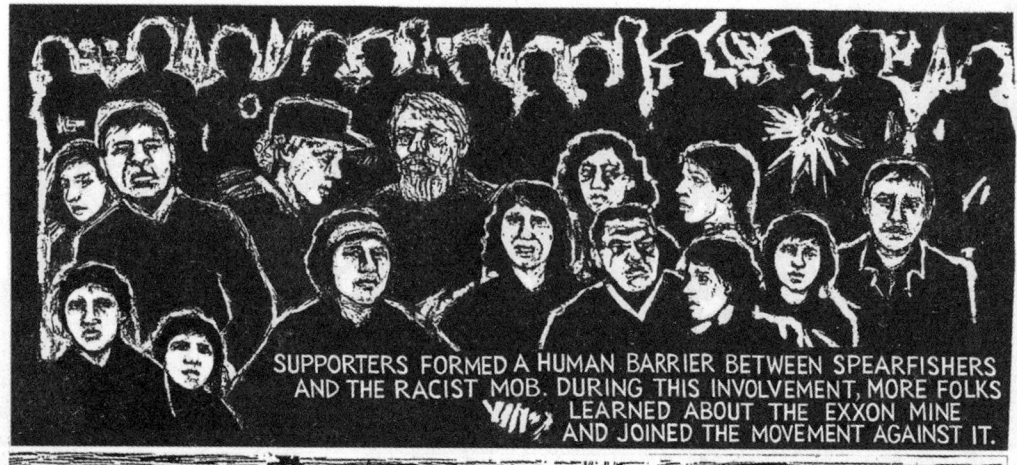

SUPPORTERS FORMED A HUMAN BARRIER BETWEEN SPEARFISHERS AND THE RACIST MOB. DURING THIS INVOLVEMENT, MORE FOLKS LEARNED ABOUT THE EXXON MINE AND JOINED THE MOVEMENT AGAINST IT.

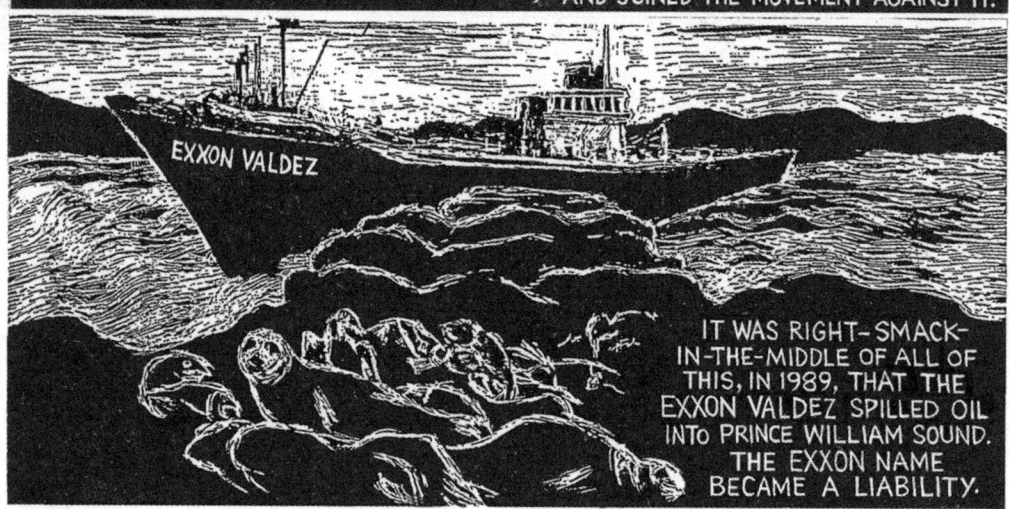

EXXON VALDEZ

IT WAS RIGHT-SMACK-IN-THE-MIDDLE OF ALL OF THIS, IN 1989, THAT THE EXXON VALDEZ SPILLED OIL INTO PRINCE WILLIAM SOUND. THE EXXON NAME BECAME A LIABILITY.

EXXON SOLD ITS INTEREST IN THE CRANDON MINE TO RIO ALGOM, A MINING COMPANY BASED IN TORONTO. THEY ALSO HAD A TERRIBLE RECORD, BUT WERE LESS INFAMOUS IN THE U.S. THEIR URANIUM MINE AT ELLIOT LAKE POISONED THE SERPENT RIVER WITH HEAVY METALS AND RADIOACTIVITY. THE SERPENT RIVER FLOWS THROUGH OJIBWE LAND IN ONTARIO.
MINERS DIED OF LUNG CANCER AS A RESULT OF BREATHING THE MINE'S TOXIC DUST.
RIO ALGOM TRIED TO UNLOAD CLEAN-UP OF THEIR POIRIER ZINC AND COPPER MINE IN QUEBEC BY SELLING IT TO THE CANADIAN GOVERNMENT FOR $1.

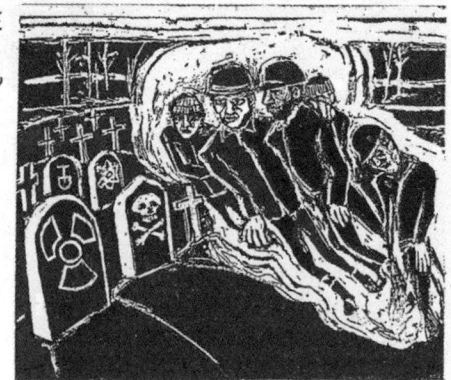

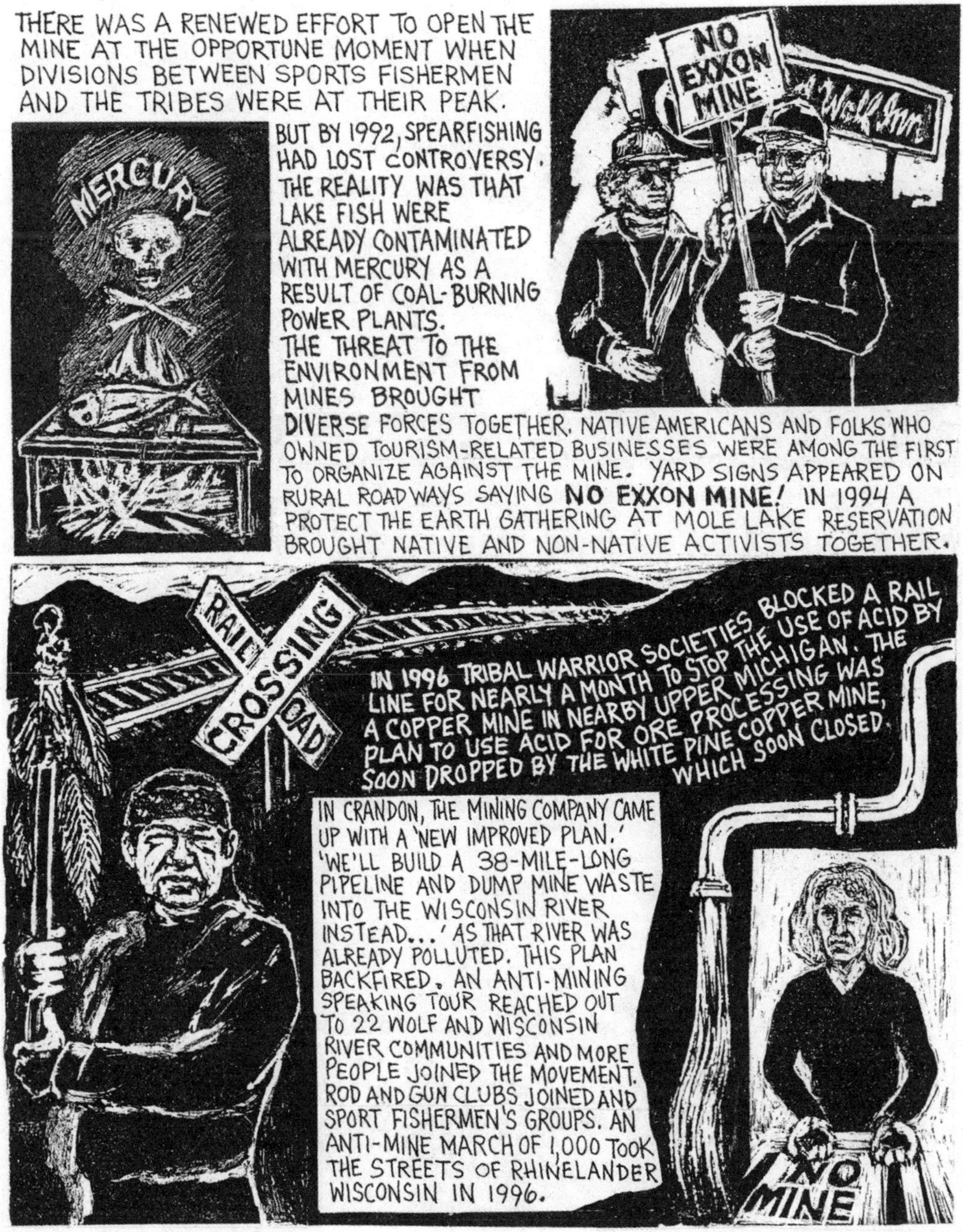

THERE WAS A RENEWED EFFORT TO OPEN THE
MINE AT THE OPPORTUNE MOMENT WHEN
DIVISIONS BETWEEN SPORTS FISHERMEN
AND THE TRIBES WERE AT THEIR PEAK.

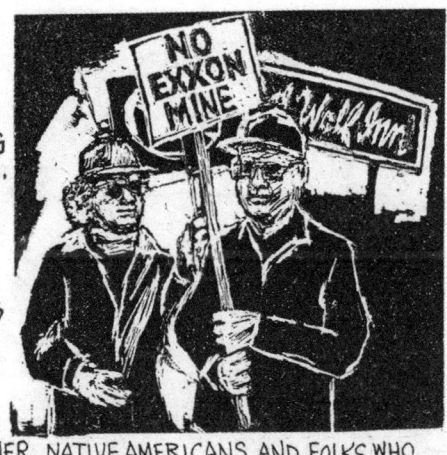

BUT BY 1992, SPEARFISHING
HAD LOST CONTROVERSY.
THE REALITY WAS THAT
LAKE FISH WERE
ALREADY CONTAMINATED
WITH MERCURY AS A
RESULT OF COAL-BURNING
POWER PLANTS.
THE THREAT TO THE
ENVIRONMENT FROM
MINES BROUGHT

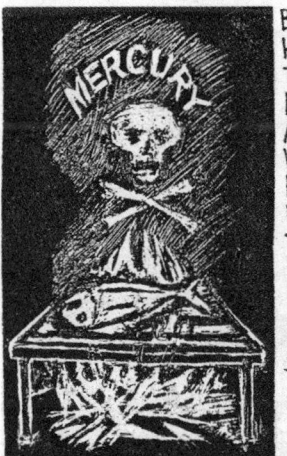

DIVERSE FORCES TOGETHER. NATIVE AMERICANS AND FOLKS WHO
OWNED TOURISM-RELATED BUSINESSES WERE AMONG THE FIRST
TO ORGANIZE AGAINST THE MINE. YARD SIGNS APPEARED ON
RURAL ROADWAYS SAYING **NO EXXON MINE!** IN 1994 A
PROTECT THE EARTH GATHERING AT MOLE LAKE RESERVATION
BROUGHT NATIVE AND NON-NATIVE ACTIVISTS TOGETHER.

IN 1996 TRIBAL WARRIOR SOCIETIES BLOCKED A RAIL
LINE FOR NEARLY A MONTH TO STOP THE USE OF ACID BY
A COPPER MINE IN NEARBY UPPER MICHIGAN. THE
PLAN TO USE ACID FOR ORE PROCESSING WAS
SOON DROPPED BY THE WHITE PINE COPPER MINE,
WHICH SOON CLOSED.

IN CRANDON, THE MINING COMPANY CAME
UP WITH A 'NEW IMPROVED PLAN.'
'WE'LL BUILD A 38-MILE-LONG
PIPELINE AND DUMP MINE WASTE
INTO THE WISCONSIN RIVER
INSTEAD...' AS THAT RIVER WAS
ALREADY POLLUTED. THIS PLAN
BACKFIRED. AN ANTI-MINING
SPEAKING TOUR REACHED OUT
TO 22 WOLF AND WISCONSIN
RIVER COMMUNITIES AND MORE
PEOPLE JOINED THE MOVEMENT.
ROD AND GUN CLUBS JOINED AND
SPORT FISHERMEN'S GROUPS. AN
ANTI-MINE MARCH OF 1,000 TOOK
THE STREETS OF RHINELANDER
WISCONSIN IN 1996.

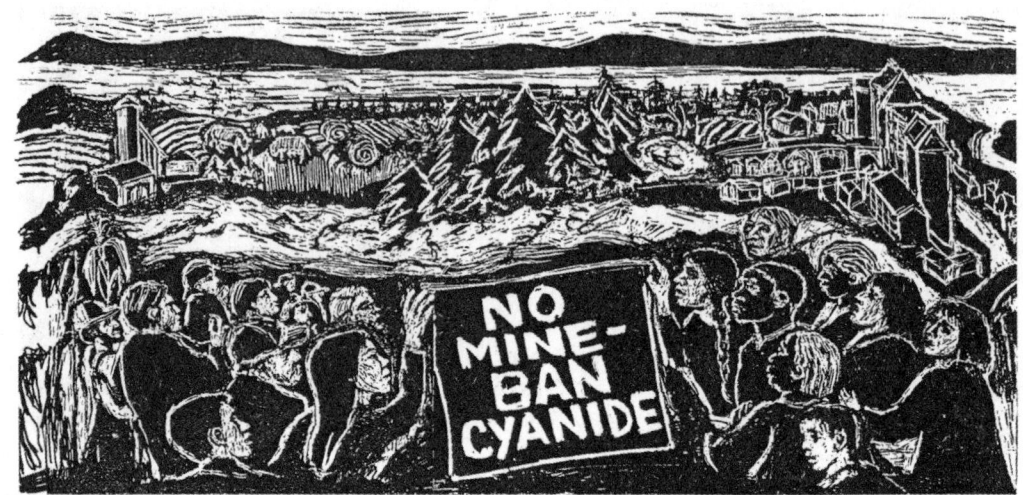

PEOPLE IN THE NORTHWOODS NEED JOBS BUT KNOW THAT MINING HAS
A BOOM AND BUST ECONOMY WITH FEW WELL-PAYING JOBS FOR LOCALS
AND SOME ADDED INCOME FOR LOCAL BUSINESSES, BUT WITH THE REAL
ADVANTAGE TO THE MULTINATIONALS — WHO CART AWAY THE WEALTH
LEAVING POISONED LAND AND A DEAD RIVER BEHIND. SO UNIONISTS
JOINED ENVIRONMENTALISTS, URBAN STUDENTS JOINED RURAL
RESIDENTS, SPORT FISHERS JOINED NATIVE AMERICANS. THE SPLITTING
TACTICS FAILED AND THE ALLIANCE CONTINUED TO GROW.

HALF OF THE MINE LAND LIES WITHIN THE TOWNSHIP OF NASHVILLE
AND THE TOWN BOARD WAS DISCOVERED TO HAVE SECRETLY NEGOTIATED
A LOCAL AGREEMENT WITH THE MINING COMPANY. IN 1997 THE PEOPLE IN

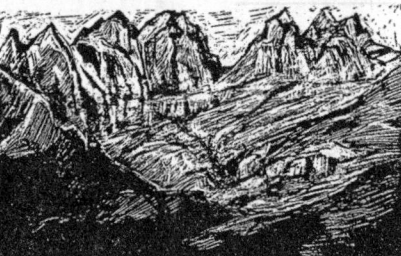

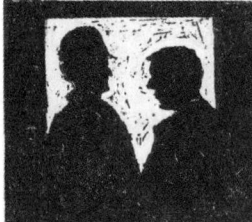

NASHVILLE ORGANIZED AND KICKED
OUT THE CORRUPT TOWN BOARD,
ELECTING AN ANTI-MINE SLATE
INCLUDING A MEMBER OF THE
MOLE LAKE SOKAOGON TRIBE.
THE NEW TOWN BOARD OVERTURNED
THE LOCAL AGREEMENT AND IS
BEING SUED TO FORCE THEM TO
NEGOTIATE AN AGREEMENT TO
PERMIT THE MINE.

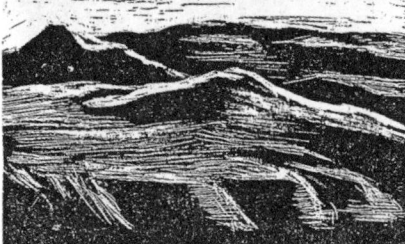

PETITION CAMPAIGNS AND RALLIES HELPED PASS THE 1998 MINING
MORATORIUM LAW WHICH SAYS THAT NO NEW MINES CAN OPEN IN
WISCONSIN UNTIL IT HAS BEEN SHOWN THAT A SIMILAR MINE

HAD NOT POLLUTED DURING
10 YEARS OF OPERATION AND
AFTER 10 YEARS CLOSED. THE
MINING COMPANY SUBMITTED
3 SAMPLE MINES TO THE DNR.
ONE IS ON A MOUNTAIN TOP,
THE SECOND IS IN PERMAFROST
AND THE LAST IS IN A DESERT.
NONE HAS ANY SIMILARITY TO
OUR NORTHWOODS' WATER TABLE.

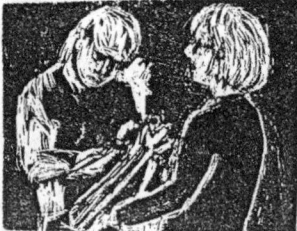

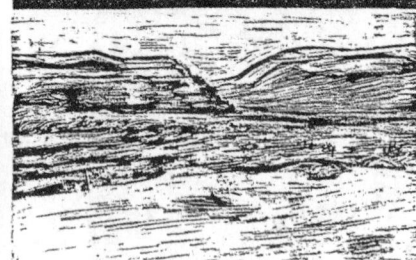

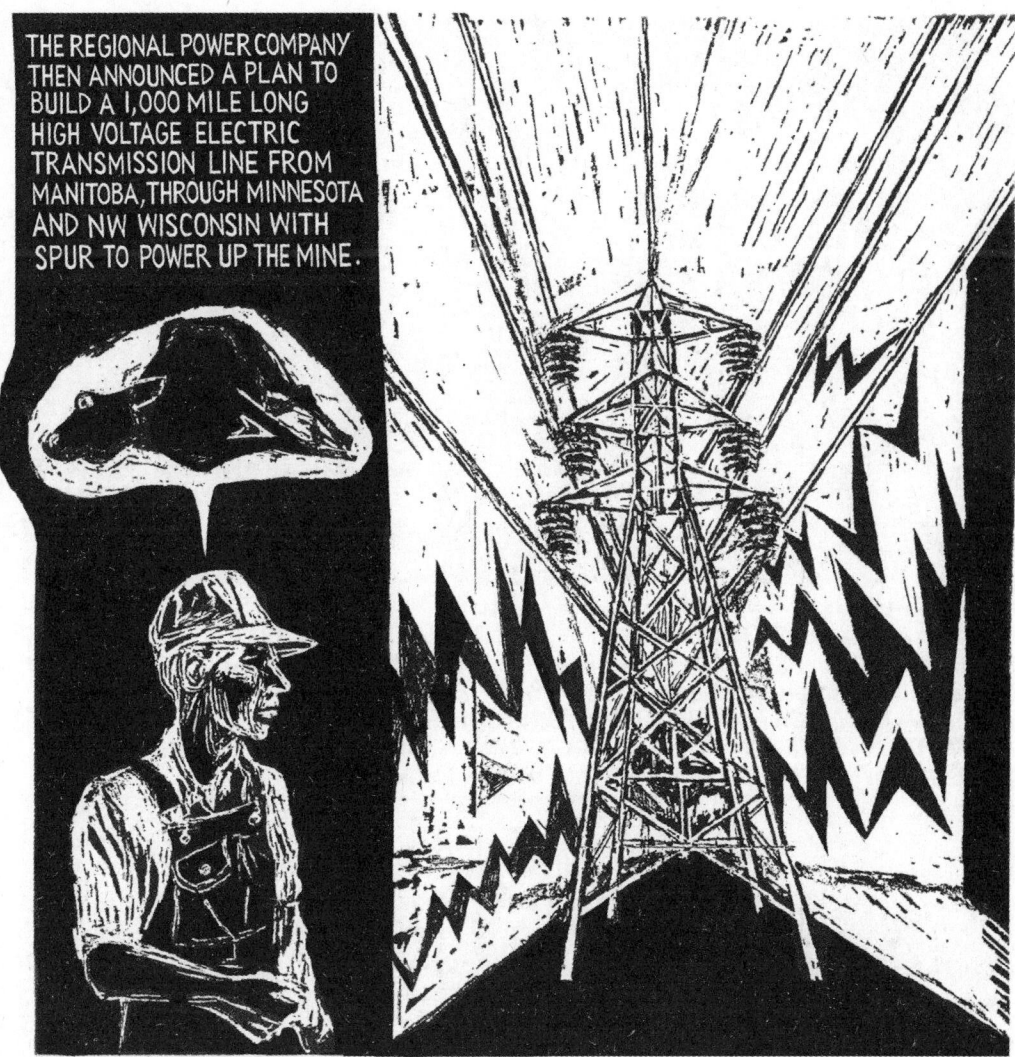

THE REGIONAL POWER COMPANY THEN ANNOUNCED A PLAN TO BUILD A 1,000 MILE LONG HIGH VOLTAGE ELECTRIC TRANSMISSION LINE FROM MANITOBA, THROUGH MINNESOTA AND NW WISCONSIN WITH SPUR TO POWER UP THE MINE.

SOME OF THE HYDROELECTRIC POWER IS GENERATED BY DAMS ON CREE LAND. THESE DAMS CAUSED DEVASTATING FLOODS LEAVING BEHIND AN EPIDEMIC OF DEPRESSION AND DESPAIR. NEITHER FOREST NOR FARM IS SAFE AS CORPORATION AND GOVERNMENT MERGE TO IMPOSE EMINENT DOMAIN. FARMERS WHOSE LAND IS IN THE PATH OF THE POWER LINE, HAVE SWORN TO STOP THE LINE BY ANY MEANS NECESSARY AND HAVE JOINED THE ALLIANCE AGAINST THE MINE.

THE ANTI-MINE ALLIANCE IS NOW CAMPAIGNING TO BAN CYANIDE IN WISCONSIN MINING. CYANIDE SPILLS HAVE POISONED RIVERS AROUND THE WORLD.

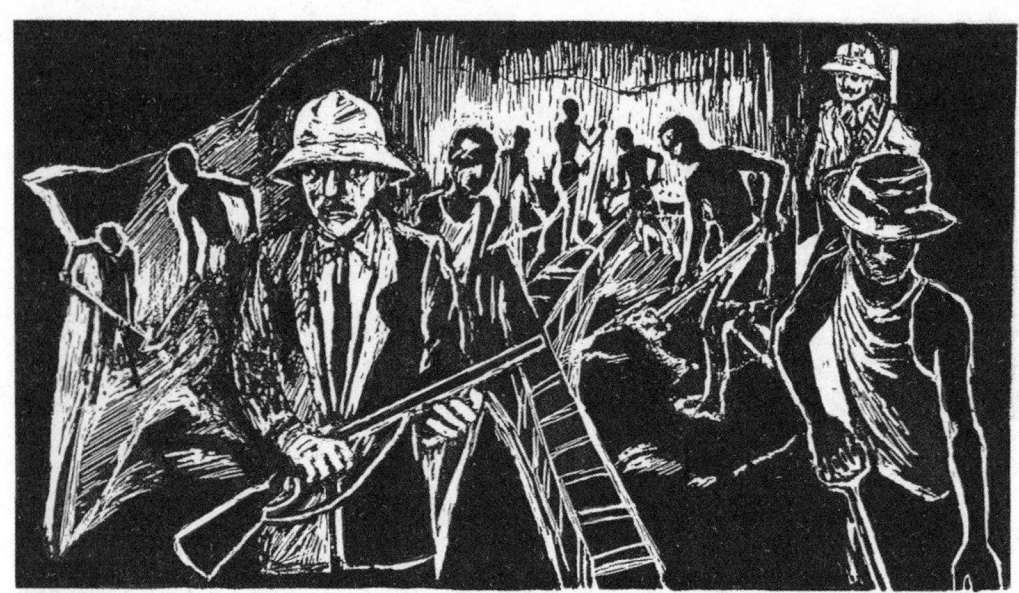

RIO ALGOM WAS THEN SOLD TO THE SOUTH AFRICAN BILLITON WHICH THEN MERGED WITH AUSTRALIAN BHP (BROKEN HILL PROPRIETARY) TO FORM THE LARGEST PRECIOUS METALS MINING CONGLOMERATE IN THE WORLD. THEY ARE AS INFAMOUS AS EXXON, BUT IN AFRICA AND THE ASIA-PACIFIC REGION. THEY CONTINUED TO DUMP MINE WASTE INTO PAPUA NEW GUINEA'S OK TEDI RIVER, KILLING ALMOST ALL THE FISH AND THE SURROUNDING FOREST.
ACTIVISTS IN AUSTRALIA ARE ALSO ORGANIZING AGAINST BHP BILLITON AND THE INDIGENOUS/NON-NATIVE ALLIANCES CONTINUE TO GROW.

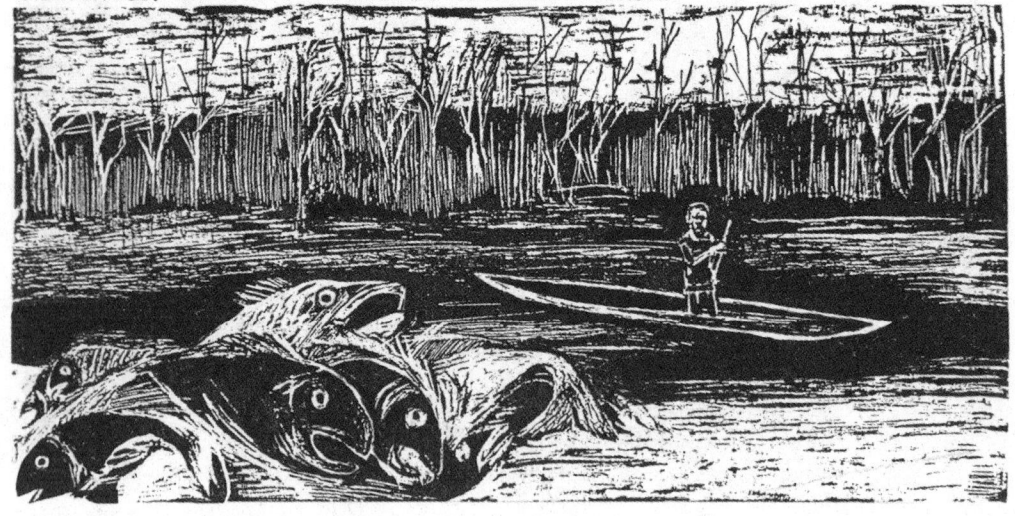

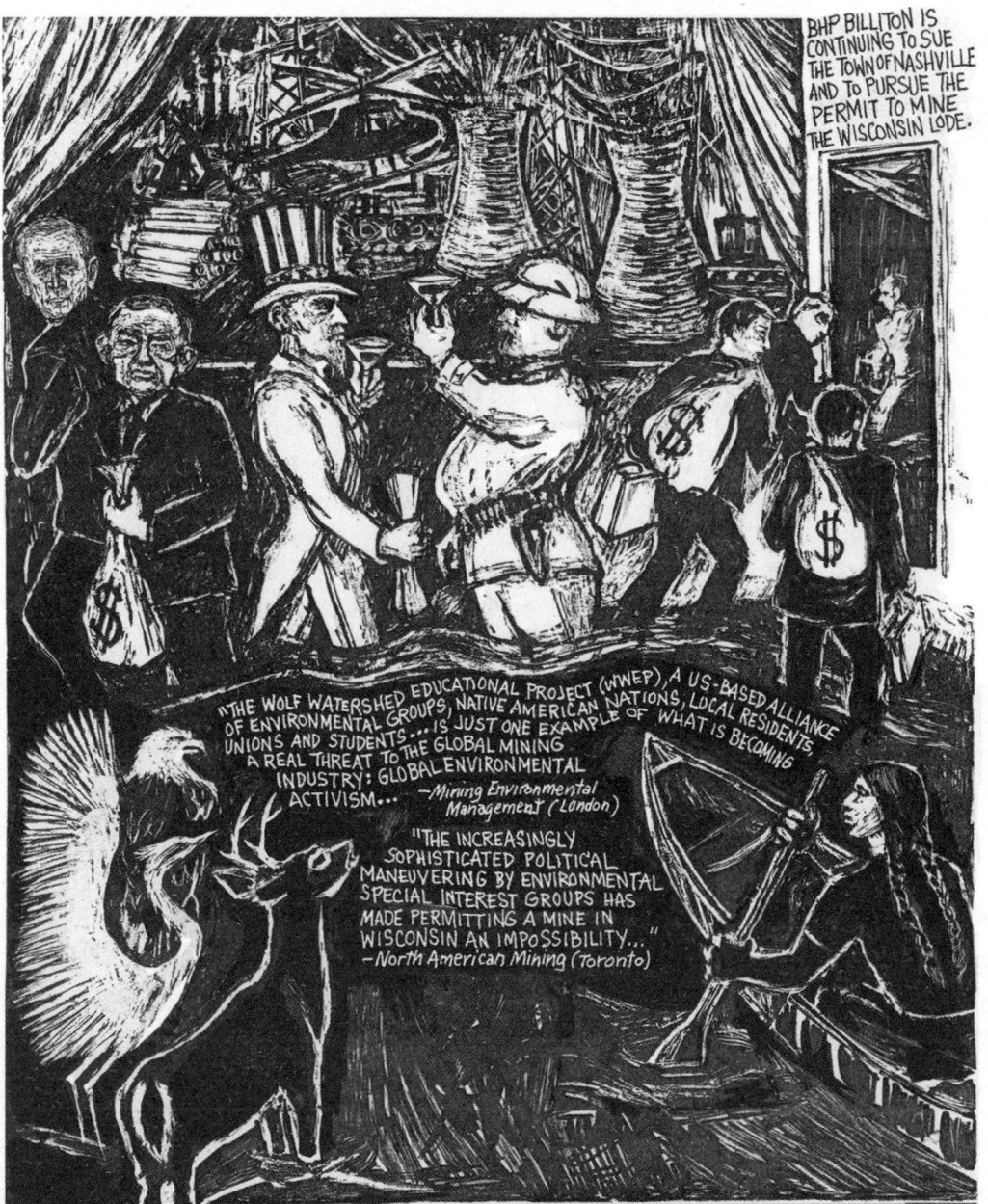

BHP BILLITON IS CONTINUING TO SUE THE TOWN OF NASHVILLE AND TO PURSUE THE PERMIT TO MINE THE WISCONSIN LODE.

"THE WOLF WATERSHED EDUCATIONAL PROJECT (WWEP), A US-BASED ALLIANCE OF ENVIRONMENTAL GROUPS, NATIVE AMERICAN NATIONS, LOCAL RESIDENTS, UNIONS AND STUDENTS... IS JUST ONE EXAMPLE OF WHAT IS BECOMING A REAL THREAT TO THE GLOBAL MINING INDUSTRY: GLOBAL ENVIRONMENTAL ACTIVISM... —Mining Environmental Management (London)

"THE INCREASINGLY SOPHISTICATED POLITICAL MANEUVERING BY ENVIRONMENTAL SPECIAL INTEREST GROUPS HAS MADE PERMITTING A MINE IN WISCONSIN AN IMPOSSIBILITY..." —North American Mining (Toronto)

WISCONSIN ANTI-MINING WEBSITES ARE OPERATED BY "BARBARIANS AT THE GATES OF CYBERSPACE." —Mining Voice

The Seattle Convergence Against the WTO

David Solnit sent me a beautiful postcard with a collage of images of giant puppets, writing that I'd really regret missing the gathering in Seattle in November 1999. It *was* going to be *that* good. The World Trade Organization (WTO) was meeting there, and this would be the first of a wave of antiglobalization demonstrations that included environmentalists *and* lumberjacks, union members *and* anarchists. The occupation of downtown Seattle surrounding the convention center was divided into wedges, with each sector making autonomous decisions about how to shut down the meeting of predatory global financial institutions and their so-called free trade agenda. Fifty thousand activists in Seattle and subsequent antiglobalization convergences between 1999 and 2002 further exposed the machinations profiting multinational cabals. They were met with raw police power exceeding what we saw in the 1960s, according to Doc Rosen, veteran street medic on the scene in Quebec City. These convergences were a prelude to the Occupy movement that rose up in 2011 and its unifying cry that "We Are the 99%."

I couldn't go to Seattle because of my weekend work schedule at the birth center. But Nicolas Lampert, and many others from Milwaukee who went to Seattle, returned home energized. Nicolas told me that during his drive back from Seattle to Milwaukee, he had taken note of corporate logos, and he suggested that we collaborate on a linocut print. He hadn't worked in this medium before. He designed the print, and we both cut the linoleum. I got out the ink and smooth old wooden spoons, and we had a printing party. This is how I had always editioned block prints. Friends took turns doing the rubbing, and we hung the prints with clothespins from strings tied across the room. Everyone took home a print, and there were plenty left to share.

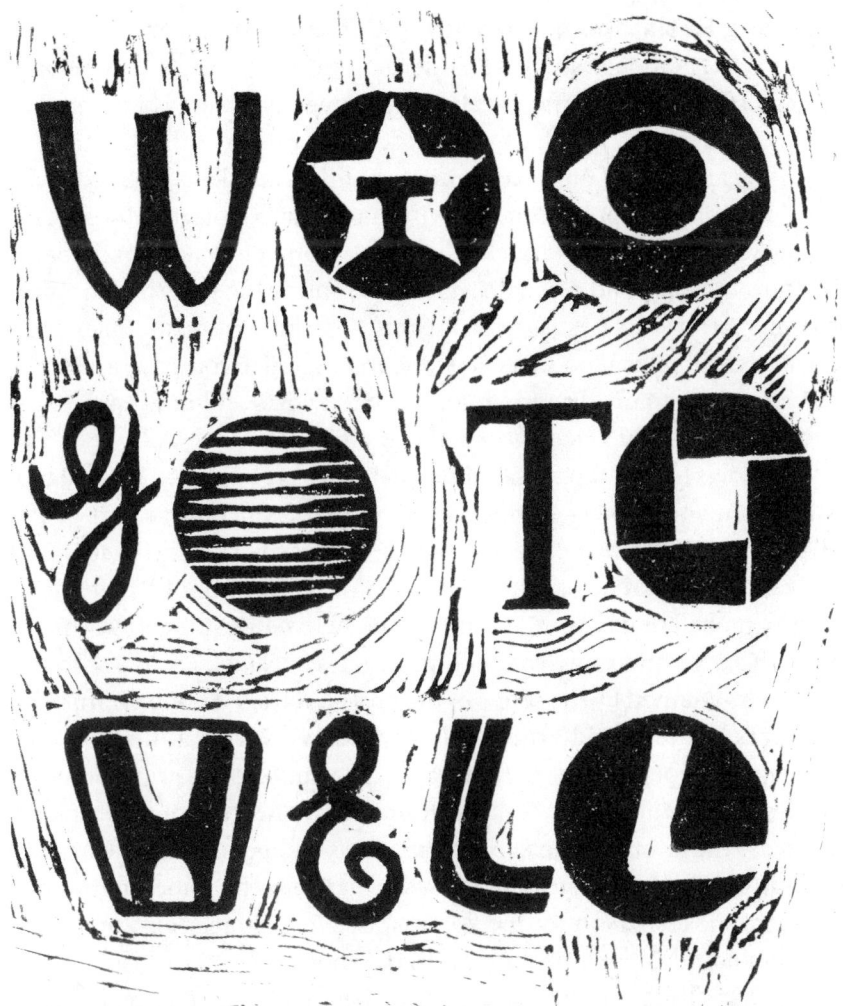

WTO Go to Hell: Nicolas Lampert designed this poster on the way home from the Seattle demonstration against the World Trade Organization. Each logo was printed with the appropriate color. We both cut the linoleum block and then held a printing party.

Drawing Resistance: A Traveling Political Art Show

At the WTO demonstration in Seattle, activist artists from all over North America found one another. Feeling the connective energy of this global justice movement, Nicolas had the idea that we needed to organize a traveling art show of up-to-the-minute political art, do-it-yourself style. (DIY remains a popular concept within activist countercultures.) The show was designed to be packed up into a minivan, "like a punk band on tour," Nicolas said. Each host group mounting the show had to agree to transport it to its next stop on the tour. The host groups were encouraged to exhibit local political artwork and organize companion events. We chose the main art and, together with artists and activist friends, identified the right places to host the exhibit.

Nicolas had a map of the route all drawn. He had lived in Oakland, so he contacted artists on the West Coast, and since I was part of the *World War 3 Illustrated* collective, I contacted artists on the East Coast. We relied on anarchist art historian Allan Antliff, whom I'd met after I photographed him in 1998 at the Toronto Active Resistance, to connect us with artists and show-space communities in Canada.

I was stunned by the scope of the project. I visited famed Industrial Workers of the World artist and poet Carlos Cortéz at his home in Chicago to explain the show to him, and he pulled out a print for me to send on the road. In New York, I fortuitously found the woman who was acting as the informal dealer for Mexico City Indigenous artist Domitila Dominguez, who illustrated *The Story of Colors* by Subcomandante Marcos, spokesperson for the Zapatistas. We included her watercolor of the masked Chiapas insurgents in the show.

It was a unique moment of coming together. The artists in the show trusted their artwork to pass through many hands, cross the continent and back, and go over the US-Canada border four times (without declaring a dollar value and without the customary insurance). We found the hosts by word of mouth and phone calls in the days before social media had developed. Unlike typical art shows, nothing was for sale. *Drawing Resistance: A Traveling Political Art Show* envisioned a long-overdue new society with noncapitalist principles.

We included artists from the *World War 3 Illustrated* collective; the Justseeds Artists' Cooperative, which came together in 1998; the Beehive Design Collective, which began in the same period; and other printmakers, poster artists, and painters who shared our worldview and

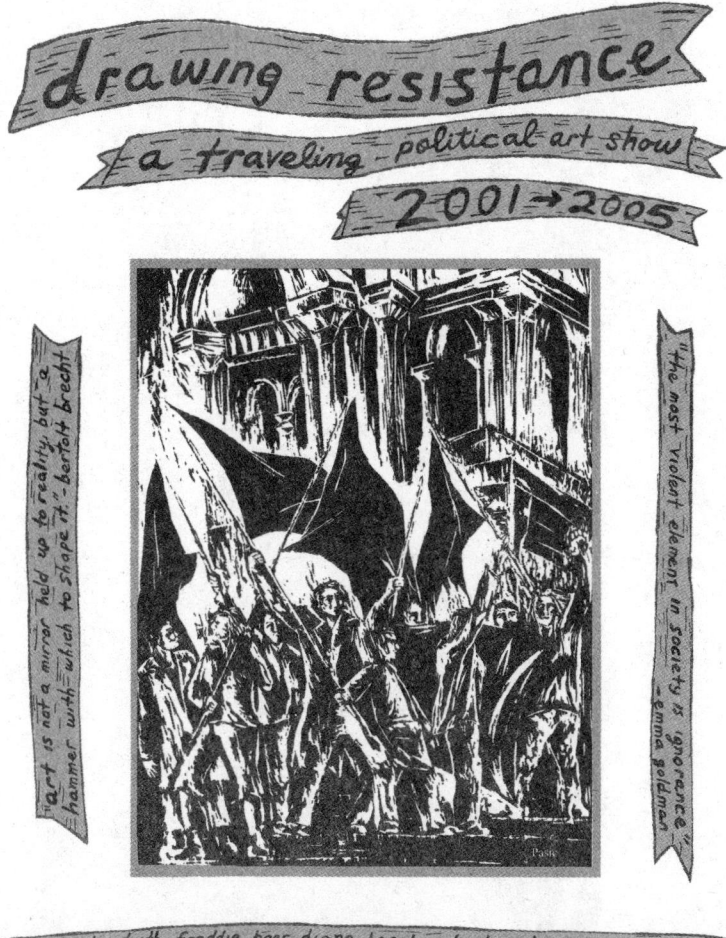

Drawing Resistance Poster: This is the original poster for *Drawing Resistance: A Traveling Political Art Show*, designed by Nicolas Lampert with the demonstration image by Iris Pasic, a young Chicago artist who periodically squatted in Riverwest. She made this 32-by-48-inch woodcut print after attending the demonstration at the Philadelphia Republican Convention in July 2000. Among others, a puppet-making crew was arrested there, accused of making chemical weapons out of jalapeño peppers while they were cooking vegan chili. Police also seized a giant puppet, accusing it of being a Trojan horse hiding weapons.

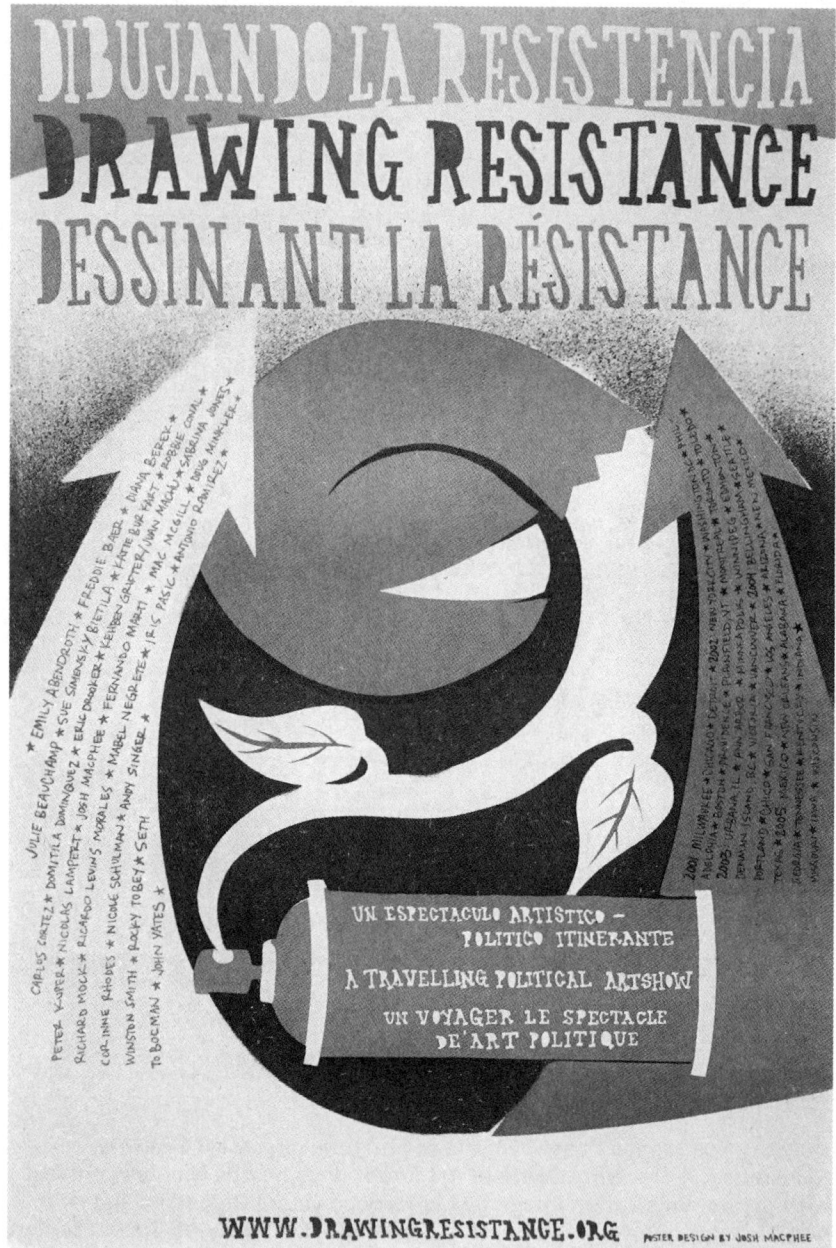

Josh MacPhee's *Drawing Resistance* Poster: A second poster for *Drawing Resistance* was designed by Josh MacPhee of Justseeds, who had an anti-incarceration stencil print in the show.

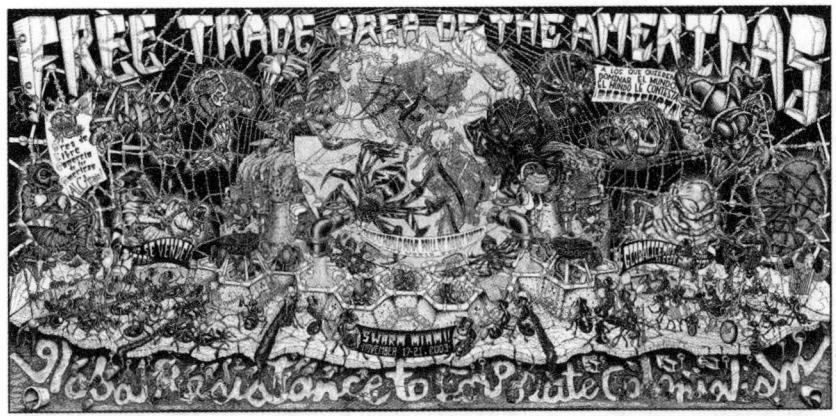

FTAA Mural by the Beehive Design Collective: Here is the Beehive Design Collective's mural *Free Trade Area of the Americas/Global Resistance to Corporate Colonialism*, which we included in *Drawing Resistance*. Their members travel, using the collective's art to present the effects of colonialism on ecosystems in the colonized Global South. The Beehive is on tour once again.

valued collaboration. Emily Abendroth from Oakland titled the quilt she included in the show *Celebrating Communities of Resistance*, and that is exactly what the show was about.

Two weeks before *Drawing Resistance* was to open in Milwaukee at the Riverwest Artists Association's gallery, the roof of the leaky old sheet-metal shop where the gallery is located fell in. Despite being a politically neutral organization, the Riverwest Artists Association members rallied, rented a storefront, and enthusiastically set about demolition, wielding sledgehammers to take down rotted walls, then installing pristine new walls and track lights. The show opened at the newly renovated gallery the day after the 9/11 attacks. With the drumbeat of nationalism and xenophobic fervor at its peak, we wondered how the show would be received. But the show became a place of solace and reassurance for many during this time of chaos.

Drawing Resistance traveled to thirty-two spaces across the US and Canada from 2001 to 2004. It was hosted by collectives, community and university art galleries, private museums, public housing community centers, and restaurants. The opening event at the Mondragon Center in Winnipeg, Manitoba, was a high point, with an enthusiastic crowd of hundreds on opening night. The show was in Houston at the Art Car Museum when Nicolas and I decided that it was time to end the tour. It was supposed to go to New Orleans next, and it would have been there

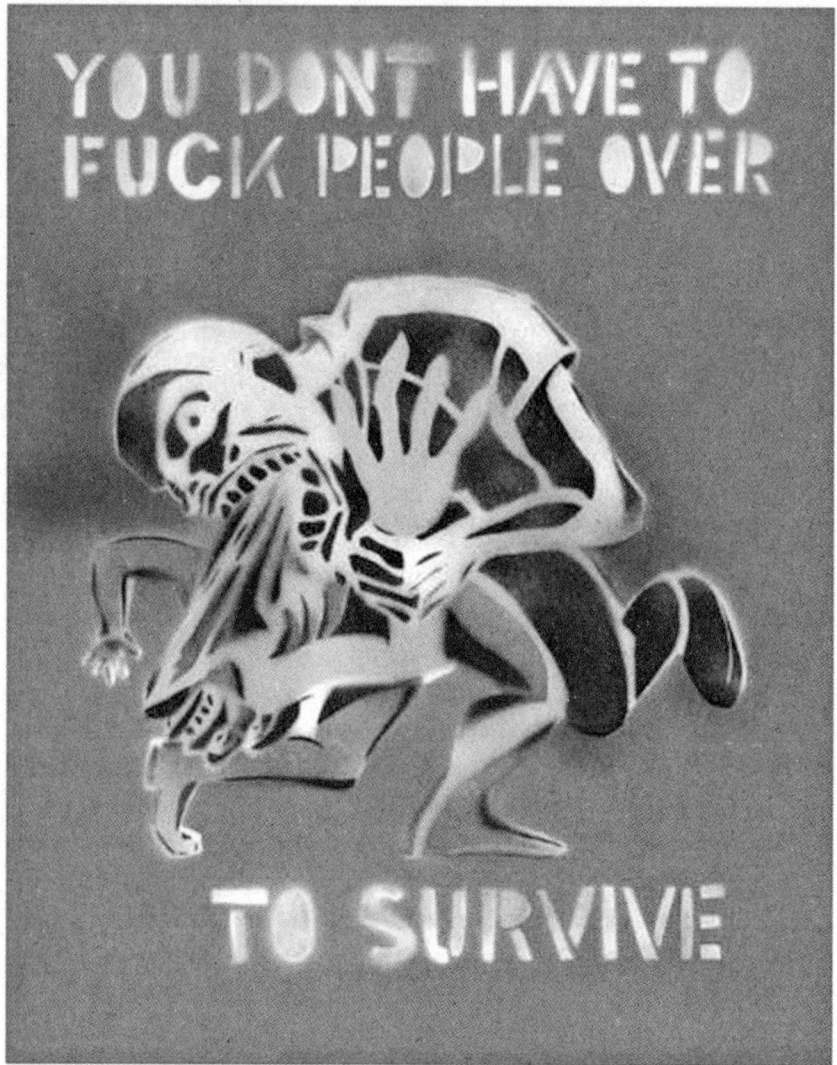

Seth Tobocman: Seth Tobocman's art needs no explanation. He is from the Lower East Side community in Manhattan, and his print in *Drawing Resistance* was *You Don't Have to Fuck People Over to Survive*. The work focused on the desperate need for housing and upholding the squatters' movement. He is a cofounder of *World War 3 Illustrated* magazine, together with Peter Kuper and Eric Drooker, who also had art in the show. John Yates's print "Democracy, We Deliver" was in the show as well. He designed the cover of this book.

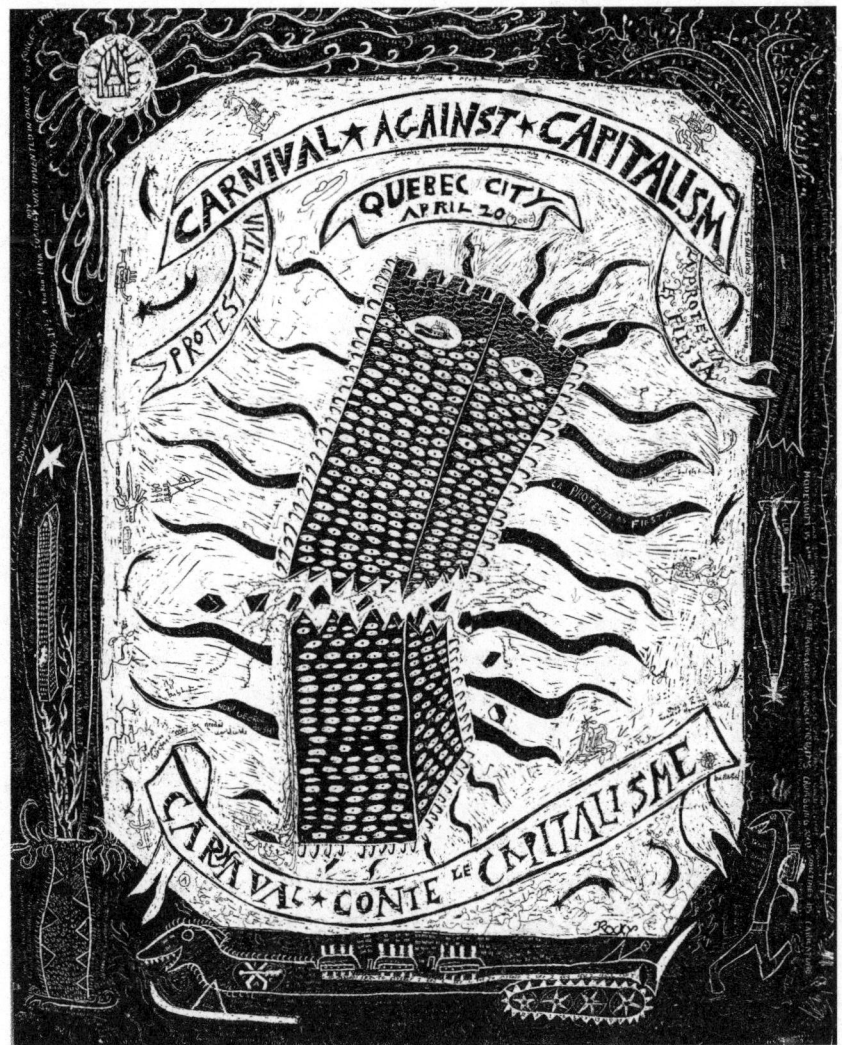

Carnival Against Capitalism: Rocky Dobey's *Carnival Against Capitalism* poster invited people to protest the FTAA (Free Trade Area of the Americas) in Quebec City. This march was met with extreme police violence. Rocky, a metal worker, is well known in Toronto for his icon-like enameled copper plaques installed permanently in the Kensington Market area.

when the catastrophic Hurricane Katrina hit the city. All the art came back to Milwaukee for one last show at the Broad Vocabulary feminist bookstore. We contacted all the artists and returned work to those who wanted it back. Many of the networks established during the show's run have lasted. The affinity and collaboration between these artists and new generations of activist artists encourages us all.

Living in the Northwoods

In 2002, while *Drawing Resistance* was still on the road, Paul, our younger son, and I moved to Ashland, Wisconsin, on the south shore of Lake Superior. After teaching freshman English as an instructor for over a decade, Paul had completed a library degree and had been hired as the reference librarian at Northland College. Our younger son, Smitty, who had traveled widely and worked on organic farms, moved north with us to finish the environmental science degree he had begun at UWM. Northland was renowned in that field, and children of staff could attend for free. Our older son, David, had gone to UW–Madison for undergraduate and graduate school and was already a librarian working in the DC area.

I was hired to work at the small local hospital in the float pool for labor and delivery. After decades of top job performance at university teaching hospitals, I never made it out of orientation there. The toxic environment was stressful, with racism both toward Ojibwe patients and staff and toward me, either for being Jewish or for not being Christian. Our next-door neighbors didn't speak to us for a year, thinking that we were "Natives living in the wrong part of town." To my great relief, I was soon hired by the Ashland County Health Department as an RN social marketing specialist. No one really knew what that entailed, so I was left to create the role. In addition to the obvious work of community education about disease threats like West Nile virus and writing the health column for the weekend edition of the *Daily Press*, I got an arts grant from the Chequamegon Bay Arts Council and hired Chris Lutter-Gardella, a giant-puppet artist, to collaborate in the creation of conceptual body systems for an event called a "BodyWalk." We worked with diverse after-school groups throughout the large county, including the Mashkisibi Boys & Girls Club on the Bad River Reservation and high school students in Marengo, where Finnish Evangelical Lutherans predominate. Then we brought the students and their body systems together for a festival at the elementary/middle school.

Working for the Ashland Health Department, I learned about the history and the politics of the region. The reservation of the Bad River Band of Lake Superior Chippewa (Ojibwe) is in Ashland County, east of the city. I suspect that one reason I was hired was because I have no family connection to the history of Ashland's white settler racism, typical of towns bordering reservations. Part of my job was to connect with the Indigenous community. I helped with tribal health screenings and spent time with the Native Gardens organizer learning about traditional raised-bed Three Sisters Gardens (corn, beans, and squash). I got to go out in the flat-bottomed boat with the Bad River Tribe invasive-species agronomist to learn about the Kakagon Sloughs wild rice beds on the Lake Superior shore—on work time. I was delighted with these opportunities. I was also welcomed into the Chequamegon Bay Arts Council to curate shows and invited by Northland College's art department chair, Jason Terry, to work in the printmaking studio to create the monoprints for a chapter about the Free Speech Movement in the 2003 book *Wobblies! A Graphic History of the Industrial Workers of the World*.

Less than three years later, Paul and I moved back to Milwaukee, because his work situation at the Northland College library had become unbearable. I still return to Ashland and the Lake Superior shore to work on art with new and old friends, collaborating on projects to protect the Great Lakes, rivers, and wild rice from the Enbridge Line 5 crude oil pipeline that crosses the Bad River Reservation and then cuts through the forests of the Upper Peninsula of Michigan, where Paul grew up. I have gone back to talk about art and activism at Northland College and have spoken on Zoom to Northwoods Unitarians.

Defending Public Education

The Republicans called it the Budget Repair Act. The purpose was to deprive public employees of collective bargaining rights, a key item of the right-wing Koch brothers' agenda. Wisconsin had been the test site for the Koch brothers–led American Legislative Exchange Council (ALEC) agenda for repression. They wrote the legislation, which was then enacted by Republican-controlled governments to dismantle the social safety net, inventing "workfare." ALEC's agenda sounds all too familiar today. They wanted to cut Medicaid, dismantle the state university system, and defund public education. Governor Scott Walker, with a Republican majority in the state assembly, went after public employee unions through Act 10. This ALEC-created legislation limited teachers' and public workers' salary raises to the cost of living and ended public employee union negotiations for health care benefits and pensions. The Koch brothers were blatantly anti-union. Act 10 was designed to bankrupt public employee unions by no longer allowing them to use payroll deduction, and to harass them by requiring yearly recertification elections.

On Valentine's Day 2011, in Madison, the capital of Wisconsin, high school students and University of Wisconsin teaching assistants walked out and marched to the capitol. The next day, public school staff and Milwaukee teachers held a sick-out and carpooled the 108 miles to the capitol. I had worked as a school nurse in Milwaukee public high schools since 2004 and was active in my union, Milwaukee Teachers' Education Association (MTEA). During the uprising, I was the spokesperson for the school nurses. A bus carried the school drumline from Riverside University High School, where I worked, to Madison, and they led our march around the capitol. We started as several thousand and grew every week, until there were over a hundred thousand people protesting from all over the state. Wisconsin Republicans and Fox News, following

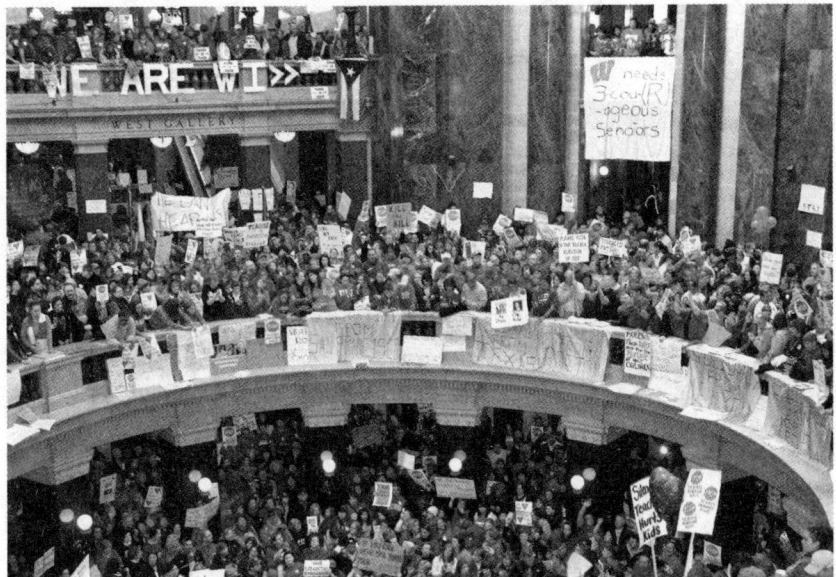

People Fill the Wisconsin State Capitol: This is the Wisconsin State Capitol in February 2011. I took many photos to use as resources for the story "Walk Like an Egyptian." This shows only a few of the circular tiers and balconies from the ground floor up into the top of the dome. And this is only the inside crowd. The four terraces and stairways outside the capitol, as well as the surrounding streets, were also filled.

their usual playbook, made accusations that we were all paid outside agitators.

On February 20, a week after the Valentine's Day protest, occupation of the state capitol became 24/7. People set up housekeeping with sleeping areas, a dining area with food donations from local businesses, a medic station, a day care and kids' play area, a sign- and banner-making area—and every other sort of mutual aid needed. The corridors of the capitol had turned into a temporary utopian society. One freezing day at the capitol, pizzas were delivered, a warm gesture of international solidarity by Egyptian demonstrators who were also fighting against their repressive government. I made a piece called "Walk Like an Egyptian," after the 1986 Bangles song, to refer to the contemporaneous occupation of Tahrir Square in Cairo. Workers from the big industrial and service unions joined us. Week after week we became more powerful. I had never imagined that suddenly Wisconsin workers could come so close to a general strike. I wonder what the result would have been if this movement had not been channeled into the usual dead-end electoral politics.

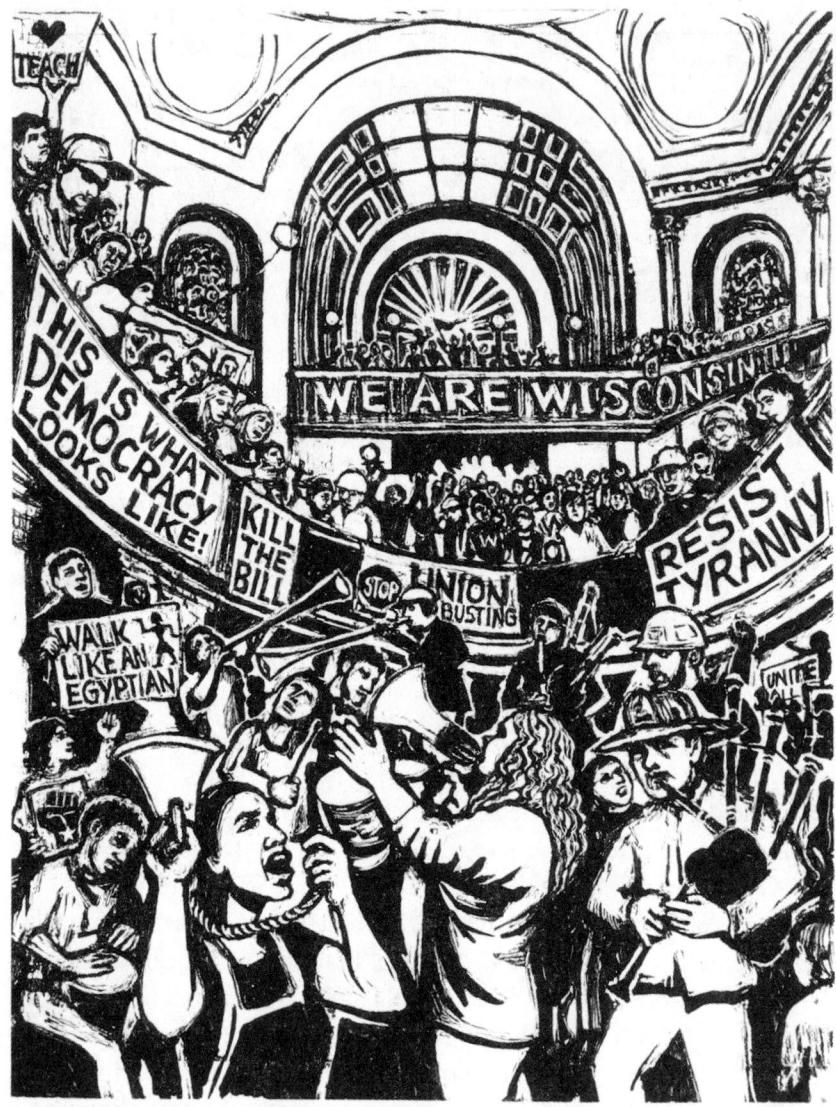

Wisconsin Workers Fight Back: I hope this drawing communicates the joyful cacophony.

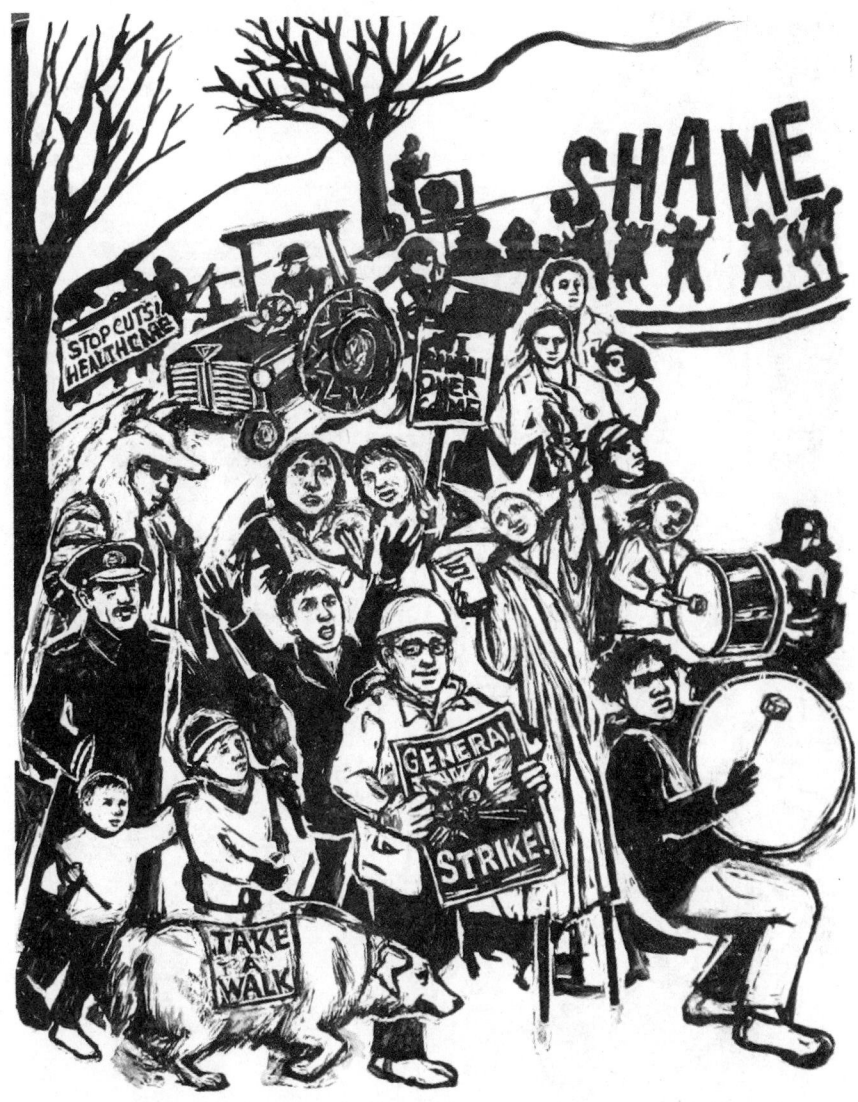

Outside the Capitol: While every layer of the inside of the capitol building was filled, thousands more packed layers of steps and the roadway around the building. We rallied in the sleet and snow. The temperature hovered around zero many days that we were there. A printed sign reading "Walker—Union Buster" and Eric Drooker's *General Strike!* poster were seen at the rally of tens of thousands of union members and supporters. Public school teachers and nurses were joined by garbage collectors from Green Bay as well as construction workers, firefighters, food industry workers, and so many more. This drawing includes special education teachers, the school social worker, and other people I know. They were delighted to be included.

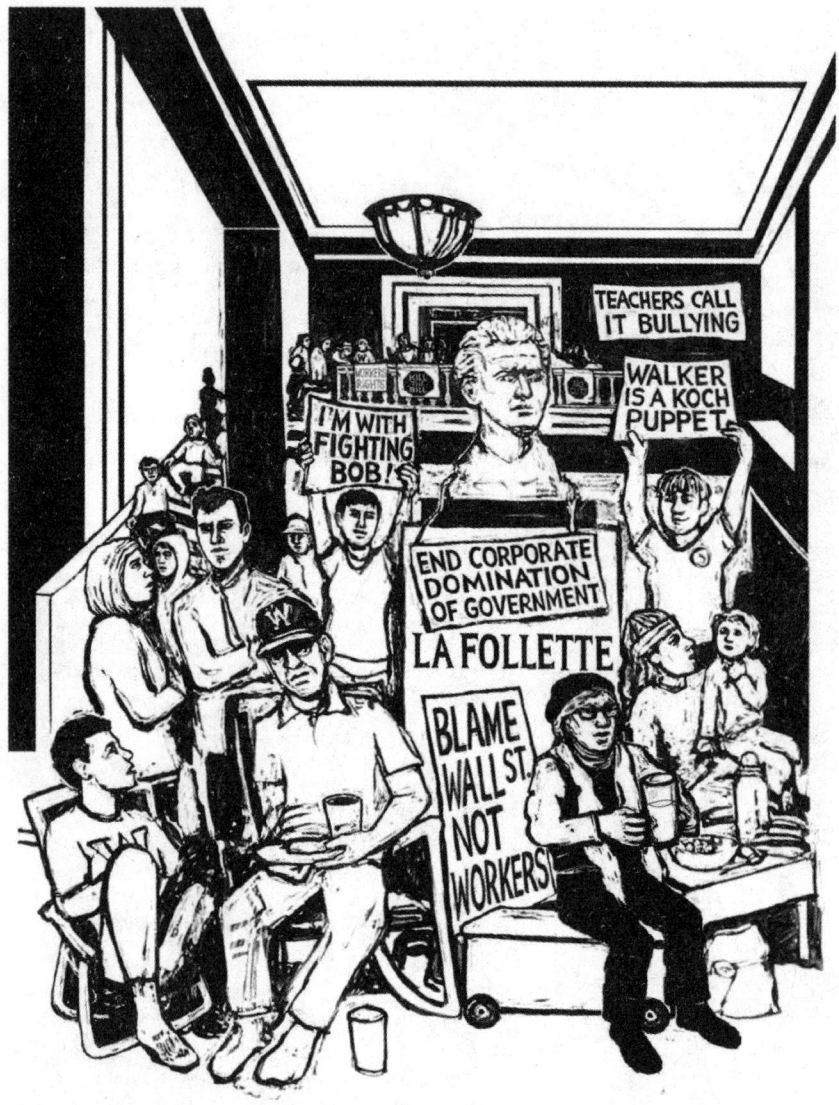

Tailgating with "Fighting Bob": Milwaukee Public Schools nurses and teachers with their extended families met at the "Fighting Bob" La Follette statue to "tailgate," as they did at Brewers baseball games. La Follette was a Progressive leader who served in Congress and the Senate and as the governor of Wisconsin.

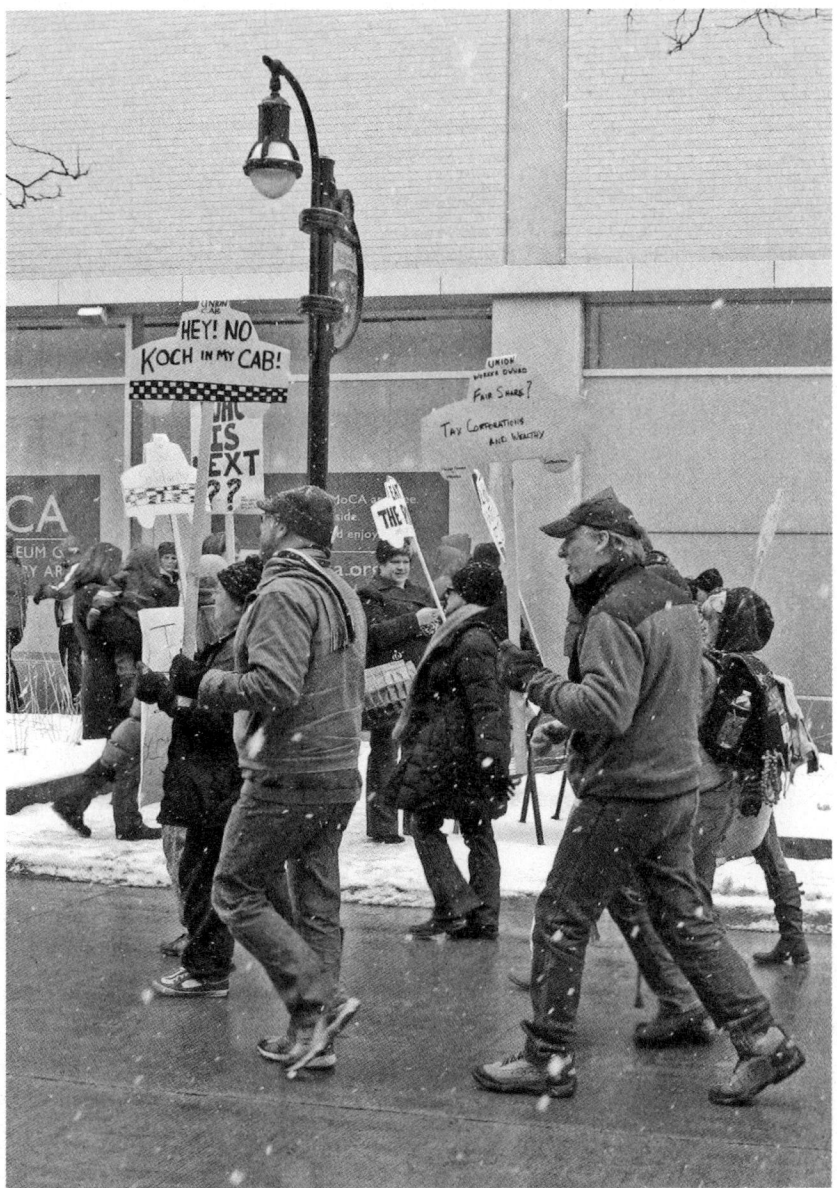

No Koch in My Cab: Cab drivers from Madison Union Cabs, a workers' cooperative since 1979, honked their horns to the cadence of "This Is What Democracy Looks Like."

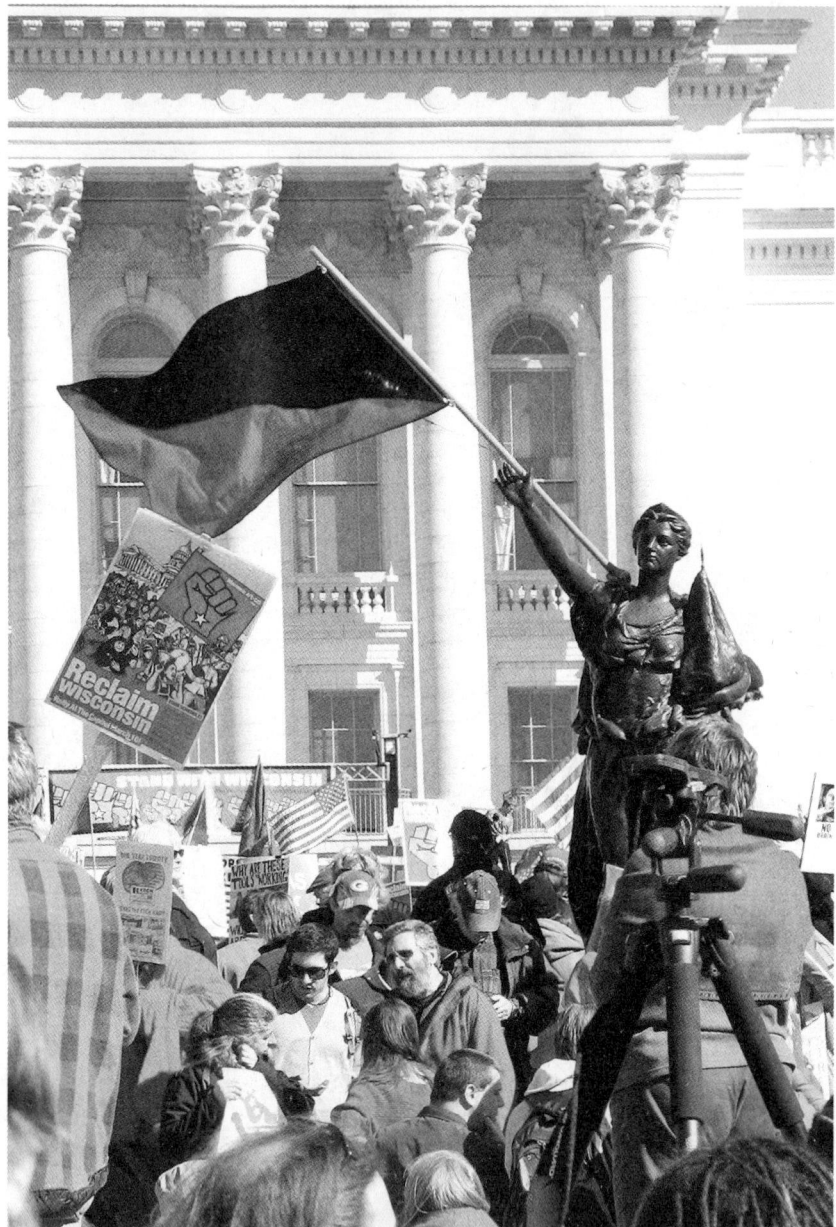

Forward Statue: Wisconsin's motto, "Forward," is represented by this statue outside the state capitol. She is often decorated in the colors of the day. Here, the *Forward* statue was given the red-and-black anarchist flag during a return march to the capitol. The union-printed poster at left used images from my drawn story (see also the poster on the facing page) and graphic designer Carrie Worthen's Big Blue Fist.

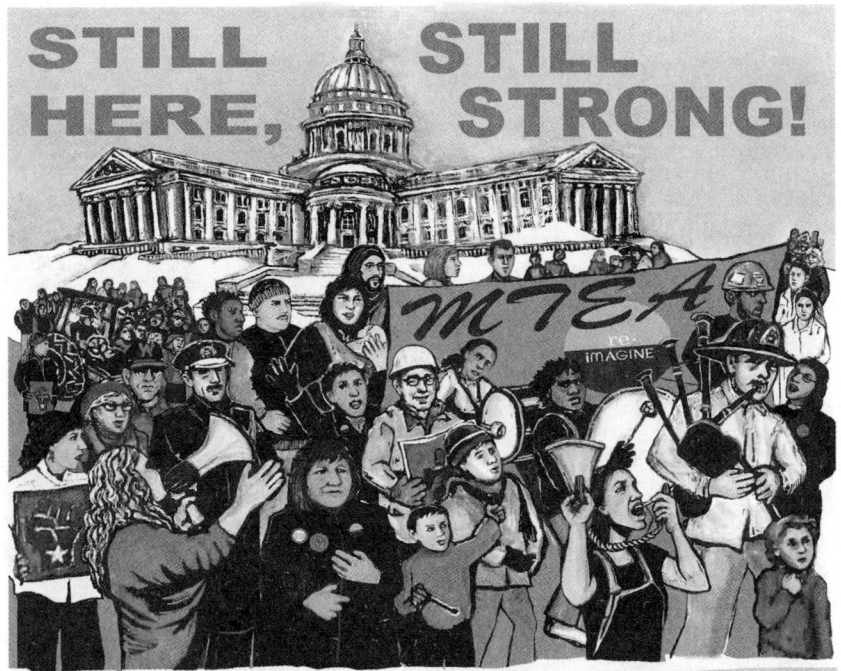

Milwaukee Teachers' Education Association Labor Day Poster: I reworked and collaged my *World War 3 Illustrated* drawings for an ad in local newspapers.

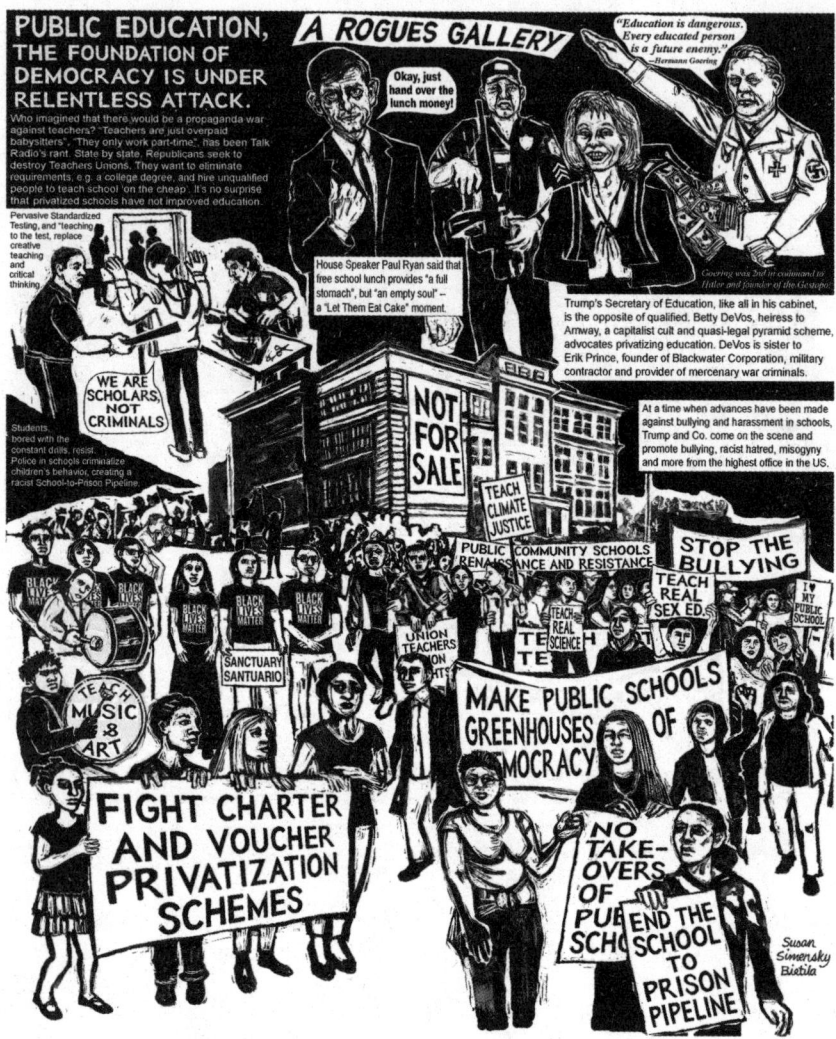

My Schools Page for the Trump Counter-Inaugural: Seth Tobocman and *World War 3 Illustrated* put together a graphic newspaper to distribute at the anti-Trump counter-inaugural demonstration in January 2017 in Washington, DC. Here is the page about public education. The bottom part of the image was published in *Rethinking Schools* and posted in faculty lounges and copying rooms in Milwaukee Public Schools.

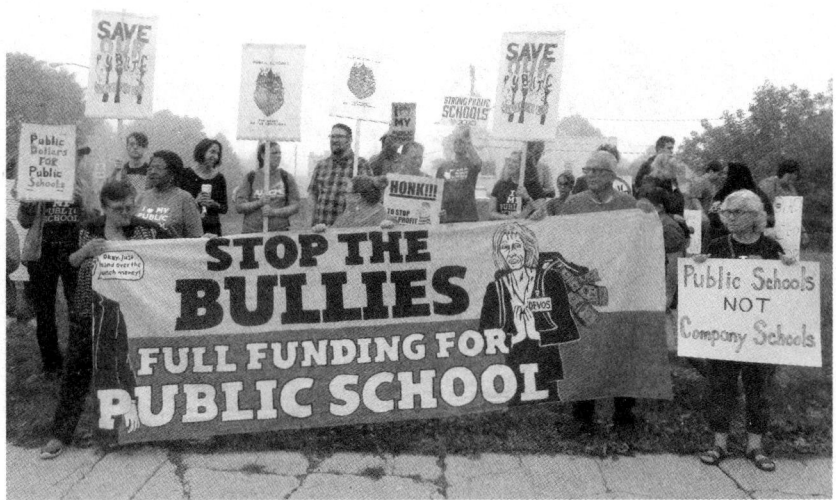

Stop the Bullies: We held art builds for public education. There were many artists involved and many designs for banners. This and the several that follow include my artwork. This banner features former Congressional Representative Paul Ryan and Secretary of Education Betsy DeVos, carried by picketing teachers. DeVos was a school voucher and Christian school advocate, appointed in Donald Trump's first term despite having no education experience or expertise. She is the sister of Erik Prince of Blackwater mercenaries infamy, and her husband is the billionaire owner of the Amway empire. Wisconsin has long been the pilot victim of ALEC's planned attacks, starting with workfare and school voucher programs. Private schools often admit students, collect the per capita state funding for them, and then expel them if they have special needs or are rebellious. The public schools are required to admit all students, even when they arrive with no state funding.

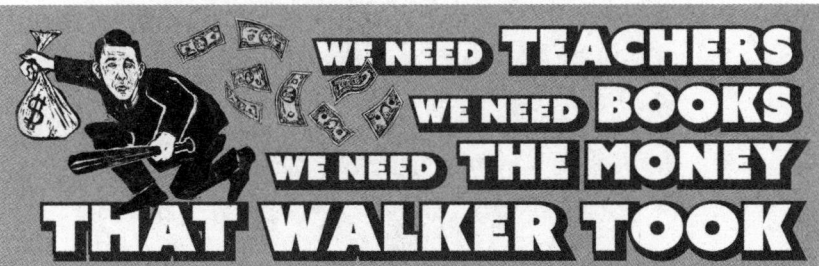

The Money That Walker Took: Wisconsin ex-governor Scott Walker cut over a billion dollars in education spending during his first five years in office.

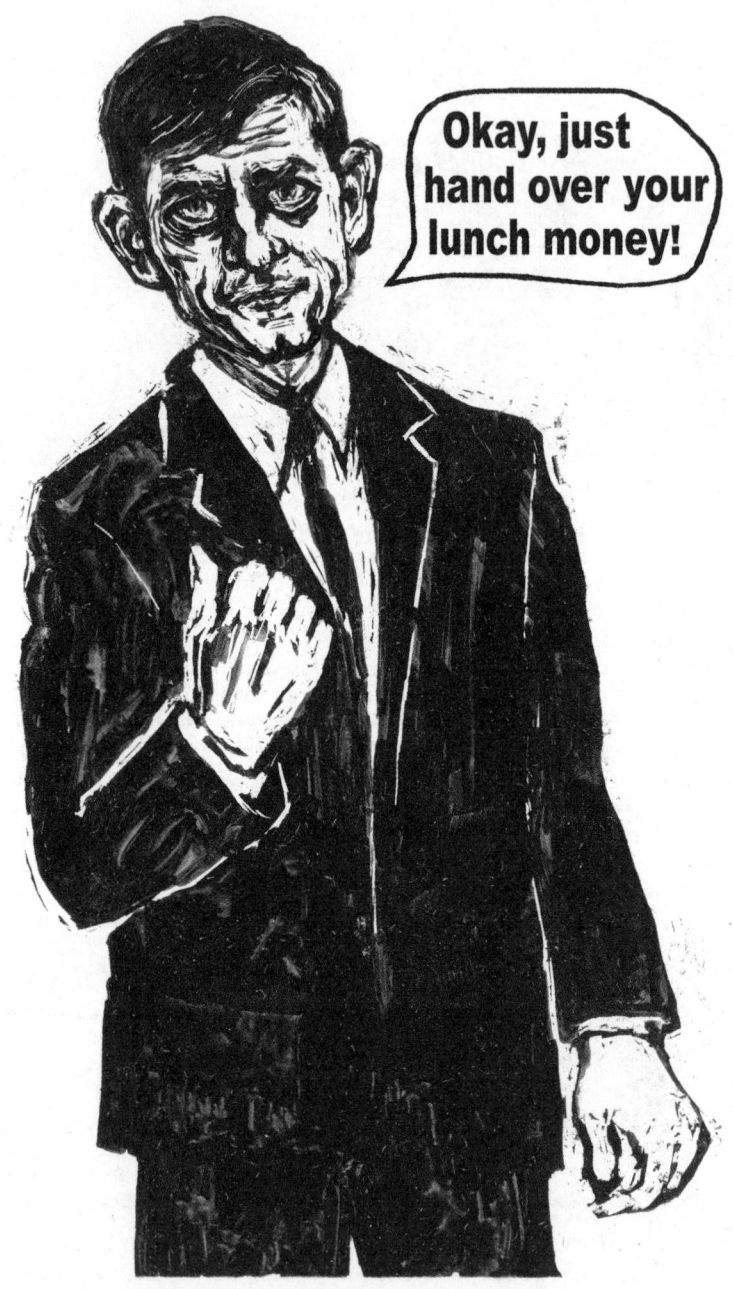

Lunch Money: Paul Ryan was Republican speaker of the House from 2015 to 2019. A bully from Janesville, Wisconsin, he is an advocate for school vouchers and cutting and privatizing Medicaid, Social Security, and everything else. Here he is taking your lunch money.

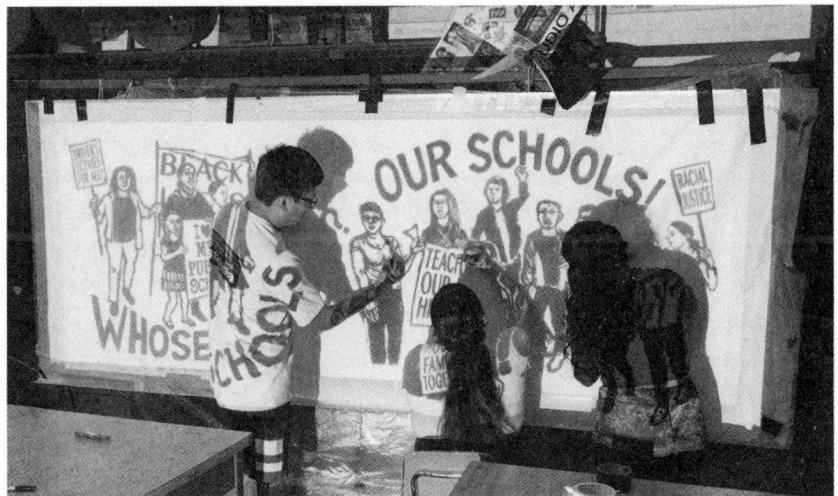

Tracing a "Whose Schools" Banner: The Milwaukee Public Schools art build crew traces a "Whose Schools? Our Schools!" banner. We tape the fabric to the wall and project the art with an LED projector from a laptop. The image is traced with chalk or pencil onto the fabric and then placed on a table for the group to paint. We provide a color picture as a painting guide. I include people in my banner designs, using photos for reference. Most of the photos are my own work, but Milwaukee has expert movement photographers, and I will reference their photos as well and give them credit.

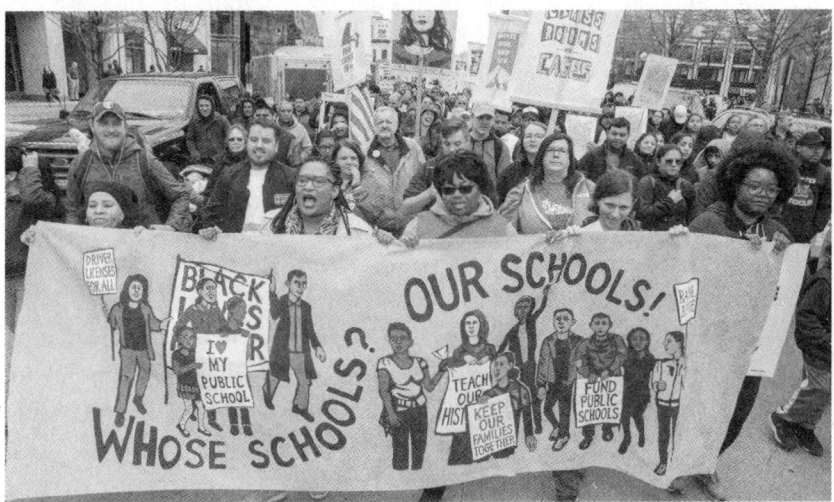

Whose Schools? Our Schools!: Here is the "Whose Schools" banner in the streets. The photo is by MTEA (the Milwaukee teachers' union) and Milwaukee photographer Joe Brusky. A core group goes on the road as the Art Build Workers. They bring a crew to lead banner-making wherever teachers in the US are going on strike.

Milwaukee Art Builds

In 2016, artist and arts organizer Nicolas Lampert was teaching art and design at UWM and invited David Solnit to speak at the Artists Now! series on campus. David asked Nicolas and I to reach out to other Milwaukee artists to organize the first art build for grassroots organizations while he was in town. Art builds are actions where artists and nonartists come together to make banners, costumes, silk screens, and papier-mâché puppets, usually using scavenged, donated, or inexpensive materials. These gatherings typically go on over a long weekend. There is plenty of time to talk and plan. The collaboration is empowering and is effective for movement building.

We rented a loft above a neighborhood microbrewery. Three groups worked side by side making art. One was Voces de la Frontera, a powerful immigrants' rights group that fights Immigration and Customs Enforcement (ICE) deportations and organizes a May Day march that draws thousands from all over the region. Art builds for Voces continue, organized by the affinity group Voces de los Artistas.

Citizens Acting for Rail Safety (CARS) made art props for their campaign against "bomb trains." These are train cars carrying dangerous explosive materials on the neglected railroad infrastructure running through populated areas. CARS built a burning oil train and fish puppets. Environmental writer Eric Hansen made sure that we didn't make generic fish, but the species indigenous to our rivers and Lake Michigan. Artists Kim Cosier, Shannon Molter, and Anne Steinberg began working on a giant blue heron, a bird that lives on the Milwaukee River. The puppet had a sixteen-foot wingspan and was completed at subsequent smaller gatherings.

The train and fish puppets were taken into the streets to warn Milwaukee about the danger of the ubiquitous tank cars traversing the entire city and crossing the its rivers. In May 2015, friends who lived near the confluence of Milwaukee's three rivers—the Milwaukee River from the north, the Menomonee River from the west, and the Kinnickinnic River from the south, just before they flow into Lake Michigan—had seen an increase of long trains pulling tank cars carrying Bakken crude oil passing by. When we heard about the Lac-Mégantic, Quebec, train disaster, we realized the potential for a disaster here. After crossing the rivers, the trains crossed a bridge over downtown's main north-south

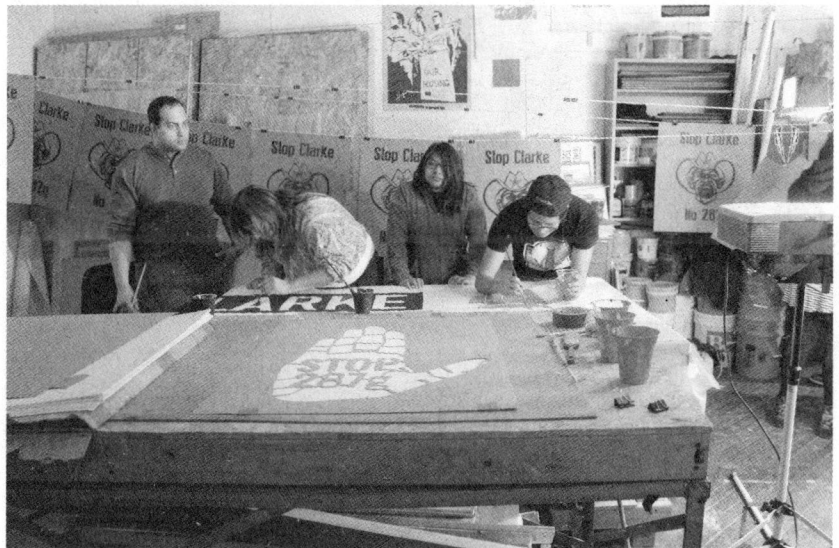

Sheriff Clarke and the 287(g) Art Build: Milwaukee County Sheriff David Clarke, a Republican, wanted his sheriffs trained and deputized by Immigration and Customs Enforcement (ICE) to interrogate, arrest, and help deport undocumented people in Milwaukee County per ICE regulation 287(g). Clarke posed on horseback, wearing a white cowboy hat and masquerading as a "good guy," referencing the old TV westerns. He didn't pull it off—collaboration between ICE and the Milwaukee Police Department is not permitted, but the mobilization against 287(g) continues statewide.

street. The trestles were rusted through, with large holes where the iron was eaten away, so we named the bridge Old Rusty.

The third group that participated in the art build was Dontre Day, an annual gathering dedicated to Dontre Hamilton, a Black man who was murdered by Milwaukee police in 2014.

Also, Nicolas and Paul Kjelland, along with other Justseeds artists, have pulled silk-screened signs and patches by the thousands at these gatherings. Other local activist artists, many of them public school art teachers, include John Fleissner, Janette Arellano, and MTEA and Voces de la Frontera photographers, including Joe Brusky, who document the creative gatherings and the public events that follow.

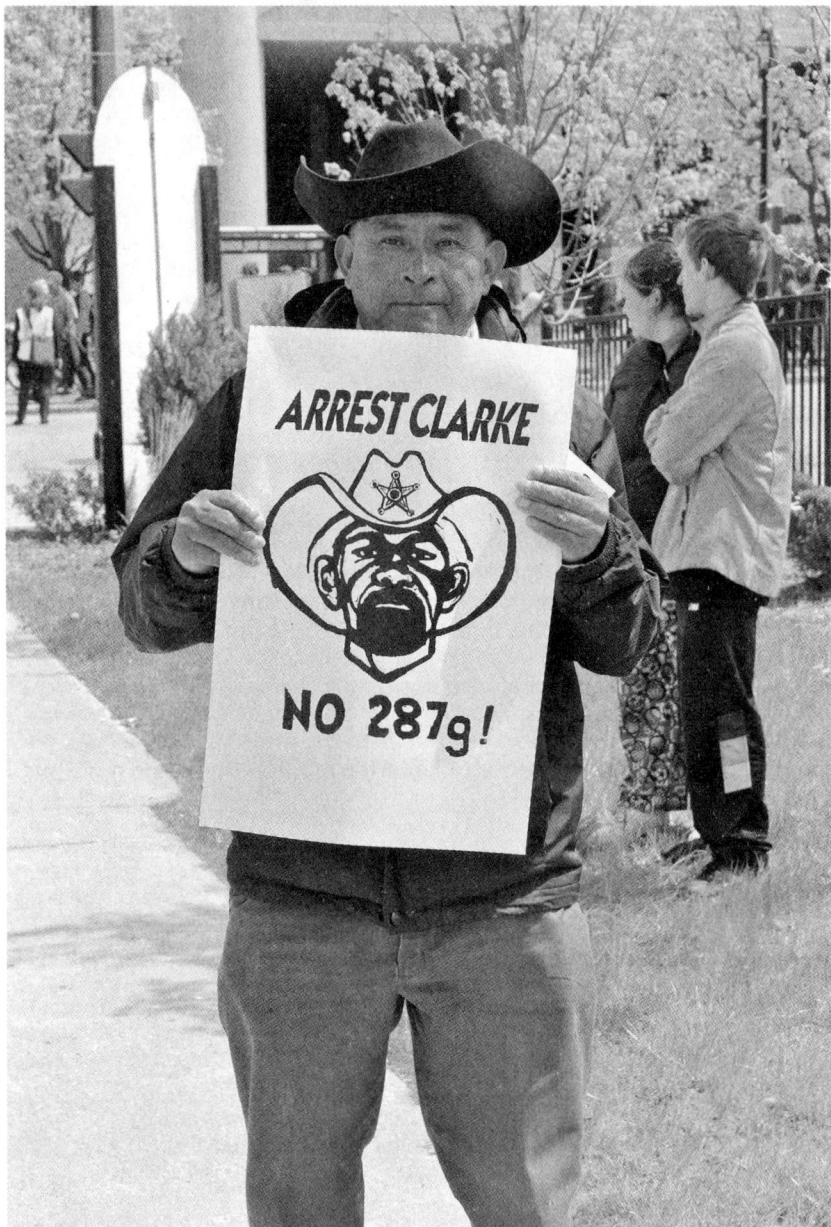

Black Hat/White Hat: Here is the Black Hat, the actual "good guy." He is active in Voces de la Frontera.

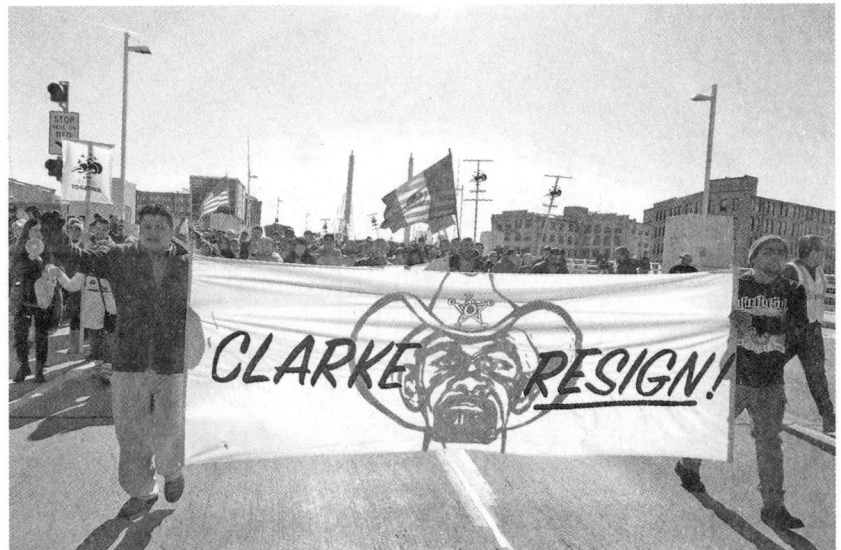

Sheriff Clarke Banner: Sheriff Clarke did resign, in hopes that Trump would appoint him to a federal post. This did not happen. Photo by C.M. DeSpears.

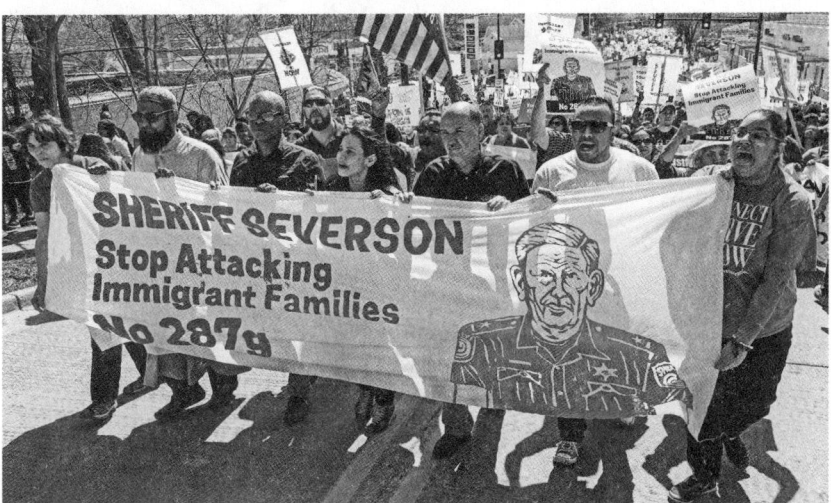

Sheriff Severson: A march in conservative Waukesha County, west of Milwaukee, against Sheriff Eric Severson, who after Clarke's resignation also sought to have his deputies deputized by ICE under 287(g). Drawing sheriffs was becoming my regular rogues' gallery thing. I drew them with brush and ink on white scratchboard and then refined the drawings with scraping tools, the way I draw my stories for *World War 3 Illustrated*. Photo by Sue Ruggles.

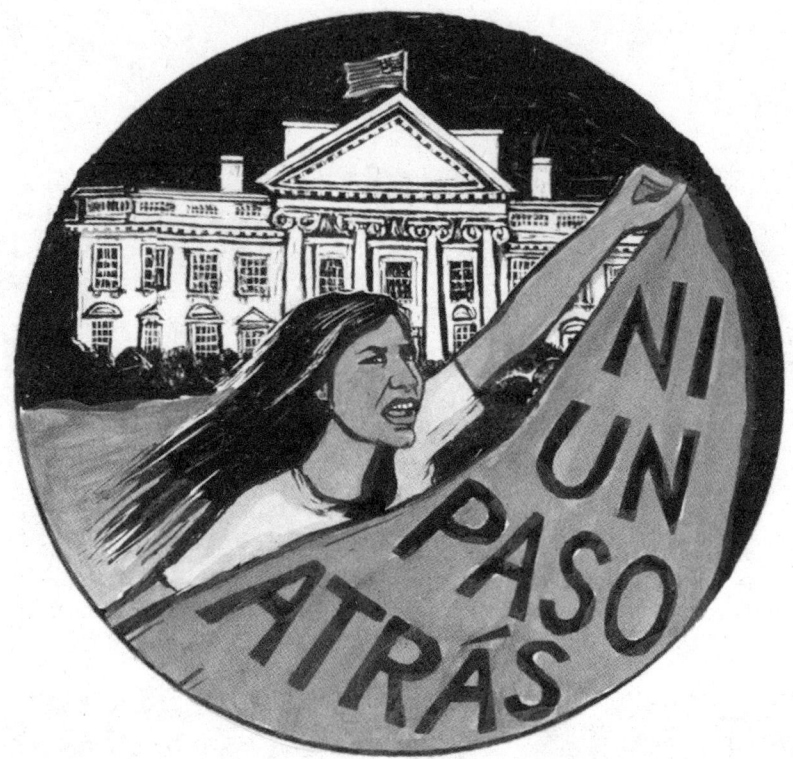

Not One Step Back: This circular design is an improved version of a women's right to choose button I made in the 1990s. Sadly, the message remains appropriate for many purposes. I made *Not One Step Back* in Spanish and English and with "Defend DACA" and "Here to Stay" versions.

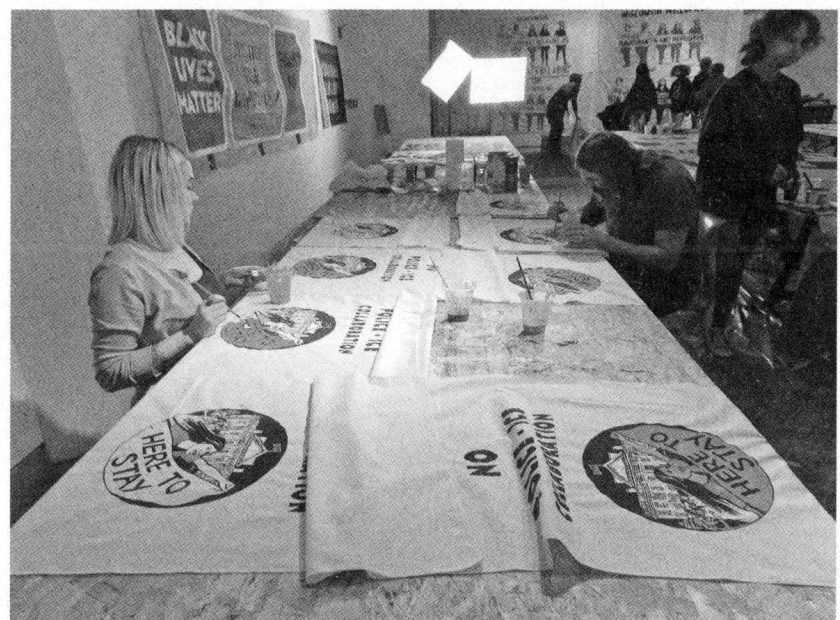

Art Build for Voces: At this art build, *Not One Step Back* was silk-screened onto signs, with color added in acrylic by many hands.

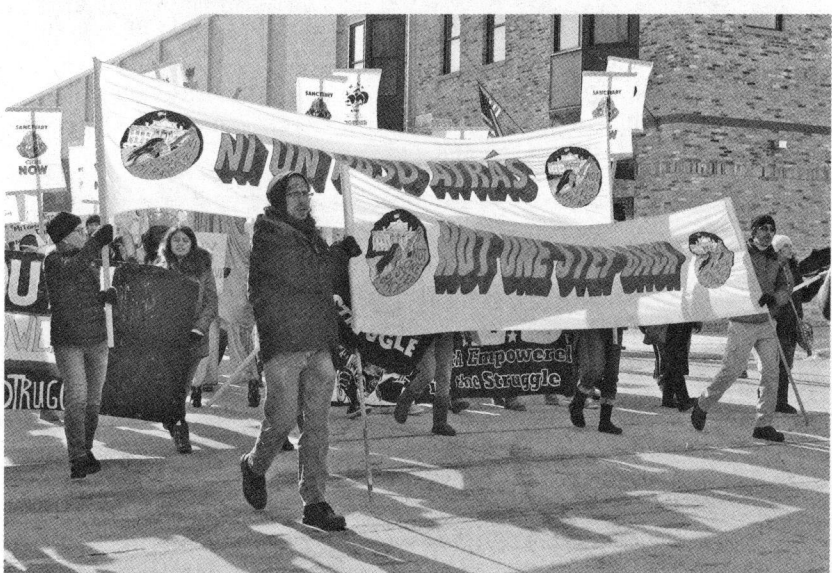

Voces de la Frontera Banner: And here is the design used on a banner carried in a Voces march.

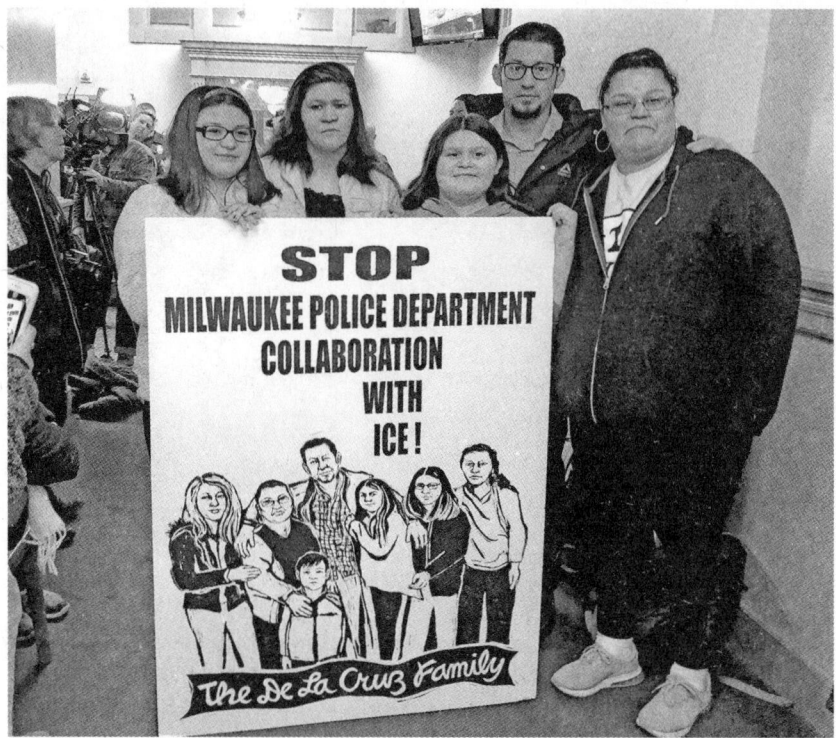

The De La Cruz Family: Voces de la Frontera asked me to draw a group portrait of the De La Cruz family for a Milwaukee City Hall news conference and city council committee hearing. We were able to stop the deportation of the father of this family.

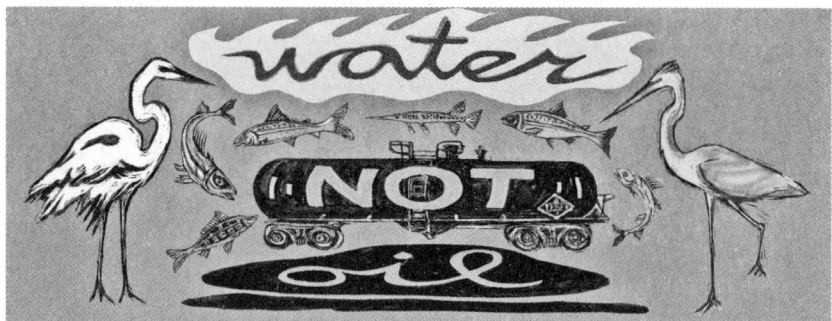

Water Not Oil: Small flags against oil by rail were silk-screened and then hand-painted. The blue heron is the bird of the Milwaukee River.

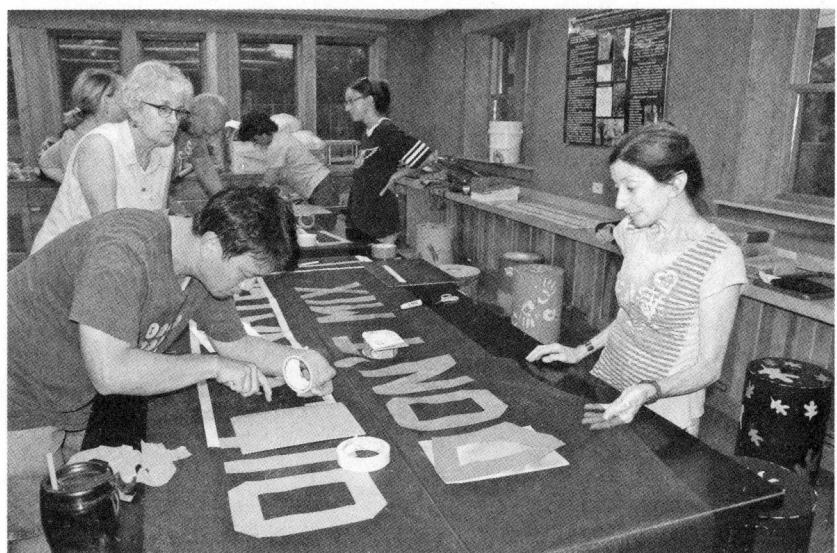

CARS Banner Making: Learning from Seattle flotilla events, we made some banners on window screening, using ever-useful duct tape to make the letters, with sticky sides facing on opposite sides of the screening.

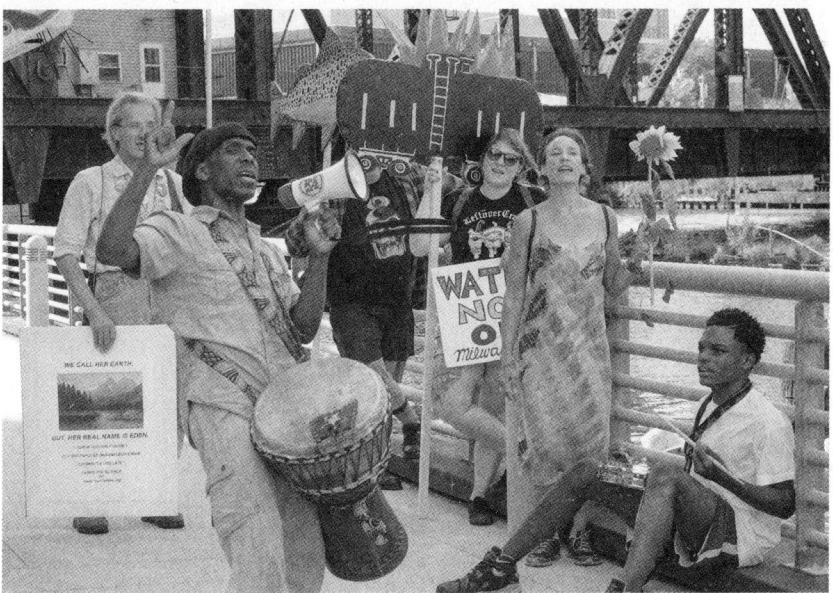

Convergence on the Shore: People joined in along the shore with the fish and flaming oil train puppets. Chants and songs were led by the passionate drummer Jahmés Finlayson, who brought joy and energy wherever he performed. He is much missed.

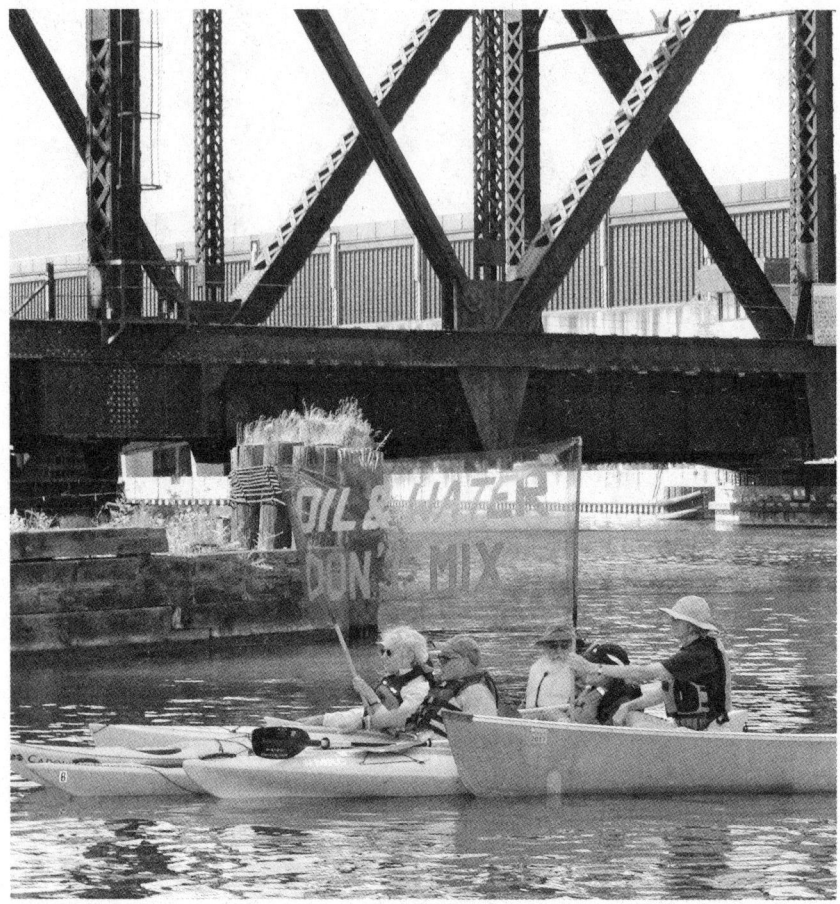

Convergence at the Confluence Kayak Banner: A kayak crew holds the banner alongside the downtown railroad bridge at the confluence of Milwaukee's three rivers during the Convergence at the Confluence event held by CARS.

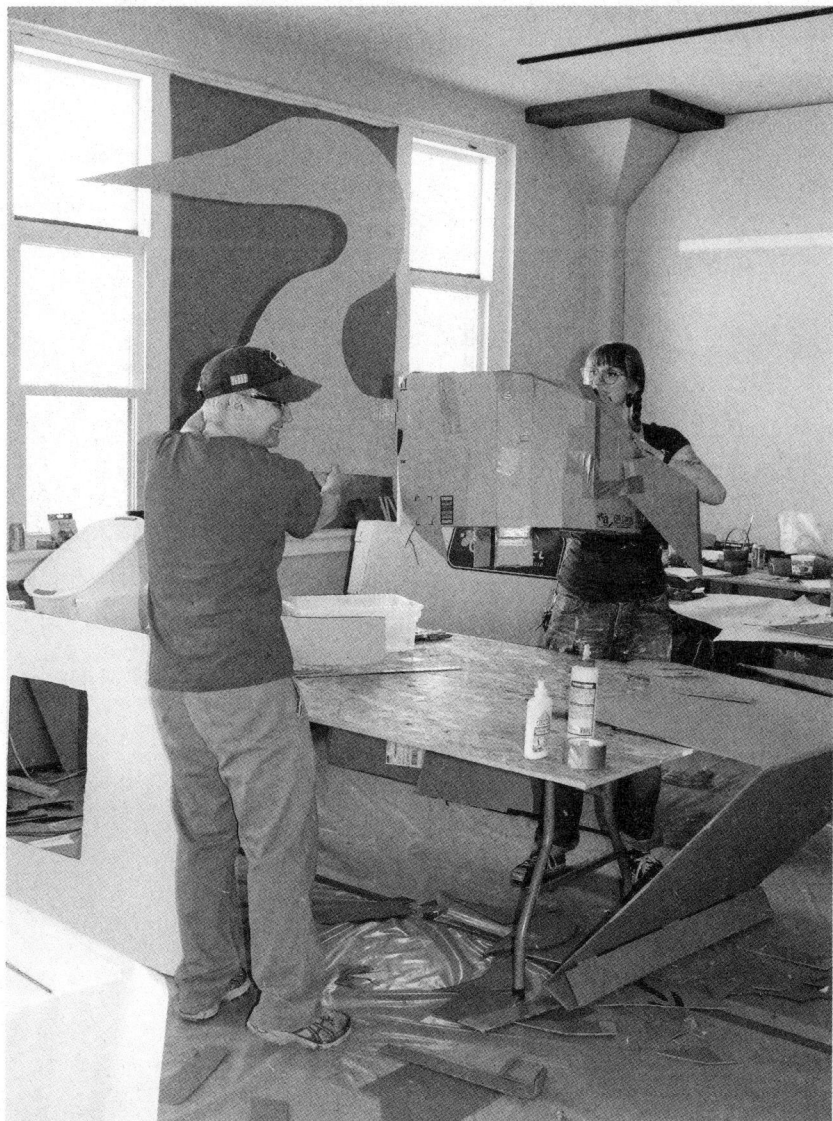

The Heron at the First Art Build: A heron with a sixteen-foot wingspan was built collaboratively over several months. It was started at the first art build by Kim Cosier, Shannon Molter, Anne Steinberg, and others.

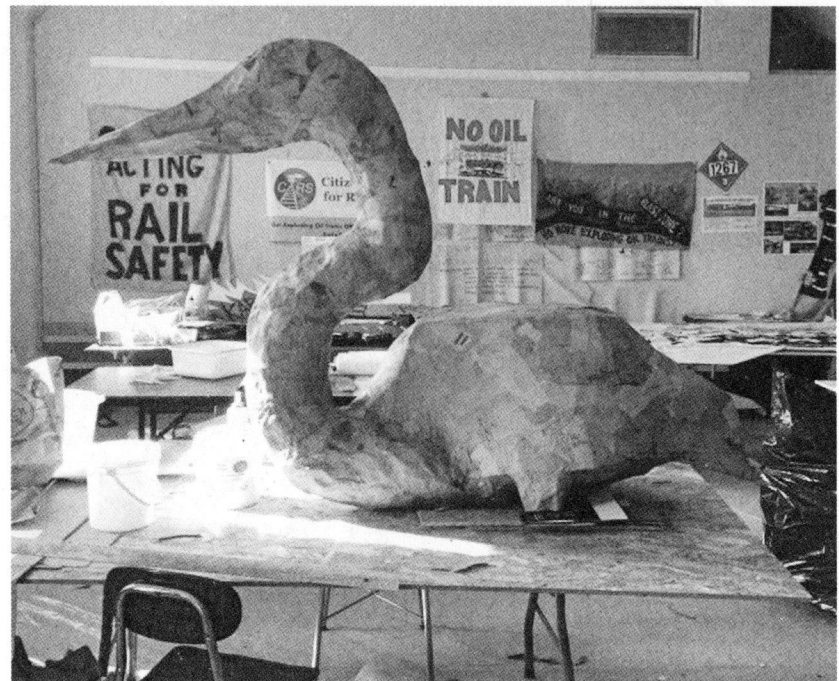

Heron Build Progress: The heron during construction, now covered with papier-mâché.

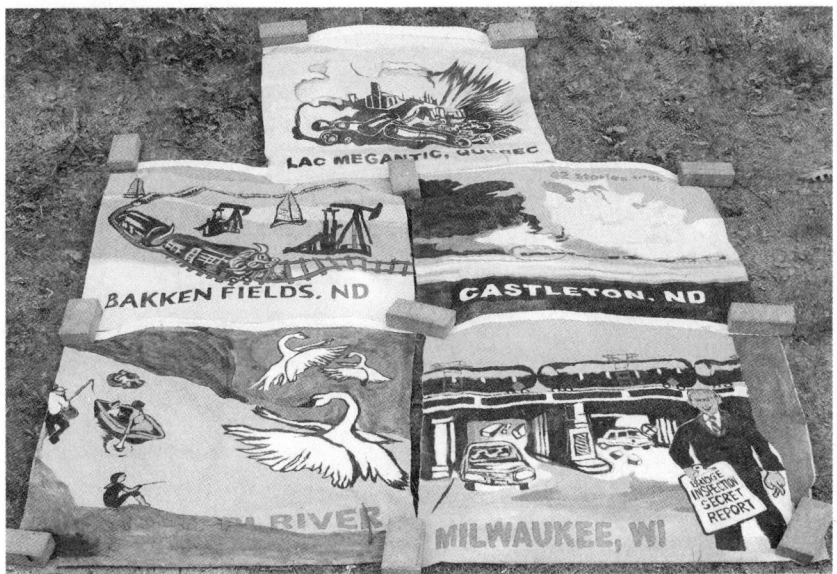

Cantastoria Paintings: These paintings on cloth are panels for a cantastoria, a form of theater where a narrator gestures to paintings while singing or speaking. This is an excellent way to do visual storytelling. When David Solnit came to the first Milwaukee art build, he brought along an anti–fossil fuel cantastoria, and we were inspired to make one about the danger of oil by rail.

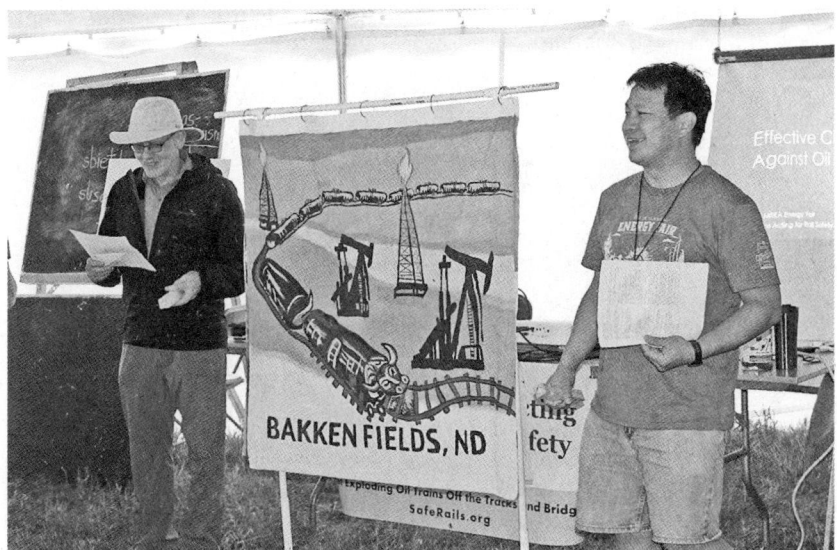

Energy Fair Cantastoria: Our cantastoria operates like a flip chart, suspended from a clothing rack. CARS used it for a presentation at the Midwest Renewable Energy Fair.

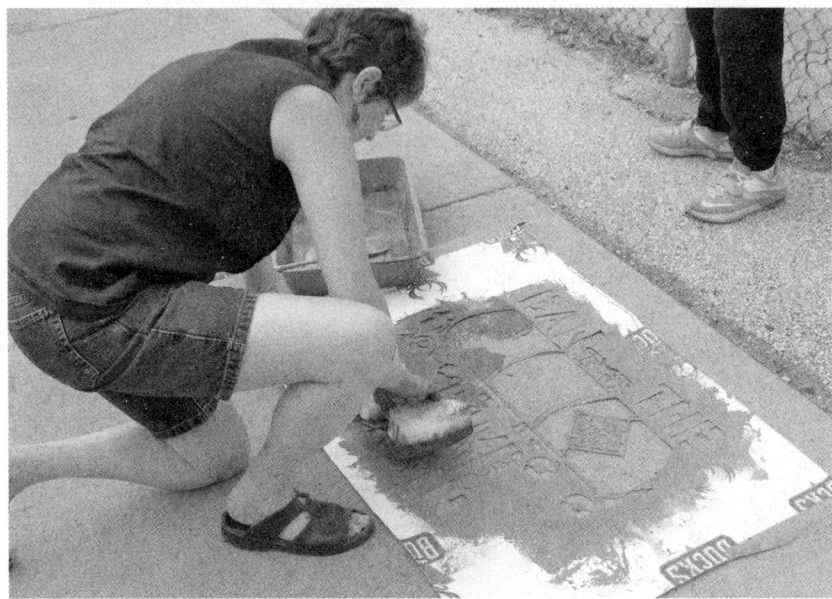

Mud Stenciling: I tried an anti–"bomb train" mud stencil. This technique was invented by artist Jesse Graves, who used to live in Milwaukee. First, I tried actual mud, but it didn't work well. I asked around at the local street festival to see if anyone had red clay. A ceramics teacher friend who lived nearby arrived in minutes. We added water to red clay to make the perfect consistency. Since it's only dirt, there is little threat of being arrested for this kind of street painting. The same is true for media using spray chalk, now available.

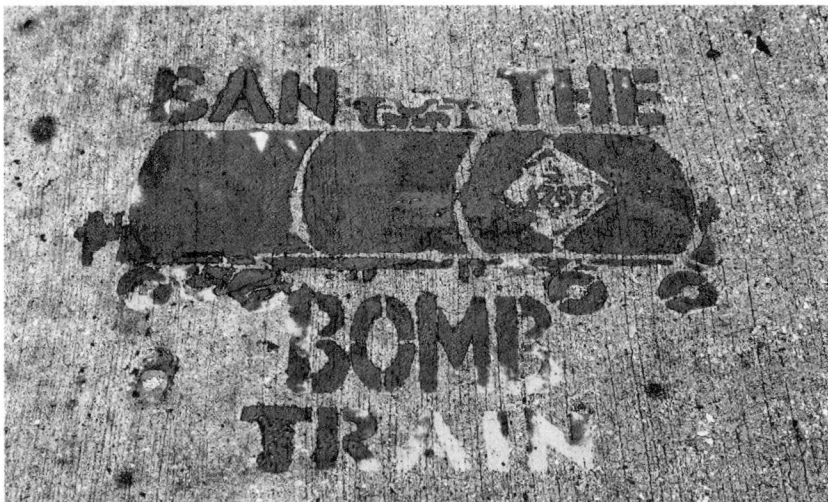

Ban the Bomb Train: Here is the "Ban the Bomb Train" mud stencil. Since it is red clay, it looks better in color.

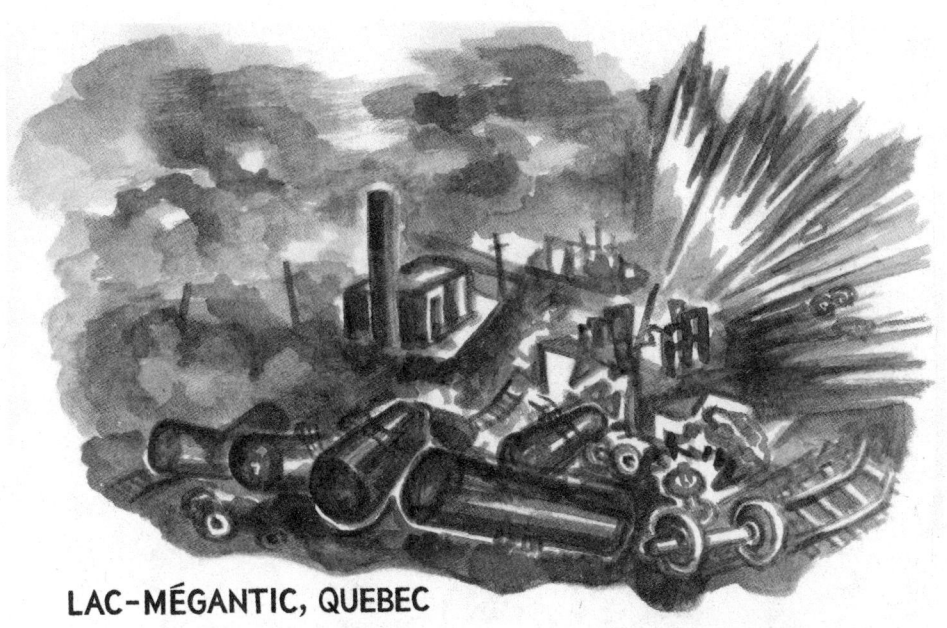

LAC-MÉGANTIC, QUEBEC

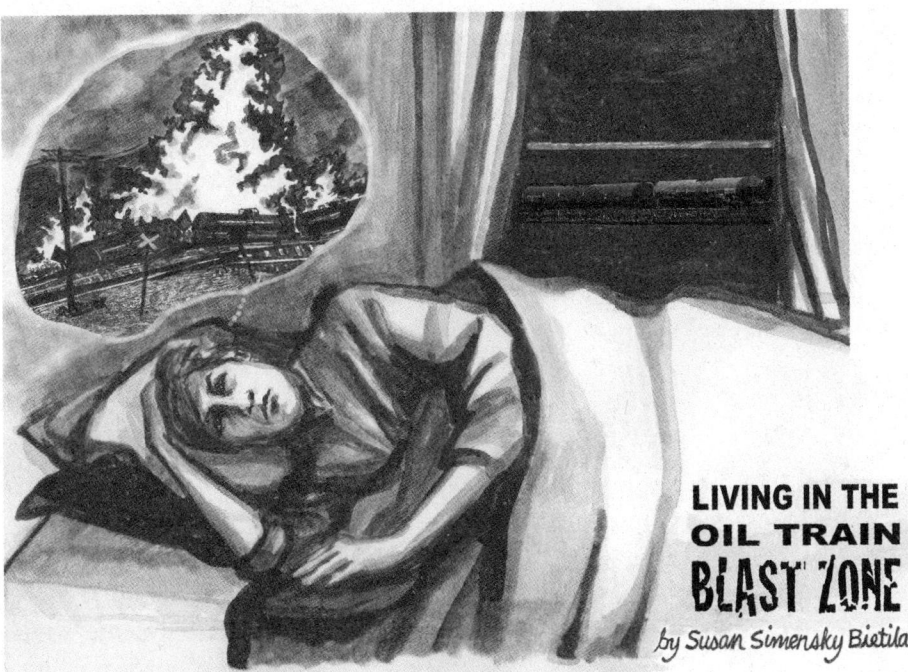

LIVING IN THE
OIL TRAIN
BLAST ZONE
by Susan Simensky Bietila

Pages 137–46: Living in the Oil Train Blast Zone
First appeared in *World War 3 Illustrated*, no. 47 (2016), "Climate Chaos" issue.

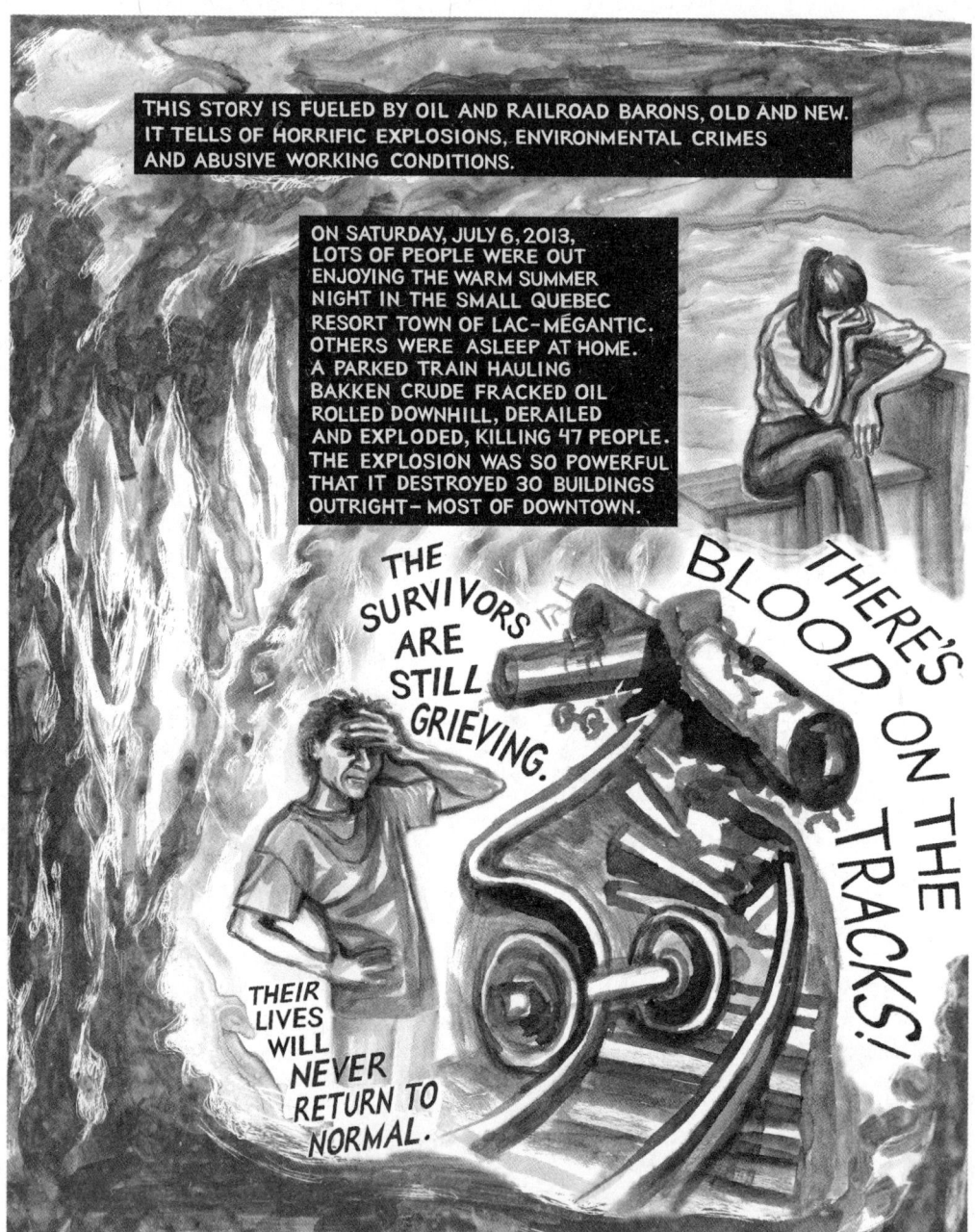

THIS STORY IS FUELED BY OIL AND RAILROAD BARONS, OLD AND NEW. IT TELLS OF HORRIFIC EXPLOSIONS, ENVIRONMENTAL CRIMES AND ABUSIVE WORKING CONDITIONS.

ON SATURDAY, JULY 6, 2013, LOTS OF PEOPLE WERE OUT ENJOYING THE WARM SUMMER NIGHT IN THE SMALL QUEBEC RESORT TOWN OF LAC-MÉGANTIC. OTHERS WERE ASLEEP AT HOME. A PARKED TRAIN HAULING BAKKEN CRUDE FRACKED OIL ROLLED DOWNHILL, DERAILED AND EXPLODED, KILLING 47 PEOPLE. THE EXPLOSION WAS SO POWERFUL THAT IT DESTROYED 30 BUILDINGS OUTRIGHT—MOST OF DOWNTOWN.

THE SURVIVORS ARE STILL GRIEVING.

THEIR LIVES WILL NEVER RETURN TO NORMAL.

THERE'S BLOOD ON THE TRACKS!

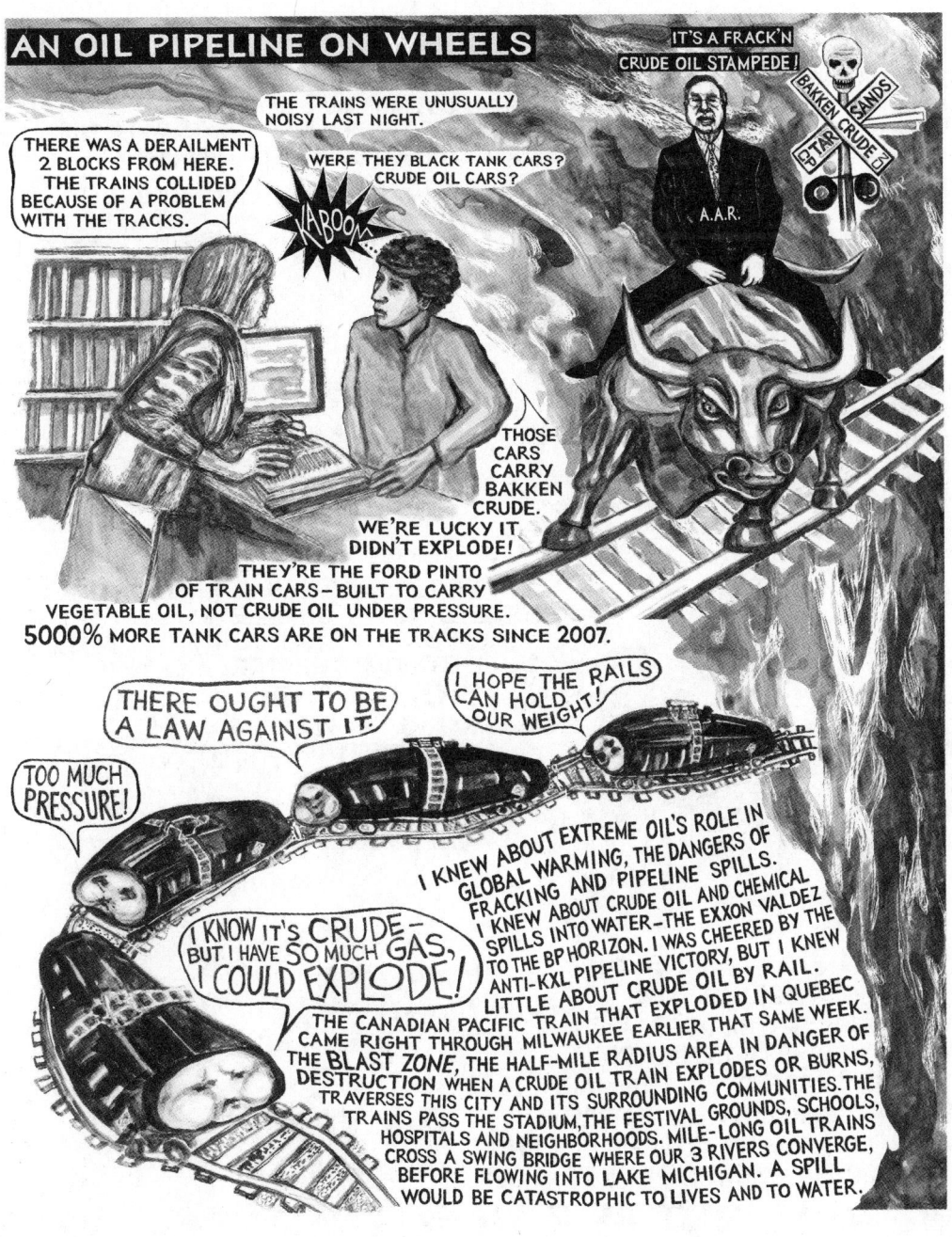

139

LAST SPRING I WENT TO A MEETING OF PEOPLE WHO LIVE RIGHT NEXT TO THE TRACKS AND ENVIRONMENTAL ACTIVISTS. THEY WERE RESEARCHING THE DANGERS OF THESE BOMB TRAINS. THEY HEARD ABOUT CRUMBLING RAILROAD BRIDGES IN NEARBY CITIES. A DECAYING 99 YEAR OLD BRIDGE WAS RIGHT OUTSIDE MY FRIEND'S WINDOW, CROSSING THE MAJOR NORTH/SOUTH DOWNTOWN STREET. THE BUILDING SHAKES WHEN THE MILE-LONG TRAINS PASS BY. I-BEAMS ARE RUSTED COMPLETELY THROUGH.

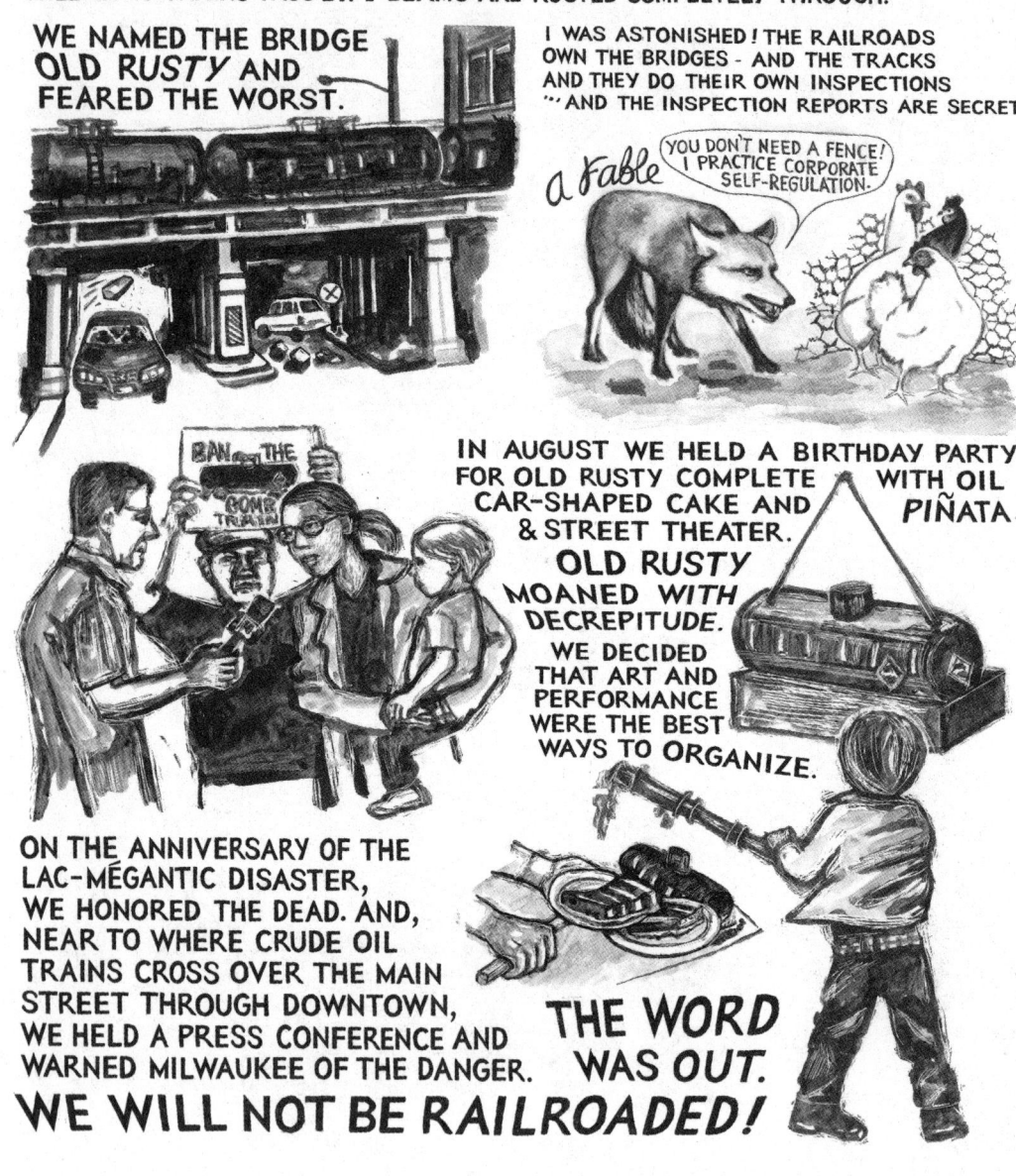

WE NAMED THE BRIDGE OLD *RUSTY* AND FEARED THE WORST.

I WAS ASTONISHED! THE RAILROADS OWN THE BRIDGES - AND THE TRACKS AND THEY DO THEIR OWN INSPECTIONS ··· AND THE INSPECTION REPORTS ARE SECRET!

a Fable

YOU DON'T NEED A FENCE! I PRACTICE CORPORATE SELF-REGULATION.

IN AUGUST WE HELD A BIRTHDAY PARTY FOR OLD RUSTY COMPLETE WITH OIL CAR-SHAPED CAKE AND PIÑATA & STREET THEATER.

OLD RUSTY MOANED *WITH* DECREPITUDE.

WE DECIDED THAT ART AND PERFORMANCE WERE THE BEST WAYS TO ORGANIZE.

BAN THE BOMB TRAINS

ON THE ANNIVERSARY OF THE LAC-MÉGANTIC DISASTER, WE HONORED THE DEAD. AND, NEAR TO WHERE CRUDE OIL TRAINS CROSS OVER THE MAIN STREET THROUGH DOWNTOWN, WE HELD A PRESS CONFERENCE AND WARNED MILWAUKEE OF THE DANGER.

THE WORD WAS *OUT*.

WE WILL NOT *BE* RAILROADED!

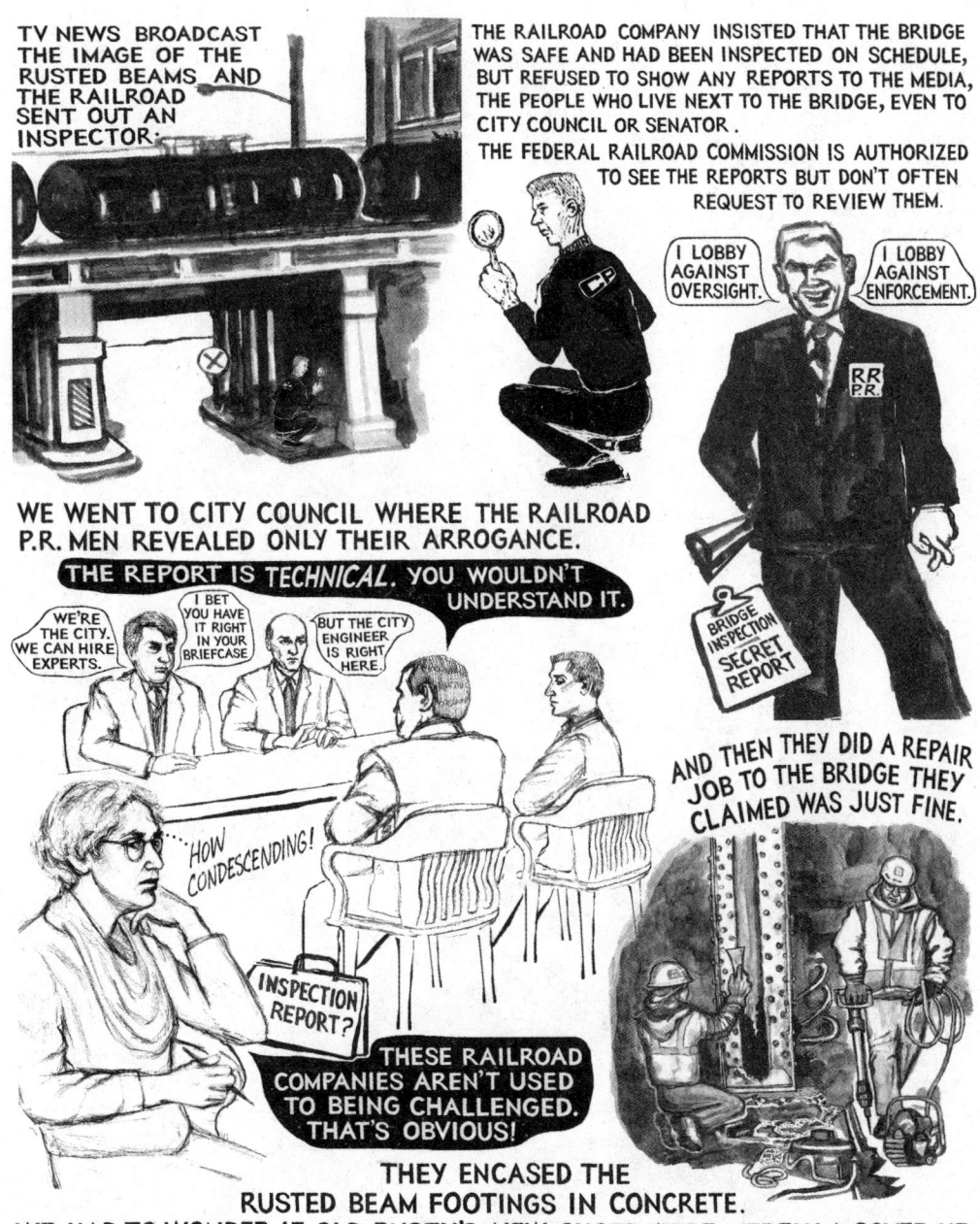

TV NEWS BROADCAST THE IMAGE OF THE RUSTED BEAMS AND THE RAILROAD SENT OUT AN INSPECTOR.

THE RAILROAD COMPANY INSISTED THAT THE BRIDGE WAS SAFE AND HAD BEEN INSPECTED ON SCHEDULE, BUT REFUSED TO SHOW ANY REPORTS TO THE MEDIA, THE PEOPLE WHO LIVE NEXT TO THE BRIDGE, EVEN TO CITY COUNCIL OR SENATOR.

THE FEDERAL RAILROAD COMMISSION IS AUTHORIZED TO SEE THE REPORTS BUT DON'T OFTEN REQUEST TO REVIEW THEM.

I LOBBY AGAINST OVERSIGHT.

I LOBBY AGAINST ENFORCEMENT.

RR P.R.

BRIDGE INSPECTION SECRET REPORT

WE WENT TO CITY COUNCIL WHERE THE RAILROAD P.R. MEN REVEALED ONLY THEIR ARROGANCE.

THE REPORT IS *TECHNICAL*. YOU WOULDN'T UNDERSTAND IT.

WE'RE THE CITY. WE CAN HIRE EXPERTS.

I BET YOU HAVE IT RIGHT IN YOUR BRIEFCASE

BUT THE CITY ENGINEER IS RIGHT HERE.

AND THEN THEY DID A REPAIR JOB TO THE BRIDGE THEY CLAIMED WAS JUST FINE.

...HOW CONDESCENDING!

INSPECTION REPORT?

THESE RAILROAD COMPANIES AREN'T USED TO BEING CHALLENGED. THAT'S OBVIOUS!

THEY ENCASED THE RUSTED BEAM FOOTINGS IN CONCRETE. WE HAD TO WONDER IF OLD RUSTY'S NEW SHOES WERE MERELY A COVER-UP.

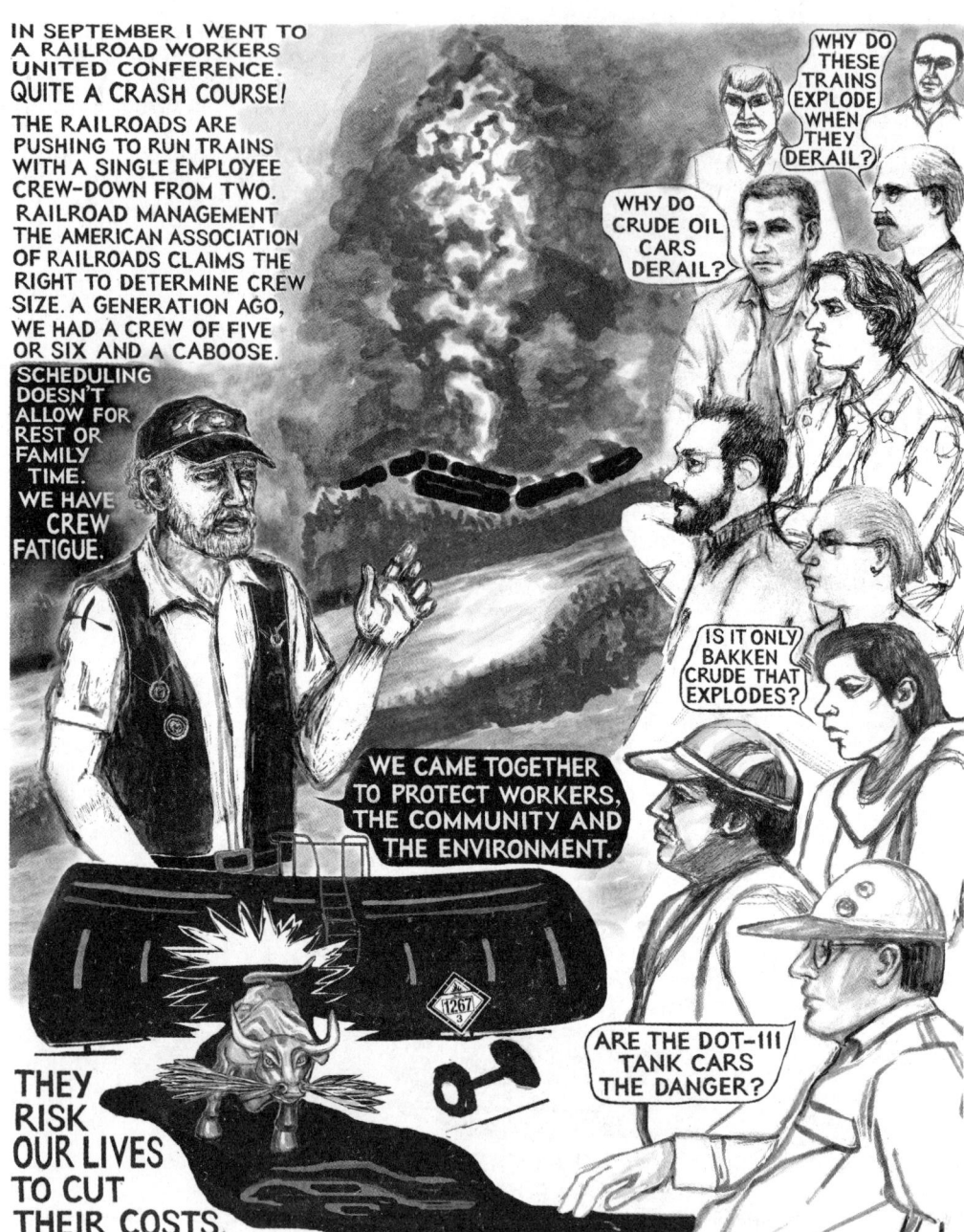

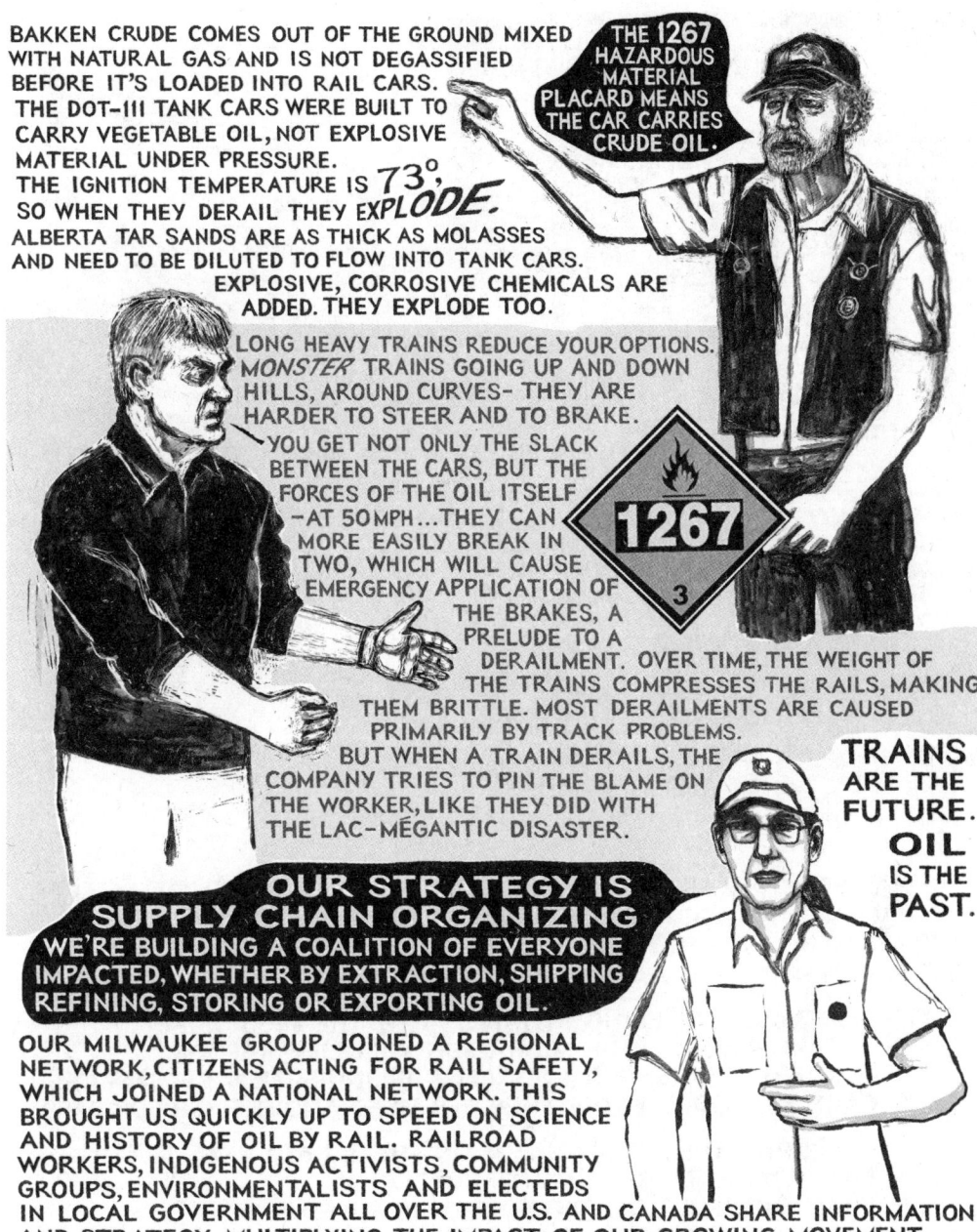

BAKKEN CRUDE COMES OUT OF THE GROUND MIXED WITH NATURAL GAS AND IS NOT DEGASSIFIED BEFORE IT'S LOADED INTO RAIL CARS. THE DOT-111 TANK CARS WERE BUILT TO CARRY VEGETABLE OIL, NOT EXPLOSIVE MATERIAL UNDER PRESSURE. THE IGNITION TEMPERATURE IS 73°, SO WHEN THEY DERAIL THEY EXPLODE. ALBERTA TAR SANDS ARE AS THICK AS MOLASSES AND NEED TO BE DILUTED TO FLOW INTO TANK CARS. EXPLOSIVE, CORROSIVE CHEMICALS ARE ADDED. THEY EXPLODE TOO.

THE 1267 HAZARDOUS MATERIAL PLACARD MEANS THE CAR CARRIES CRUDE OIL.

LONG HEAVY TRAINS REDUCE YOUR OPTIONS. MONSTER TRAINS GOING UP AND DOWN HILLS, AROUND CURVES- THEY ARE HARDER TO STEER AND TO BRAKE. YOU GET NOT ONLY THE SLACK BETWEEN THE CARS, BUT THE FORCES OF THE OIL ITSELF —AT 50 MPH...THEY CAN MORE EASILY BREAK IN TWO, WHICH WILL CAUSE EMERGENCY APPLICATION OF THE BRAKES, A PRELUDE TO A DERAILMENT. OVER TIME, THE WEIGHT OF THE TRAINS COMPRESSES THE RAILS, MAKING THEM BRITTLE. MOST DERAILMENTS ARE CAUSED PRIMARILY BY TRACK PROBLEMS. BUT WHEN A TRAIN DERAILS, THE COMPANY TRIES TO PIN THE BLAME ON THE WORKER, LIKE THEY DID WITH THE LAC-MÉGANTIC DISASTER.

1267
3

TRAINS ARE THE FUTURE. OIL IS THE PAST.

OUR STRATEGY IS SUPPLY CHAIN ORGANIZING WE'RE BUILDING A COALITION OF EVERYONE IMPACTED, WHETHER BY EXTRACTION, SHIPPING REFINING, STORING OR EXPORTING OIL.

OUR MILWAUKEE GROUP JOINED A REGIONAL NETWORK, CITIZENS ACTING FOR RAIL SAFETY, WHICH JOINED A NATIONAL NETWORK. THIS BROUGHT US QUICKLY UP TO SPEED ON SCIENCE AND HISTORY OF OIL BY RAIL. RAILROAD WORKERS, INDIGENOUS ACTIVISTS, COMMUNITY GROUPS, ENVIRONMENTALISTS AND ELECTEDS IN LOCAL GOVERNMENT ALL OVER THE U.S. AND CANADA SHARE INFORMATION AND STRATEGY, MULTIPLYING THE IMPACT OF OUR GROWING MOVEMENT.

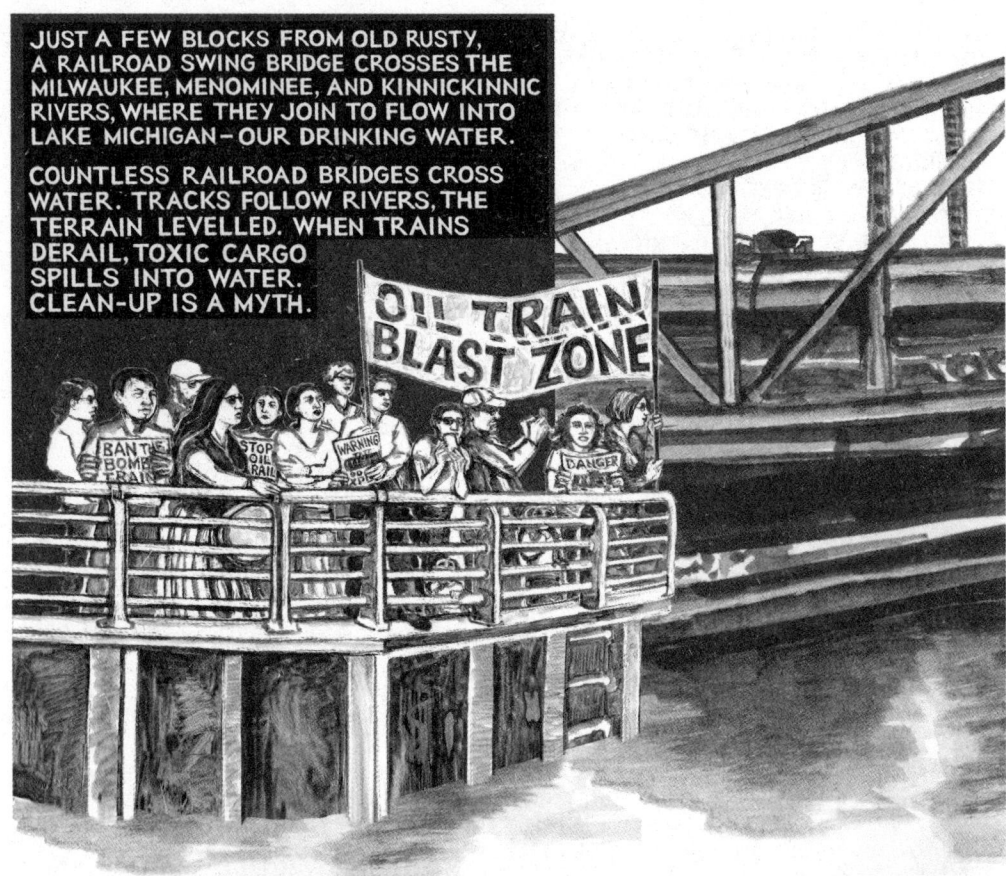

JUST A FEW BLOCKS FROM OLD RUSTY,
A RAILROAD SWING BRIDGE CROSSES THE
MILWAUKEE, MENOMINEE, AND KINNICKINNIC
RIVERS, WHERE THEY JOIN TO FLOW INTO
LAKE MICHIGAN – OUR DRINKING WATER.

COUNTLESS RAILROAD BRIDGES CROSS
WATER. TRACKS FOLLOW RIVERS, THE
TERRAIN LEVELLED. WHEN TRAINS
DERAIL, TOXIC CARGO SPILLS INTO WATER.
CLEAN-UP IS A MYTH.

WE HAD FOUR DERAILMENTS LAST YEAR–TWO IN A RESIDENTIAL AREA
IN WATERTOWN, WISCONSIN, NEAR THE ROCK RIVER. BAKKEN CRUDE
SPILLED NEXT TO A REPAIR SHOP. A FIREFIGHTER RUSHED IN AND SHUT
DOWN POWER TO A TRANSFORMER. NO FIREBALL *THIS TIME. WHEW!*

A TRAIN DERAILED SPILLING ETHANOL INTO THE MISSISSIPPI
RIVER INTERNATIONAL BIRD MIGRATION WILDLIFE REFUGE.
AND, NEAR THE MISSISSIPPI IN GALENA, ILLINOIS, NEW REINFORCED
TANK CARS EXPLODED WHEN THEY DERAILED AND BURNED FOR DAYS.

A PLAN TO SHIP CRUDE OIL BY BARGE ON THE GREAT LAKES IS BEING
FLOATED. SHIPPING BY BARGE CUTS COSTS.
NOW THAT THE CRUDE OIL EXPORT BAN IS ENDED AND
OIL PRICES ARE RISING.....WHAT COULD GO *WRONG???*

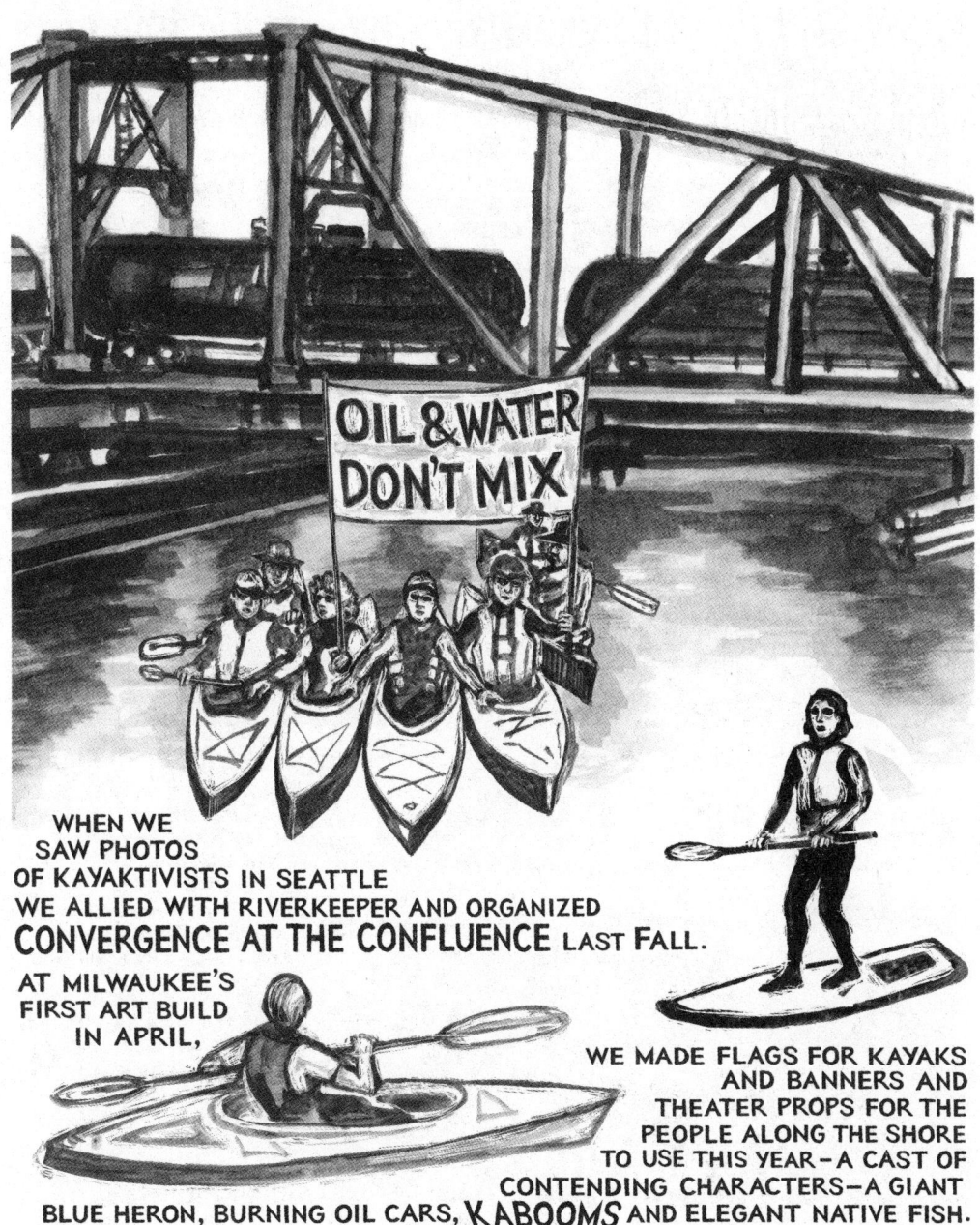

WHEN WE
SAW PHOTOS
OF KAYAKTIVISTS IN SEATTLE
WE ALLIED WITH RIVERKEEPER AND ORGANIZED
CONVERGENCE AT THE CONFLUENCE LAST FALL.

AT MILWAUKEE'S
FIRST ART BUILD
IN APRIL,

WE MADE FLAGS FOR KAYAKS
AND BANNERS AND
THEATER PROPS FOR THE
PEOPLE ALONG THE SHORE
TO USE THIS YEAR – A CAST OF
CONTENDING CHARACTERS – A GIANT
BLUE HERON, BURNING OIL CARS, KABOOMS AND ELEGANT NATIVE FISH.

ACTIVISM CAN HALT EXPANSION OF A DYING INDUSTRY

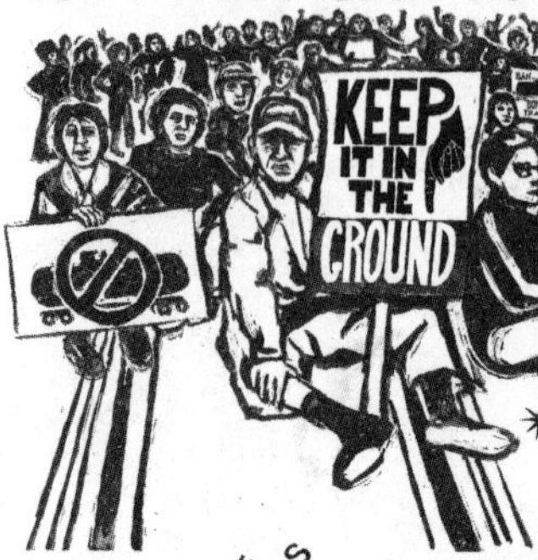

THE LINK IN THE SUPPLY CHAIN MOST VULNERABLE TO PUBLIC OPPOSITION IS WHEN LOCAL GOVERNMENT APPROVAL IS NEEDED FOR NEW INFRASTRUCTURE.

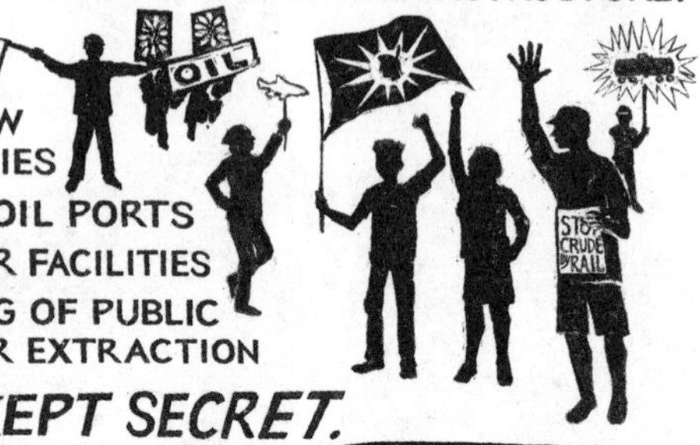

STOP OIL

* NO NEW REFINERIES
* NO NEW OIL PORTS
* NO NEW TRANSFER FACILITIES
* NO LEASING OF PUBLIC LANDS FOR EXTRACTION

DANGERS ARE KEPT SECRET.

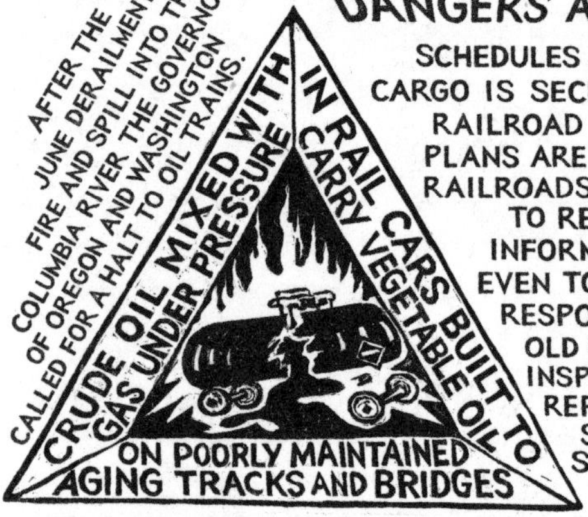

SCHEDULES ARE SECRET, CARGO IS SECRET AND THE RAILROAD EMERGENCY PLANS ARE SECRET. RAILROADS REFUSE TO RELEASE INFORMATION EVEN TO FIRST RESPONDERS. OLD RUSTY'S INSPECTION REPORT IS STILL SECRET.

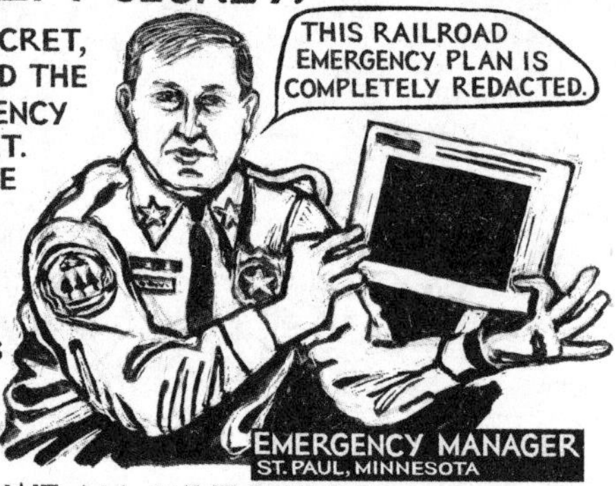

AFTER THE JUNE DERAILMENT, FIRE AND SPILL INTO THE COLUMBIA RIVER OF OREGON AND WASHINGTON CALLED FOR A HALT TO OIL TRAINS.

CRUDE OIL MIXED WITH VEGETABLE OIL GAS UNDER PRESSURE IN RAIL CARS BUILT TO CARRY ON POORLY MAINTAINED AGING TRACKS AND BRIDGES

THIS RAILROAD EMERGENCY PLAN IS COMPLETELY REDACTED.

EMERGENCY MANAGER
ST. PAUL, MINNESOTA

WE ALL HAVE THE RIGHT TO KNOW!

SAFETY UPGRADES WERE ORDERED A YEAR AGO ON THE DOT-111 TANK CARS, BUT ONLY 225 WERE RETROFITTED OF 100,000. AT THIS RATE IT WOULD TAKE 500 YEARS TO COMPLETE THE JOB. UPGRADED CARS STILL EXPLODE.

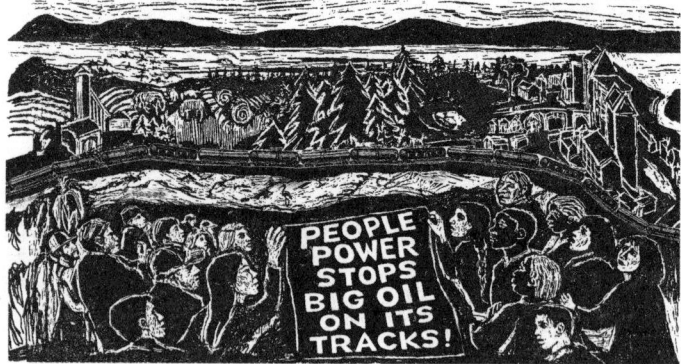

PEOPLE POWER STOPS BIG OIL ON ITS TRACKS!

WE HAVE A 60-YEAR-OLD ENBRIDGE PIPELINE UNDER THE MACKINAC STRAITS AT THE NORTH END OF LAKE MICHIGAN, FRAC SANDS MINING TO THE WEST, TRIPLING CAPACITY OF THE ENBRIDGE PIPELINE THROUGH THE CENTER OF WISCONSIN, AND PLANS FOR NEW RAIL TO THE SOUTH TO BYPASS CHICAGO—CUTTING CRUDE'S TRIP TIME TO REFINERY OR EXPORT.

THE PLAN TO MAKE WISCONSIN A CRUDE OIL SUPERHIGHWAY MUST BE STOPPED.

Love Water, Not Oil

The fish and heron puppets made during the art build for Convergence at the Confluence continue to be used. They were next used in a performance at the annual We Are Water gathering, sponsored by Milwaukee Water Commons. The heron was met with delight as its sixteen-foot wings swooped from behind the seated crowd and soared overhead to the water's edge. Milwaukee's Overpass Light Brigade spelled out water words with letters made of tiny LED lights. Melanie Ariens, the artist in residence at Milwaukee Water Commons, gave me a gift of LED lights. She had been using them to highlight a Great Lakes cutout and thought that they would enhance the fish puppets at night. So I outlined the brown trout, smallmouth bass, and northern pike with LED lights.

After the event, respected Indigenous educator Mark Denning asked me, "Where are the sturgeon?" As a member of the Menominee Sturgeon Clan, Mark explained the cultural and historical significance of this aquatic behemoth that is virtually unchanged from the age of the dinosaurs. Every spring, when the ice melts and the water warms, sturgeon swim up the rivers from Lake Michigan to spawn. For millennia, they have provided the Menominee Nation with a feast, marking the end of winter and lean times.

Grateful for Mark's teaching, I traveled the shore of the Wolf River in April 2017 to watch the six-to-nine-foot-long fish, with their gleaming, scaleless bodies and rows of spiky white scutes, gliding upstream to spawn, leaping and clustering in the shallows. I built a life-size sturgeon puppet, then sturgeon hats. Groups gathered to make banners, T-shirts, and patches for water protector events.

When the building of an enormous open-pit iron mine in the Penokee Mountains south of Lake Superior was proposed, the CARS group repurposed itself to support the community in northern Wisconsin

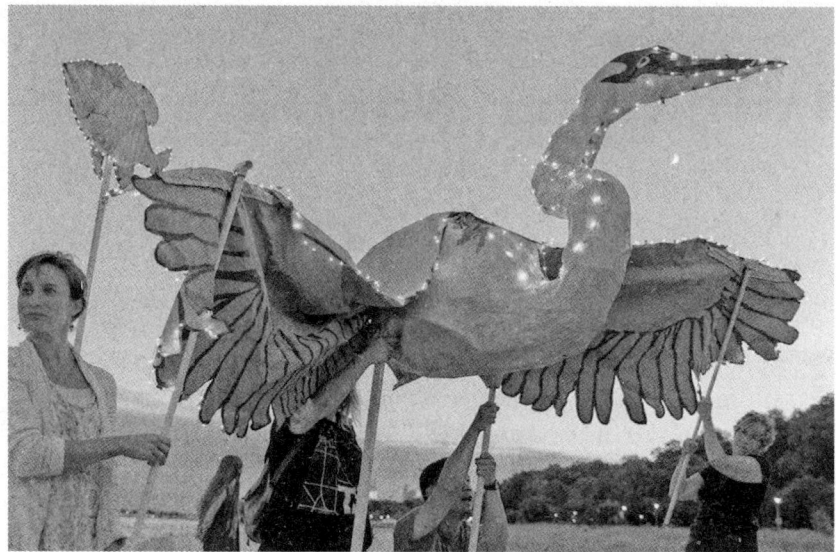

The Heron Puppet at the We Are Water Celebration: Milwaukee Water Commons, a multicultural organization connecting communities to Lake Michigan and the rivers, hosts an annual celebration with performance, poetry, and group participation. We Are Water is held at dusk on the Lake Michigan shore. CARS brought our fish and heron puppets to the event. The Water Commons artist-in-residence, Melanie Ariens, choreographs the creation of an outline of the Great Lakes with candles, everyone participating. She suggested that I outline the puppets in LED lights for night events. The puppets continue to travel to water protector events in Wisconsin, Michigan, and Minnesota. The Madison 350.org art team have created many more water critter hats. Photo by Joe Brusky.

fighting this Penokee Mine. Our antimine group was invited to the Menominee Nation Sturgeon Feast Pow Wow held on the Menominee Reservation, which the Wolf River runs through. We brought the fish puppets along but were unsure how they would be received, given that we are not Indigenous people and are unfamiliar with Menominee traditions. Also, the tombstone installation, dedicated to rivers poisoned by mining, had been criticized by some Menominee and Ojibwe activists for being negative. I stood the puppets just outside the gym where people were dancing. When Dawn Wilbur, a well-known tribal member and the cultural teacher at Menominee Indian High School, gleefully picked up a sturgeon puppet and brought it to "visit" smiling elders seated on the sidelines and then carried it into the round dance, I had my answer. Art expressing love for water and *all our relatives* is appreciated. At events where people don't know my name, they call me "the Sturgeon Lady."

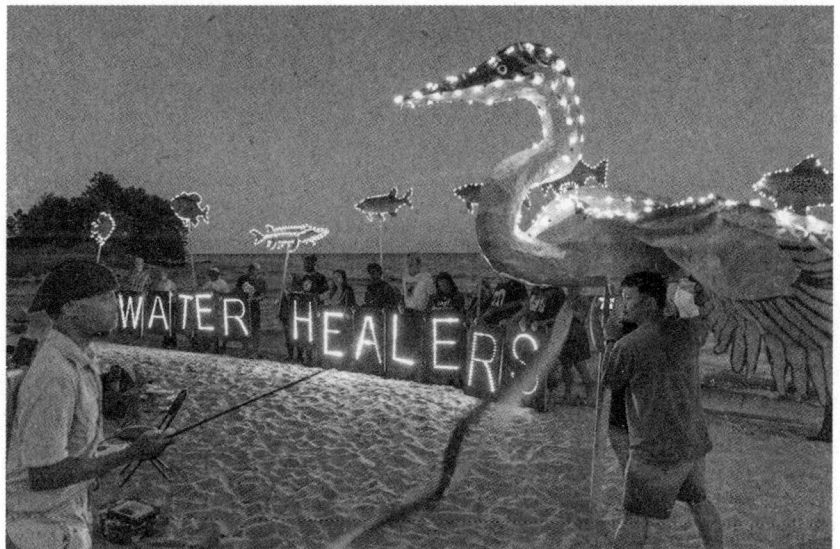

The Overpass Light Brigade: Founded by Milwaukee artists Lane Hall, Lisa Moline, and Joe Brusky, the Overpass Light Brigade is an artist collective that grew out of the 2011 uprising at the Wisconsin State Capitol. Using LED lights to spell out critical messages on highway overpasses, each letter is held by one person to make the words. The collective has inspired groups far and wide to make their own LED letter signs. Projecting onto buildings has also become a popular way to make public statements. Here they are not above a highway but at We Are Water, with the fish puppets swimming behind the words and the heron soaring. Photo by Joe Brusky.

The epic Standing Rock occupation in North Dakota to stop the Dakota Access Pipeline, from the spring of 2016 to the winter of 2017, brought together a massive Indigenous movement. Almost everyone I know went to the camp on the Standing Rock Sioux Reservation in support. Unable to go, I supported the No DAPL movement by finding artists worldwide to create button designs to spread the word and to use at fundraising events. Dylan Miner, a Justseeds artist, made indispensable designs. I did guest-teaching gigs on Zoom, having students create posters and buttons against the "big black snakes," the leaking pipelines carrying Alberta tar sands crude oil across the Upper Midwest in the US to Sarnia, Ontario—down from Canada and then back to Canada for refining and export. Their art went to the front lines of the occupation and still travels to water protector events against Enbridge Line 5. I make it a point to share photos of art being used in the movements with the artists. Some of this art was used in a Standing Rock/No DAPL

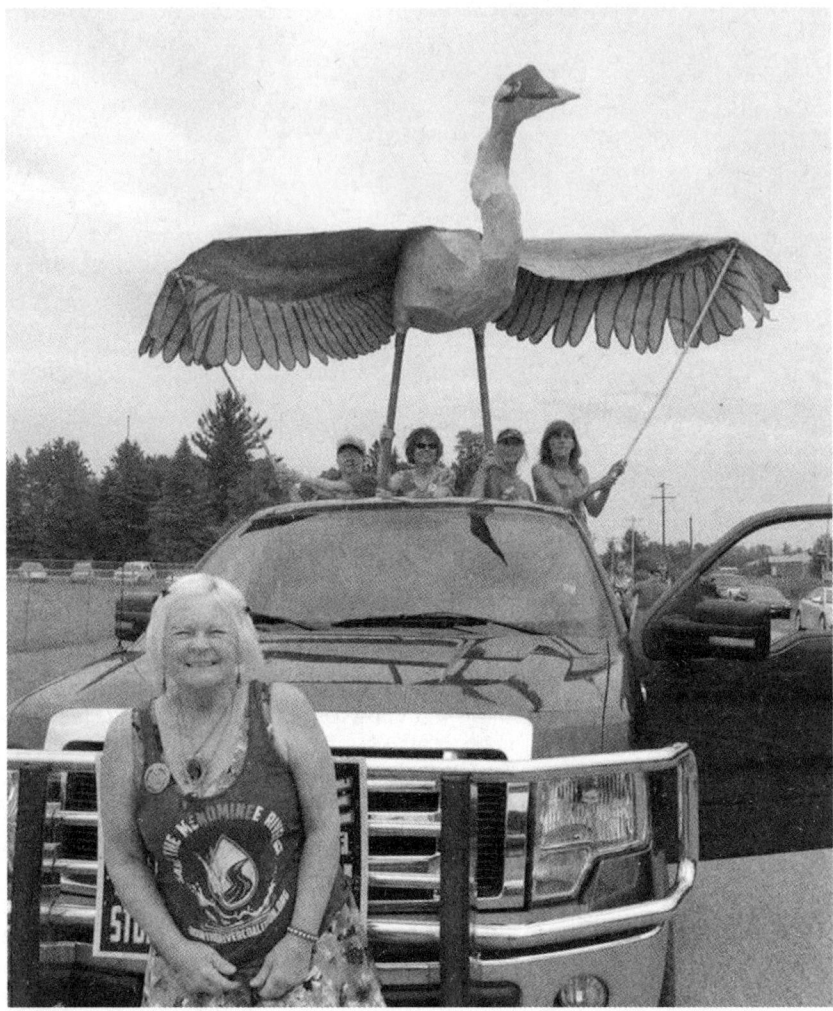

The Heron Puppet Up North in a Rural Parade: The heron puppet is now kept near the Menominee River, at the border between Wisconsin and Michigan. It is carried in small rural parades on the No Back Forty Mine float. The wings rise and fall, operated by a person on each side. The structure has been improved, and it is safely stored between events. This 2023 photo by Robin Hanson features the heron and Robin's mother, Mary Hanson, an organizer of No Back Forty Mine events (see more on the Back Forty Mine later in this chapter).

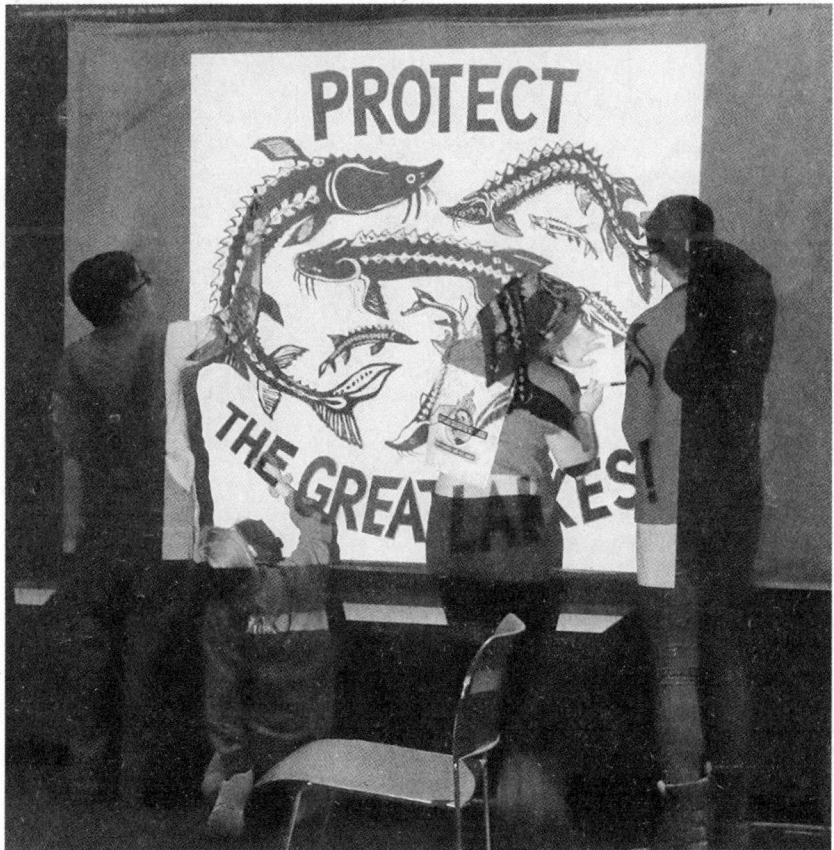

Sturgeon Banner Tracing: Here are some photos of water protector art being made. The sturgeon banner art is projected onto fabric and traced for painting.

calendar to raise money for needed supplies to aid the people camped out in cold and windy North Dakota. This project was a collaboration with poets from Woodland Pattern Book Center, who also organized a poetry and art fundraising event that was jam-packed, with people lined up outside the door.

In 2016, I was invited to facilitate an art build in Madison held by the 350.org art team to make art protesting the Enbridge pipeline. The group included Paul Fieber, who is a professional kite maker. He stitched together an enormous river in various shades of blue out of ripstop nylon. We made critter hats. Each person decided what animal, fish, or bird they wanted to wear. The river ripples down the street, and the critter hats bob.

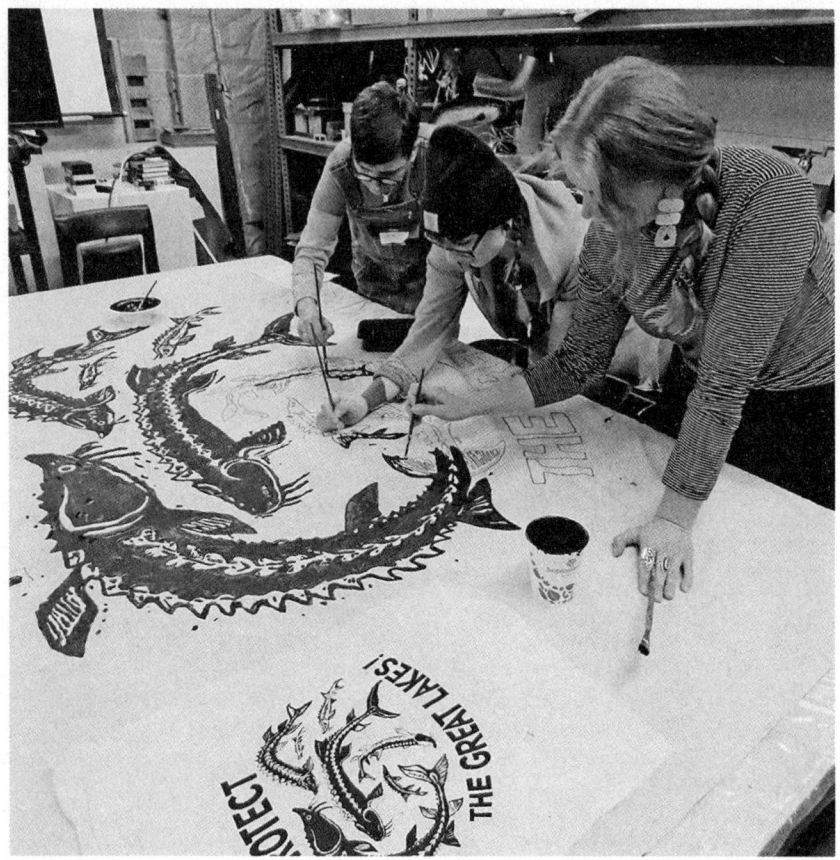

Painting the Banner: Several artists fill in the outlined sturgeon with paint.

In Milwaukee, we built wooden frames to mount flags on kayaks for the 2016 anti–oil train event. We got the instructions to build them from David Solnit and Art and Revolution friends in San Francisco. In 2023, I drove the frames to a gathering of non-Indigenous water protectors in Michigan for a flotilla in Ann Arbor. Michigan people then drove them 620 miles to Ashland to make sure the frames would make it in time for a flotilla on Fish Creek, which flows into Lake Superior. The Madison 350.org art team drove there with the animal hats and their descendants made at the 2016 art build. The Ashland art build team brought colorful banners, flags, and silk-screened patches to decorate the boats. We were sent out on the water with Ojibwe blessings and drumming. The communication and travel to one another's events and

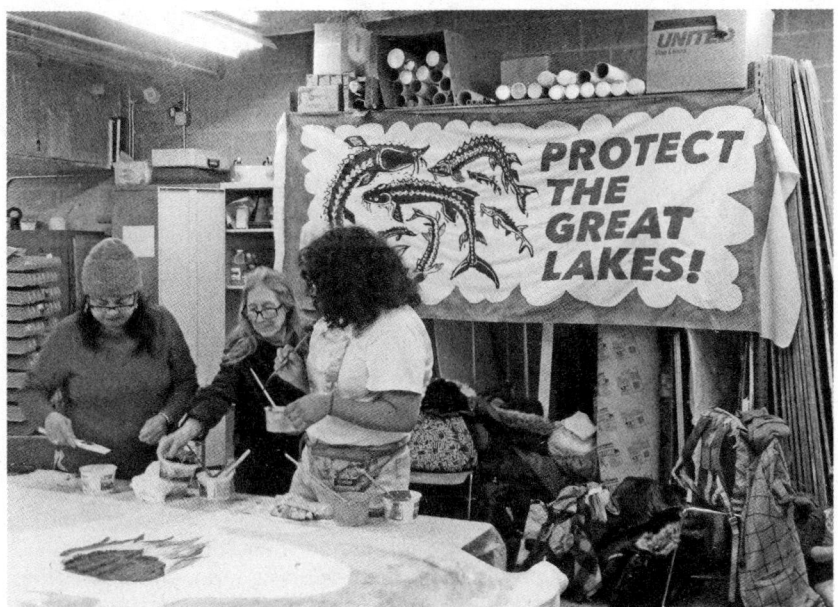

Sturgeon Banner Painted: A variation on the sturgeon banner hangs at a Milwaukee art build.

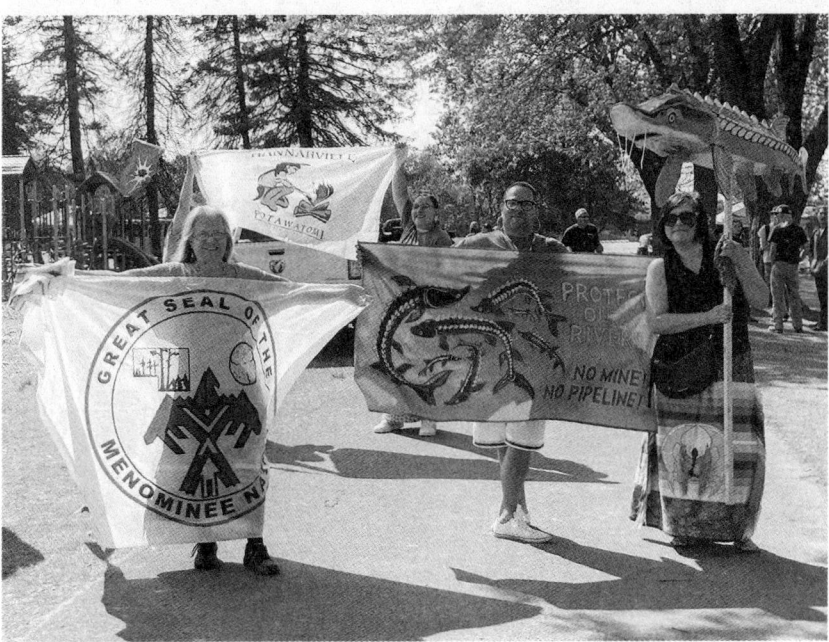

No Pipeline, No Back Forty Mine: A "Protect Our Rivers" version of the sturgeon banner design is held by Menominee Nation water walkers at the Menominee River.

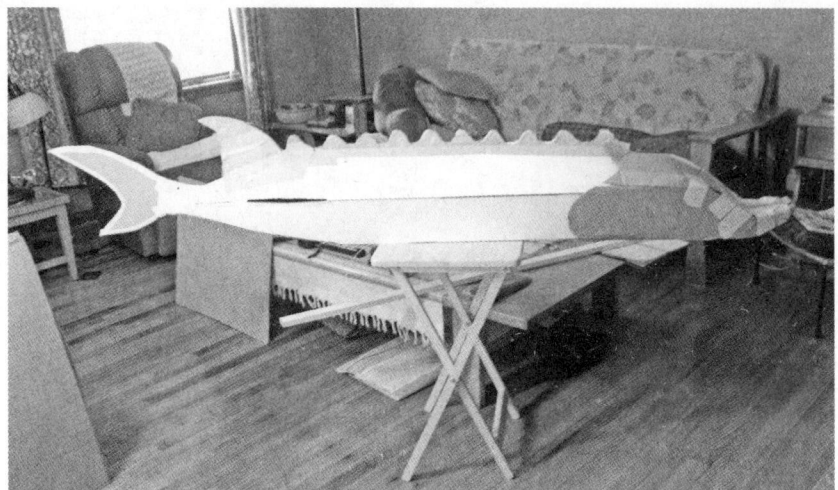

Making a Cardboard Sturgeon: To make the basic sturgeon shape out of cardboard, first, the pieces are cut, scored, and folded. Next, they are fixed in place, joined using a sword stapler, masking tape, and wood glue, and then covered in places with papier-mâché. Bicycle boxes are nice and big sources for materials.

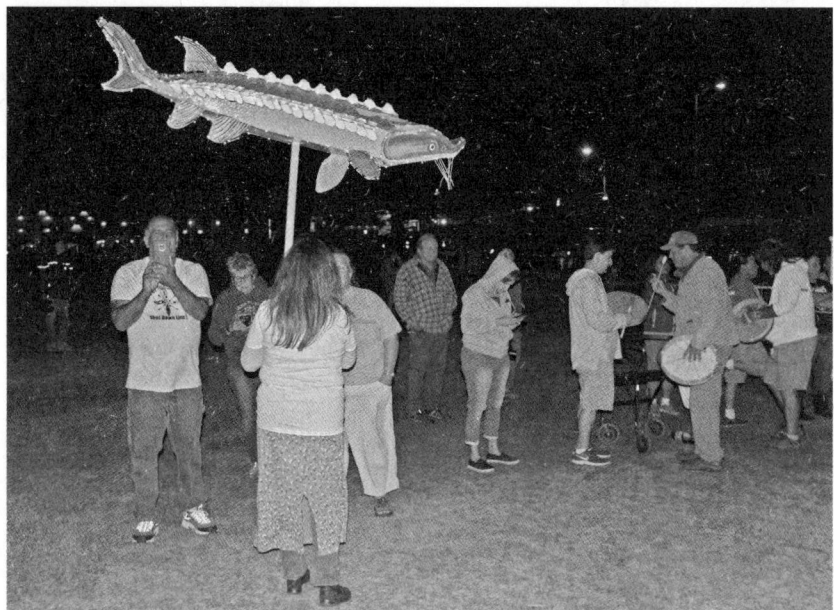

Sturgeon at Night at the Mackinac Straits: Here is the big sturgeon puppet at the Mackinac Straits at an annual Labor Day weekend gathering against the proposed Enbridge Line 5 crude oil tunnel under the straits between Lake Michigan and Lake Huron, between Lower Michigan and the Upper Peninsula. The LED lights work well at night.

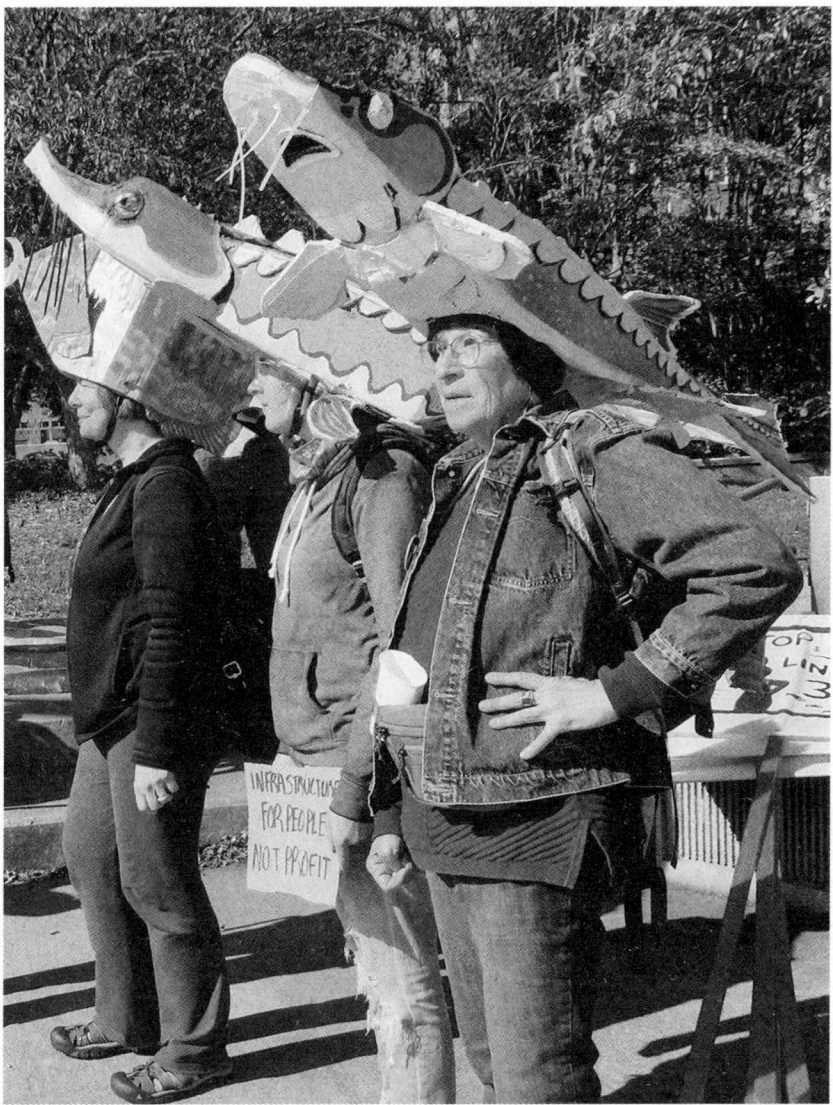

Duluth Sturgeon Hats: I was invited to lead a puppet hat build by the Madison 350.org art team in 2017, and they maintained and improved the hats and made more. Several sturgeon hats were worn at the march in Duluth, Minnesota, to protest Enbridge Line 3 and honor and remember MMIW (Missing and Murdered Indigenous Women). "Man camps" of itinerant pipeline construction crews bring increased sex trafficking and drugs to Indigenous communities, leading to a rise in violence against women. One of the sturgeon hats is now in Madison with the environmentalist group 350.org, another is in Ashland, Wisconsin, with the No Enbridge Line 5 art team, and the third is temporarily at the Indian Community School in Franklin, Wisconsin.

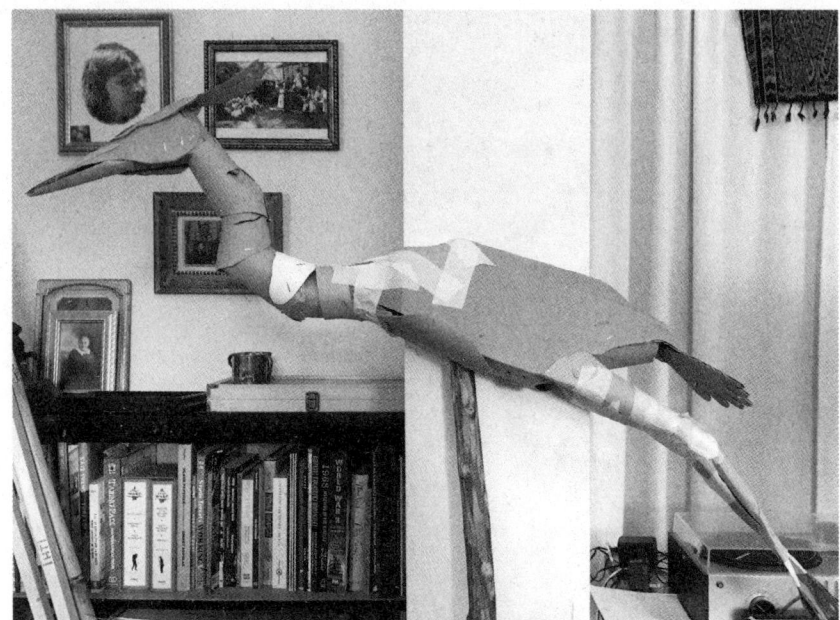

A Heron Puppet Is Started: The cardboard armature of a life-size blue heron puppet shows how the pieces are joined.

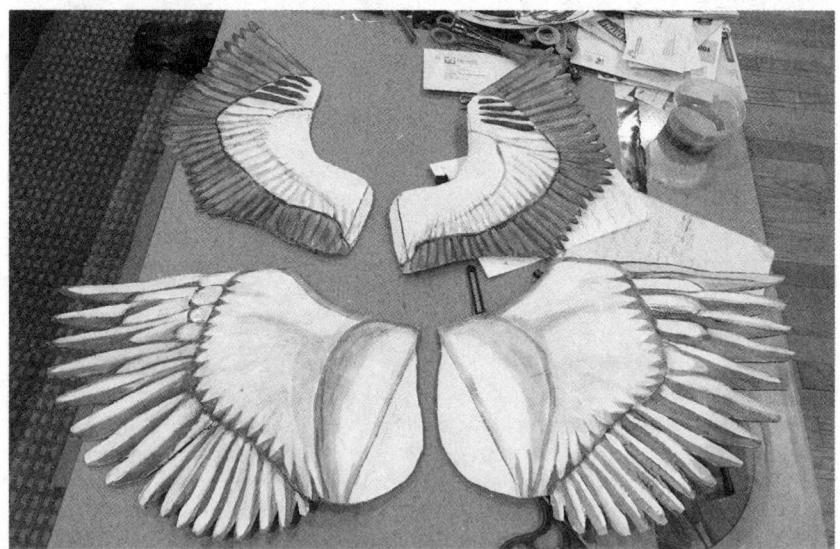

The Wings Are Made: And here are two pairs of heron wings cut out and painted, with tabs that will slot into the bodies.

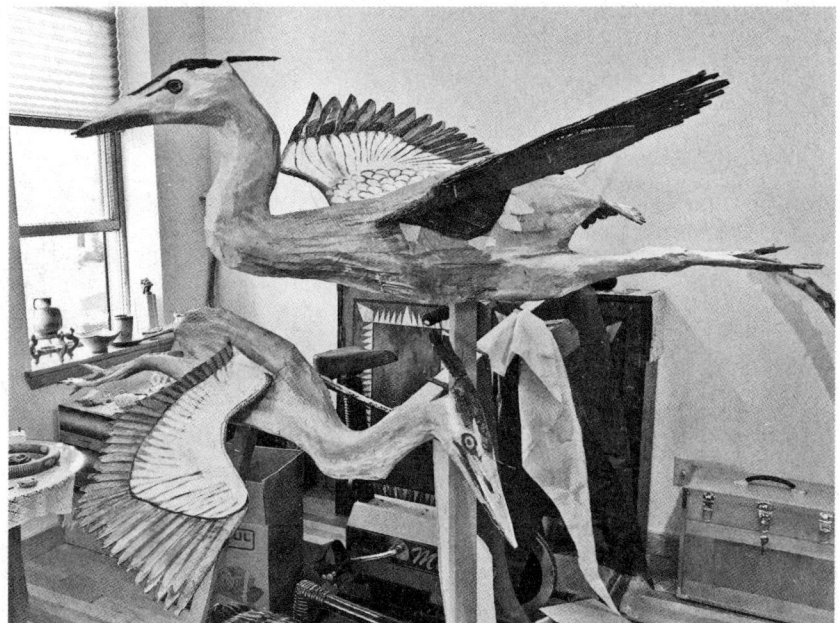

The Heron Puppets Completed: The two life-size heron puppets were in the 2021 Milwaukee Riverkeeper Boat Parade, celebrating the return of the sturgeon to the Milwaukee River. Our boat went downstream through downtown and then into the industrial harbor, where a real live blue heron perched on a dock lined with boathouses, glaring suspiciously at the invasion of its territory.

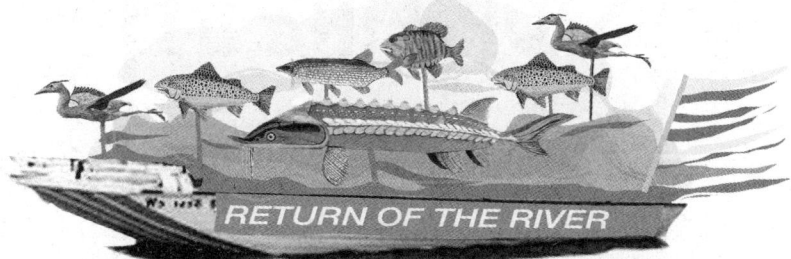

Float Drawing: This mock-up shows the plan for the placement of puppets on a boat for the Riverkeeper flotilla. Photos of the puppets are photoshopped onto the scale drawing.

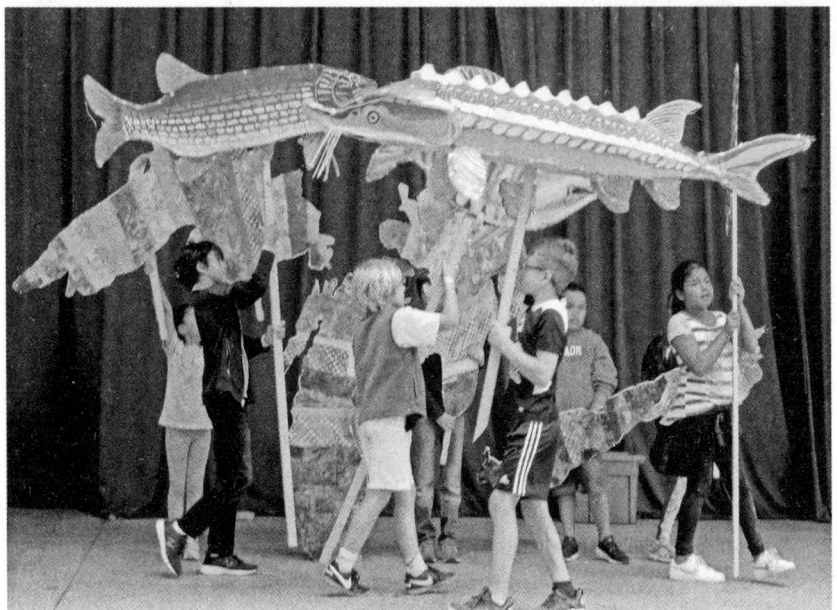

Indian Summer Festival: The children's stage at the 2021 Indian Summer Festival, the largest Native American gathering in the US, was sponsored by Woodland Pattern, a small-press poetry center and art gallery. Elementary school classes went onstage to parade the fish puppets in front of Melanie Ariens's Great Lakes installation while an Ojibwe story was read.

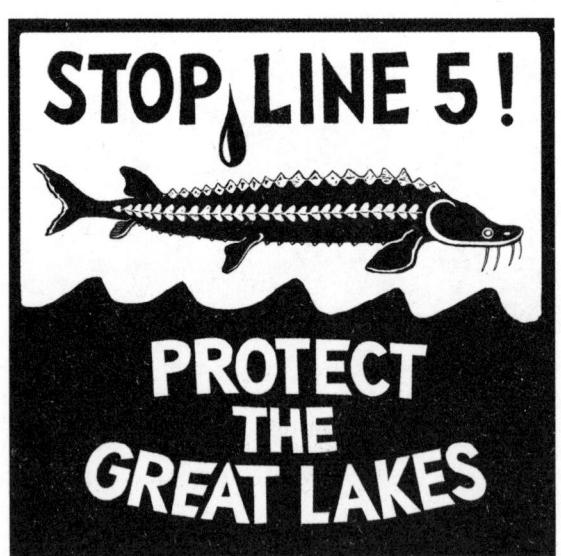

"Protect the Great Lakes" Sturgeon Patch: This "Stop Line 5!" art was made into a patch.

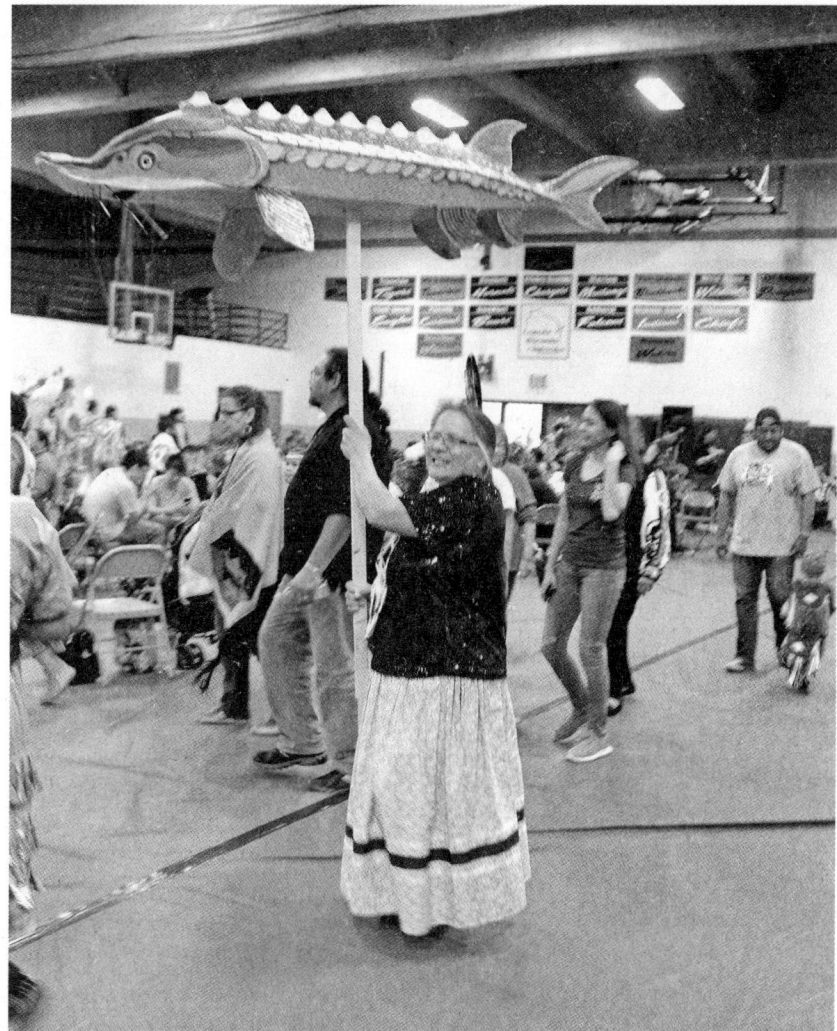

The Sturgeon Puppet in the Round Dance: The big sturgeon puppet was carried in the Menominee Sturgeon Feast Pow Wow round dance by Menominee Indian High School cultural teacher Dawn Wilbur.

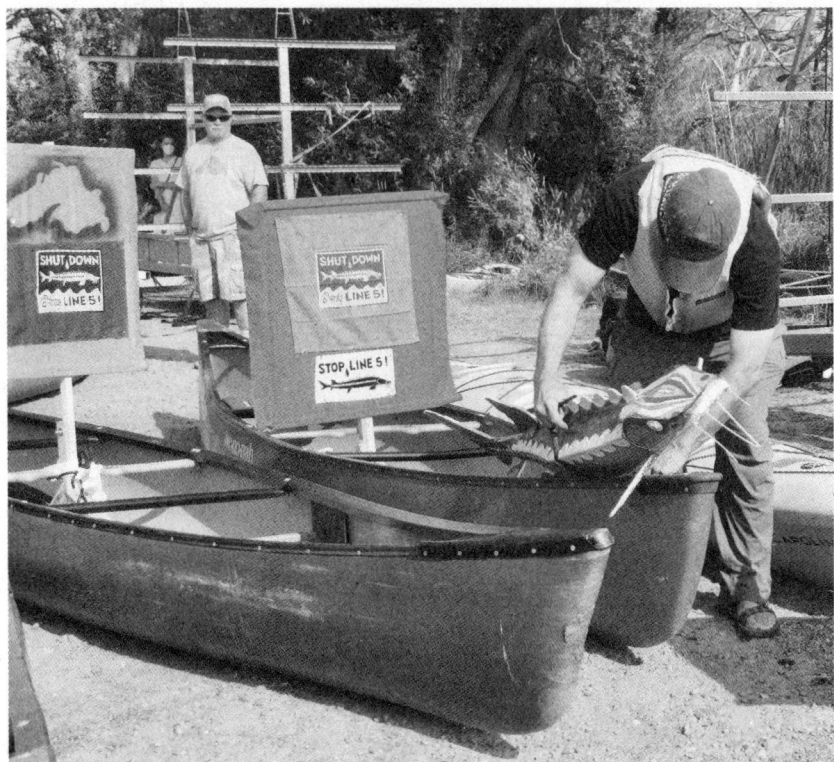

Kayak Flags: Silk-screened flags for kayaks were assembled in Ashland, Wisconsin. Here they are being attached to a kayak for the No Line 5 Flotilla at Fish Creek, west of Ashland.

sharing artwork between Wisconsin, Michigan, Minnesota, Ontario, and Quebec strengthens our network.

All over the Upper Midwest, with radio ads and full-page newspaper ads as far as Chicago, Enbridge spends millions on advertising and public relations. In Ashland, along the Line 5, Enbridge held a weekly dinner. They bait their dog-and-pony propaganda shows with free food, just like the Jewel-Osco PR people did in Milwaukee, using the people who show up to eat as proof of their traction in the community.

They lie about their safety record and promise well-paying jobs in the depressed post-mining Northwoods economy. The truth is that the jobs go mainly to transient workers or technical experts from afar. My friends' Shut Down Enbridge Line 5 group rented the same hall for weekly potluck dinners at which neighbors were given accurate information, countering Enbridge's lies. The Enbridge Line 5 pipeline carries fracked crude oil through the forest, its route marked with orange flags.

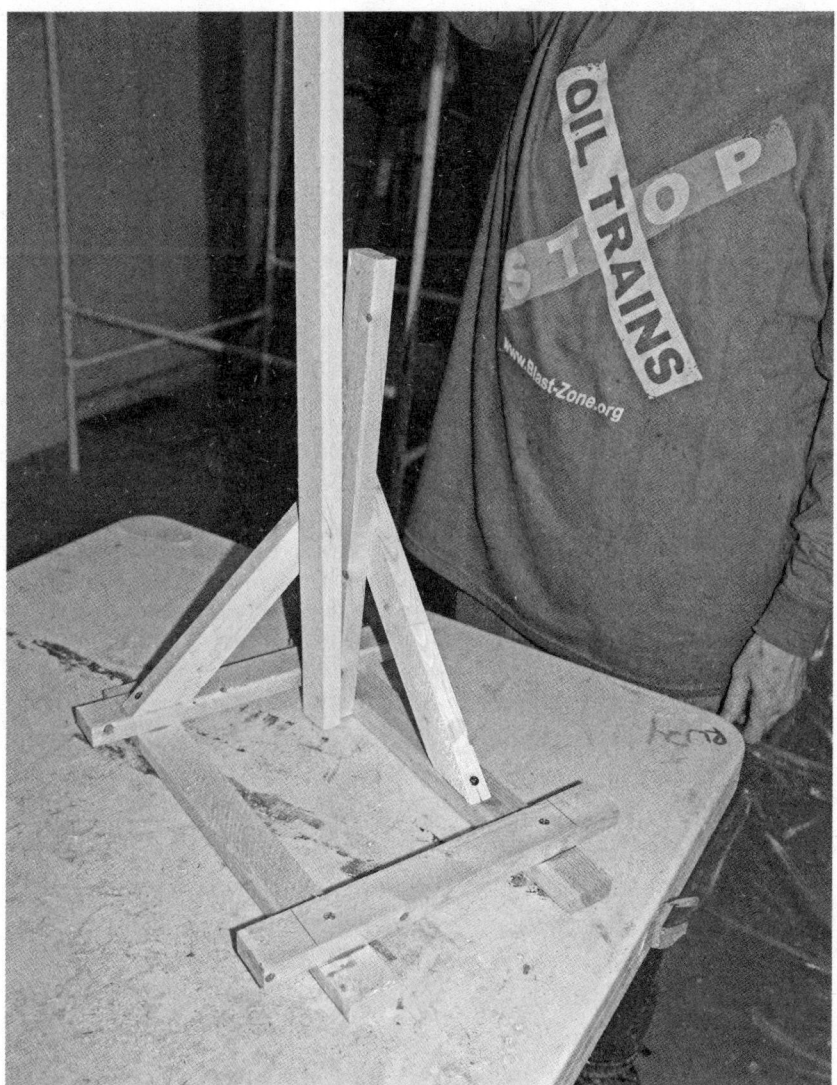

A Wood Frame to Put Flags onto Kayaks or Canoes: A close-up of the kayak frame shows how they are constructed.

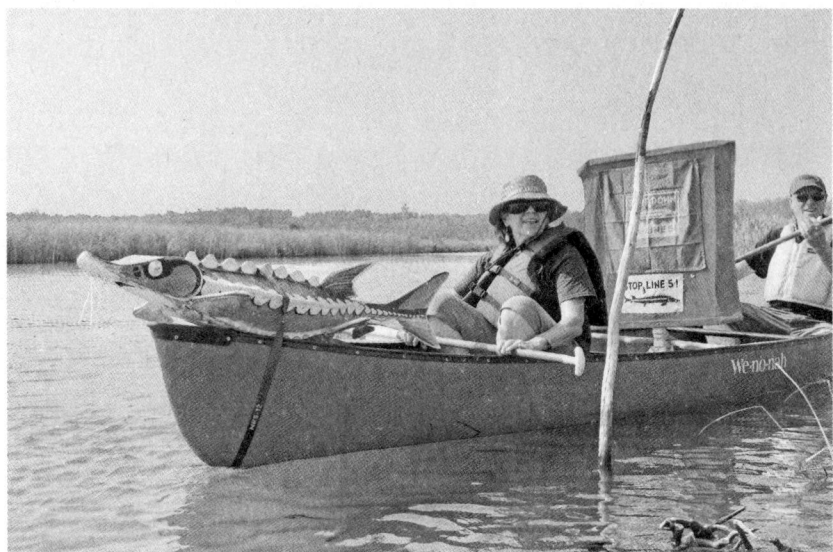

Sturgeon Figureheads: The Madison 350.org art team attached the fish and animal hats to the bows of kayaks as figureheads, replacing the archetypal wood carving of a woman on sailing ships of old.

All pipelines leak, but the corporations don't do anything about these breaches until someone reports seeing the greasy black slick in the forest or on the water. Closing Line 5 at one location would stop the flow of oil all along the route.

We are part of a growing worldwide movement to protect water and end fossil fuels. Despite the resounding victory we had a decade ago stopping the Crandon Mine, international mining companies continue their quest to make the northern Great Lakes region a resource extraction colony and crude oil pipeline corridor.

In 2011, the mining company Gogebic Taconite proposed a giant open-pit iron ore mine in the Penokee Hills, an ancient mountain range south of Ashland. Indigenous and non-Native water protectors set up a protest encampment, Harvest Camp, and camped through the frigid northern winter, living off the land. After five years of organized opposition, Gogebic Taconite withdrew their bid to mine, claiming they couldn't mine the wetlands, as they were too wet!

For over a decade, Canadian company Highland Copper has been planning a new sulfide mine just west of Michigan's Porcupine Mountains Wilderness State Park, where the Lake of the Clouds is a popular destination. The proposed Copperwood Mine would drill for

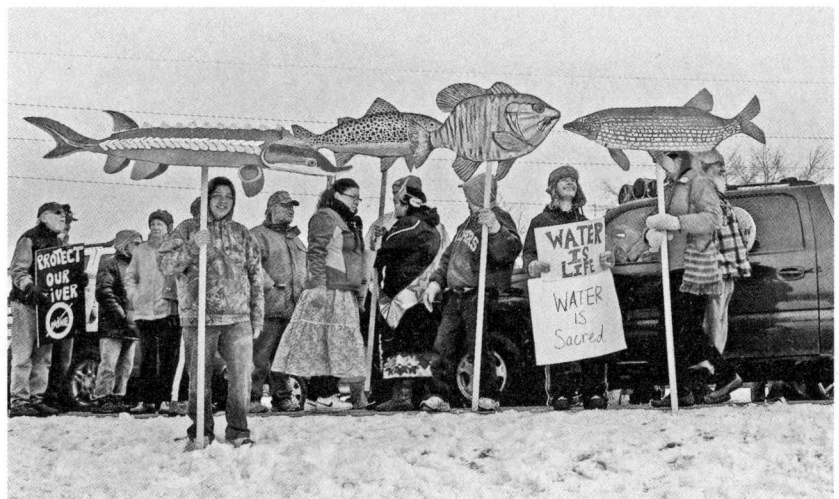

No Back Forty Mine Winter Bridge Walk: The sturgeon and other fish puppets, originally made for the movement against oil trains, were used for a No Back Forty Mine bridge walk across the Menominee River, connecting Menominee, Wisconsin, to Marinette, Michigan.

ore beneath the bed of Lake Superior and deposit the waste uphill. Local people and regional tribal members in the sparsely populated area of the Upper Peninsula have rapidly organized opposition, learning from previous antimine campaigns.

The Back Forty Mine was proposed by Aquila Resources in 2015, and we're still fighting it. (Gold Resource Corporation acquired Aquila and the project in 2021.) This would be an open-pit mine for extracting sulfide ore containing gold, zinc, and other metals. The mine is proposed on a site that is only fifty feet from the Menominee River, bordering Wisconsin and the Michigan's Upper Peninsula. An on-site processing mill would dump cyanide near the twin cities of Marinette, Wisconsin, and Menominee, Michigan, at the mouth of the river as it flows into Lake Michigan.

And, significantly, the sturgeon have returned to the Menominee River, showing that when we stop the mining, the water quality improves.

In 2023, the annual Labor Day weekend Water Is Life Festival was held in Petoskey, Michigan, south of the Mackinac Straits. The day before the festival, people who live all along the Enbridge Line 5 pipeline route, including Québécois activists, came together to paint protest banners in English and French. The Detroit Light Brigade also refurbished their signs. Ojibwe tribal members hosted us, allowing us

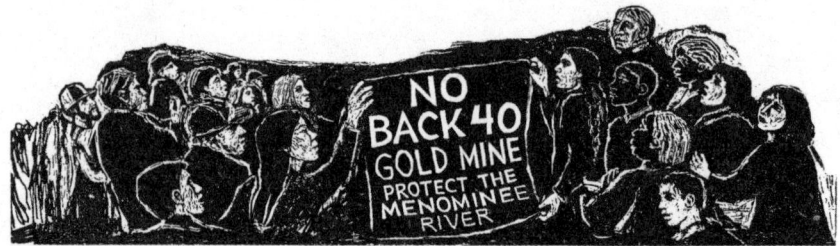

No Back 40: We are still fighting the Back Forty Mine, although the value of the mining company is spiraling downward, hopefully into oblivion. This scratchboard drawing was first used in art against the Crandon Mine and continues to circulate. The people and the lay of the land are a good likeness.

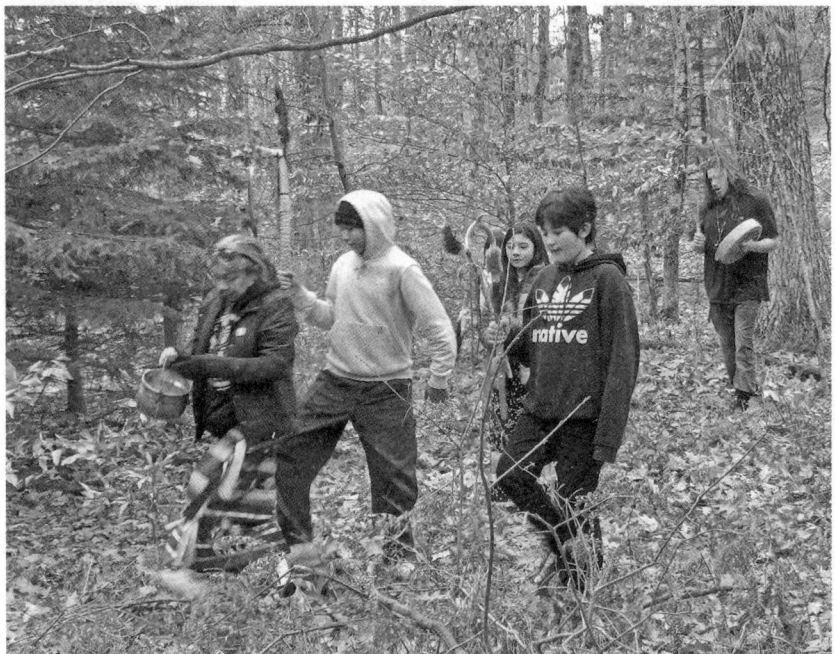

A Little Civil Disobedience on a Public Road: In November 2023, I joined Menominee friends walking Boneyard Road, near the Back Forty Mine site. Archeologists have documented that this area and nearby islands are cultural sites of ancient farming communities. The road passes through an area called Dogs Belly, which has been added to the National Register of Historic Places. Menominee researchers found that the road is public property even though it passes through land claimed by the mining company Gold Resource Corporation. The road was chained off and posted with No Trespassing signs. When we walked the forest road, we encountered private security guards and deputy sheriffs standing by, with an attack dog in the cruiser. Targeted people were cited for trespassing in later weeks.

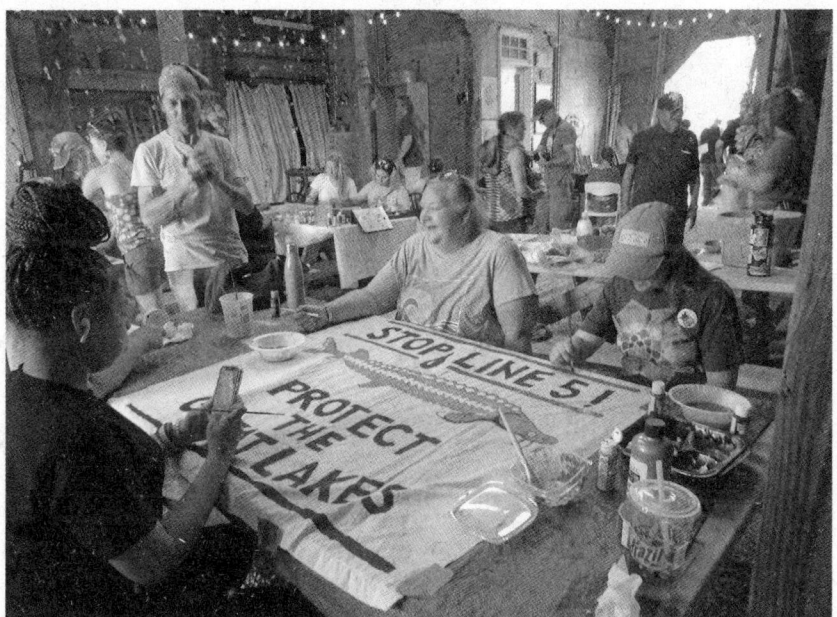

The Art Build at the Mackinac Straits: We had access to a wonderful barn at the 2023 Labor Day convergence near the Mackinac Straits.

to prepare for the demonstration in a beautiful barn and kitchen. Our hosts served platters of locally caught and smoked fish and crackers as an appetizer, followed by a memorable Ojibwe meal that included fish, wild rice, blueberries, and venison. Three hundred people feasted on more than enough to eat and were then gifted bags of wild rice from the wetlands of the Bad River Ojibwe sloughs. The Ojibwe and Odawa hosts were most certainly "doing things in a good way."

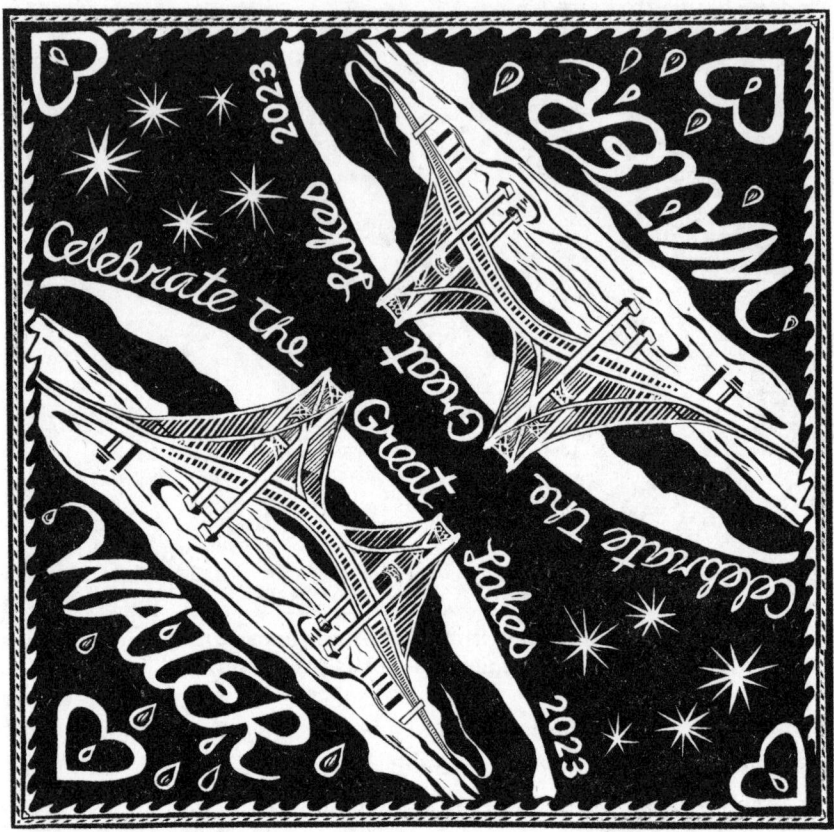

A Souvenir Scarf for the Mackinac Bridge Walk: Every Labor Day the Mackinac Bridge Walk draws huge crowds. People against Enbridge building a tunnel under the Mackinac Straits joined the walk and distributed silk-screened royal-blue scarves. The scarves were made to look like tourist items.

Pages 167–77: Water Protectors
First appeared in *World War 3 Illustrated*, no. 51 (2020), "The World We Are Fighting For" issue.

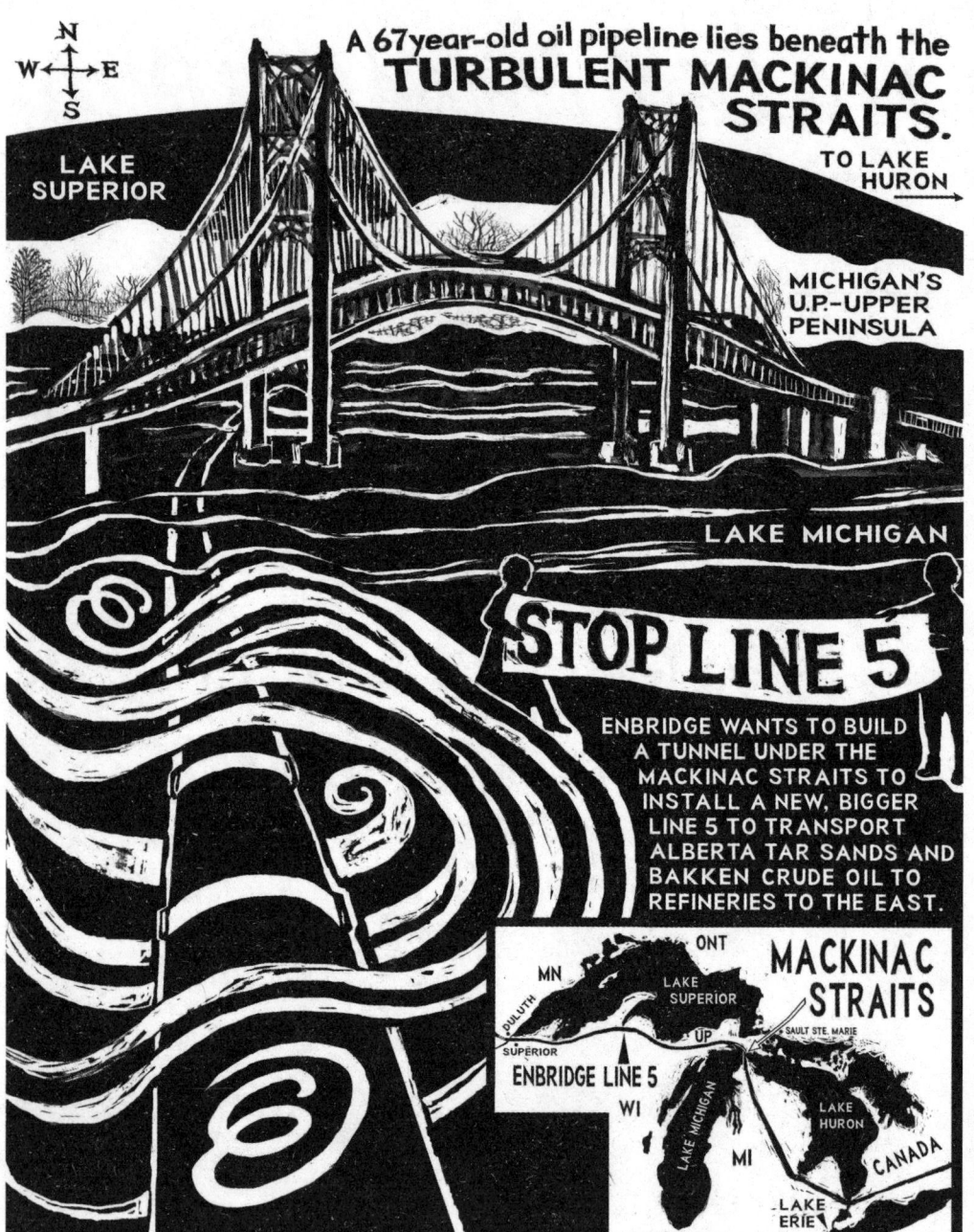

A 67 year-old oil pipeline lies beneath the
TURBULENT MACKINAC STRAITS.

LAKE SUPERIOR

TO LAKE HURON →

MICHIGAN'S U.P.–UPPER PENINSULA

LAKE MICHIGAN

STOP LINE 5

ENBRIDGE WANTS TO BUILD A TUNNEL UNDER THE MACKINAC STRAITS TO INSTALL A NEW, BIGGER LINE 5 TO TRANSPORT ALBERTA TAR SANDS AND BAKKEN CRUDE OIL TO REFINERIES TO THE EAST.

MACKINAC STRAITS

MN
ONT
LAKE SUPERIOR
DULUTH
UP
SAULT STE. MARIE
SUPERIOR
ENBRIDGE LINE 5
WI
LAKE MICHIGAN
MI
LAKE HURON
CANADA
LAKE ERIE

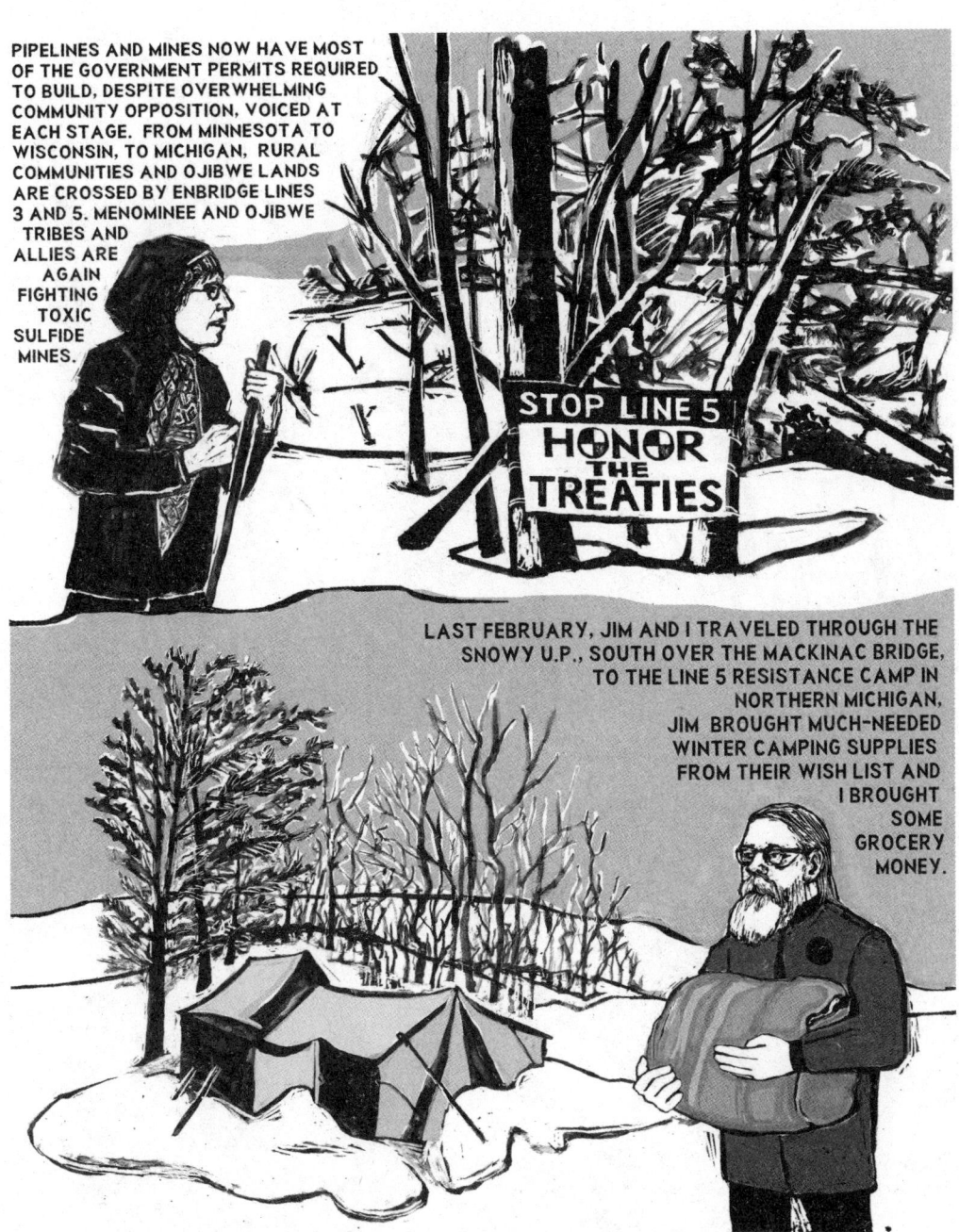

PIPELINES AND MINES NOW HAVE MOST OF THE GOVERNMENT PERMITS REQUIRED TO BUILD, DESPITE OVERWHELMING COMMUNITY OPPOSITION, VOICED AT EACH STAGE. FROM MINNESOTA TO WISCONSIN, TO MICHIGAN, RURAL COMMUNITIES AND OJIBWE LANDS ARE CROSSED BY ENBRIDGE LINES 3 AND 5. MENOMINEE AND OJIBWE TRIBES AND ALLIES ARE AGAIN FIGHTING TOXIC SULFIDE MINES.

STOP LINE 5
HONOR THE TREATIES

LAST FEBRUARY, JIM AND I TRAVELED THROUGH THE SNOWY U.P., SOUTH OVER THE MACKINAC BRIDGE, TO THE LINE 5 RESISTANCE CAMP IN NORTHERN MICHIGAN. JIM BROUGHT MUCH-NEEDED WINTER CAMPING SUPPLIES FROM THEIR WISH LIST AND I BROUGHT SOME GROCERY MONEY.

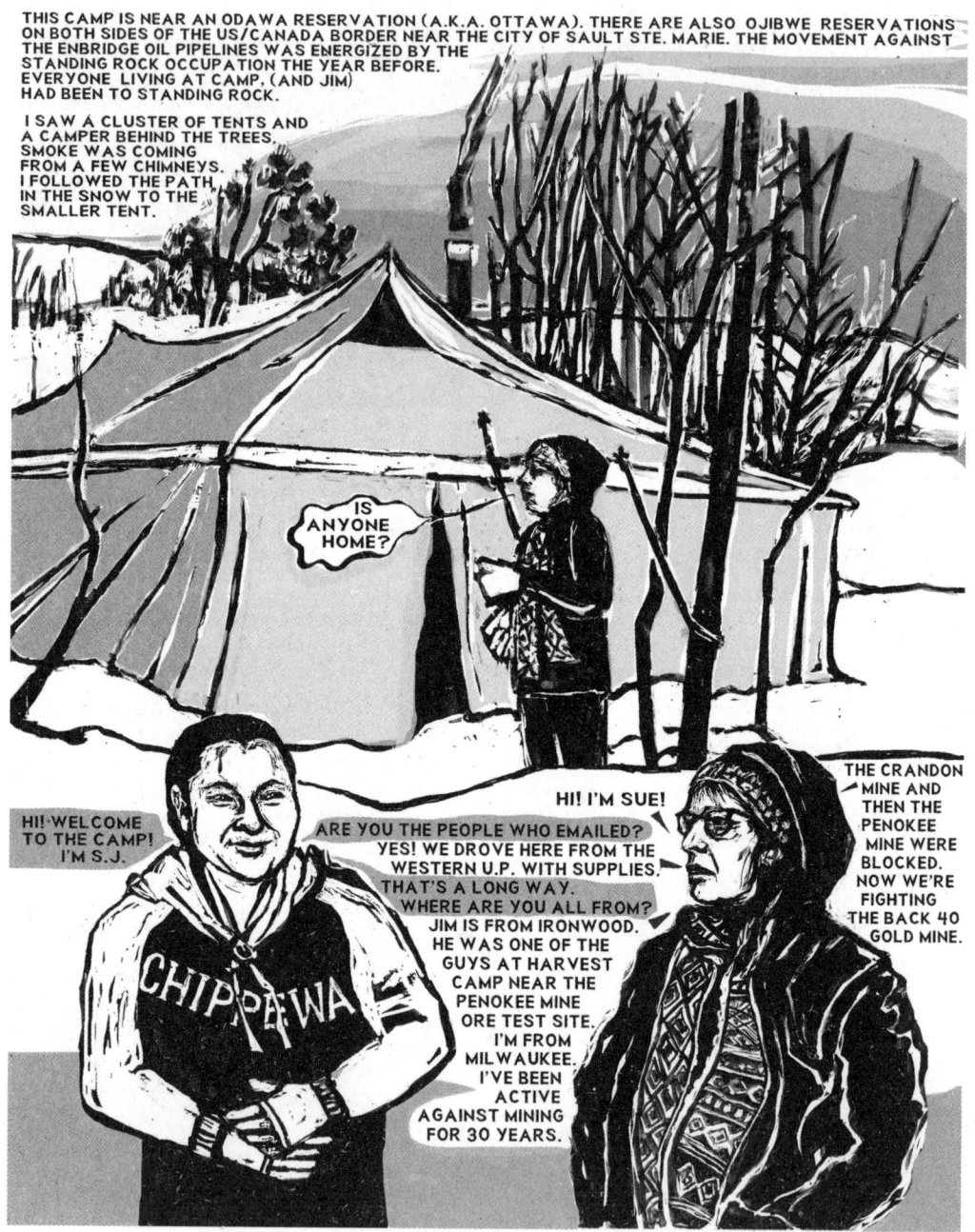

THIS CAMP IS NEAR AN ODAWA RESERVATION (A.K.A. OTTAWA). THERE ARE ALSO OJIBWE RESERVATIONS ON BOTH SIDES OF THE US/CANADA BORDER NEAR THE CITY OF SAULT STE. MARIE. THE MOVEMENT AGAINST THE ENBRIDGE OIL PIPELINES WAS ENERGIZED BY THE STANDING ROCK OCCUPATION THE YEAR BEFORE. EVERYONE LIVING AT CAMP, (AND JIM) HAD BEEN TO STANDING ROCK.

I SAW A CLUSTER OF TENTS AND A CAMPER BEHIND THE TREES. SMOKE WAS COMING FROM A FEW CHIMNEYS. I FOLLOWED THE PATH IN THE SNOW TO THE SMALLER TENT.

IS ANYONE HOME?

HI! WELCOME TO THE CAMP! I'M S.J.

HI! I'M SUE!

ARE YOU THE PEOPLE WHO EMAILED? YES! WE DROVE HERE FROM THE WESTERN U.P. WITH SUPPLIES. THAT'S A LONG WAY. WHERE ARE YOU ALL FROM? JIM IS FROM IRONWOOD. HE WAS ONE OF THE GUYS AT HARVEST CAMP NEAR THE PENOKEE MINE ORE TEST SITE. I'M FROM MILWAUKEE. I'VE BEEN ACTIVE AGAINST MINING FOR 30 YEARS.

CHIPPEWA

THE CRANDON MINE AND THEN THE PENOKEE MINE WERE BLOCKED. NOW WE'RE FIGHTING THE BACK 40 GOLD MINE.

170

WHAT BRINGS YOU HERE?

WE'VE BEEN WORKING TO STOP THE BACK 40 GOLD MINE, NEXT
TO THE MENOMINEE RIVER ON THE MICHIGAN/WISCONSIN BORDER,
WITH THE WATER PROTECTORS FROM THE MENOMINEE TRIBE AND
FROM THE TOWNS NEARBY. WE HEARD ABOUT YOUR CAMP AND
WANTED TO VISIT AND BRING SUPPLIES. WE WANT TO SPREAD
THE WORD ABOUT LINE 5'S THREAT TO THE GREAT LAKES TOO.

BUT WHAT BRINGS YOU HERE?

... STOPPING THE PIPELINES CARRYING TOXIC CRUDE OIL GOES
UP AGAINST THE HEART OF MULTINATIONAL CAPITALISM. WE
MUST STOP NEW OIL INFRASTRUCTURE TO STOP GLOBAL
WARMING AND PROTECT THE GREAT LAKES FROM OIL SPILLS.

YES, BUT THAT'S NOT IT!

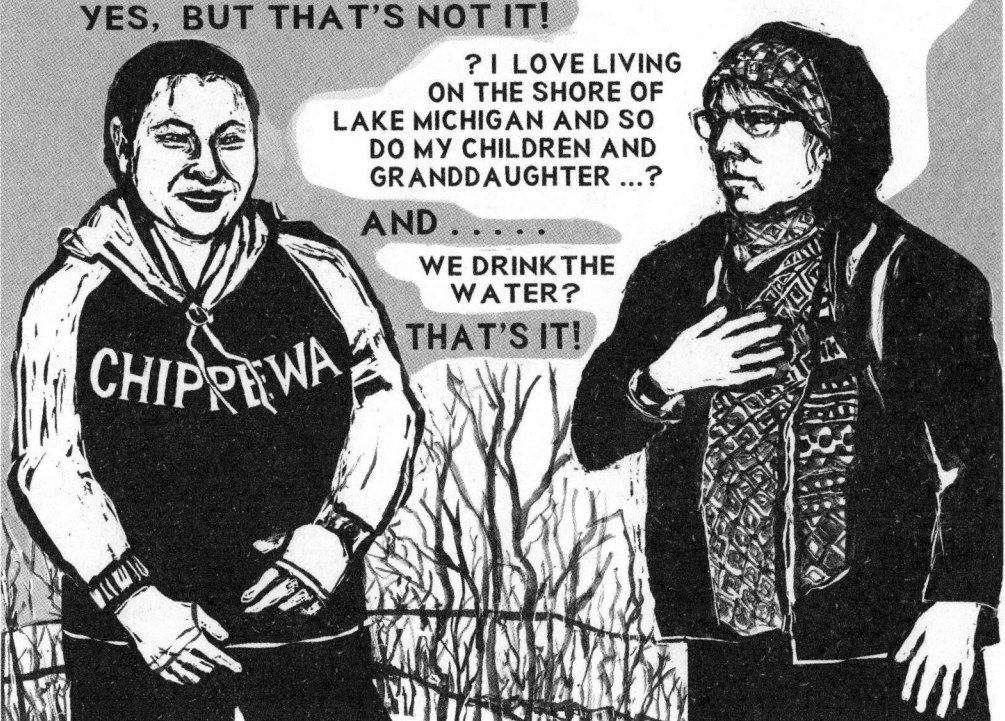

? I LOVE LIVING
ON THE SHORE OF
LAKE MICHIGAN AND SO
DO MY CHILDREN AND
GRANDDAUGHTER ...?

AND . . . . .

WE DRINK THE
WATER?

THAT'S IT!

CHIPPEWA

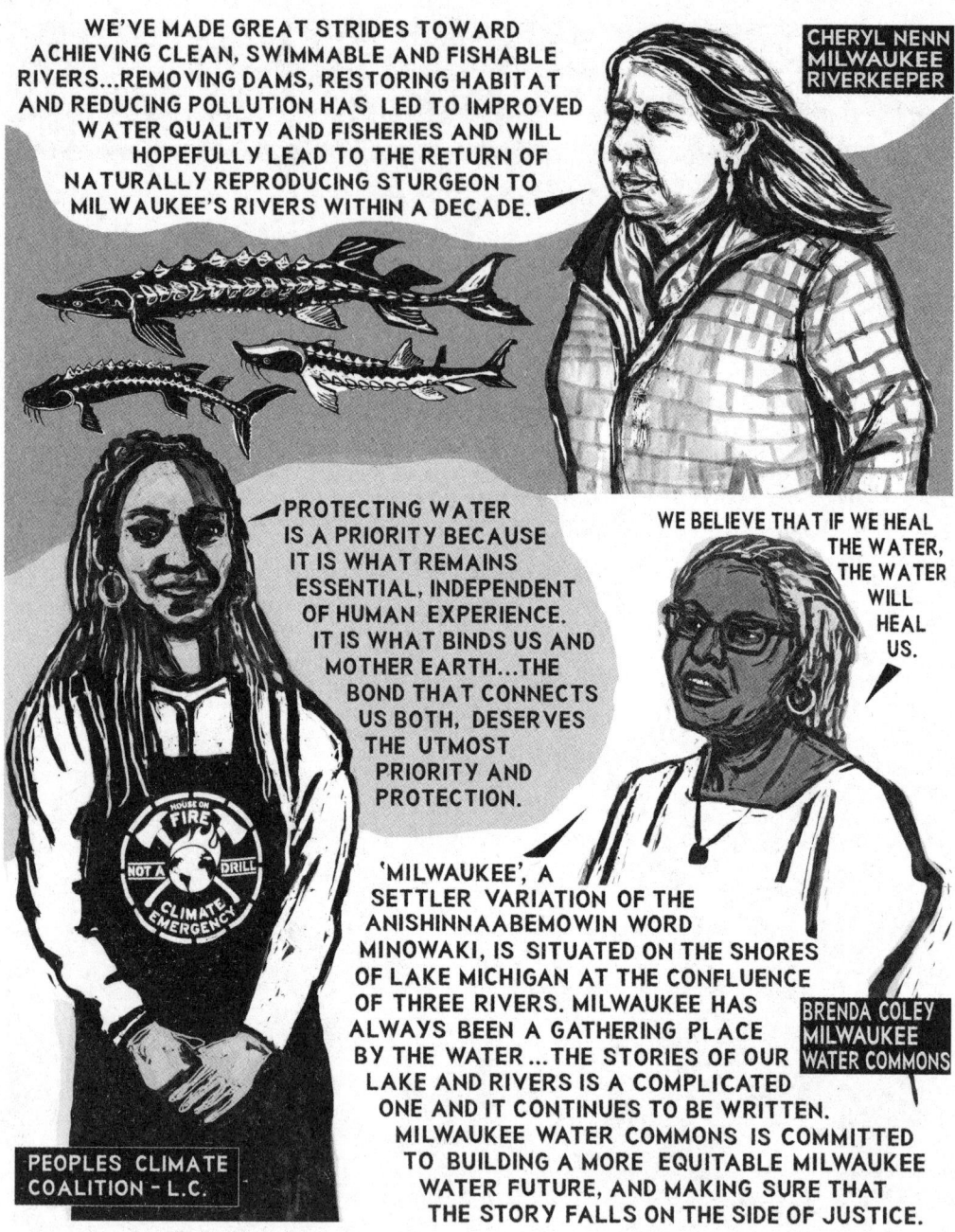

WE'VE MADE GREAT STRIDES TOWARD ACHIEVING CLEAN, SWIMMABLE AND FISHABLE RIVERS...REMOVING DAMS, RESTORING HABITAT AND REDUCING POLLUTION HAS LED TO IMPROVED WATER QUALITY AND FISHERIES AND WILL HOPEFULLY LEAD TO THE RETURN OF NATURALLY REPRODUCING STURGEON TO MILWAUKEE'S RIVERS WITHIN A DECADE.

CHERYL NENN
MILWAUKEE
RIVERKEEPER

PROTECTING WATER IS A PRIORITY BECAUSE IT IS WHAT REMAINS ESSENTIAL, INDEPENDENT OF HUMAN EXPERIENCE. IT IS WHAT BINDS US AND MOTHER EARTH...THE BOND THAT CONNECTS US BOTH, DESERVES THE UTMOST PRIORITY AND PROTECTION.

WE BELIEVE THAT IF WE HEAL THE WATER, THE WATER WILL HEAL US.

'MILWAUKEE', A SETTLER VARIATION OF THE ANISHINNAABEMOWIN WORD MINOWAKI, IS SITUATED ON THE SHORES OF LAKE MICHIGAN AT THE CONFLUENCE OF THREE RIVERS. MILWAUKEE HAS ALWAYS BEEN A GATHERING PLACE BY THE WATER...THE STORIES OF OUR LAKE AND RIVERS IS A COMPLICATED ONE AND IT CONTINUES TO BE WRITTEN. MILWAUKEE WATER COMMONS IS COMMITTED TO BUILDING A MORE EQUITABLE MILWAUKEE WATER FUTURE, AND MAKING SURE THAT THE STORY FALLS ON THE SIDE OF JUSTICE.

BRENDA COLEY
MILWAUKEE
WATER COMMONS

PEOPLES CLIMATE
COALITION - L.C.

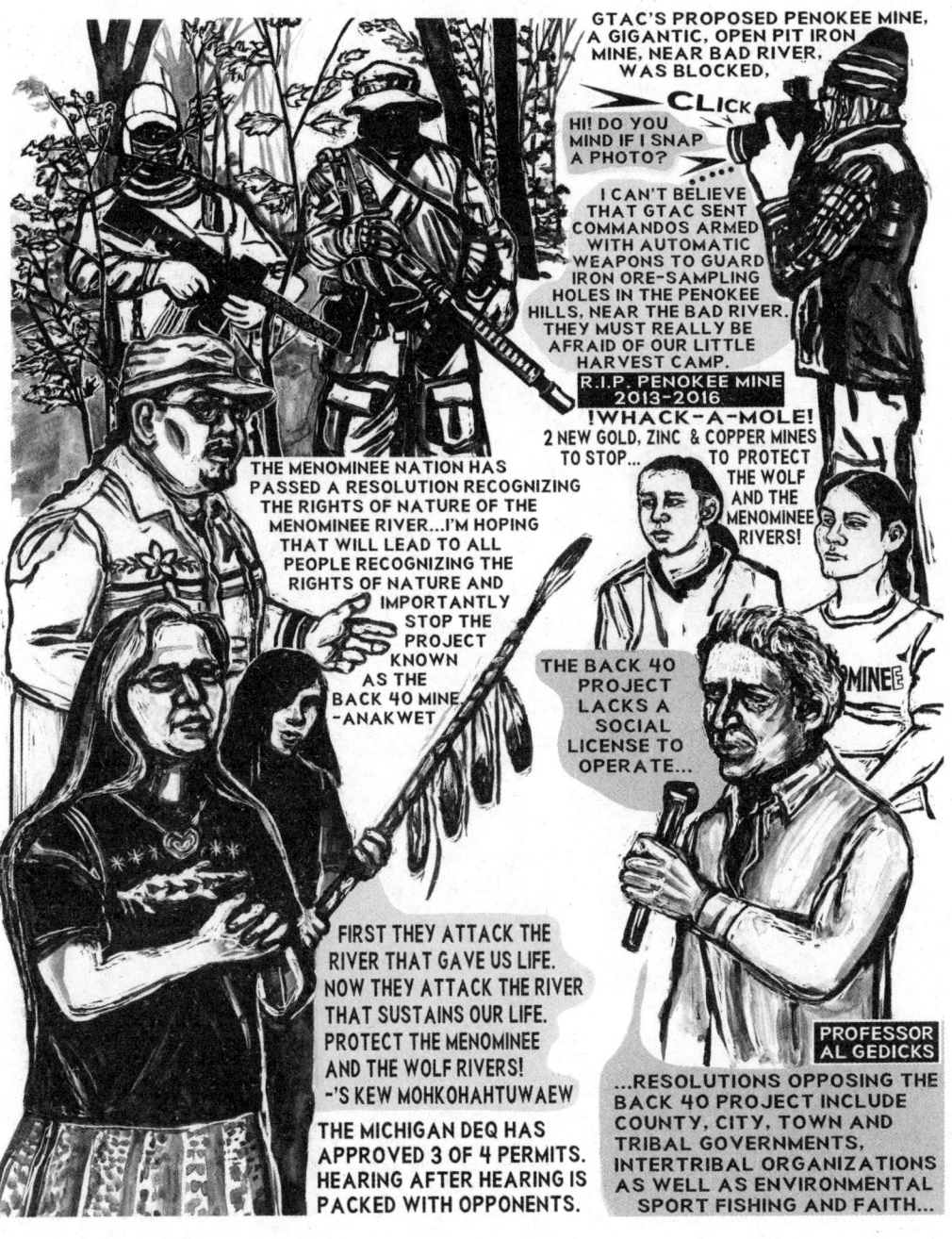

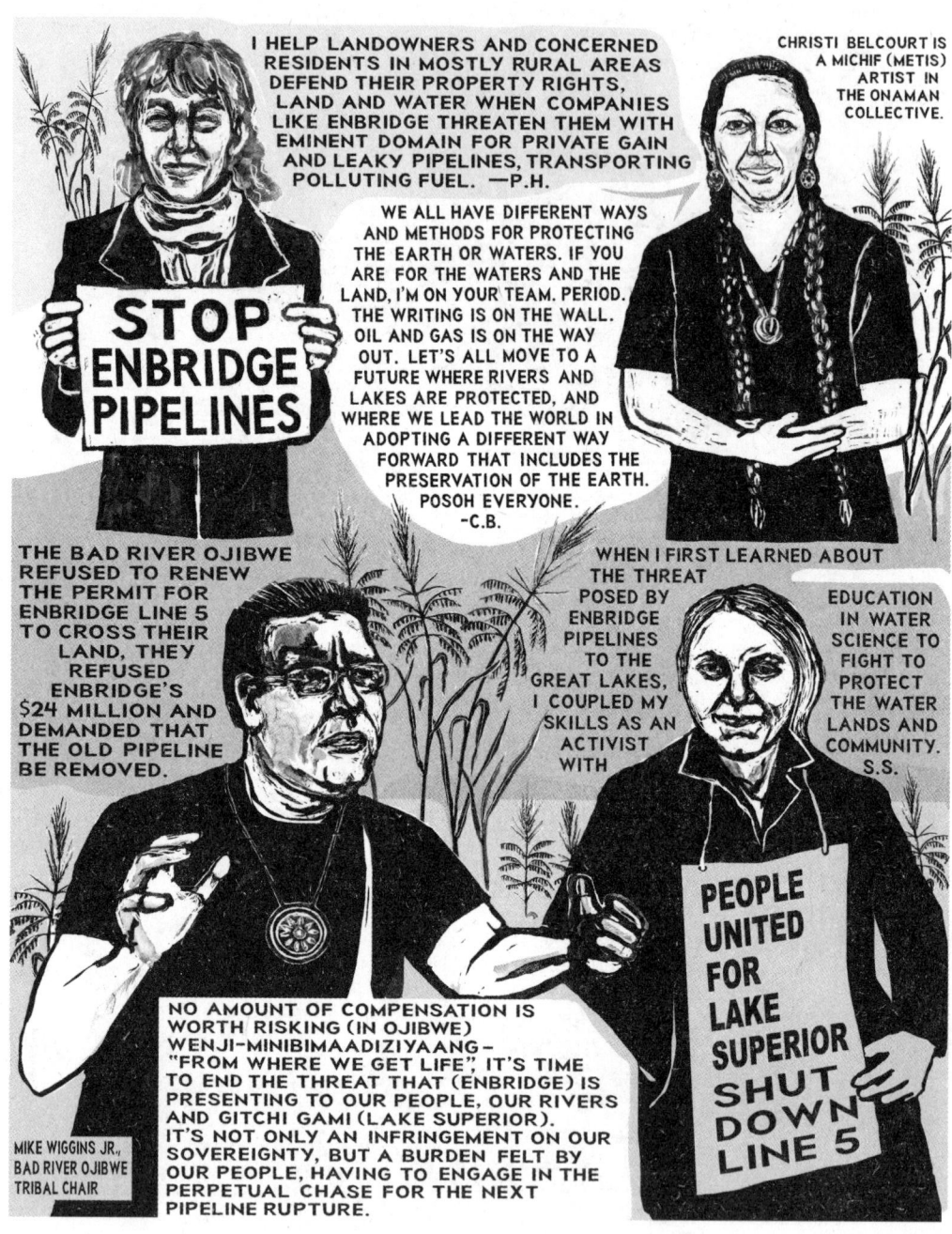

174

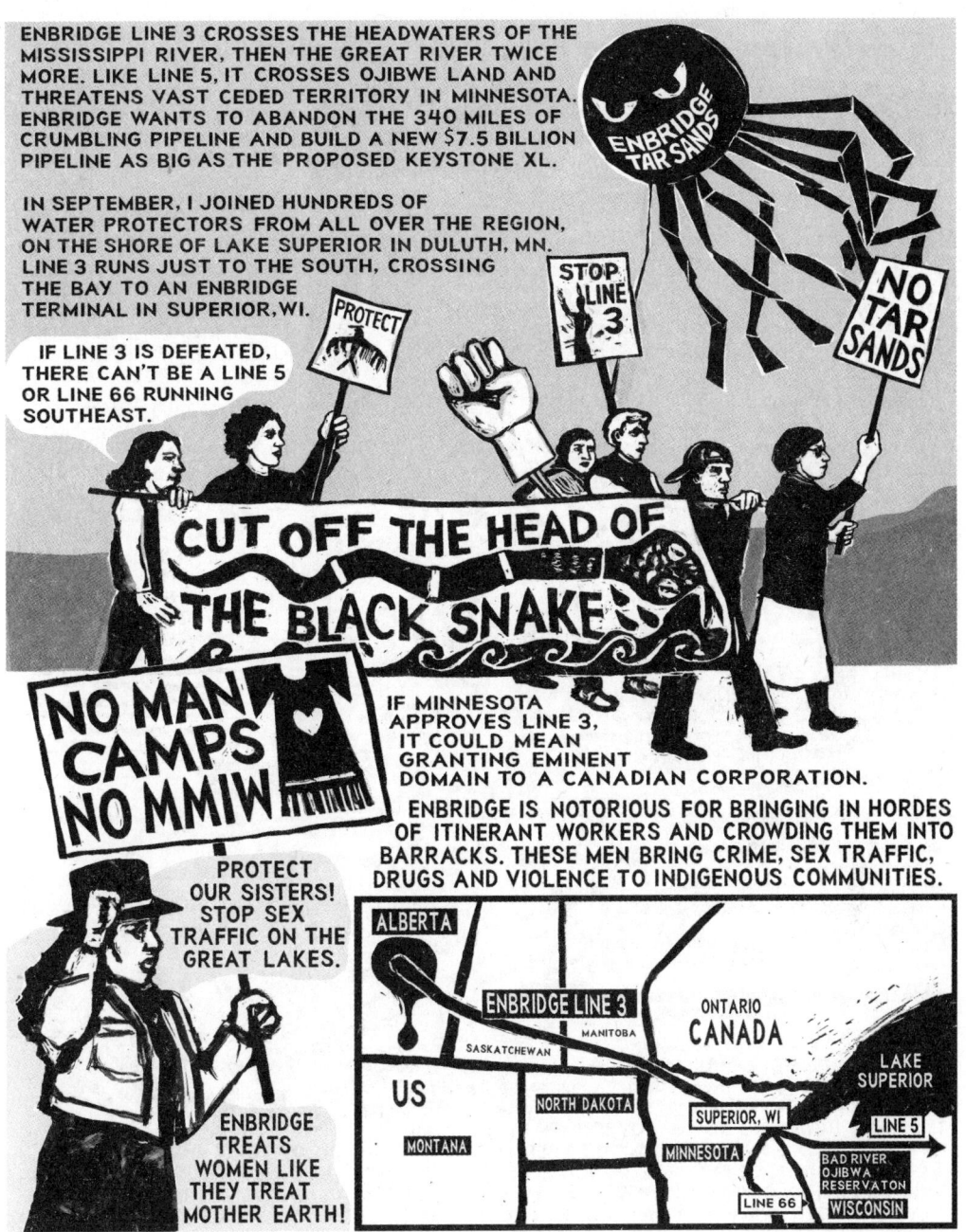

ENBRIDGE LINE 3 CROSSES THE HEADWATERS OF THE MISSISSIPPI RIVER, THEN THE GREAT RIVER TWICE MORE. LIKE LINE 5, IT CROSSES OJIBWE LAND AND THREATENS VAST CEDED TERRITORY IN MINNESOTA. ENBRIDGE WANTS TO ABANDON THE 340 MILES OF CRUMBLING PIPELINE AND BUILD A NEW $7.5 BILLION PIPELINE AS BIG AS THE PROPOSED KEYSTONE XL.

IN SEPTEMBER, I JOINED HUNDREDS OF WATER PROTECTORS FROM ALL OVER THE REGION, ON THE SHORE OF LAKE SUPERIOR IN DULUTH, MN. LINE 3 RUNS JUST TO THE SOUTH, CROSSING THE BAY TO AN ENBRIDGE TERMINAL IN SUPERIOR, WI.

IF LINE 3 IS DEFEATED, THERE CAN'T BE A LINE 5 OR LINE 66 RUNNING SOUTHEAST.

ENBRIDGE TAR SANDS

PROTECT

STOP LINE 3

NO TAR SANDS

CUT OFF THE HEAD OF THE BLACK SNAKE

NO MAN CAMPS NO MMIW

IF MINNESOTA APPROVES LINE 3, IT COULD MEAN GRANTING EMINENT DOMAIN TO A CANADIAN CORPORATION.

ENBRIDGE IS NOTORIOUS FOR BRINGING IN HORDES OF ITINERANT WORKERS AND CROWDING THEM INTO BARRACKS. THESE MEN BRING CRIME, SEX TRAFFIC, DRUGS AND VIOLENCE TO INDIGENOUS COMMUNITIES.

PROTECT OUR SISTERS! STOP SEX TRAFFIC ON THE GREAT LAKES.

ENBRIDGE TREATS WOMEN LIKE THEY TREAT MOTHER EARTH!

ALBERTA

ENBRIDGE LINE 3

SASKATCHEWAN

MANITOBA

ONTARIO
CANADA

US

NORTH DAKOTA

MONTANA

SUPERIOR, WI

MINNESOTA

LINE 66

LINE 5

LAKE SUPERIOR

BAD RIVER OJIBWA RESERVATON

WISCONSIN

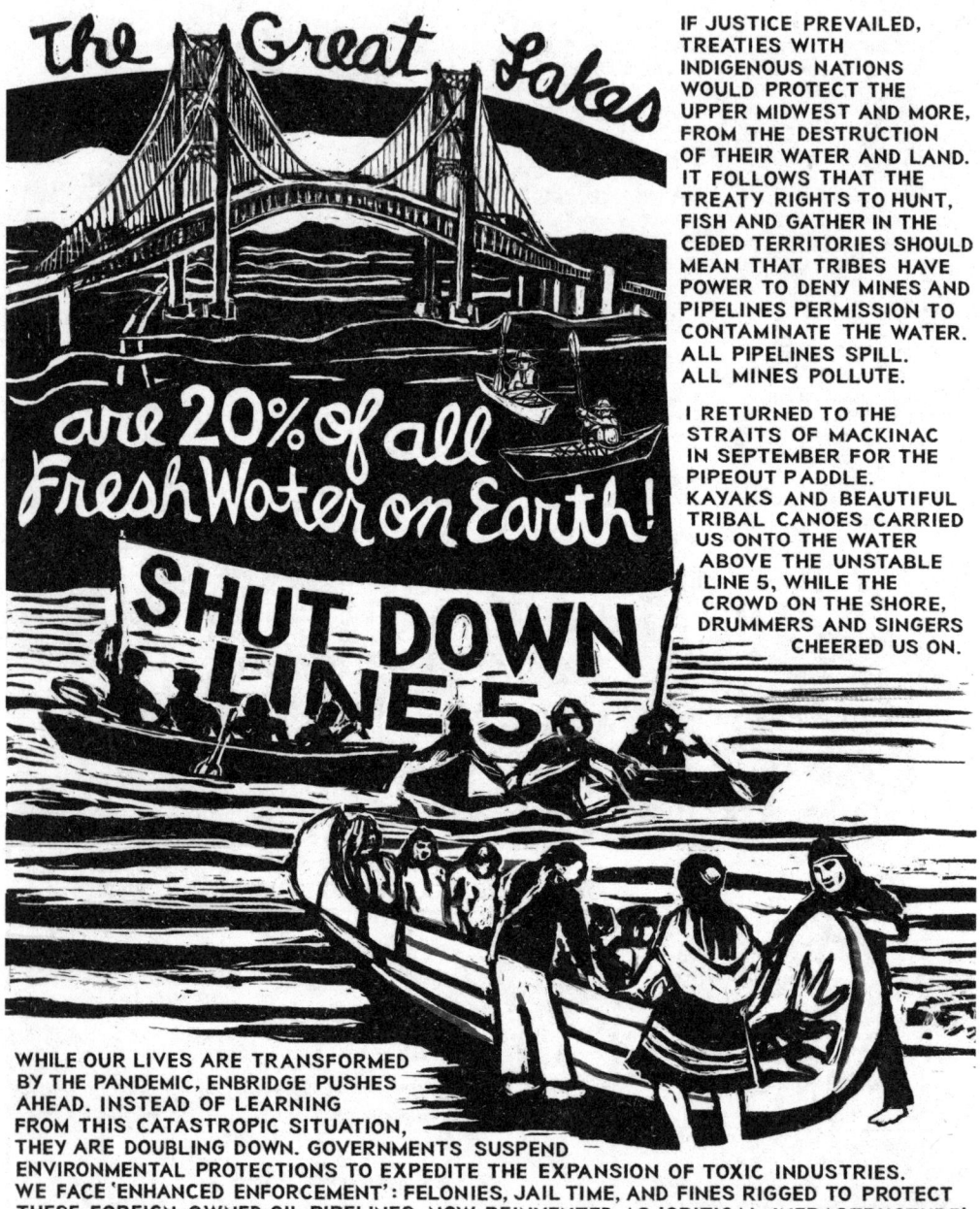

The Great Lakes are 20% of all Fresh Water on Earth!

SHUT DOWN LINE 5

IF JUSTICE PREVAILED, TREATIES WITH INDIGENOUS NATIONS WOULD PROTECT THE UPPER MIDWEST AND MORE, FROM THE DESTRUCTION OF THEIR WATER AND LAND. IT FOLLOWS THAT THE TREATY RIGHTS TO HUNT, FISH AND GATHER IN THE CEDED TERRITORIES SHOULD MEAN THAT TRIBES HAVE POWER TO DENY MINES AND PIPELINES PERMISSION TO CONTAMINATE THE WATER. ALL PIPELINES SPILL. ALL MINES POLLUTE.

I RETURNED TO THE STRAITS OF MACKINAC IN SEPTEMBER FOR THE PIPEOUT PADDLE. KAYAKS AND BEAUTIFUL TRIBAL CANOES CARRIED US ONTO THE WATER ABOVE THE UNSTABLE LINE 5, WHILE THE CROWD ON THE SHORE, DRUMMERS AND SINGERS CHEERED US ON.

WHILE OUR LIVES ARE TRANSFORMED BY THE PANDEMIC, ENBRIDGE PUSHES AHEAD. INSTEAD OF LEARNING FROM THIS CATASTROPIC SITUATION, THEY ARE DOUBLING DOWN. GOVERNMENTS SUSPEND ENVIRONMENTAL PROTECTIONS TO EXPEDITE THE EXPANSION OF TOXIC INDUSTRIES. WE FACE 'ENHANCED ENFORCEMENT': FELONIES, JAIL TIME, AND FINES RIGGED TO PROTECT THESE FOREIGN-OWNED OIL PIPELINES, NOW REINVENTED AS 'CRITICAL INFRASTRUCTURE'. NEVERTHELESS, WE WILL CONTINUE TO PROTECT THE WATER AND PROTECT ONE ANOTHER.

THIS PAGE IS DEDICATED TO THE VICTORY OF THE NATIVE/NON-NATIVE COALITION WHICH FOUGHT A TOXIC ZINC AND COPPER SULFIDE-ORE MINE FOR 28 YEARS TO PROTECT THE WOLF RIVER AND, IN 2003, WON... AND DEDICATED TO THE STURGEON, WHICH SWIM UPSTREAM FROM LAKE WINNEBAGO IN APRIL. PEOPLE LINE THE RIVERBANKS BY DAY, WATCHING THE DINOSAUR-AGE GIANTS PARADE BY, AND BY NIGHT, LANTERNS IN THEIR HANDS, GUARD THE STURGEON TO PROTECT THEM FROM POACHERS.

NO MINE ON WISCONSIN'S WOLF RIVER

FOR THOUSANDS OF YEARS THE STURGEON RUN MARKED THE END OF THE STARVING TIME, PROVIDING FOOD FOR THE PEOPLE LIVING ALONG THE RIVERS.

AND, LIKE THE PROVERBIAL CANARY SINGING IN THE COAL MINE, THE STURGEON'S RETURN IS EVIDENCE THAT THE WATER HAS BEEN PROTECTED.

177

The Long Haul

Many '60s radicals did not "burn out." We went on to "serve the people" as teachers, union organizers, writers, community garden organizers, and health professionals and can be found in the places where we can support new sparks of resistance. Working as a nurse for fifty years kept me real, grounded, and intimately connected to resistance movements when holding down a job was a necessity for me, not a choice.

Are there steps to revolution in everyday life?

When students at the high school where I worked demanded an end to the school-to-prison pipeline and police in the schools, I was there with them when they chanted, "We are scholars, not criminals!" I worked with other union members to successfully abolish the budget line that paid for police in Milwaukee Public Schools. Our success ended up being overturned by Republican state legislators a few years later, but we know we can win again.

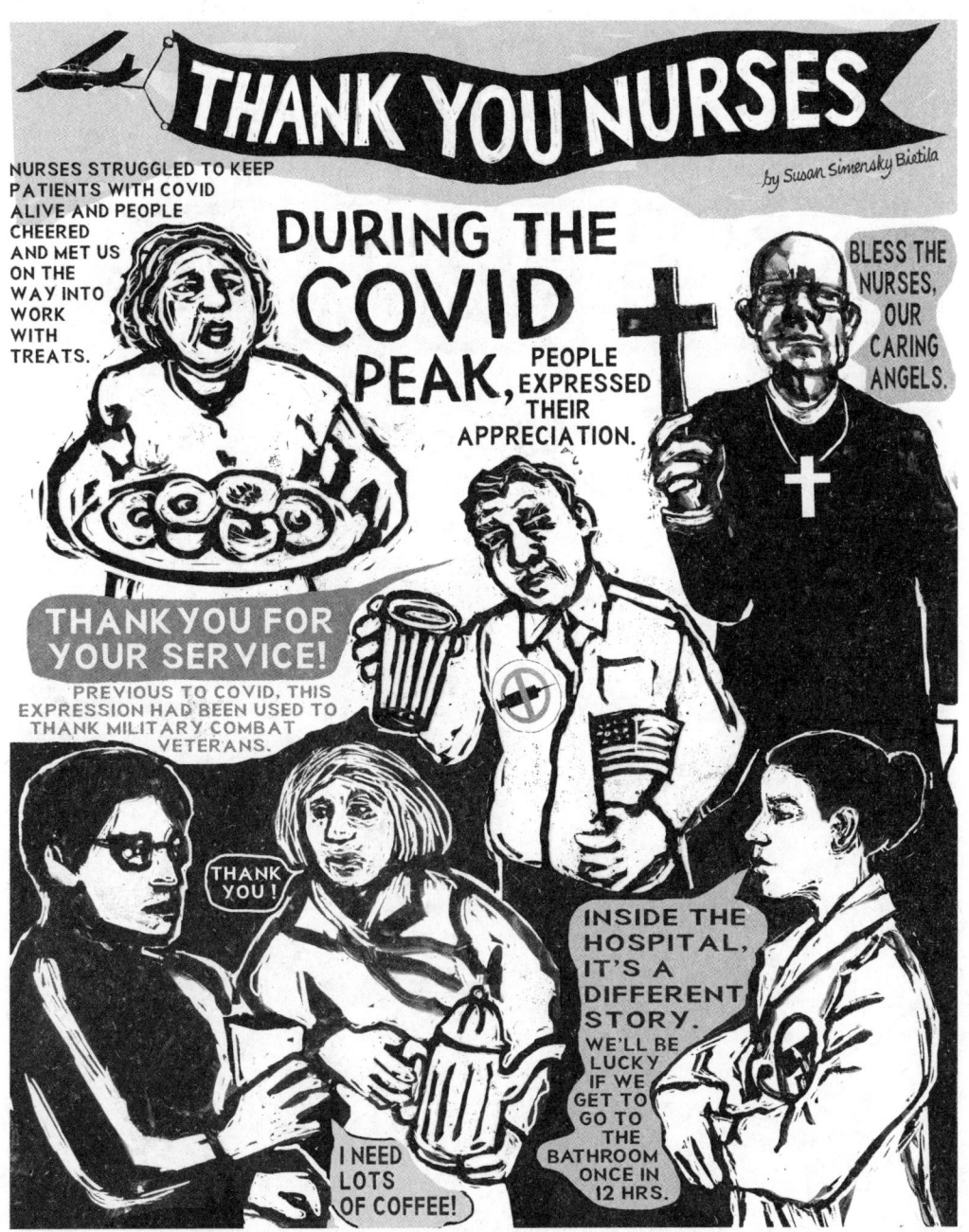

Pages 179–82: Thank You Nurses
And then came COVID—pandemic capitalism. Here is a day in the life, from a nurse's point of view. The story first appeared in *World War 3 Illustrated*, no. 53 (2023), "My Body, Our Rights" issue.

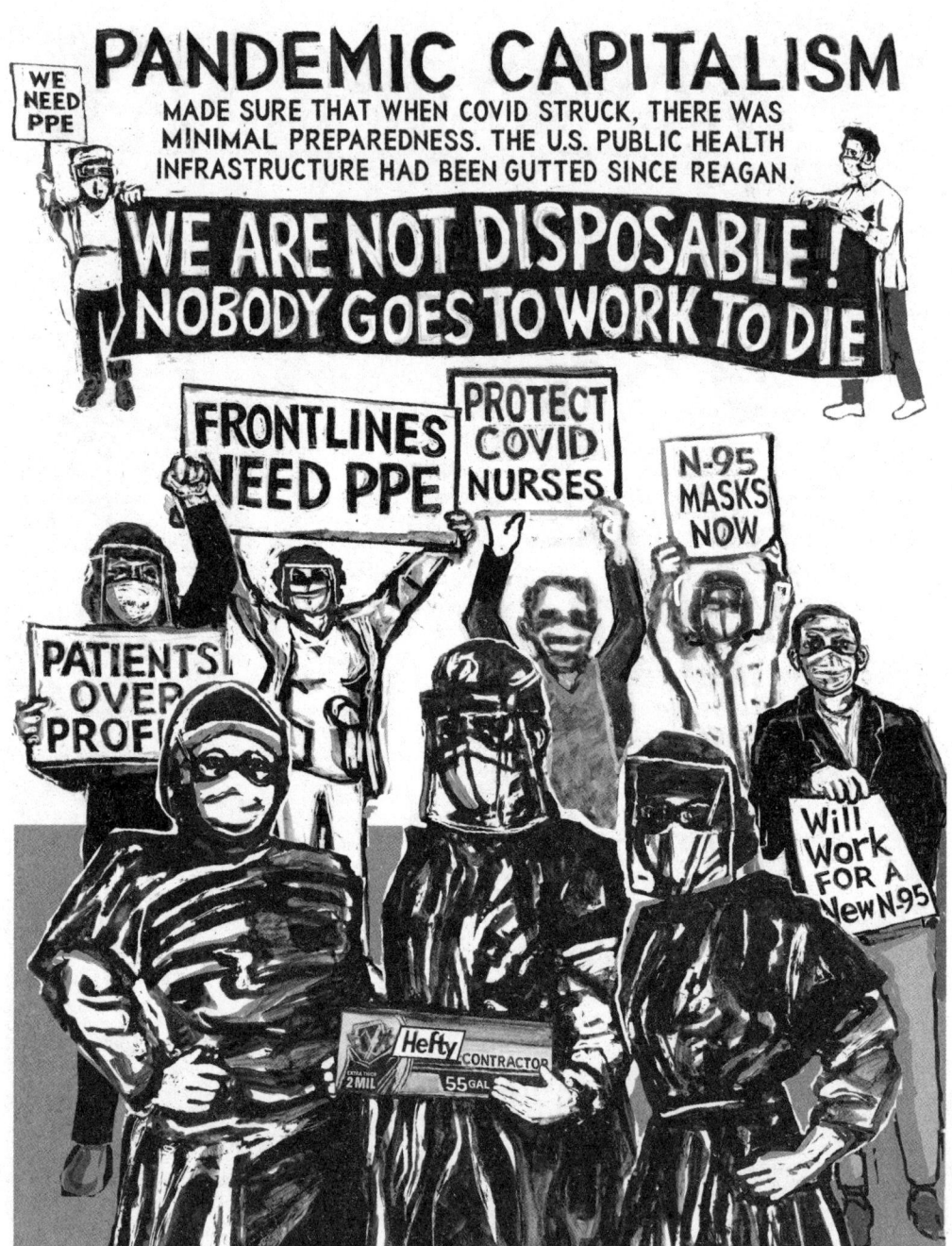

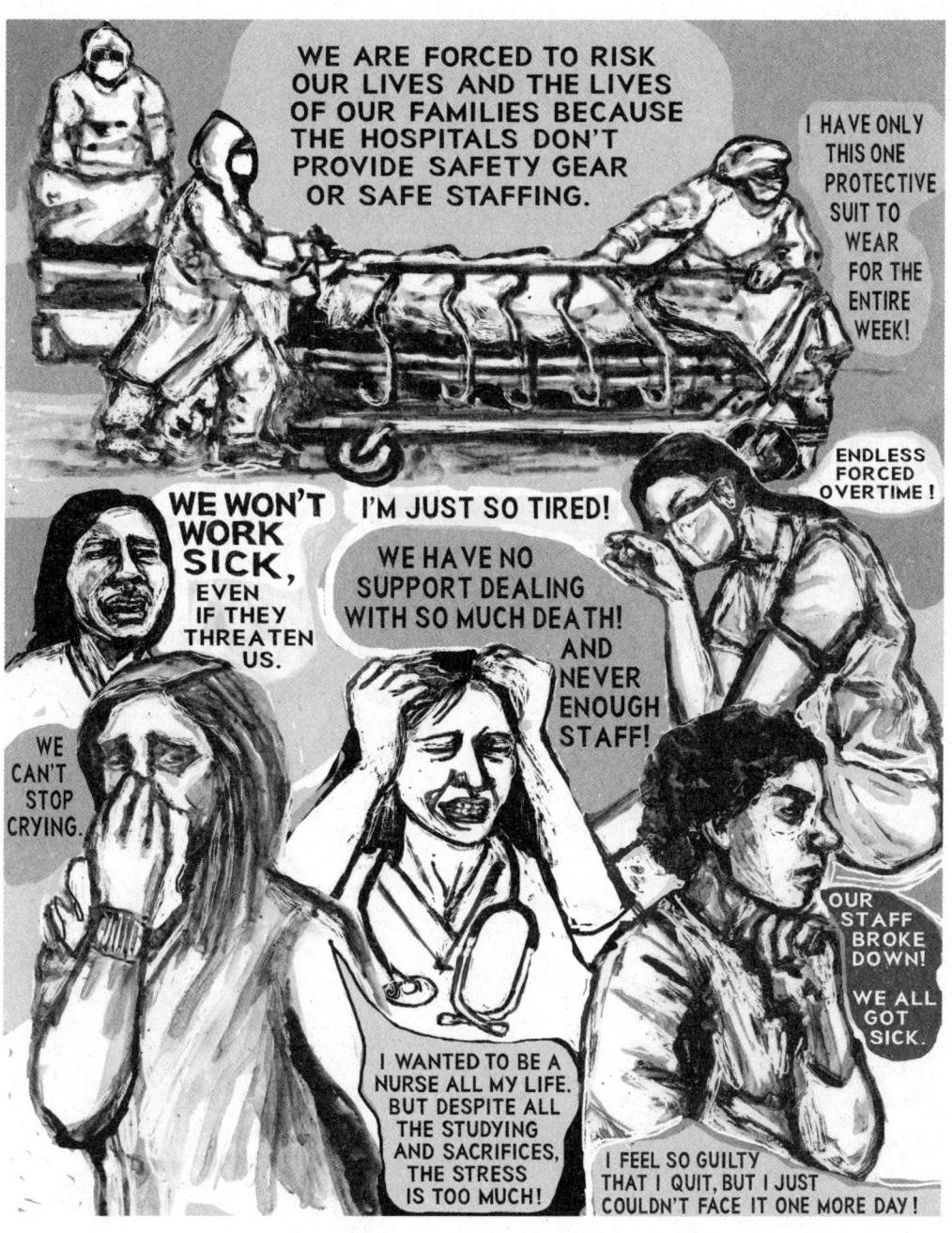

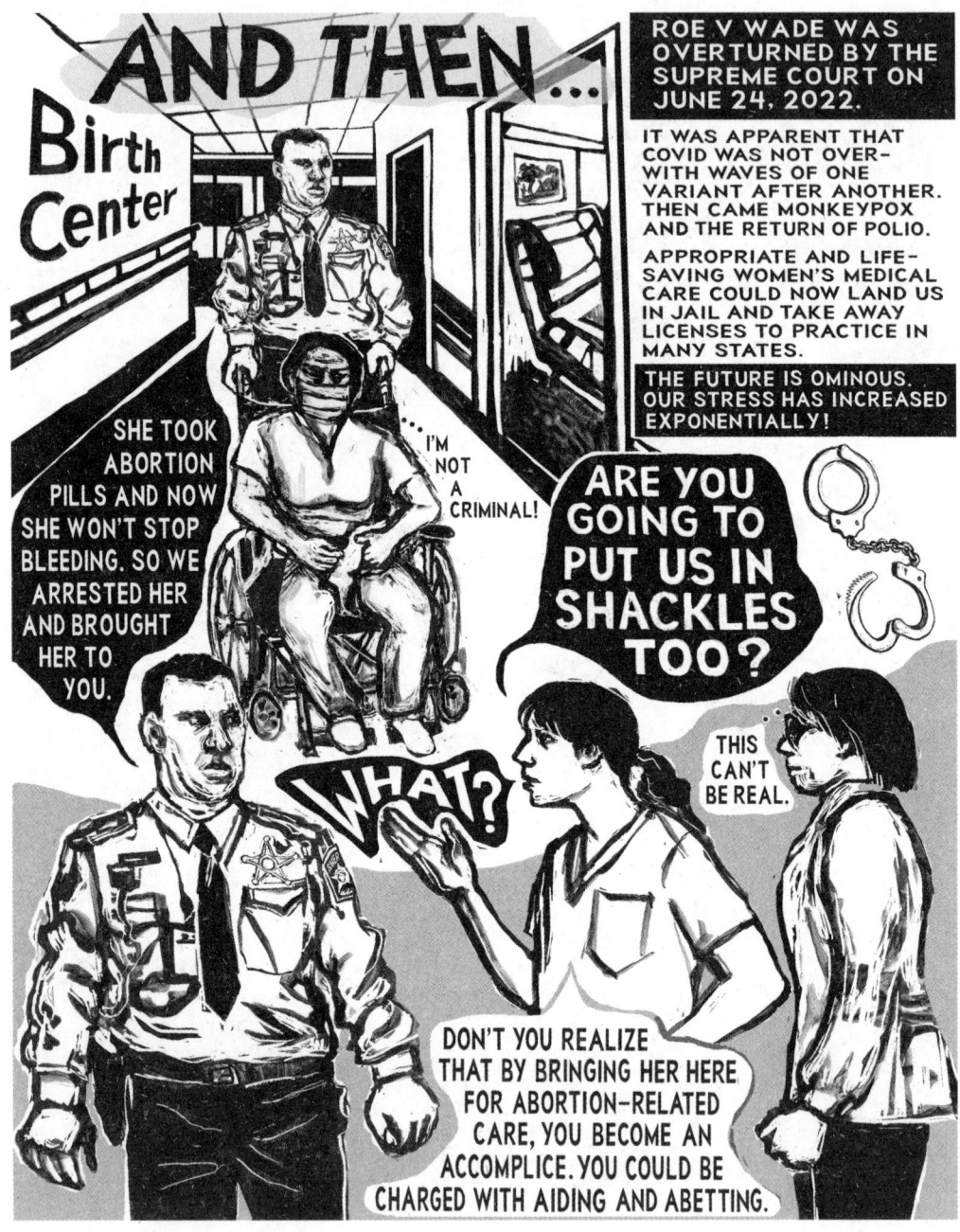

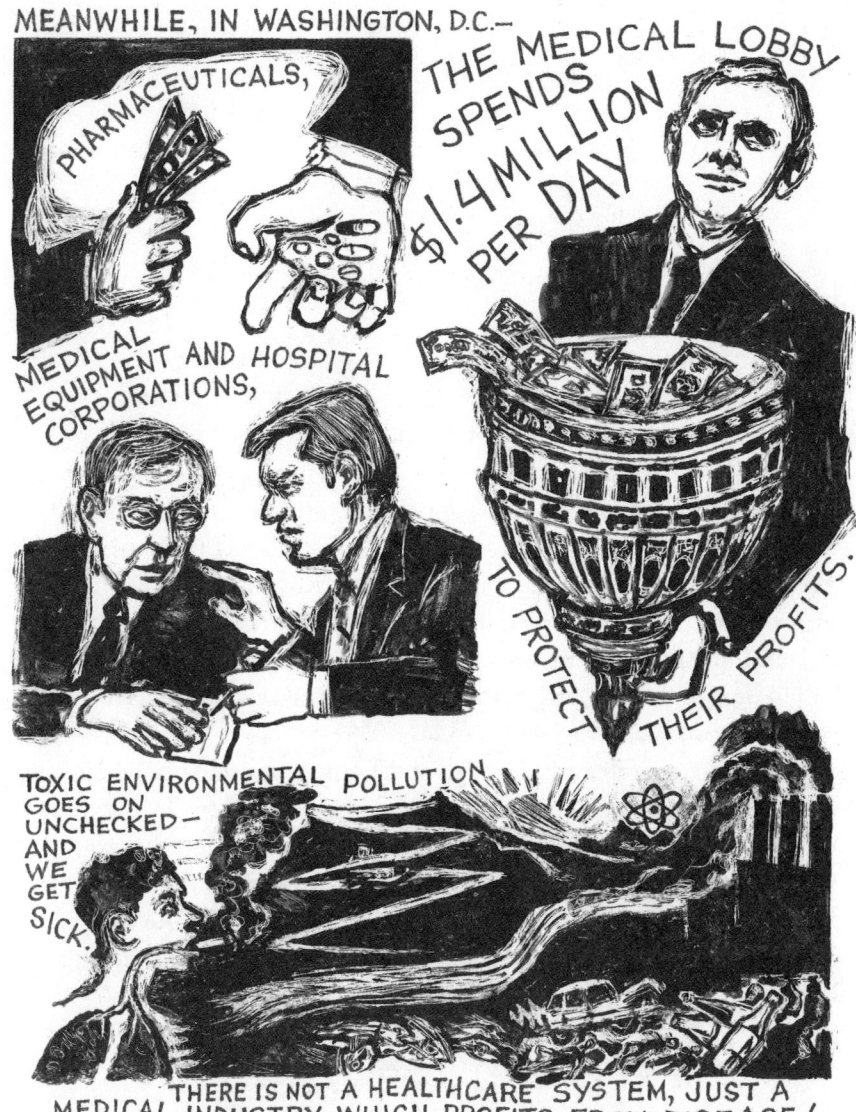

A Page from "American Travesty": A sample of the crisis in the medical care system in ordinary times. It makes no sense to call it health care. The full story is in *World War 3 Illustrated*, no. 40 (2009), "What We Want" issue.

Street Medics

Milwaukee Industrial Workers of the World (IWW) invited me to talk about my experience as a street medic in their series of talks at public libraries. Fifty people showed up. The 2017 program was covered by the *Milwaukee Courier*, an African American community newspaper. The headline was "Street Medic or Simply Being a Good Citizen?" When people who had been medics at Standing Rock returned home, the experience fueled the forming of a local group. We organized a series of trainings taught by medics from regional action medic groups and called our group Forward Action Medics. "Forward" is the Wisconsin state motto.

As police murdered Black men and women here and elsewhere with impunity, the movement against police violence grew in Milwaukee. When George Floyd was murdered in Minneapolis, people surrounded notorious police precincts and then marched for two hundred days. Black Lives Matter street medics were there with their go bags. A vast mutual aid network arose alongside the demonstrations. This was during the height of the COVID pandemic.

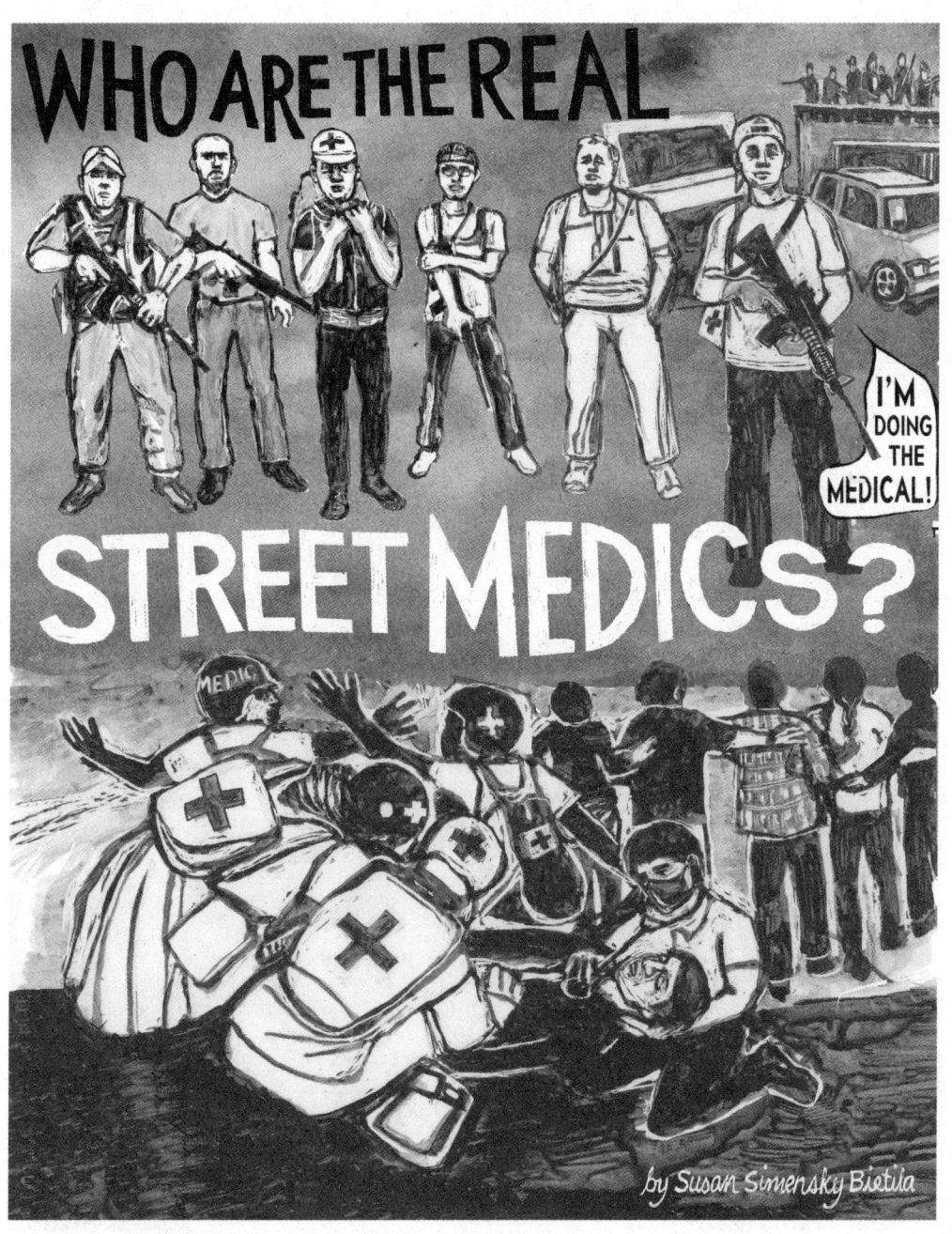

Pages 185–96: Who Are the Real Street Medics?
First appeared in *World War 3 Illustrated*, no. 52 (2020), "Frontiers of Repair" issue.

CIVIL RIGHTS MARCHERS NEEDED MEDICS

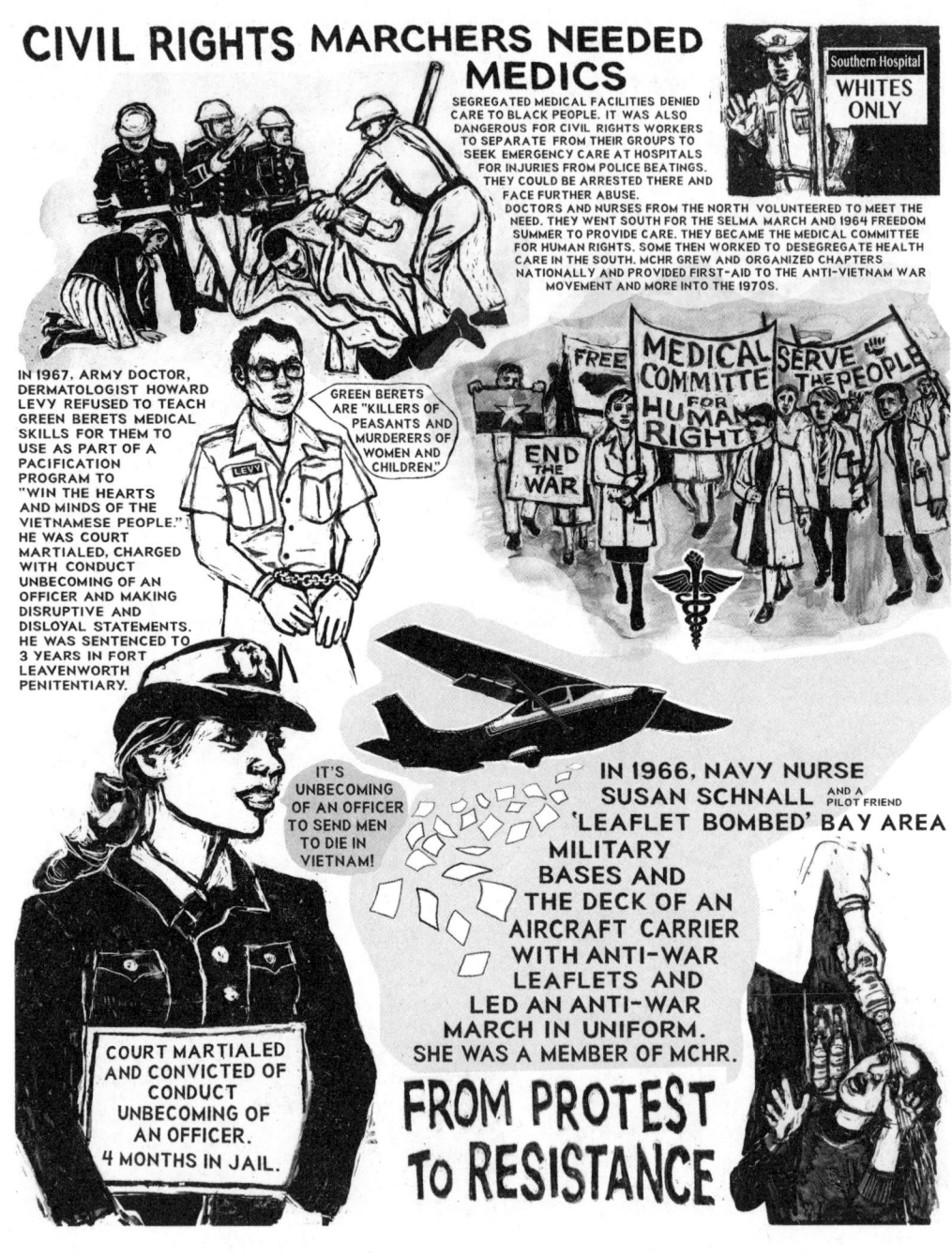

SEGREGATED MEDICAL FACILITIES DENIED CARE TO BLACK PEOPLE. IT WAS ALSO DANGEROUS FOR CIVIL RIGHTS WORKERS TO SEPARATE FROM THEIR GROUPS TO SEEK EMERGENCY CARE AT HOSPITALS FOR INJURIES FROM POLICE BEATINGS. THEY COULD BE ARRESTED THERE AND FACE FURTHER ABUSE.

DOCTORS AND NURSES FROM THE NORTH VOLUNTEERED TO MEET THE NEED. THEY WENT SOUTH FOR THE SELMA MARCH AND 1964 FREEDOM SUMMER TO PROVIDE CARE. THEY BECAME THE MEDICAL COMMITTEE FOR HUMAN RIGHTS. SOME THEN WORKED TO DESEGREGATE HEALTH CARE IN THE SOUTH. MCHR GREW AND ORGANIZED CHAPTERS NATIONALLY AND PROVIDED FIRST-AID TO THE ANTI-VIETNAM WAR MOVEMENT AND MORE INTO THE 1970S.

Southern Hospital
WHITES ONLY

IN 1967, ARMY DOCTOR, DERMATOLOGIST HOWARD LEVY REFUSED TO TEACH GREEN BERETS MEDICAL SKILLS FOR THEM TO USE AS PART OF A PACIFICATION PROGRAM TO "WIN THE HEARTS AND MINDS OF THE VIETNAMESE PEOPLE." HE WAS COURT MARTIALED, CHARGED WITH CONDUCT UNBECOMING OF AN OFFICER AND MAKING DISRUPTIVE AND DISLOYAL STATEMENTS. HE WAS SENTENCED TO 3 YEARS IN FORT LEAVENWORTH PENITENTIARY.

LEVY

GREEN BERETS ARE "KILLERS OF PEASANTS AND MURDERERS OF WOMEN AND CHILDREN."

FREE MEDICAL COMMITTEE FOR HUMAN RIGHTS SERVE THE PEOPLE
END THE WAR

IT'S UNBECOMING OF AN OFFICER TO SEND MEN TO DIE IN VIETNAM!

IN 1966, NAVY NURSE SUSAN SCHNALL AND A PILOT FRIEND 'LEAFLET BOMBED' BAY AREA MILITARY BASES AND THE DECK OF AN AIRCRAFT CARRIER WITH ANTI-WAR LEAFLETS AND LED AN ANTI-WAR MARCH IN UNIFORM. SHE WAS A MEMBER OF MCHR.

COURT MARTIALED AND CONVICTED OF CONDUCT UNBECOMING OF AN OFFICER. 4 MONTHS IN JAIL.

FROM PROTEST To RESISTANCE

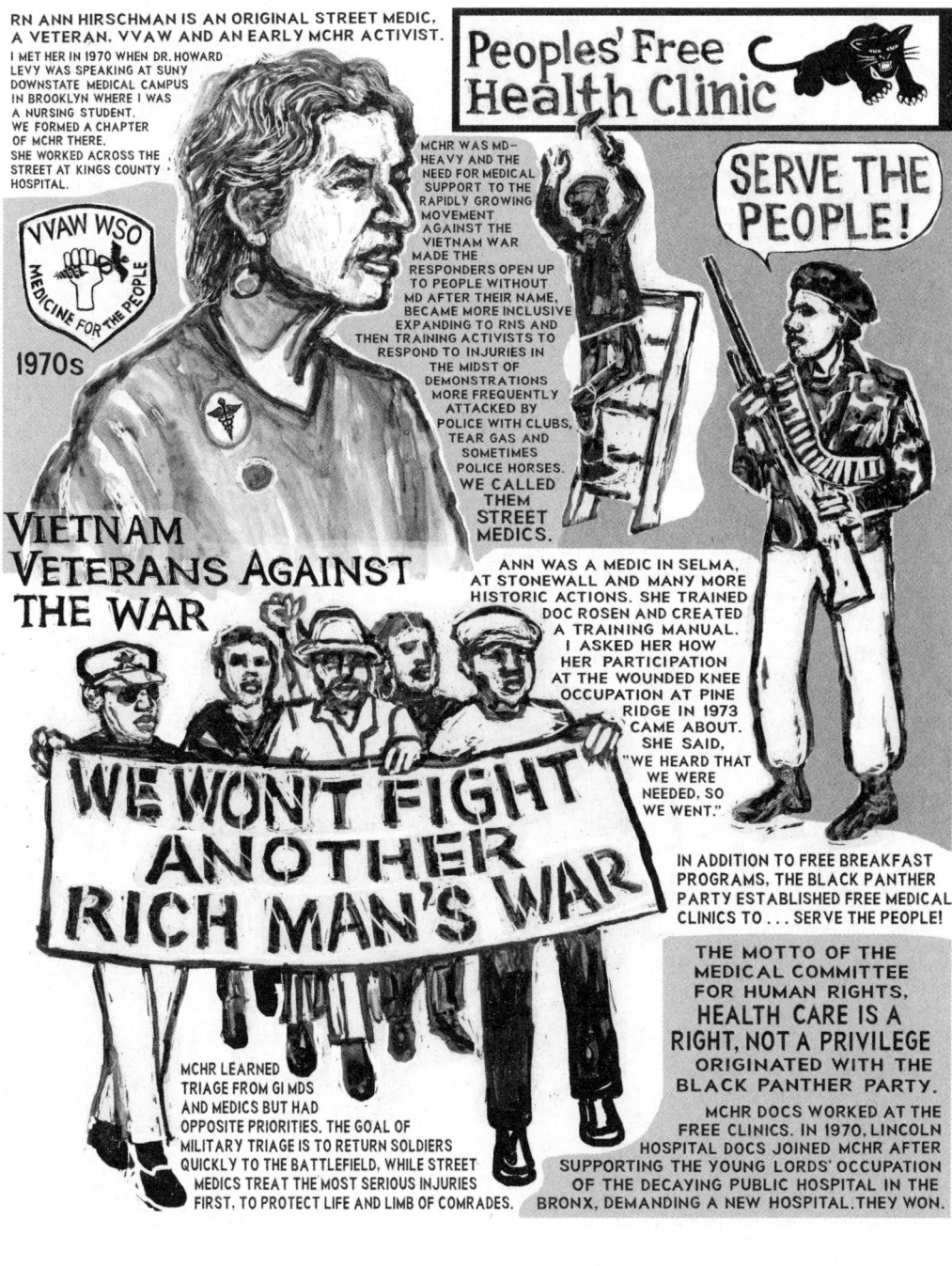

RN ANN HIRSCHMAN IS AN ORIGINAL STREET MEDIC, A VETERAN, VVAW AND AN EARLY MCHR ACTIVIST.

I MET HER IN 1970 WHEN DR. HOWARD LEVY WAS SPEAKING AT SUNY DOWNSTATE MEDICAL CAMPUS IN BROOKLYN WHERE I WAS A NURSING STUDENT. WE FORMED A CHAPTER OF MCHR THERE. SHE WORKED ACROSS THE STREET AT KINGS COUNTY HOSPITAL.

VVAW WSO
MEDICINE FOR THE PEOPLE

1970s

MCHR WAS MD-HEAVY AND THE NEED FOR MEDICAL SUPPORT TO THE RAPIDLY GROWING MOVEMENT AGAINST THE VIETNAM WAR MADE THE RESPONDERS OPEN UP TO PEOPLE WITHOUT MD AFTER THEIR NAME, BECAME MORE INCLUSIVE EXPANDING TO RNS AND THEN TRAINING ACTIVISTS TO RESPOND TO INJURIES IN THE MIDST OF DEMONSTRATIONS MORE FREQUENTLY ATTACKED BY POLICE WITH CLUBS, TEAR GAS AND SOMETIMES POLICE HORSES. WE CALLED THEM STREET MEDICS.

Peoples' Free Health Clinic

SERVE THE PEOPLE!

VIETNAM VETERANS AGAINST THE WAR

ANN WAS A MEDIC IN SELMA, AT STONEWALL AND MANY MORE HISTORIC ACTIONS. SHE TRAINED DOC ROSEN AND CREATED A TRAINING MANUAL. I ASKED HER HOW HER PARTICIPATION AT THE WOUNDED KNEE OCCUPATION AT PINE RIDGE IN 1973 CAME ABOUT. SHE SAID, "WE HEARD THAT WE WERE NEEDED, SO WE WENT."

WE WON'T FIGHT ANOTHER RICH MAN'S WAR

IN ADDITION TO FREE BREAKFAST PROGRAMS, THE BLACK PANTHER PARTY ESTABLISHED FREE MEDICAL CLINICS TO ... SERVE THE PEOPLE!

THE MOTTO OF THE MEDICAL COMMITTEE FOR HUMAN RIGHTS, HEALTH CARE IS A RIGHT, NOT A PRIVILEGE ORIGINATED WITH THE BLACK PANTHER PARTY.

MCHR DOCS WORKED AT THE FREE CLINICS. IN 1970, LINCOLN HOSPITAL DOCS JOINED MCHR AFTER SUPPORTING THE YOUNG LORDS' OCCUPATION OF THE DECAYING PUBLIC HOSPITAL IN THE BRONX, DEMANDING A NEW HOSPITAL. THEY WON.

MCHR LEARNED TRIAGE FROM GI MDS AND MEDICS BUT HAD OPPOSITE PRIORITIES. THE GOAL OF MILITARY TRIAGE IS TO RETURN SOLDIERS QUICKLY TO THE BATTLEFIELD, WHILE STREET MEDICS TREAT THE MOST SERIOUS INJURIES FIRST, TO PROTECT LIFE AND LIMB OF COMRADES.

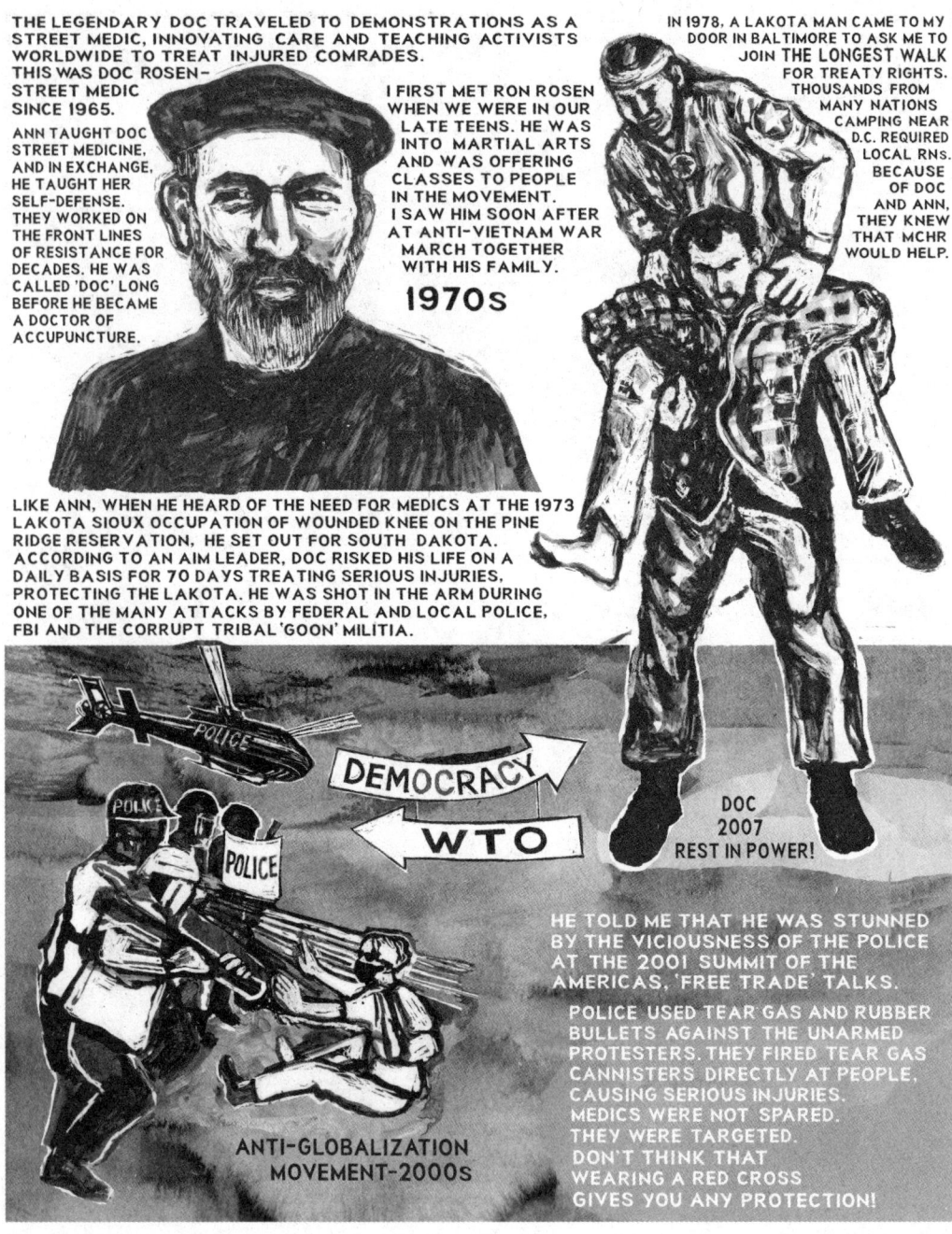

THE LEGENDARY DOC TRAVELED TO DEMONSTRATIONS AS A STREET MEDIC, INNOVATING CARE AND TEACHING ACTIVISTS WORLDWIDE TO TREAT INJURED COMRADES. THIS WAS DOC ROSEN- STREET MEDIC SINCE 1965.

ANN TAUGHT DOC STREET MEDICINE, AND IN EXCHANGE, HE TAUGHT HER SELF-DEFENSE. THEY WORKED ON THE FRONT LINES OF RESISTANCE FOR DECADES. HE WAS CALLED 'DOC' LONG BEFORE HE BECAME A DOCTOR OF ACCUPUNCTURE.

I FIRST MET RON ROSEN WHEN WE WERE IN OUR LATE TEENS. HE WAS INTO MARTIAL ARTS AND WAS OFFERING CLASSES TO PEOPLE IN THE MOVEMENT. I SAW HIM SOON AFTER AT ANTI-VIETNAM WAR MARCH TOGETHER WITH HIS FAMILY.

1970s

IN 1978, A LAKOTA MAN CAME TO MY DOOR IN BALTIMORE TO ASK ME TO JOIN THE LONGEST WALK FOR TREATY RIGHTS. THOUSANDS FROM MANY NATIONS CAMPING NEAR D.C. REQUIRED LOCAL RNs. BECAUSE OF DOC AND ANN, THEY KNEW THAT MCHR WOULD HELP.

LIKE ANN, WHEN HE HEARD OF THE NEED FOR MEDICS AT THE 1973 LAKOTA SIOUX OCCUPATION OF WOUNDED KNEE ON THE PINE RIDGE RESERVATION, HE SET OUT FOR SOUTH DAKOTA. ACCORDING TO AN AIM LEADER, DOC RISKED HIS LIFE ON A DAILY BASIS FOR 70 DAYS TREATING SERIOUS INJURIES, PROTECTING THE LAKOTA. HE WAS SHOT IN THE ARM DURING ONE OF THE MANY ATTACKS BY FEDERAL AND LOCAL POLICE, FBI AND THE CORRUPT TRIBAL 'GOON' MILITIA.

DEMOCRACY

WTO

DOC 2007 REST IN POWER!

POLICE

POLICE

ANTI-GLOBALIZATION MOVEMENT-2000s

HE TOLD ME THAT HE WAS STUNNED BY THE VICIOUSNESS OF THE POLICE AT THE 2001 SUMMIT OF THE AMERICAS, 'FREE TRADE' TALKS.

POLICE USED TEAR GAS AND RUBBER BULLETS AGAINST THE UNARMED PROTESTERS. THEY FIRED TEAR GAS CANNISTERS DIRECTLY AT PEOPLE, CAUSING SERIOUS INJURIES. MEDICS WERE NOT SPARED. THEY WERE TARGETED. DON'T THINK THAT WEARING A RED CROSS GIVES YOU ANY PROTECTION!

IN 2016, MEDICS RETURNED HOME TO MILWAUKEE FROM THE HISTORIC INDIGENOUS STANDING ROCK OCCUPATION TO PROTECT THE WATER AND ALL LIFE FROM THE DAKOTA ACCESS TAR SANDS OIL PIPELINE. THERE HAD BEEN TALK ABOUT STARTING A STREET MEDIC GROUP HERE FOR A YEAR OR TWO. NOW THERE WERE PEOPLE WHO HAD REAL EXPERIENCE. THEY HAD WORKED WITH ACTION MEDIC MENTORS AND WERE NOW READY TO GET GOING. A 20-HR MEDIC TRAINING WAS ORGANIZED. WORD SPREAD QUICKLY AND THE TRAINING FILLED.

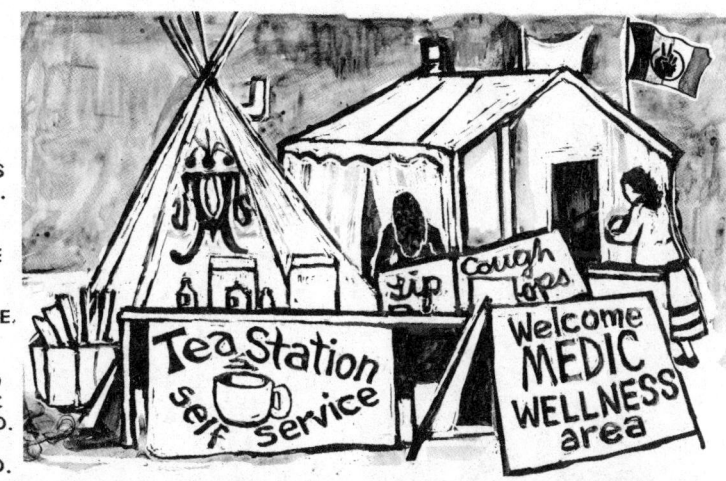

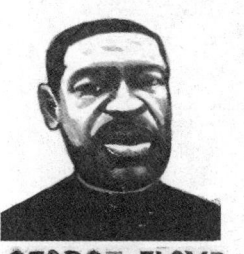

GEORGE FLOYD

WHEN GEORGE FLOYD WAS MURDERED BY POLICE IN MINNEAPOLIS, OUTRAGED MILWAUKEANS—BLACKS AND OTHERS—GATHERED AT THE NOTORIOUS 5TH PRECINCT. THE FIRST NIGHT, THERE WAS SOME PROPERTY DESTRUCTION NEARBY. POLICE FORTIFIED THE PRECINCT, POSTED OFFICERS WITH AUTOMATIC WEAPONS ON THE ROOF AND BROUGHT OUT ARMORED VEHICLES. THE NATIONAL GUARD WAS MOBILIZED. BUT AFTER THE FIRST FEW DAYS, AN ORGANIZED RESPONSE CONSCIOUSLY ECHOED THE ICONIC OPEN-HOUSING MARCHES OF THE 1960s. 200 DAYS OF MARCHES DEMANDING **DEFUND THE POLICE** BEGAN.

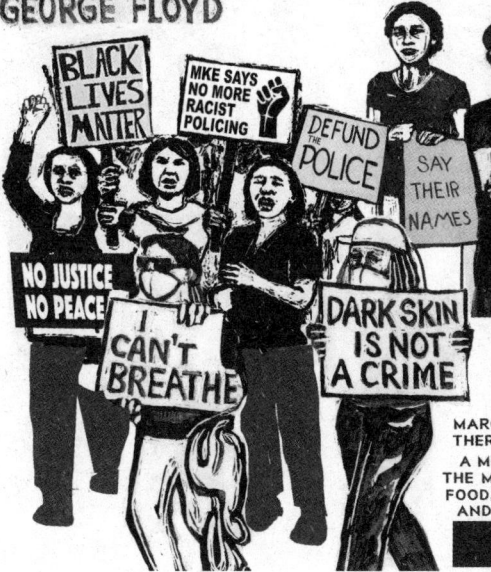

AND MARCH THEY DID—EVERY EVENING. THERE WAS NO ROAD MAP. HUNDREDS OF PEOPLE WALKING, FOLLOWED BY A CAR CARAVAN, PEOPLE HANGING OUT OF THE CAR WINDOW OR SUN ROOF, FOR MILES THROUGH EVERY NEIGHBORHOOD OF THE CITY AND INTO THE SUBURBS. PEOPLE JOINED IN AS THE MARCH WENT BY—ALL THIS DURING COVID. STREET MEDICS WERE THERE FOR THE BLACK LIVES MATTER MOVEMENT.

A MUTUAL AID NETWORK WAS CREATED TO MEET THE NEEDS OF THE MARCHERS—A HUGE COORDINATED SUPPLY CHAIN OF WATER, FOOD, MEDICAL SUPPLIES AND ALSO BULLHORNS, A P.A. SYSTEM, AND EVEN A PORTABLE STAGE. THERE WAS ALSO A BAIL FUND.

THIS COLLABORATION WAS A GLIMPSE OF THE FUTURE WE WANT AND NEED.

189

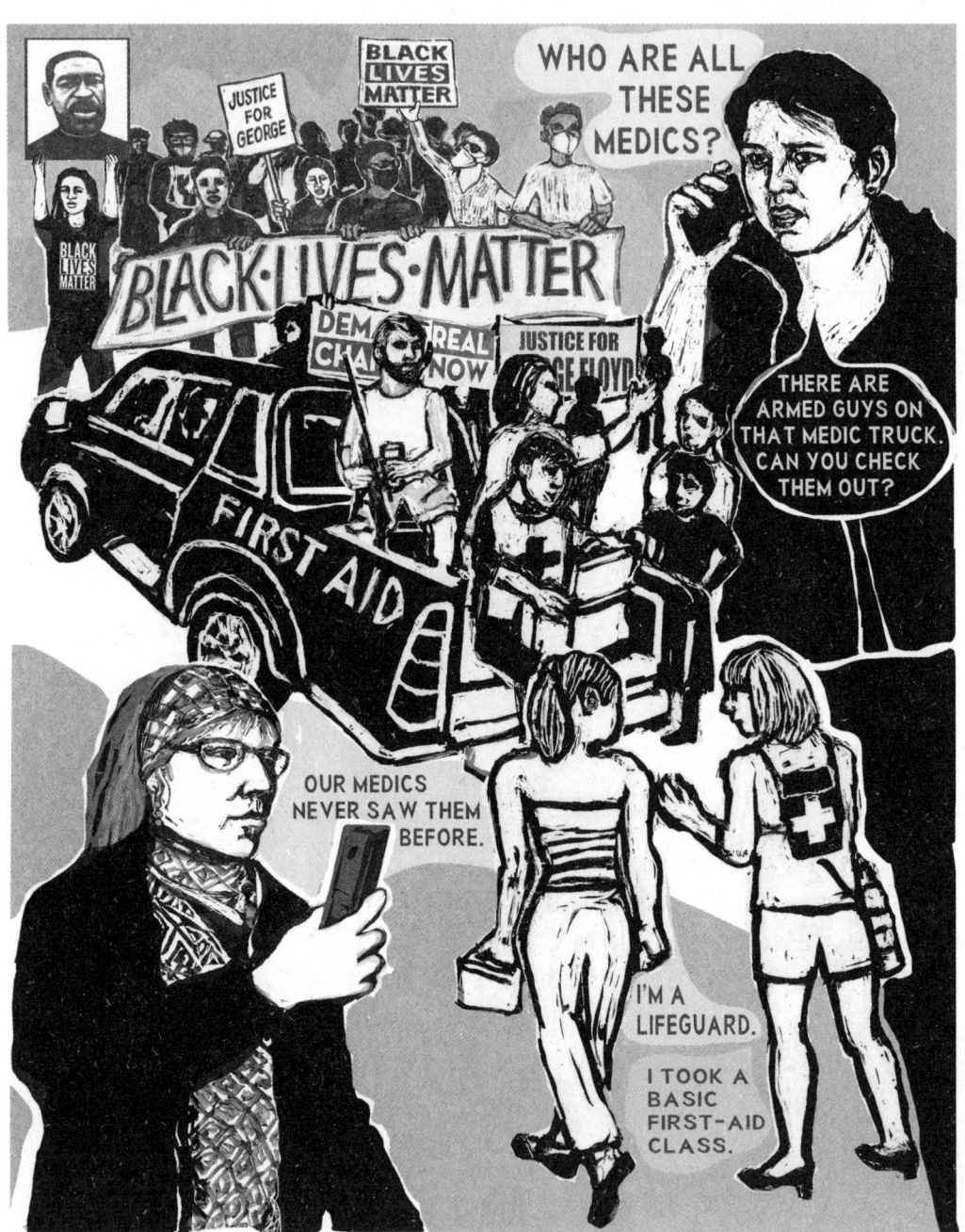

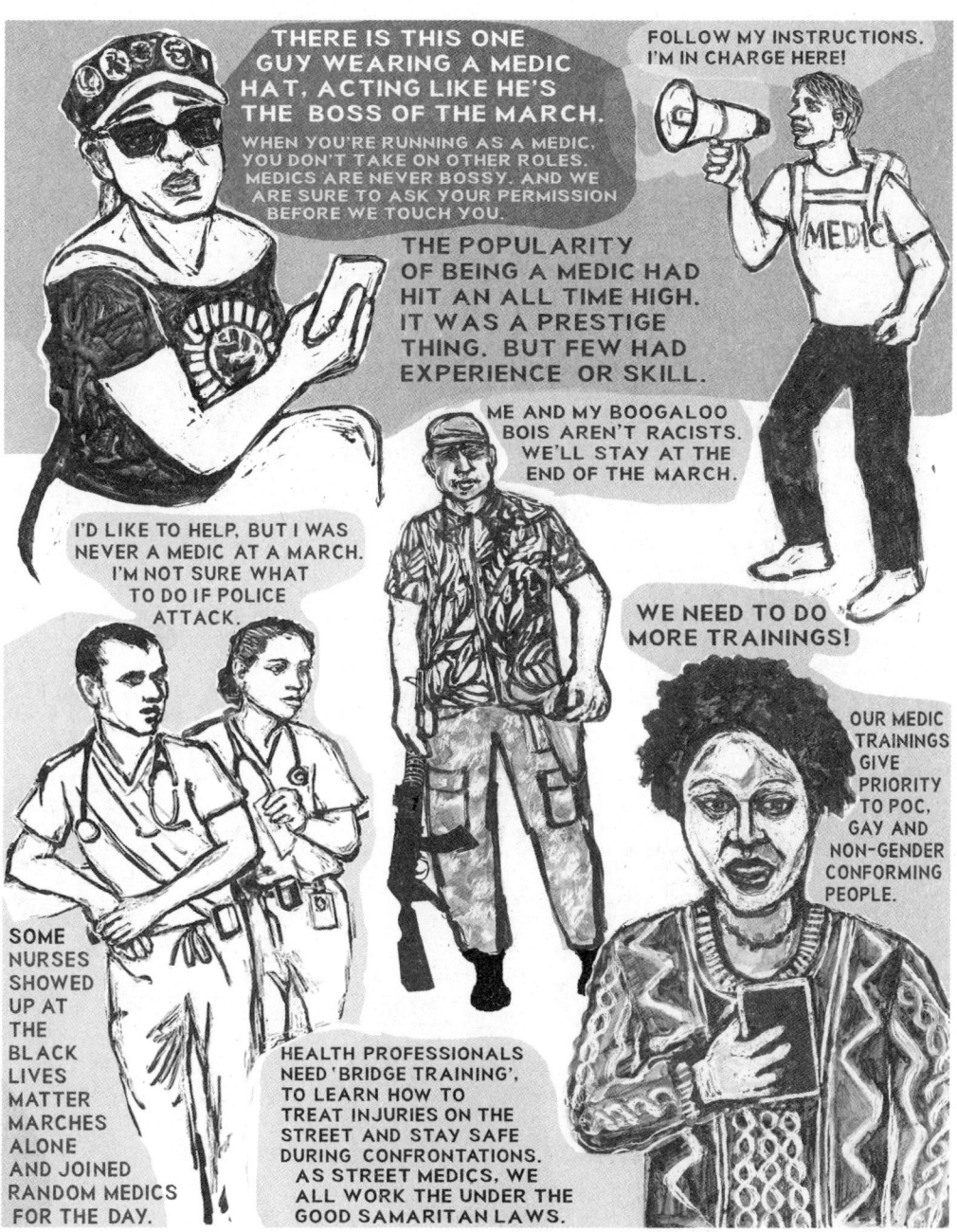

7 BULLETS IN THE BACK

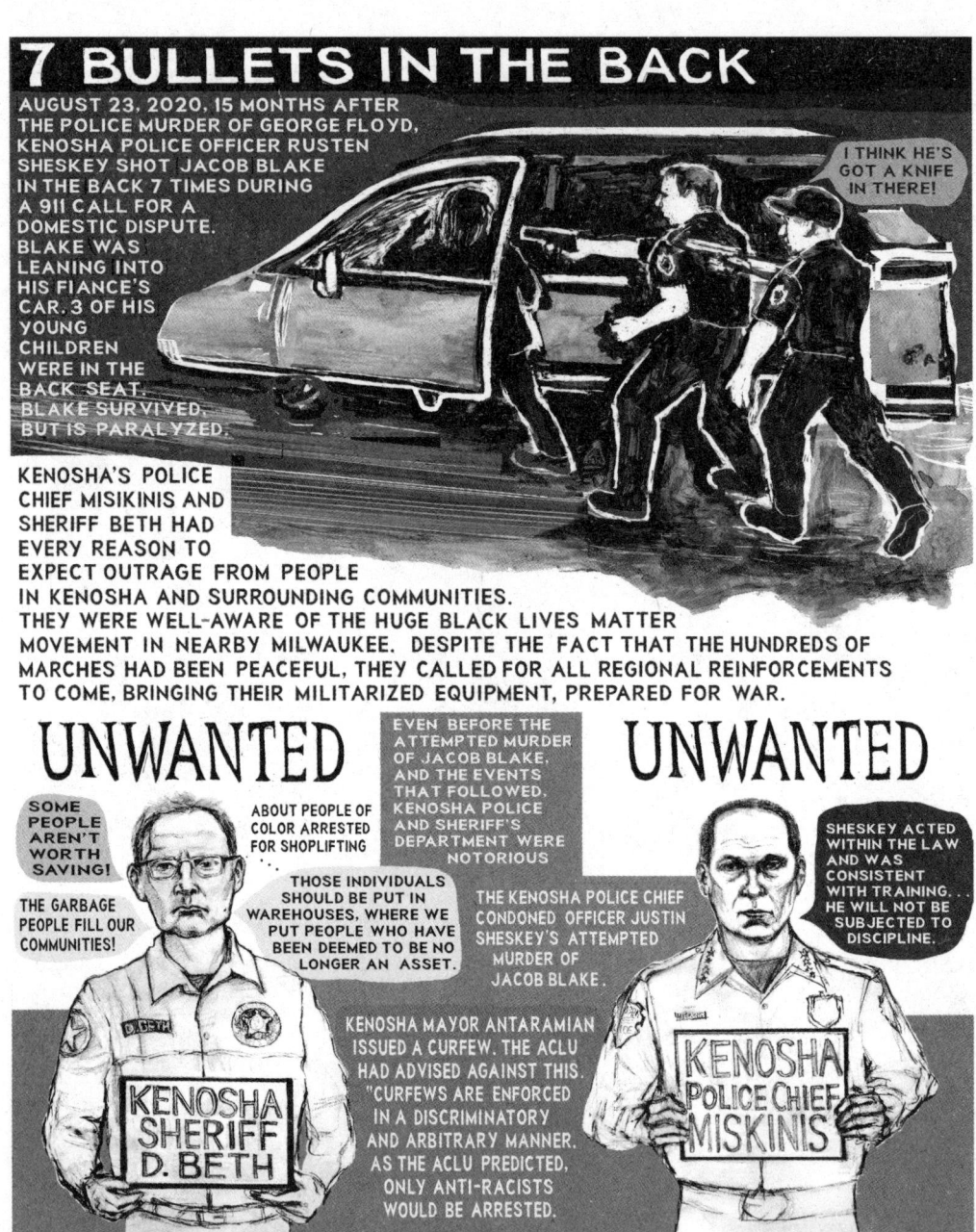

AUGUST 23, 2020, 15 MONTHS AFTER THE POLICE MURDER OF GEORGE FLOYD, KENOSHA POLICE OFFICER RUSTEN SHESKEY SHOT JACOB BLAKE IN THE BACK 7 TIMES DURING A 911 CALL FOR A DOMESTIC DISPUTE. BLAKE WAS LEANING INTO HIS FIANCE'S CAR. 3 OF HIS YOUNG CHILDREN WERE IN THE BACK SEAT. BLAKE SURVIVED, BUT IS PARALYZED.

I THINK HE'S GOT A KNIFE IN THERE!

KENOSHA'S POLICE CHIEF MISIKINIS AND SHERIFF BETH HAD EVERY REASON TO EXPECT OUTRAGE FROM PEOPLE IN KENOSHA AND SURROUNDING COMMUNITIES. THEY WERE WELL-AWARE OF THE HUGE BLACK LIVES MATTER MOVEMENT IN NEARBY MILWAUKEE. DESPITE THE FACT THAT THE HUNDREDS OF MARCHES HAD BEEN PEACEFUL, THEY CALLED FOR ALL REGIONAL REINFORCEMENTS TO COME, BRINGING THEIR MILITARIZED EQUIPMENT, PREPARED FOR WAR.

UNWANTED

SOME PEOPLE AREN'T WORTH SAVING!

THE GARBAGE PEOPLE FILL OUR COMMUNITIES!

ABOUT PEOPLE OF COLOR ARRESTED FOR SHOPLIFTING

THOSE INDIVIDUALS SHOULD BE PUT IN WAREHOUSES, WHERE WE PUT PEOPLE WHO HAVE BEEN DEEMED TO BE NO LONGER AN ASSET.

KENOSHA SHERIFF D. BETH

EVEN BEFORE THE ATTEMPTED MURDER OF JACOB BLAKE, AND THE EVENTS THAT FOLLOWED, KENOSHA POLICE AND SHERIFF'S DEPARTMENT WERE NOTORIOUS

THE KENOSHA POLICE CHIEF CONDONED OFFICER JUSTIN SHESKEY'S ATTEMPTED MURDER OF JACOB BLAKE.

KENOSHA MAYOR ANTARAMIAN ISSUED A CURFEW. THE ACLU HAD ADVISED AGAINST THIS. "CURFEWS ARE ENFORCED IN A DISCRIMINATORY AND ARBITRARY MANNER. AS THE ACLU PREDICTED, ONLY ANTI-RACISTS WOULD BE ARRESTED.

UNWANTED

SHESKEY ACTED WITHIN THE LAW AND WAS CONSISTENT WITH TRAINING... HE WILL NOT BE SUBJECTED TO DISCIPLINE.

KENOSHA POLICE CHIEF MISKINIS

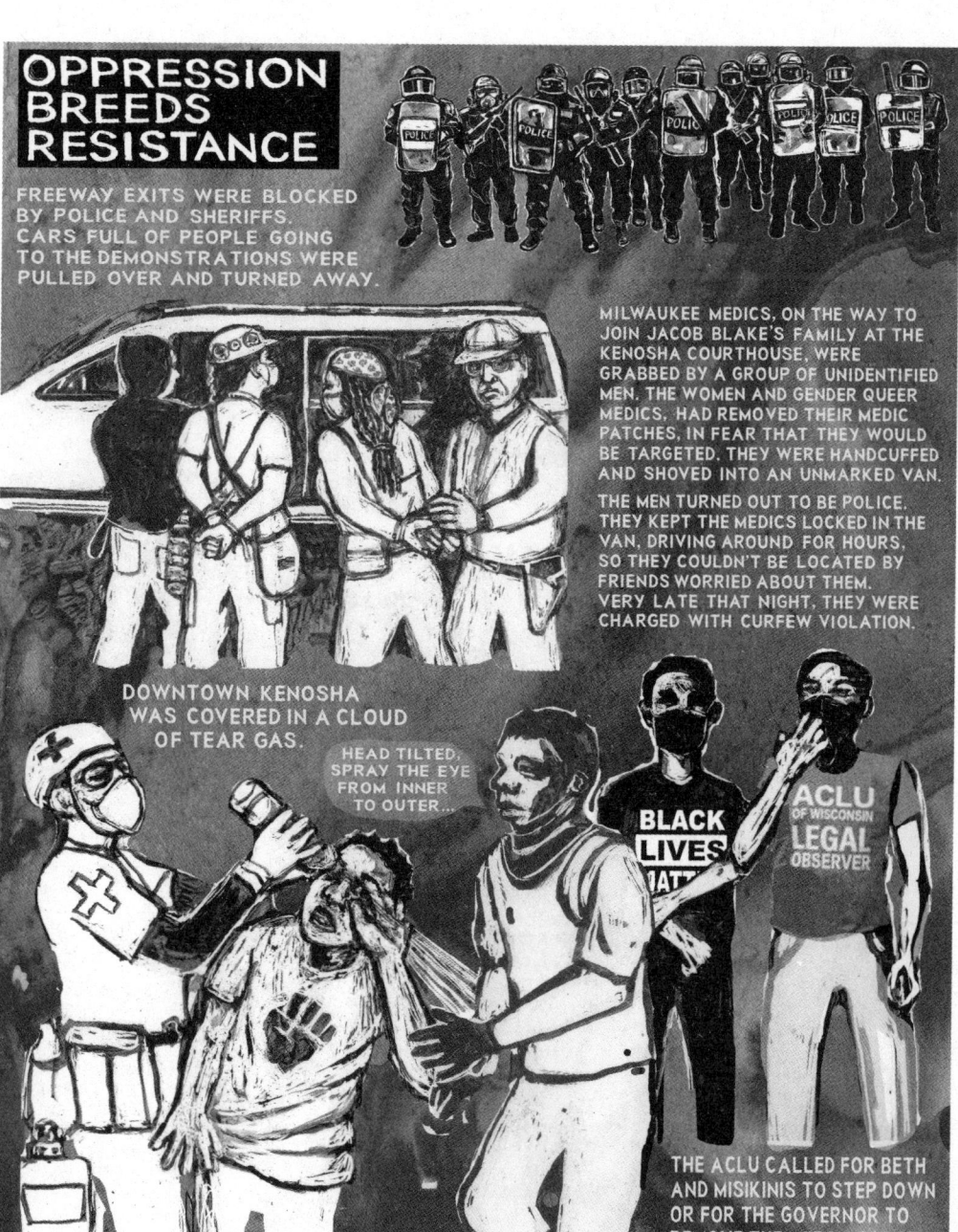

OPPRESSION BREEDS RESISTANCE

FREEWAY EXITS WERE BLOCKED BY POLICE AND SHERIFFS. CARS FULL OF PEOPLE GOING TO THE DEMONSTRATIONS WERE PULLED OVER AND TURNED AWAY.

MILWAUKEE MEDICS, ON THE WAY TO JOIN JACOB BLAKE'S FAMILY AT THE KENOSHA COURTHOUSE, WERE GRABBED BY A GROUP OF UNIDENTIFIED MEN. THE WOMEN AND GENDER QUEER MEDICS, HAD REMOVED THEIR MEDIC PATCHES, IN FEAR THAT THEY WOULD BE TARGETED. THEY WERE HANDCUFFED AND SHOVED INTO AN UNMARKED VAN.

THE MEN TURNED OUT TO BE POLICE. THEY KEPT THE MEDICS LOCKED IN THE VAN, DRIVING AROUND FOR HOURS, SO THEY COULDN'T BE LOCATED BY FRIENDS WORRIED ABOUT THEM. VERY LATE THAT NIGHT, THEY WERE CHARGED WITH CURFEW VIOLATION.

DOWNTOWN KENOSHA WAS COVERED IN A CLOUD OF TEAR GAS.

HEAD TILTED, SPRAY THE EYE FROM INNER TO OUTER...

BLACK LIVES MATTER

ACLU OF WISCONSIN LEGAL OBSERVER

THE ACLU CALLED FOR BETH AND MISIKINIS TO STEP DOWN OR FOR THE GOVERNOR TO REMOVE THEM FROM OFFICE.

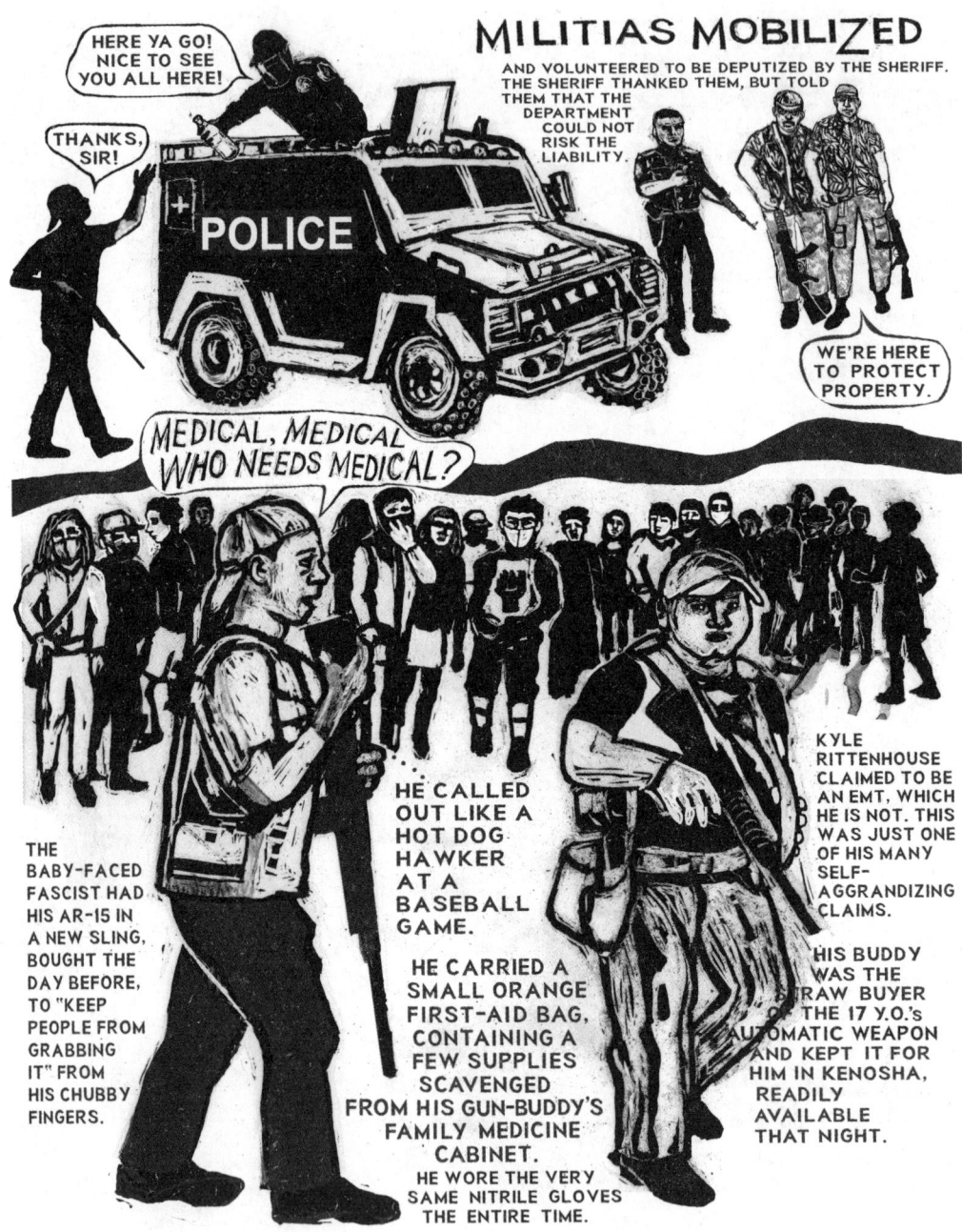

MILITIAS MOBILIZED

AND VOLUNTEERED TO BE DEPUTIZED BY THE SHERIFF. THE SHERIFF THANKED THEM, BUT TOLD THEM THAT THE DEPARTMENT COULD NOT RISK THE LIABILITY.

HERE YA GO! NICE TO SEE YOU ALL HERE!

THANKS, SIR!

WE'RE HERE TO PROTECT PROPERTY.

POLICE

MEDICAL, MEDICAL WHO NEEDS MEDICAL?

THE BABY-FACED FASCIST HAD HIS AR-15 IN A NEW SLING, BOUGHT THE DAY BEFORE, TO "KEEP PEOPLE FROM GRABBING IT" FROM HIS CHUBBY FINGERS.

HE CALLED OUT LIKE A HOT DOG HAWKER AT A BASEBALL GAME.

HE CARRIED A SMALL ORANGE FIRST-AID BAG, CONTAINING A FEW SUPPLIES SCAVENGED FROM HIS GUN-BUDDY'S FAMILY MEDICINE CABINET.

HE WORE THE VERY SAME NITRILE GLOVES THE ENTIRE TIME.

KYLE RITTENHOUSE CLAIMED TO BE AN EMT, WHICH HE IS NOT. THIS WAS JUST ONE OF HIS MANY SELF-AGGRANDIZING CLAIMS.

HIS BUDDY WAS THE STRAW BUYER OF THE 17 Y.O.'s AUTOMATIC WEAPON AND KEPT IT FOR HIM IN KENOSHA, READILY AVAILABLE THAT NIGHT.

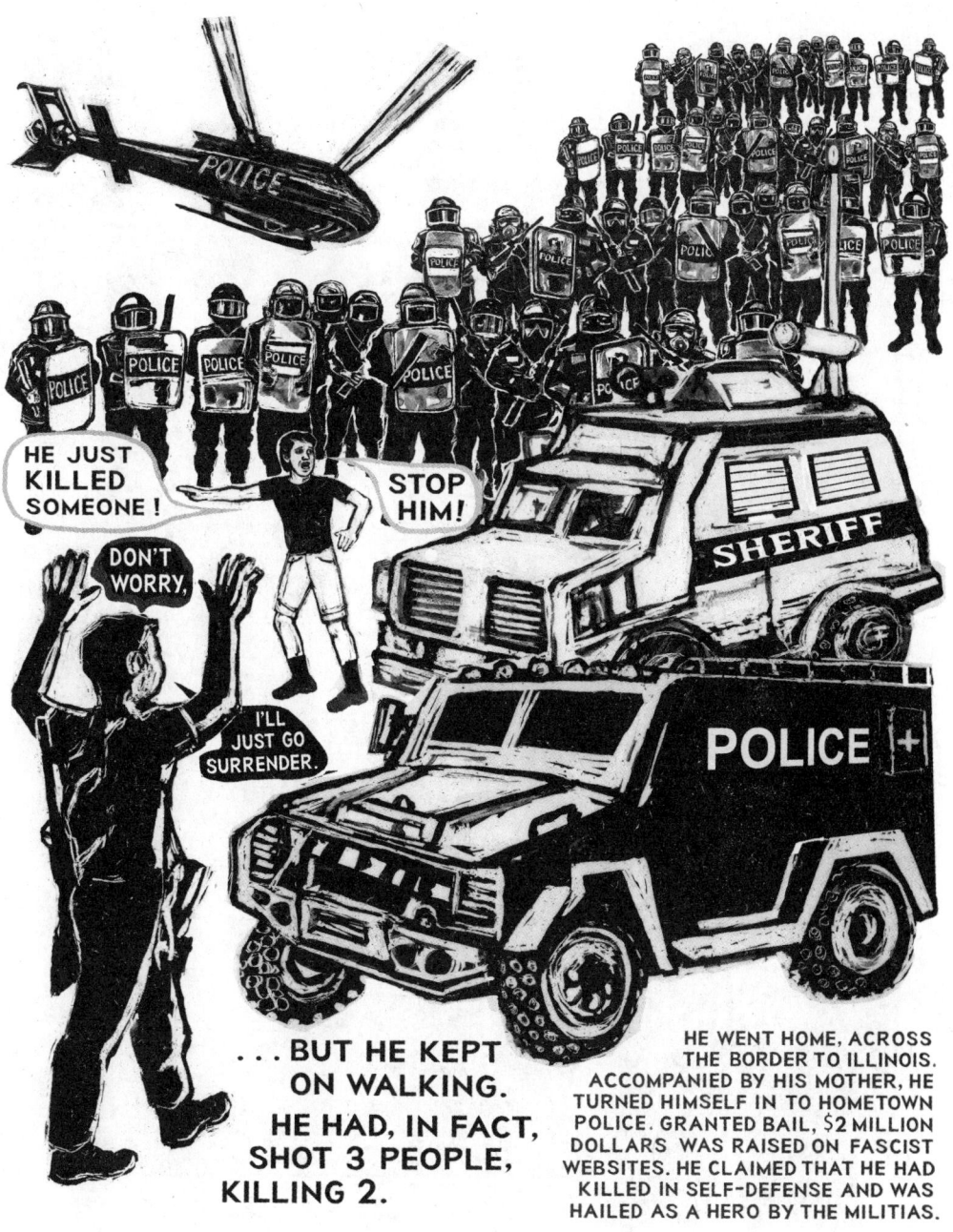

...BUT HE KEPT ON WALKING.

HE HAD, IN FACT, SHOT 3 PEOPLE, KILLING 2.

HE WENT HOME, ACROSS THE BORDER TO ILLINOIS. ACCOMPANIED BY HIS MOTHER, HE TURNED HIMSELF IN TO HOMETOWN POLICE. GRANTED BAIL, $2 MILLION DOLLARS WAS RAISED ON FASCIST WEBSITES. HE CLAIMED THAT HE HAD KILLED IN SELF-DEFENSE AND WAS HAILED AS A HERO BY THE MILITIAS.

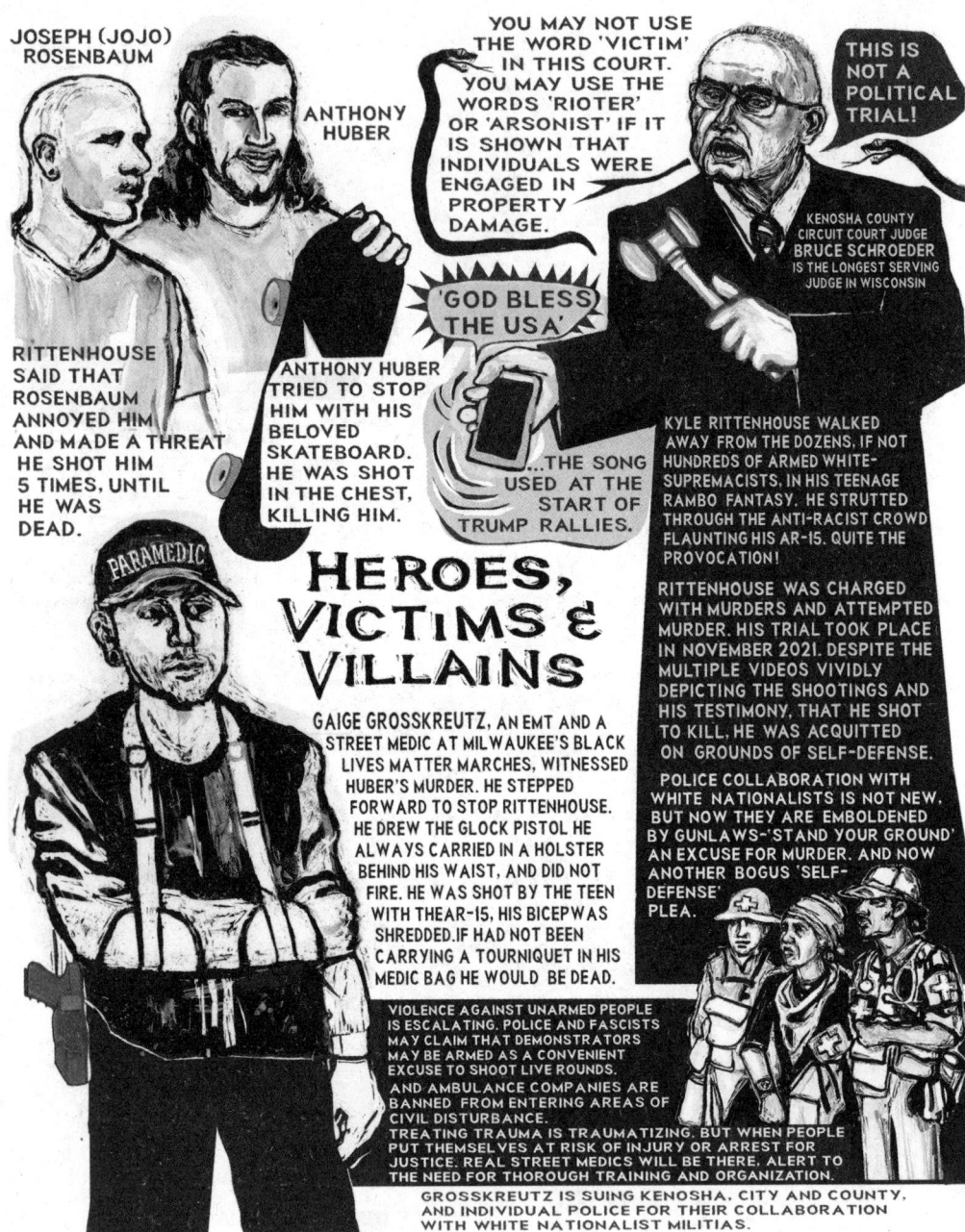

Foreshadowings of Fascism

Brazilian educator Paulo Freire taught adults literacy by having students analyze personal experience and connect it to the causality of oppression. Collective power comes from putting personal experience into the social context and revealing the root causes we must overturn, together. The 1970s women's movement consciousness-raising saying "the personal is political" was originally much the same. The women's liberation movement won victories that gave women more power over pregnancy and contraception. As a nurse, I was on the front lines of resisting retrogressive control of women's bodies. But a regime of fascist misogyny is attacking these gains and has instituted dystopic retribution. In response, I drew "An Unshackled Birth"—a true story of how nurses stand up for women.

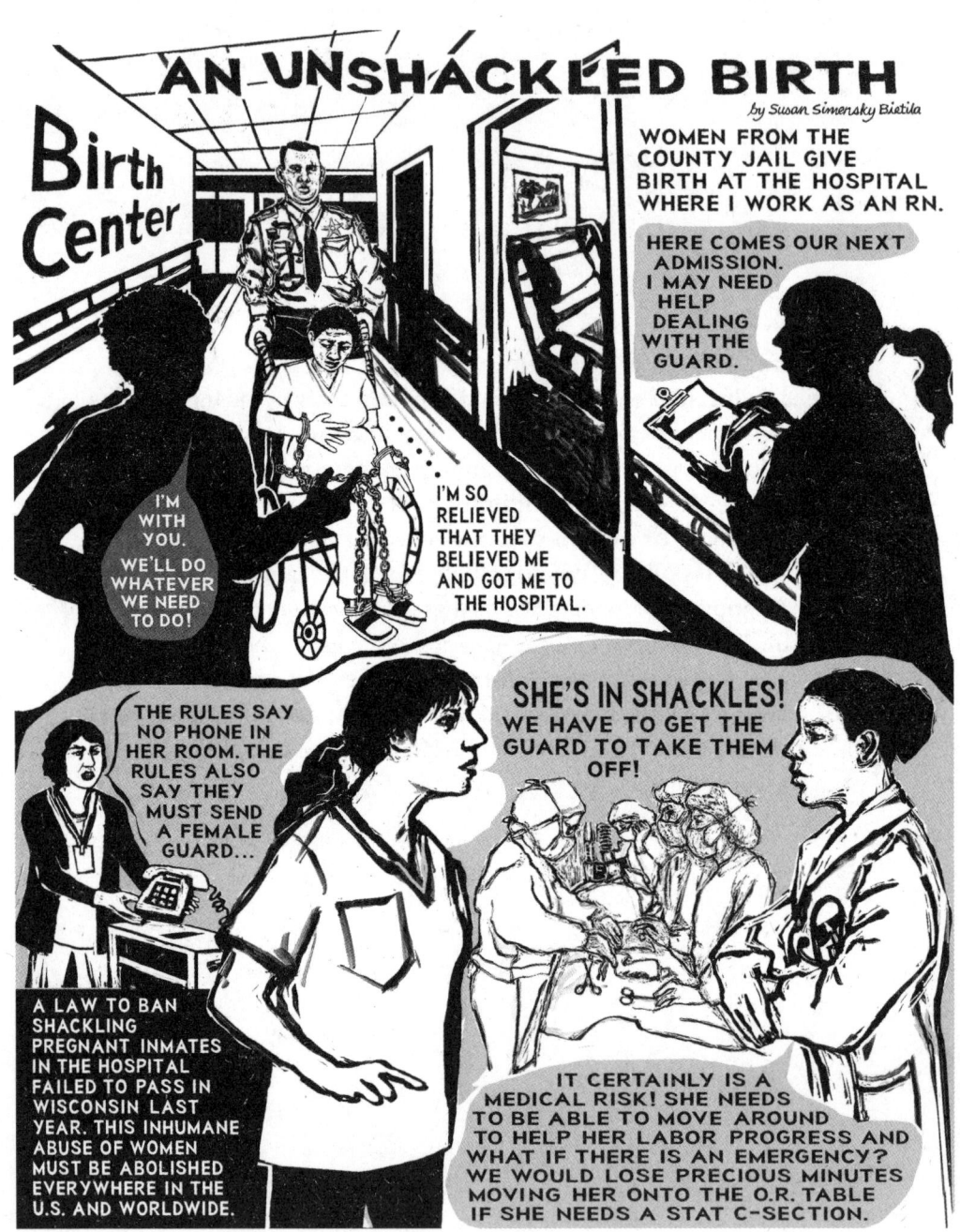

Pages 198–200: An Unshackled Birth
First appeared in *World War 3 Illustrated*, no. 53 (2023), "Shameless Feminists" issue.

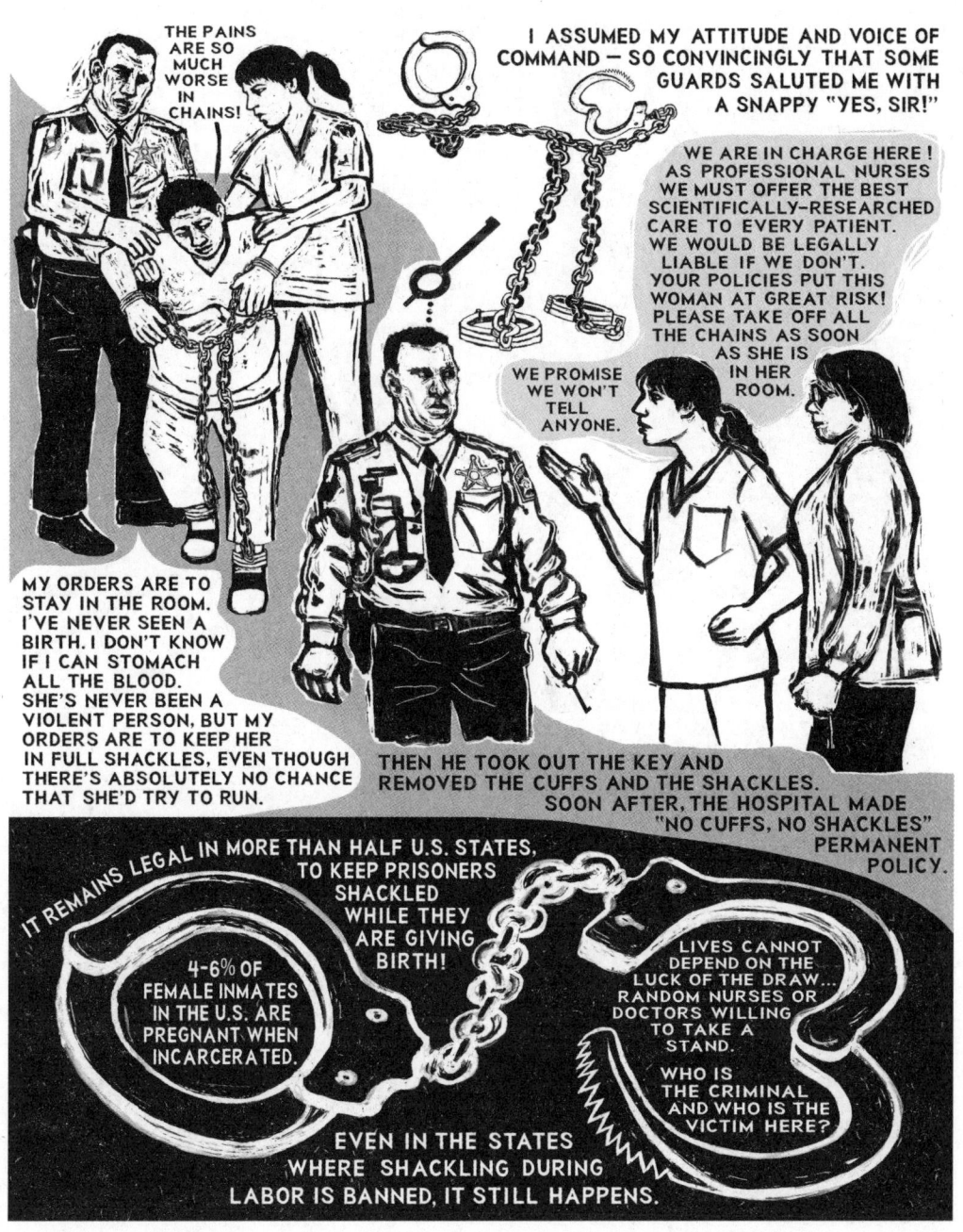

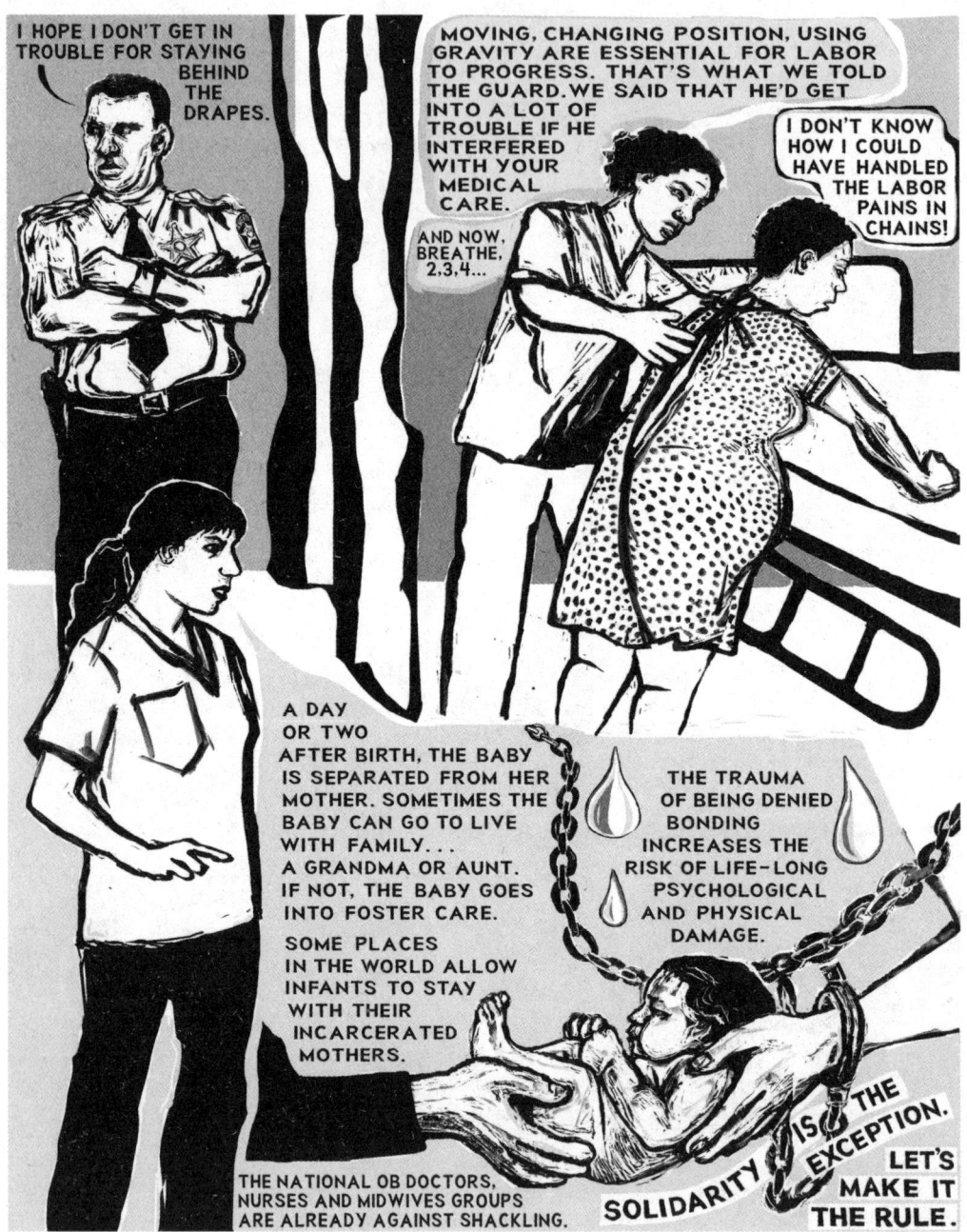

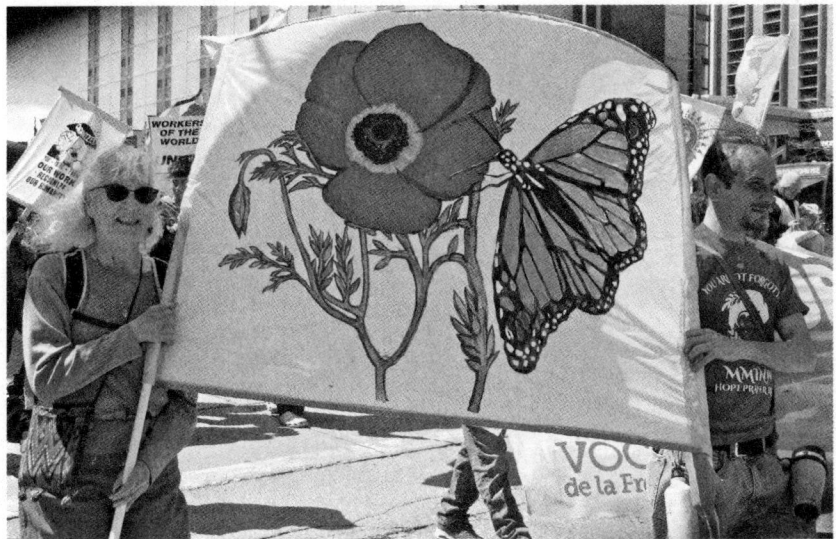

May Day 2024—A Poppy for Palestine, a Monarch Butterfly for Immigrants and Refugees: May Day marches in Milwaukee are held on May 1 each year and are led by Voces de la Frontera, a powerful and loving group protecting undocumented people from deportation by ICE, and much more. May Day here is a one-day strike, with the demonstration titled "A Day Without Immigrants and Workers." When Palestinians are being targeted, we step up to defend them. The monarch butterfly is a symbol for "No Borders" as they fly from Michoacán, Mexico, to us. The red poppy represents solidarity with the Palestinian people.

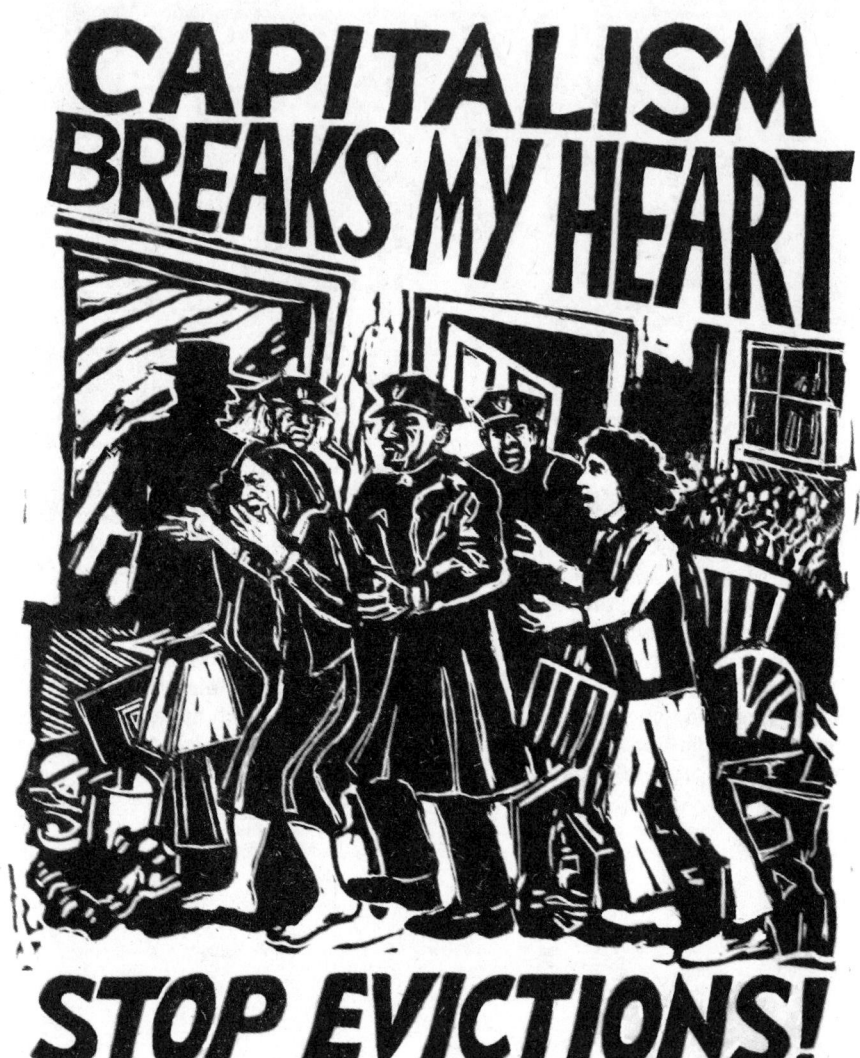

Capitalism Breaks My Heart: I made this linoleum block print around 2010 for an exhibit at the Cream City Collective's infoshop that never happened. So I shared it on the Justseeds website as a downloadable graphic. Around 2020, I got a request to use the print in a brochure for a conference on the housing crisis happening at the New School in New York. I was surprised they'd found the print online, so I did an internet search for the poster and was delighted to find photographs of it pasted on walls in Berlin, Germany, and Adelaide, Australia. It obviously had gone far and wide. When I did art for *RAT*, it showed up in underground papers from coast to coast, but this print traveled so much farther.

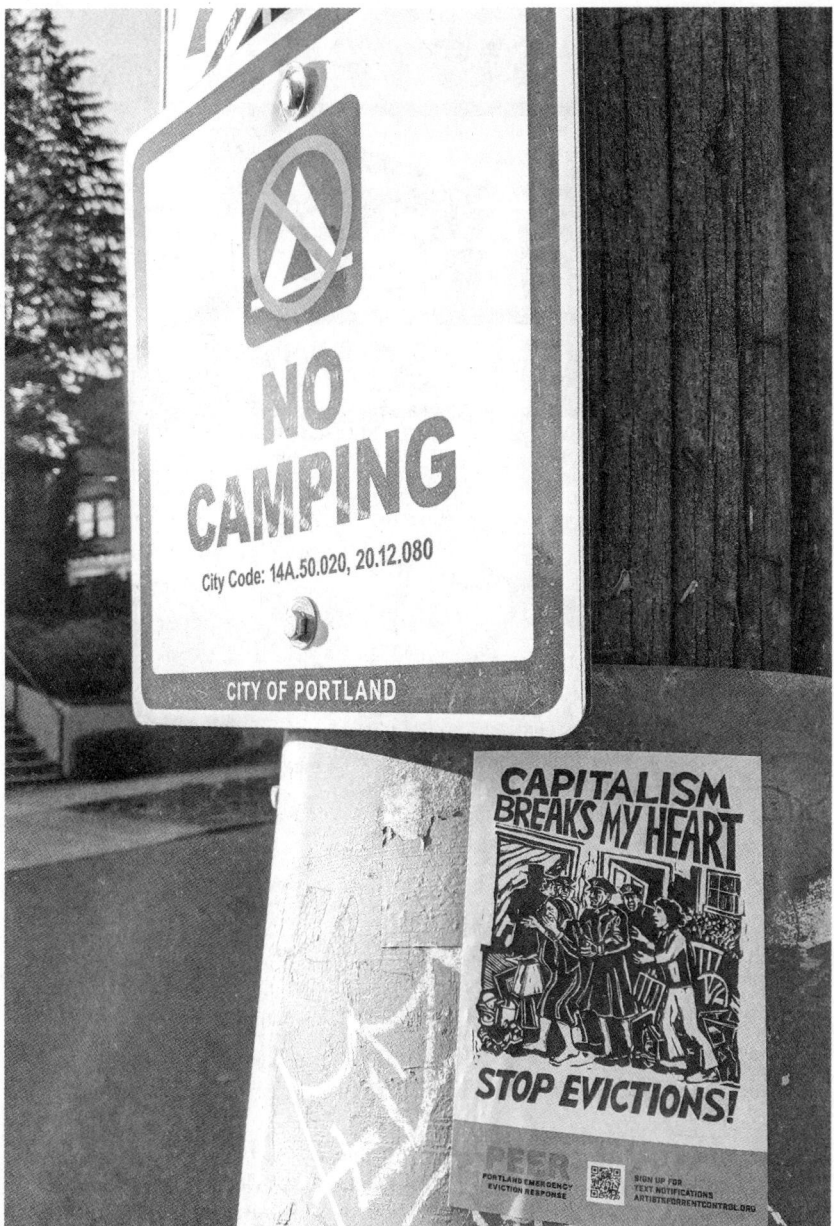

No Camping: I thank singer-songwriter David Rovics for photographing *Capitalism Breaks My Heart—Stop Evictions!* at an unhoused people's encampment in Portland, Oregon. David shared the poster with tenants unions in Portland and Olympia, Washington. I can't think of a more appropriate place for it to be exhibited.

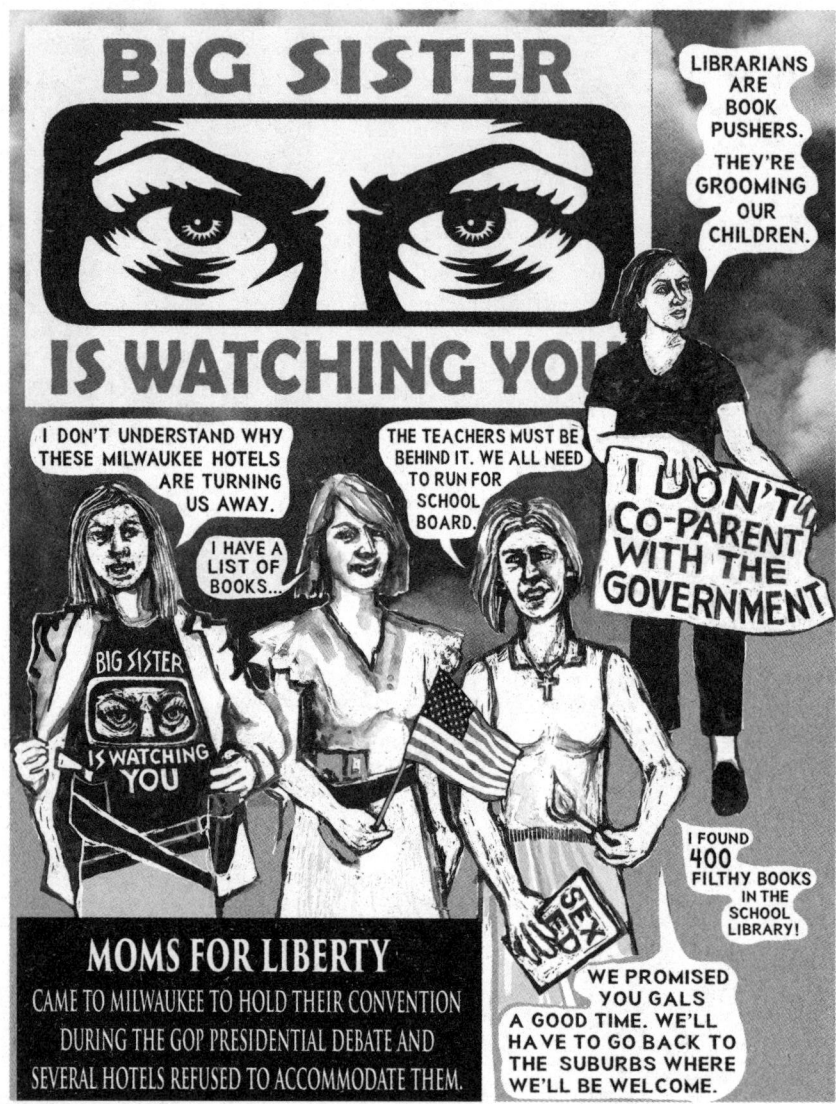

Big Sister Is Watching You: Although *Big Sister* is an integral part of the story of the impact of the Republican National Convention coming to Milwaukee, it developed a story of its own. I was invited to include it in the art show *POW-litical Comics: From Ripon to the RNC*, featuring comics and cartoons about the Republican Party. It was curated by the wonderful Museum of Wisconsin Art, to show at their annex gallery at the Saint Kate—The Arts Hotel, in the heart of downtown, during the time that GOP delegates would be staying there. But at the show's opening night, the hotel owner demanded that my art be removed. She stated that it would "cause riots, like during Black Lives Matter." This was strange

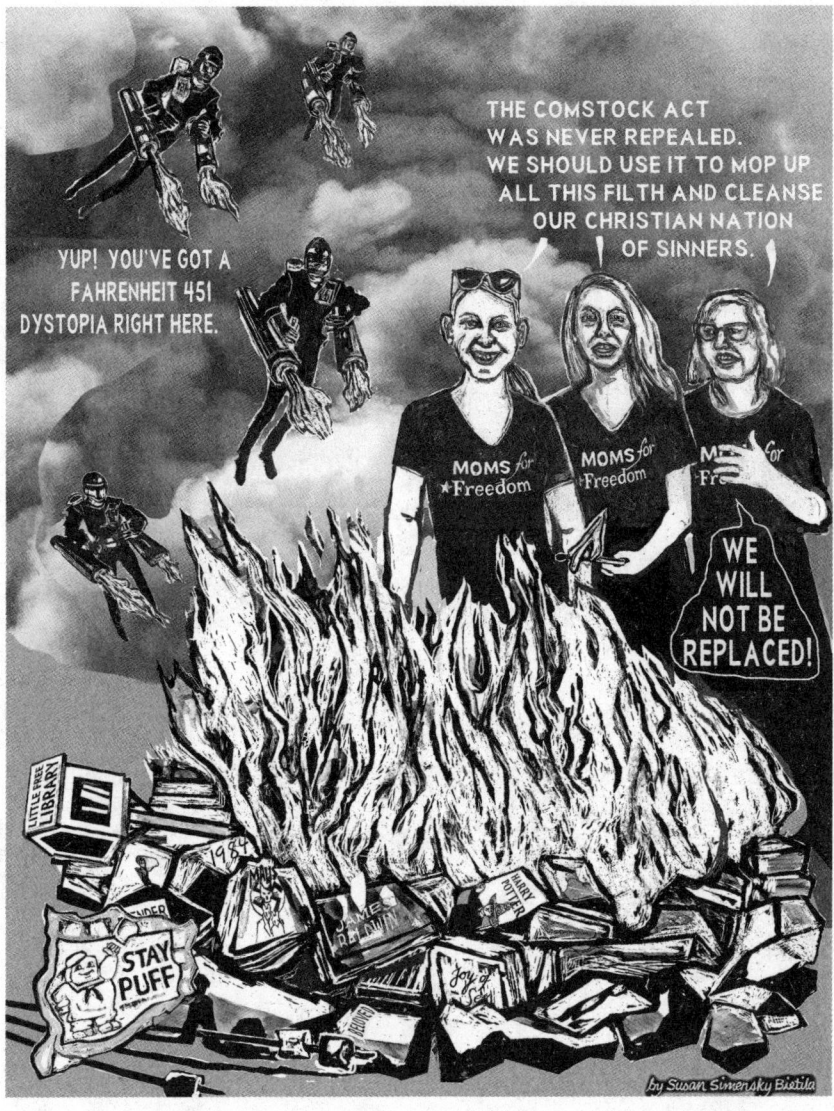

not only because other art in the show was more inflammatory, but also because there were no riots in downtown Milwaukee during Black Lives Matter. The story "Don't Be Conned by FoxConn" (which follows), much more directly insulting to the GOP, was a mutually acceptable replacement and hung in its place. But the entire show was taken down well before the closing date and the GOP convention. Press coverage and interviews about the censorship followed. Helped by the notoriety, *Big Sister* has been popular in three more shows thus far. It appeared as part of the story "Elephant Stampede in Milwaukee," *World War 3 Illustrated*, no. 54 (2024), "Now?" issue.

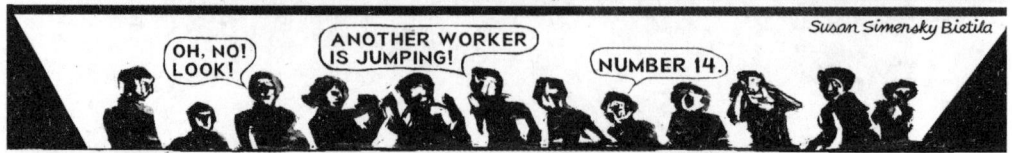

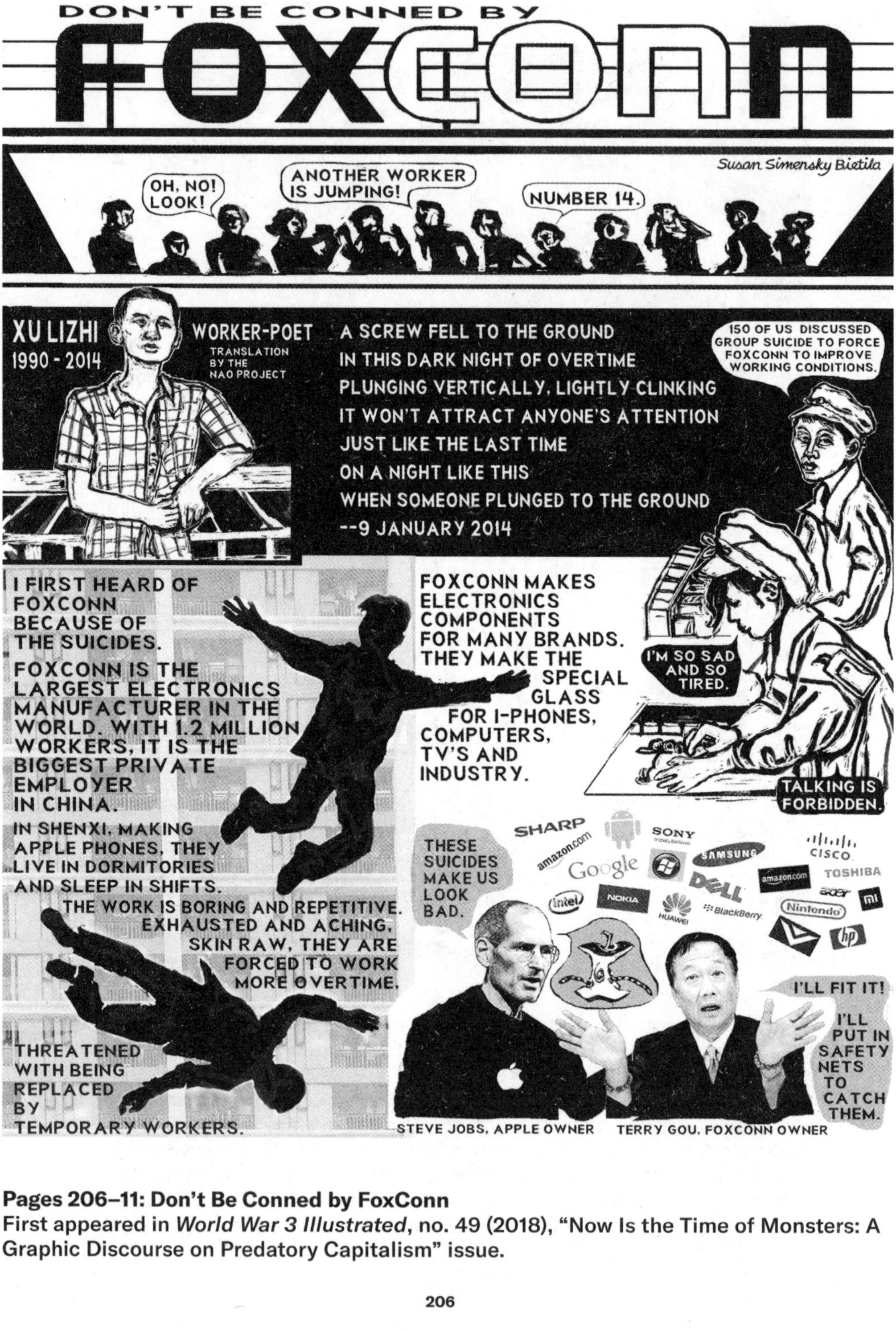

Pages 206–11: Don't Be Conned by FoxConn
First appeared in *World War 3 Illustrated*, no. 49 (2018), "Now Is the Time of Monsters: A Graphic Discourse on Predatory Capitalism" issue.

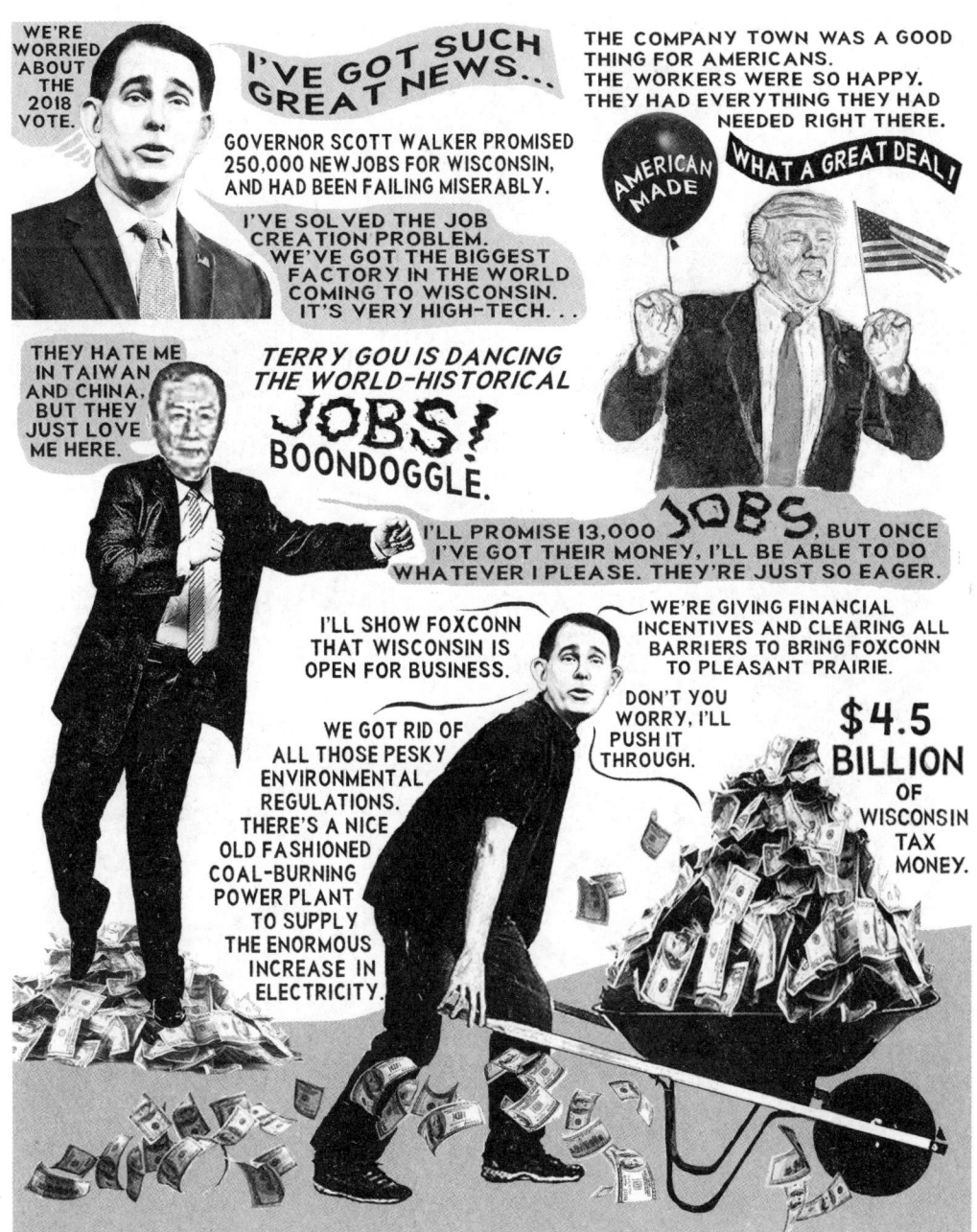

WE'RE WORRIED ABOUT THE 2018 VOTE.

I'VE GOT SUCH GREAT NEWS...

GOVERNOR SCOTT WALKER PROMISED 250,000 NEW JOBS FOR WISCONSIN, AND HAD BEEN FAILING MISERABLY.

I'VE SOLVED THE JOB CREATION PROBLEM. WE'VE GOT THE BIGGEST FACTORY IN THE WORLD COMING TO WISCONSIN. IT'S VERY HIGH-TECH...

THE COMPANY TOWN WAS A GOOD THING FOR AMERICANS. THE WORKERS WERE SO HAPPY. THEY HAD EVERYTHING THEY HAD NEEDED RIGHT THERE.

AMERICAN MADE

WHAT A GREAT DEAL!

THEY HATE ME IN TAIWAN AND CHINA, BUT THEY JUST LOVE ME HERE.

TERRY GOU IS DANCING THE WORLD-HISTORICAL

JOBS! BOONDOGGLE.

I'LL PROMISE 13,000 JOBS, BUT ONCE I'VE GOT THEIR MONEY, I'LL BE ABLE TO DO WHATEVER I PLEASE. THEY'RE JUST SO EAGER.

I'LL SHOW FOXCONN THAT WISCONSIN IS OPEN FOR BUSINESS.

WE'RE GIVING FINANCIAL INCENTIVES AND CLEARING ALL BARRIERS TO BRING FOXCONN TO PLEASANT PRAIRIE.

WE GOT RID OF ALL THOSE PESKY ENVIRONMENTAL REGULATIONS. THERE'S A NICE OLD FASHIONED COAL-BURNING POWER PLANT TO SUPPLY THE ENORMOUS INCREASE IN ELECTRICITY.

DON'T YOU WORRY, I'LL PUSH IT THROUGH.

$4.5 BILLION OF WISCONSIN TAX MONEY.

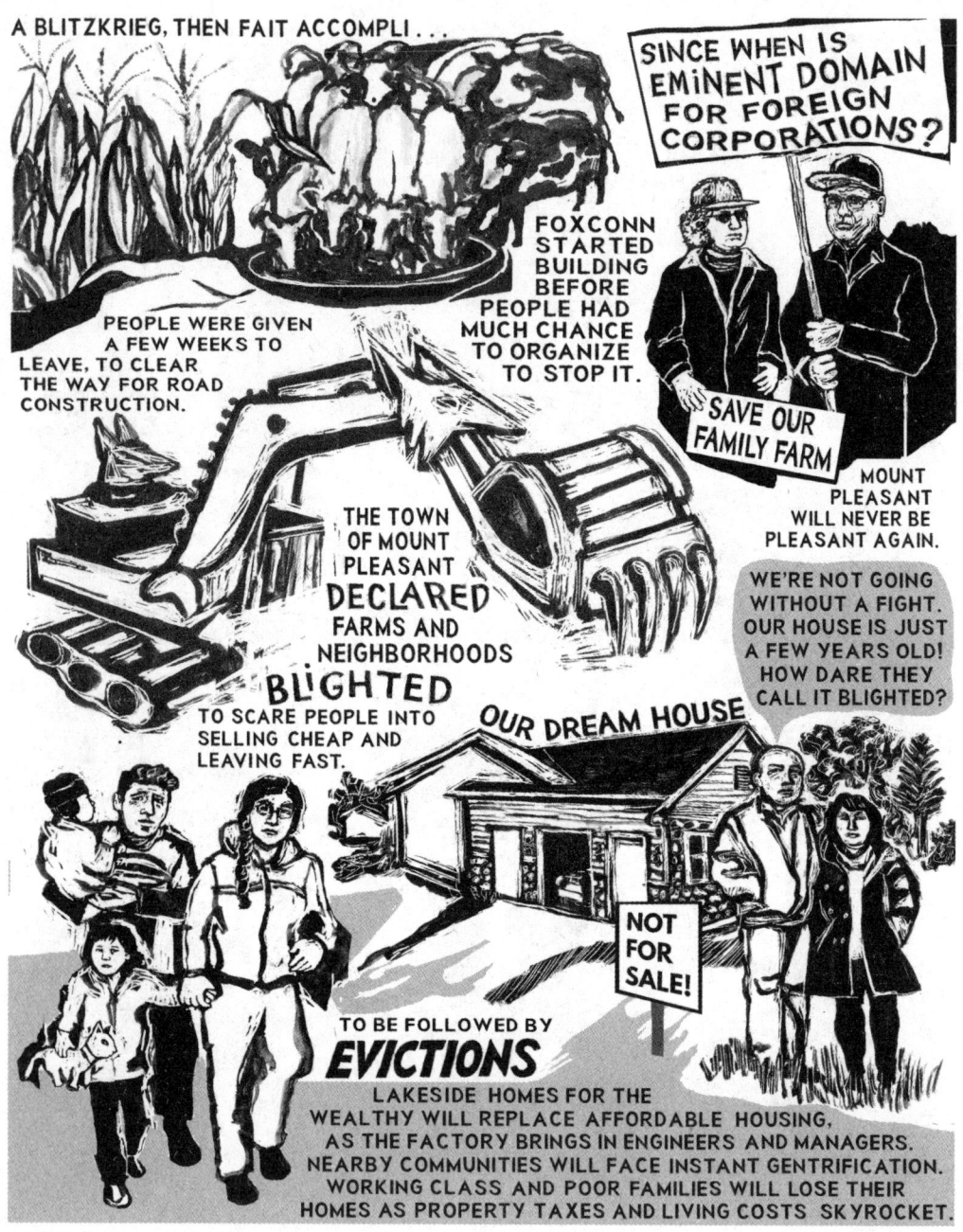

A BLITZKRIEG, THEN FAIT ACCOMPLI...

SINCE WHEN IS EMiNENT DOMAIN FOR FOREIGN CORPORATIONS?

PEOPLE WERE GIVEN A FEW WEEKS TO LEAVE, TO CLEAR THE WAY FOR ROAD CONSTRUCTION.

FOXCONN STARTED BUILDING BEFORE PEOPLE HAD MUCH CHANCE TO ORGANIZE TO STOP IT.

SAVE OUR FAMILY FARM

MOUNT PLEASANT WILL NEVER BE PLEASANT AGAIN.

THE TOWN OF MOUNT PLEASANT DECLARED FARMS AND NEIGHBORHOODS BLIGHTED TO SCARE PEOPLE INTO SELLING CHEAP AND LEAVING FAST.

WE'RE NOT GOING WITHOUT A FIGHT. OUR HOUSE IS JUST A FEW YEARS OLD! HOW DARE THEY CALL IT BLIGHTED?

OUR DREAM HOUSE

NOT FOR SALE!

TO BE FOLLOWED BY EVICTIONS

LAKESIDE HOMES FOR THE WEALTHY WILL REPLACE AFFORDABLE HOUSING, AS THE FACTORY BRINGS IN ENGINEERS AND MANAGERS. NEARBY COMMUNITIES WILL FACE INSTANT GENTRIFICATION. WORKING CLASS AND POOR FAMILIES WILL LOSE THEIR HOMES AS PROPERTY TAXES AND LIVING COSTS SKYROCKET.

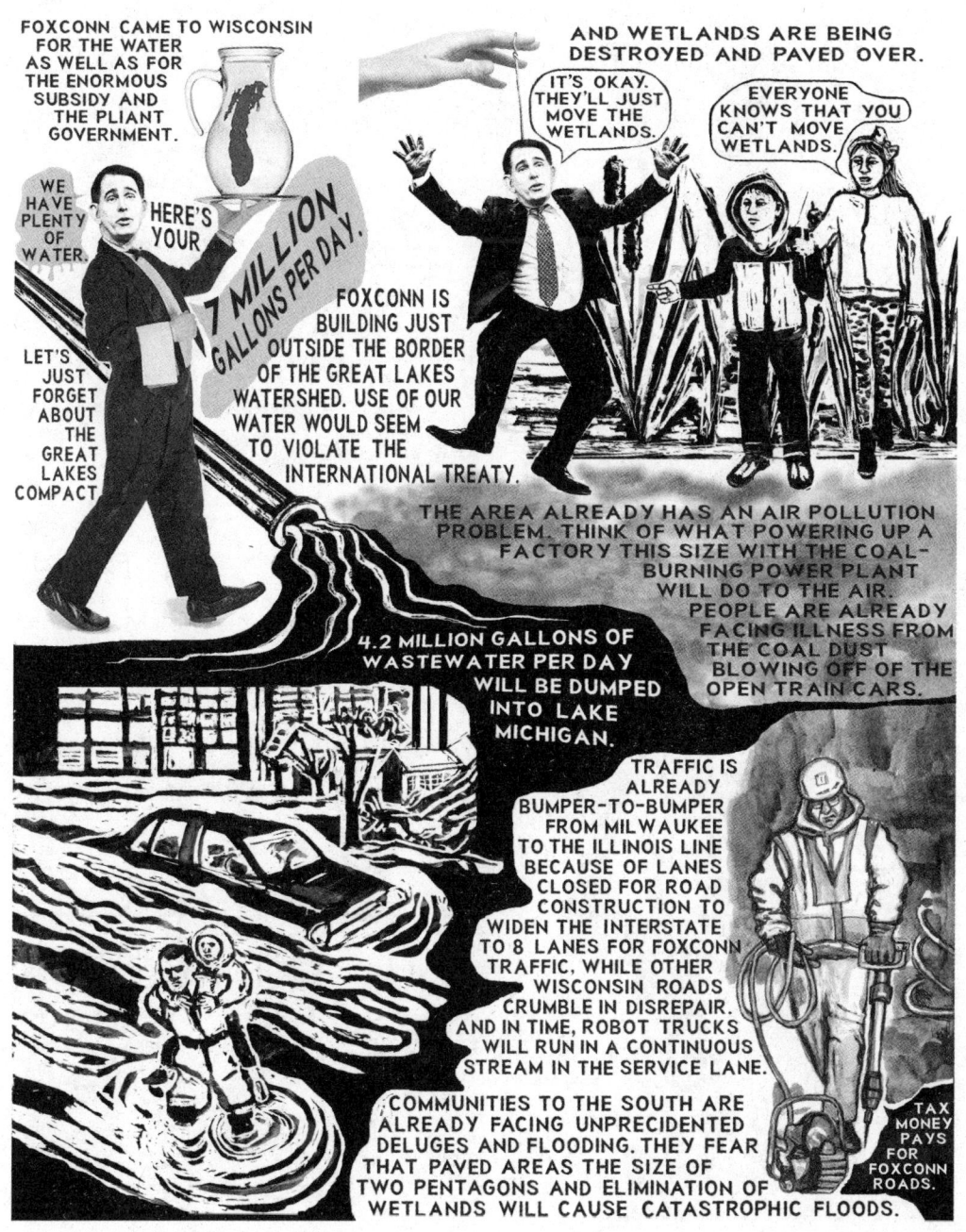

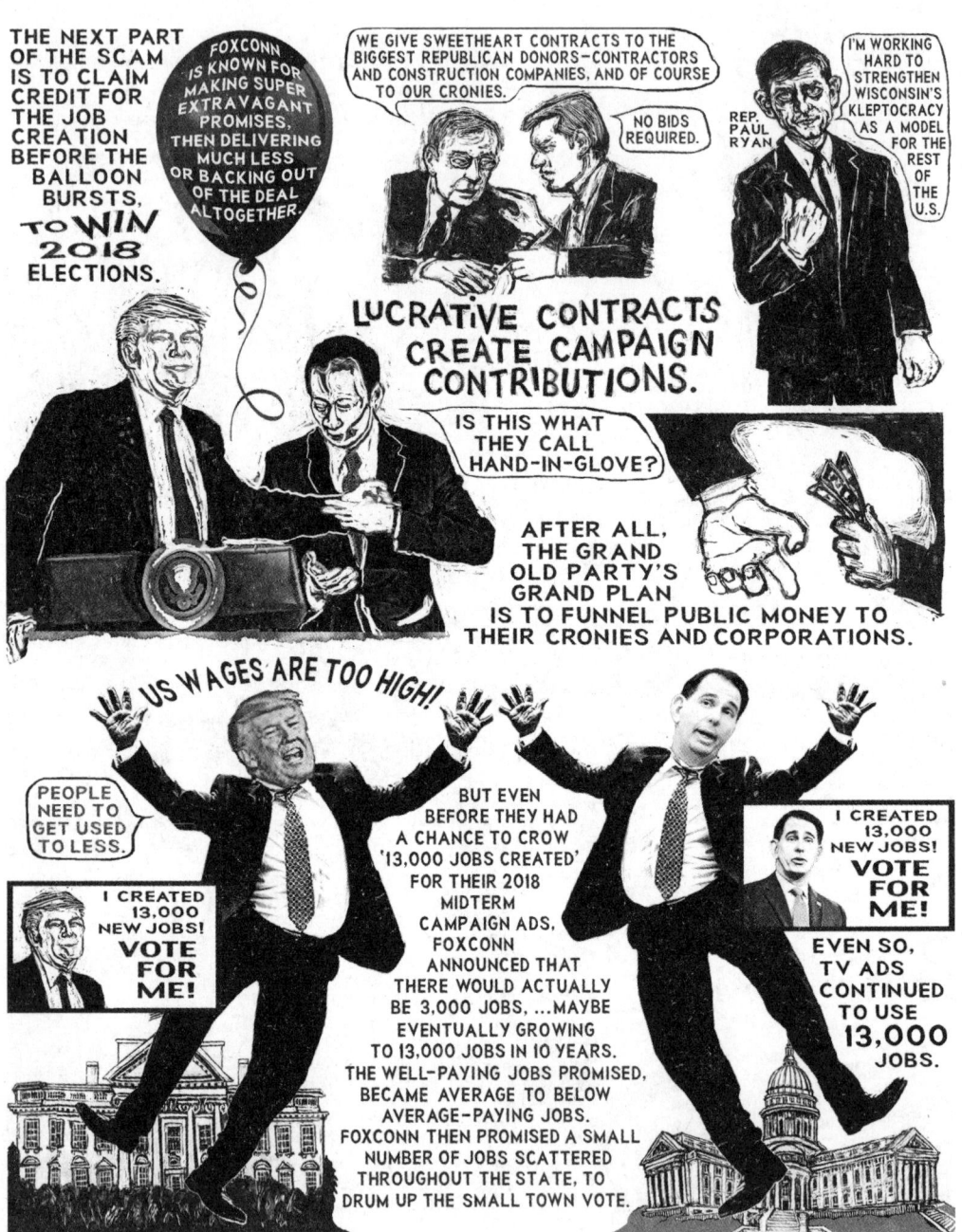

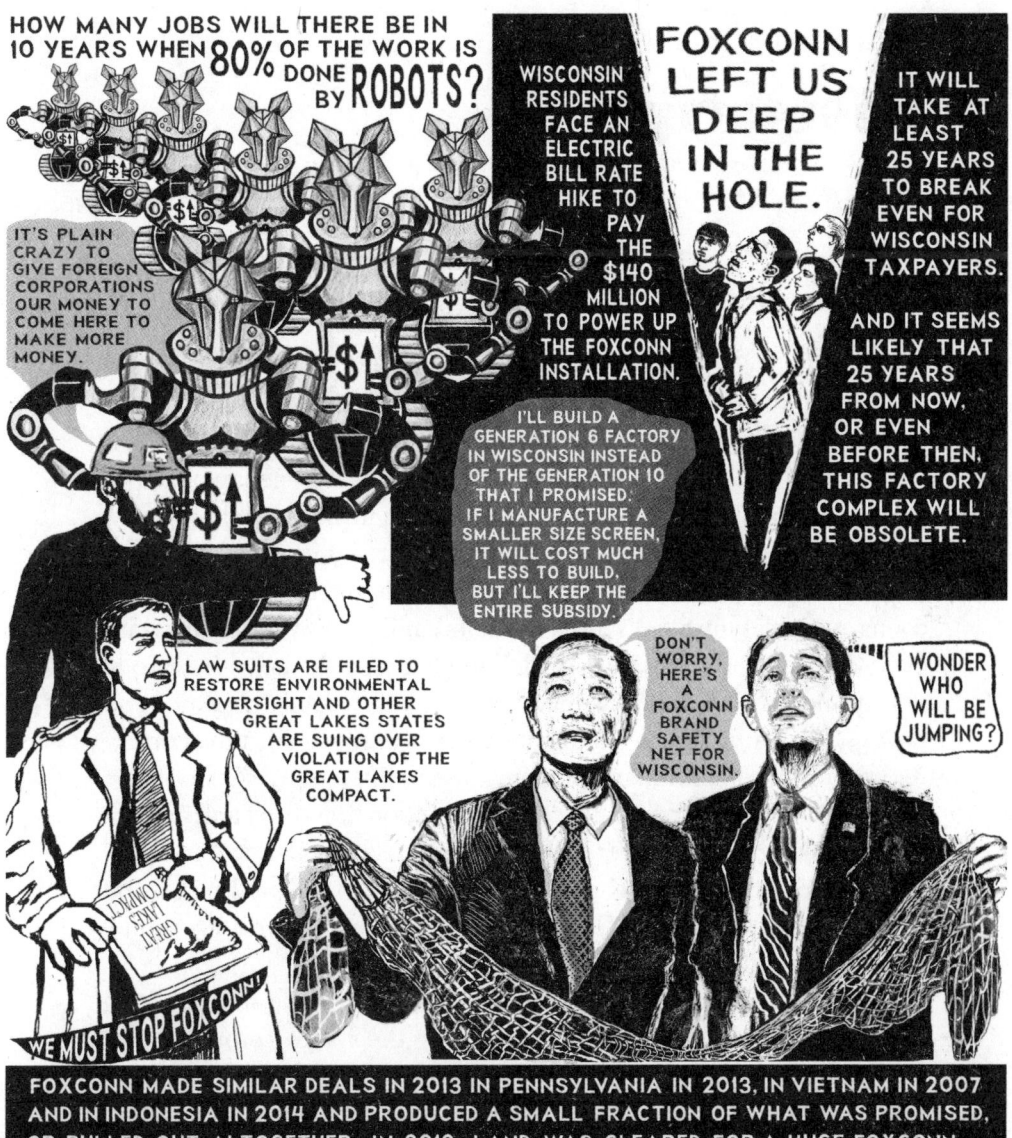

FOXCONN MADE SIMILAR DEALS IN 2013 IN PENNSYLVANIA IN 2013, IN VIETNAM IN 2007 AND IN INDONESIA IN 2014 AND PRODUCED A SMALL FRACTION OF WHAT WAS PROMISED, OR PULLED OUT ALTOGETHER. IN 2012, LAND WAS CLEARED FOR A HUGE FOXCONN COMPLEX IN SAO PAULO, BRAZIL. THE GOVERNMENT NEGOTIATED TO GIVE FOXCONN LARGE INCENTIVES AND PROMISED 100,000 JOBS. FOXCONN ALL BUT VANISHED WITH SHOCKING SPEED AND THE GOVERNMENT, WHICH PROMISED THESE JOBS AND AN ERA OF PROSPERITY, WAS IMPEACHED AMIDST A STORM OF CORRUPTION SCANDALS.

Postscript

Paul died of cancer on March 8, 2015. He got sick right after I retired from nursing. He was only sixty-six. We had been together for over forty years and had expected many more. He was diagnosed with a rare cancer that had already spread. He had been exposed to carcinogens much of his life. First, he grew up in an iron-mining town in Michigan, where everything was covered in red dust. He had worked at several small factories full of toxic chemicals and then atop the coke ovens at Bethlehem Steel's Sparrows Point mill in Maryland. I miss him every day. He was my home. I am delighted to spend time with my sons, Smitty and David. David became a librarian before Paul did. David and my only grandchild, now a teen, march in Chicago against the current regime, for the environment and for women's liberation. Our sons have inherited a love of similar music, science fiction literature, and international cooking. My daughter-in-law knows which books and films I will enjoy. I cherish memories of going out to world beat and punk bands and dancing with my children. The Clash remains our favorite. My family and my community are there for me.

When I first started writing my drawn stories, Blake, a writer, long ago one of the anarchist punks who rode in the van to Toronto Active Resistance with Smitty and me in 1998, taught me the idea of the story arc. So here, in the postscript, I return to the first story in the book, "Cossacks." Where I grew up in Brooklyn, the fathers in the Boulevard Houses project were veterans who had fought fascism in World War II. My neighborhood was home to many who had volunteered to fight the fascists in the Spanish Civil War. Most of them were Jewish and, like my family, intimately aware of the horrors of nationalist violence. Orthodox Jewish men from outside the neighborhood went door to door shaking cans decorated with the Star of David, collecting money to plant trees in Israel, a campaign to portray the land of Palestine as barren desert. They were not welcomed. My working-class Jewish neighbors were critical, did not support Zionism, and saw Israel as on a dangerous trajectory toward ethnic nationalism and violence.

Today I live in a neighborhood where so many of us are antifascist and active against Israel's genocide in Palestine and against ICE terrorism. I look forward to new and creative forms of mutual aid and to ever-broadening circles of resistance in these extraordinary times. We will win.

Acknowledgments

In normal times, here is where I would thank all the people who have been important to my development as an activist artist. Some of you have been mentioned in this history. But now, in the present context, this could easily be turned into "naming names." So thank you to all the people on the front lines, as well as my first readers, my editors, and PM Press for making this book possible.

About the Author

Susan Simensky Bietila is based in Wisconsin and works with Indigenous water protectors and allies to stop toxic mines and oil pipelines by organizing art builds and creating banners, puppets, and masks. She works with social justice movements including Voces de la Frontera, Jewish Voice for Peace, Communities United by Water, and many others. She was a coeditor and collective member of *RAT*—the pioneering second-wave feminist newspaper—and later joined the *World War 3 Illustrated* collective, where she continues to create graphic nonfiction rooted in her activist experience. Her work has appeared in the streets, on the shores, in halls of power, and in galleries, as well as in magazines, including *Fifth Estate*, *The Nation*, and *In These Times*, and books, including *Anarchy and Art: From the Paris Commune to the Fall of the Berlin Wall*; *Wobblies! A Graphic History of the Industrial Workers of the World*; and *World War 3 Illustrated: 1979–2014*.

ABOUT PM PRESS

PM Press is an independent, radical publisher of critically necessary books for our tumultuous times. Our aim is to deliver bold political ideas and vital stories to all walks of life and arm the dreamers to demand the impossible. Founded in 2007 by a small group of people with decades of publishing, media, and organizing experience, we have sold millions of copies of our books, most often one at a time, face to face. We're old enough to know what we're doing and young enough to know what's at stake. Join us to create a better world.

PM Press
PO Box 23912
Oakland, CA 94623
www.pmpress.org

PM Press in Europe
europe@pmpress.org
www.pmpress.org.uk

FRIENDS OF PM PRESS

These are indisputably momentous times—the financial system is melting down globally and the Empire is stumbling. Now more than ever there is a vital need for radical ideas.

In the many years since its founding—and on a mere shoestring—PM Press has risen to the formidable challenge of publishing and distributing knowledge and entertainment for the struggles ahead. With hundreds of releases to date, we have published an impressive and stimulating array of literature, art, music, politics, and culture. Using every available medium, we've succeeded in connecting those hungry for ideas and information to those putting them into practice.

Friends of PM allows you to directly help impact, amplify, and revitalize the discourse and actions of radical writers, filmmakers, and artists. It provides us with a stable foundation from which we can build upon our early successes and provides a much-needed subsidy for the materials that can't necessarily pay their own way. You can help make that happen—and receive every new title automatically delivered to your door once a month—by joining as a Friend of PM Press. And, we'll throw in a free T-shirt when you sign up.

Here are your options:

- **$30 a month** Get all books and pamphlets plus a 50% discount on all webstore purchases

- **$40 a month** Get all PM Press releases (including CDs and DVDs) plus a 50% discount on all webstore purchases

- **$100 a month** Superstar—Everything plus PM merchandise, free downloads, and a 50% discount on all webstore purchases

For those who can't afford $30 or more a month, we have **Sustainer Rates** at $15, $10, and $5. Sustainers get a free PM Press T-shirt and a 50% discount on all purchases from our website.

Your Visa or Mastercard will be billed once a month, until you tell us to stop. Or until our efforts succeed in bringing the revolution around. Or the financial meltdown of Capital makes plastic redundant. Whichever comes first.

World War 3 Illustrated: 1979–2014

Edited by Peter Kuper and Seth Tobocman with an introduction by Bill Ayers

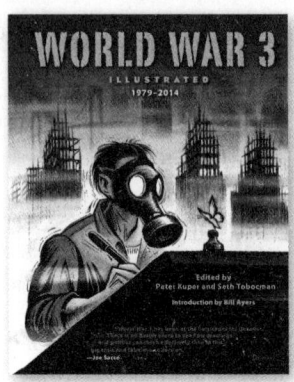

ISBN: 978-1-60486-958-3
$29.95   320 pages

Founded in 1979 by Seth Tobocman and Peter Kuper, *World War 3 Illustrated* is a labor of love run by a collective of artists (both first-timers and established professionals) and political activists working with the unified goal of creating a home for political comics, graphics, and stirring personal stories. Their confrontational comics shine a little reality on the fantasy world of the American kleptocracy, and have inspired the developing popularity and recognition of comics as a respected art form.

This full-color retrospective exhibition is arranged thematically, including housing rights, feminism, environmental issues, religion, police brutality, globalization, and depictions of conflicts from the Middle East to the Midwest. *World War 3 Illustrated* isn't about a war that may happen; it's about the ongoing wars being waged around the world and on our very own doorsteps. *World War 3 Illustrated* also illuminates the war we wage on each other—and sometimes the one taking place in our own minds. *World War 3* artists have been covering the topics that matter for over 30 years, and they're just getting warmed up.

Contributors include Sue Coe, Eric Drooker, Fly, Sandy Jimenez, Sabrina Jones, Peter Kuper, Mac McGill, Kevin Pyle, Spain Rodriguez, Nicole Schulman, Seth Tobocman, Susan Willmarth, and dozens more.

"World War 3 Illustrated *is the real thing. . . . As always it mixes newcomers and veterans, emphasizes content over style (but has plenty of style), keeps that content accessible and critical, and pays its printers and distributors but no one else. If it had nothing more than that kind of dedication to recommend it, it would be invaluable. But it has much, much more."*
—New York Times*

"Reading WW3 *is both a cleansing and an enraging experience. The graphics remind us how very serious the problems and how vile the institutions that cause them really are."*
—Utne Reader*

Paper Politics: Socially Engaged Printmaking Today

Edited by Josh MacPhee

ISBN: 978-1-60486-090-0
$24.95   160 pages

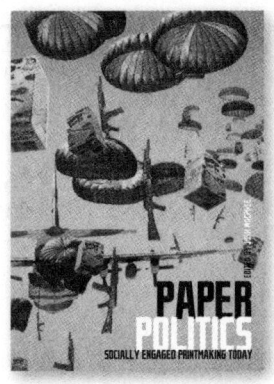

Paper Politics: Socially Engaged Printmaking Today is a major collection of contemporary politically and socially engaged printmaking. This full-color book showcases print art that uses themes of social justice and global equity to engage community members in political conversation. Based on an art exhibition that has traveled to a dozen cities in North America, *Paper Politics* features artwork by over 200 international artists; an eclectic collection of work by both activist and non-activist printmakers who have felt the need to respond to the monumental trends and events of our times.

Paper Politics presents a breathtaking tour of the many modalities of printing by hand: relief, intaglio, lithography, serigraph, collagraph, monotype, and photography. In addition to these techniques, included are more traditional media used to convey political thought, finely crafted stencils and silk-screens intended for wheat pasting in the street. Artists range from the well established (Sue Coe, Swoon, Carlos Cortez) to the up-and-coming (Favianna Rodriguez, Chris Stain, Nicole Schulman), from street artists (BORF, You Are Beautiful) to rock poster makers (EMEK, Bughouse).

"Let's face it, most collections of activist art suck. Either esthetic concerns are front and center and the politics that motivate such creation are pushed to the margin, or politics prevail and artistic quality is an afterthought. With the heart of an activist and the eye of an artist, Josh MacPhee miraculously manages to do justice to both. Paper Politics *is singularly impressive."*
—Stephen Duncombe, author of *Dream: Re-imagining Progressive Politics in an Age of Fantasy*

"For all of those who claim that poster art is dead in the age of YouTube and Blogs, Paper Politics *will wheatpaste another message over your computer monitor. This exhibition and book is a testament to the vibrant trajectory of printmaking in the service of social change, including examples of earlier movements and artists as well as the graphics popping up right now. Obscure and familiar subjects are presented with wit, joy, and searing satire, guaranteed to snap your senses and challenge your opinions. It took a village to make this show, and the world will benefit from seeing it."*
—Lincoln Cushing, author of *Revolución! Cuban Poster Art*

Slingshot: 40 Postcards by Eric Drooker

Eric Drooker

ISBN: 978-1-62963-508-8
Price: $19.95   84 pages

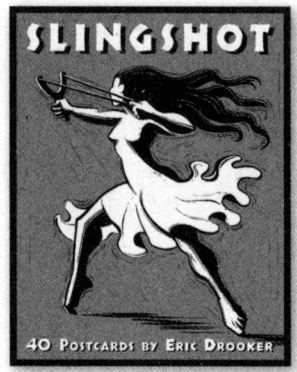

Disguised as a book of innocent postcards, *Slingshot* is a dangerous collection of Eric Drooker's most notorious posters. Plastered on brick walls from New York to Berlin, tattooed on bodies from Kansas to Mexico City, Drooker's graphics continue to infiltrate and inflame the body politic. Drooker is the author of the graphic novels *Flood! A Novel in Pictures* (winner of the American Book Award) and *Blood Song: A Silent Ballad*. He collaborated with Beat poet Allen Ginsberg on the underground classic *Illuminated Poems*. His provocative art has appeared on countless posters and book covers, and his hard-edged graphics are a familiar sight on street corners throughout the world. Eric Drooker is a third-generation New Yorker, born and raised on Manhattan Island. His paintings are frequently seen on covers of the New Yorker and hang in various art collections throughout the U.S. and Europe.

"Drooker's old Poe hallucinations of beauteous deathly reality transcend political hang-up and fix our present American dreams."
—Allen Ginsberg

"When the rush of war parades are over, a simple and elegant reminder of humanity remains—in the work of Eric Drooker."
—Sue Coe

White and Black: Political Cartoons from Palestine

Mohammad Sabaaneh
with a Foreword by Seth Tobocman

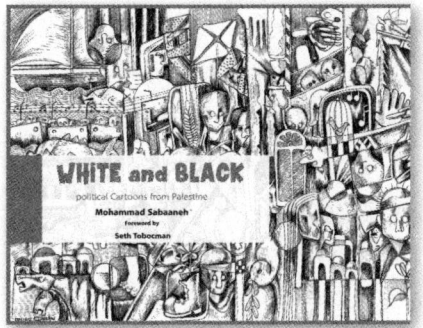

ISBN: 978-1-68257-067-8
   (paperback)
   978-1-68257-092-0
   (hardcover)
$19.95/$49.95   212 pages

Palestinian political cartoonist Mohammad Sabaaneh has gained renown worldwide for his stark black-and-white drawings that express the numerous abuses and losses that his countrymen suffer under Israel's occupation and celebrate their popular resistance. This collection includes 180 of Sabaaneh's best cartoons, including some depicting the privations he and other Palestinian political prisoners have suffered in Israel's many prisons. This book offers profound insights into the political and social struggles facing the Palestinian people and a pointed critique of the inaction or complicity of the "international community." Veteran graphic artist Seth Tobocman contributes a foreword.

"Each of Mohammad Sabaaneh's powerful drawings is like a gut punch that gets straight to the essence of the stark reality of Palestinian life under Israeli occupation. This is how an artist resists."
—Joe Sacco, author and illustrator whose books include *Palestine* and *Footnotes in Gaza*

"Despite working at a very complicated crossroads of ideology and political pressures, Mohammad Sabaaneh continues to produce sharp, incisive cartoons. His tenacity and courage is an inspiration for cartoonists around the world."
—Matt Wuerker, Pulitzer Prize-winning editorial cartoonist at *Politico*

"If you want to get a smart Palestinian's view of what's happening in the Middle East, you can't do better than look at Mohammad Sabaaneh's cartoons—they tell you more than words can say."
—Victor Navasky, publisher emeritus, *The Nation*

"Sabaaneh's illustrations are intricate and moving—stark, striking, and rich with Palestinian visual traditions and symbols. The result is a series of intimate portraits of Palestinian life under occupation that combines history and present-day reality. These cartoons are a powerful call to action, both to the international community and to the Palestinian people, serving as a reminder that at the end of the day it is we—Palestinians around the world—who will be the masters of our own destiny."
—Leila Abdelrazaq, graphic artist and author of *Baddawi*

Baddawi

Leila Abdelrazaq

ISBN: 978-1-93598-240-1
$19.99   128 pages

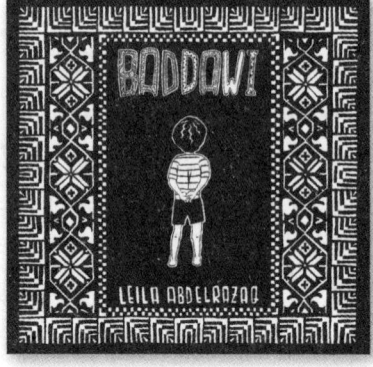

An arrestingly drawn debut graphic novel, *Baddawi* is the story of a young boy named Ahmad struggling to find his place in the world.

Baddawi explores the childhood of the author's father from a determinedly boy's-eye view as he witnesses the world crumbling around him and attempts to carry on, forging his own path in the midst of terrible uncertainty. Ahmed was raised in the refugee camp of Baddawi in northern Lebanon, one of many thousands of children born to Palestinians who fled (or were expelled from) their homeland during the 1948 war that established the state of Israel. Ahmad's dogged pursuit of education and opportunity echoes the journey of the Palestinian people, as they make the best of their existing circumstances while remaining determined to one day return to their homeland.

"At turns heartbreaking and humorous, this coming-of-age story is a must read."
—*Foreword Reviews*

"In Baddawi, *Leila Abdelrazaq tells a coming-of-age story that is funny, angry, and deeply human. The bold blacks of her drawing remind one of Marjane Satrapi, or the legendary French artist David B. But she transforms the style, infusing it with design elements from Palestinian embroidery.* Baddawi *is the story of her father's childhood in a Lebanese refugee camp. It is also the story of hundreds of thousands of displaced Palestinians."*
—Molly Crabapple, author of *Drawing Blood*

"Leila Abdelrazaq is a fresh and exciting artist and writer. Baddawi *is heartfelt and poignant and is told from an often-underrepresented perspective. It is a vital read for anyone curious about the plight of the Palestinian people."*
—Toufic El Rassi, author of *Arab in America*

"This book is a substantial accomplishment, a serious story in comic-book form containing magnificent drawing by a young artist of promise."
—Samia A. Halaby, painter, writer, and author of *Liberation Art of Palestine*

"Leila Abdelrazaq blends beauty, politics, humor, rich Palestinian traditions, and the humanity of everyday life during historic times into her delicate lines and powerful compositions."
—Ethan Heitner, cartoonist and illustrator, *Freedom Funnies*

Diario De Oaxaca:
A Sketchbook Journal of Two Years in Mexico

Peter Kuper, with an Introduction
by Martín Solares

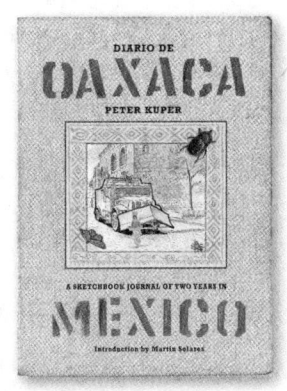

ISBN: 978-1-60486-071-9
$24.95   240 pages

Painting a vivid, personal portrait of social and
political upheaval in Oaxaca, Mexico, this unique
memoir employs comics, bilingual essays, photos, and sketches to chronicle the
events that unfolded around a teachers' strike and led to a seven-month siege.

When award-winning cartoonist Peter Kuper and his wife and daughter moved
to the beautiful 16th-century colonial town of Oaxaca in 2006, they planned
to spend a quiet year or two enjoying a different culture and taking a break
from the U.S. political climate under the Bush administration. What they hadn't
counted on was landing in the epicenter of Mexico's biggest political struggle
in recent years. Timely and compelling, this extraordinary firsthand account
presents a distinct artistic vision of Oaxacan life, from explorations of the
beauty of the environment to graphic portrayals of the fight between strikers
and government troops that left more than 20 people dead, including American
journalist Brad Will.

*"Kuper is a colossus; I have been in awe of him for over 20 years. Teachers and
students everywhere take heart: Kuper has in these pages born witness to our
seemingly endless struggle to educate and to be educated in the face of institutions
that really don't give a damn. In this ruined age we need Kuper's unsparing
compassionate visionary artistry like we need hope."*
—Junot Díaz, Pulitzer Prize winning author of *The Brief Wondrous Life of Oscar
Wao*

*"Peter Kuper is undoubtedly the modern master whose work has refined the socially
relevant comic to the highest point yet achieved."*
—*Newsarama*

"An artist at the top of his form."
—*Publishers Weekly*

*"Oaxaca Diary reveals to us how so many aspects of a city can be combined on the
same page by an adept artist; poetry, magic, beauty, mystery, fear, as well as the
different faces that protest can assume when politicians hold a city hostage."*
— Martín Solares, from his introduction

Mutual Aid: An Illuminated Factor of Evolution

Peter Kropotkin
Illustrated by N.O. Bonzo with an
Introduction by David Graeber &
Andrej Grubačić, Foreword by Ruth
Kinna, Postscript by GATS, and an
Afterword by Allan Antliff

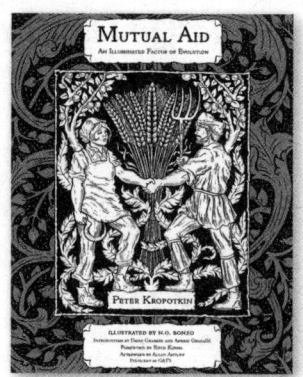

ISBN: 978-1-62963-874-4 (paperback)
    978-1-62963-875-1 (hardcover)
$30.00/$70.00   336 pages

One hundred years after his death, Peter Kropotkin is still one of the most inspirational figures of the anarchist movement. It is often forgotten that Kropotkin was also a world-renowned geographer whose seminal critique of the hypothesis of competition promoted by social Darwinism helped revolutionize modern evolutionary theory. An admirer of Darwin, he used his observations of life in Siberia as the basis for his 1902 collection of essays *Mutual Aid: A Factor of Evolution*. Kropotkin demonstrated that mutually beneficial cooperation and reciprocity—in both individuals and as a species—plays a far more important role in the animal kingdom and human societies than does individualized competitive struggle. Kropotkin carefully crafted his theory making the science accessible. His account of nature rejected Rousseau's romantic depictions and ethical socialist ideas that cooperation was motivated by the notion of "universal love." His understanding of the dynamics of social evolution shows us the power of cooperation—whether it is bison defending themselves against a predator or workers unionizing against their boss. His message is clear: solidarity is strength!

Every page of this new edition of *Mutual Aid* has been beautifully illustrated by one of anarchism's most celebrated current artists, N.O. Bonzo. The reader will also enjoy original artwork by GATS and insightful commentary by David Graeber, Ruth Kinna, Andrej Grubačić, and Allan Antliff.

"N.O. Bonzo has created a rare document, updating Kropotkin's anarchist classic Mutual Aid, *by intertwining compelling imagery with an updated text. Filled with illustrious examples, their art gives the words and histories, past and present, resonance for new generations to seed flowers of cooperation to push through the concrete of resistance to show liberatory possibilities for collective futures."*
—scott crow, author of *Black Flags and Windmills* and *Setting Sights*